MW00808134

THE COMPLETE BOOK OF GHOSTS AND POLTERGEISTS

OTHER BOOKS BY LEONARD R.N. ASHLEY

George Alfred Henty and the Victorian Mind
Turkey: Names and Naming Practices
The Complete Book of Spells, Curses, and Magical Recipes
The Complete Book of the Devil's Disciples
The Complete Book of Devils and Demons
The Complete Book of Magic and Witchcraft
The Complete Book Superstition, Prophecy, and Luck
What's in a Name?
Elizabethan Popular Culture
Colley Cibber
Authorship and Evidence in Renaissance Drama
George Peele: The Man and His Work
Ripley's "Believe It Or Not" Book of The Military
The Air Defence of North America (NORAD)
Nineteenth-Century British Drama
Mirrors for the Man: 26 Plays of World Drama
The History of the Short Story
Other People's Lives
Tales of Mystery and Melodrama

editor

Phantasms of the Living
Reliques of Irish Poetry
The Ballad Poetry of Ireland
Shakespeare's Jest Book
Soohrab and Rustum
A Narrative of the Life of Mrs. Charolotte Charke

co-editor

British Short Stories: Classics and Criticism
Geolinguistic Perspectives
Language in Contemporary Society
Constructed Languages and Language Construction
Geolinguistics 1997
Geolinguistics 1998
Language and Communication in the New Century

THE COMPLETE BOOK OF
GHOSTS AND POLTERGEISTS

Leonard R.N. Ashley

PROFESSOR *EMERITUS*, BROOKLYN COLLEGE
OF THE CITY UNIVERSITY OF NEW YORK

BARRICADE BOOKS / NEW YORK

Published by Barricade Books Inc.
150 Fifth Avenue, Suite 700
New York, NY 10011

Copyright © 2000 by Leonard R. N. Ashley

All rights reserved.

No part of this book may be reproduced, stored in a retrieval system, or transmitted in any form, by any means, including mechanical, electronic, photocopying, recording, or otherwise, without the prior written permission of the publisher, except by a reviewer who wishes to quote brief passages in connection with a review written for inclusion in a magazine, newspaper, or broadcast.

Printed in the United States of America.
Designed by Cindy LaBreacht

Library of Congress Cataloging-in-Publication Data
Ashley, Leonard R. N.
    The complete book of ghosts & poltergeists / Leonard R.N. Ashley.
        p. cm.
    Includes index.
    ISBN: 1-56980-138-X
    1. Ghosts. 2. Poltergeists. I. Title: Complete book of ghosts and poltergeists.
BF1461.A745 2000
133.1--dc21   99-055375

10 9 8 7 6 5 4 3 2 1

FOR
MARK

Do you know what fear is? Not ordinary fear of insult, injury or death, but abject, quivering dread of something that you cannot see—fear that dries the inside of the mouth and half of the throat—fear that makes you sweat on the palms of the hands, and gulp in order to keep the uvula at work? This is a fine Fear—a great cowardice, and must be felt to be appreciated.

—Rudyard Kipling, *My Own True Ghost Story*

In memoriam

RICHARD CHINTALIN
22 May 1939–6 July 1999

Table of Contents

A daguerreotype of 1852 on which is written: "Kate & Maggie Fox, Rochester Mediums. T.M. Easterly Daguerrean."

Read This First

I have often said that people seldom or never read the introductions to books. I keep on hoping they will read mine, because an introduction helps to put a book in context. This one will be brief.

Here is the seventh book in my Barricade Books series on the occult. The earlier books in the series are *The Complete Book of Superstition, Prophecy, and Luck* (1995), *The Complete Book of Magic and Witchcraft* (1995), *The Complete Book of Devils and Demons* (1996), *The Complete Book of the Devil's Disciples* (1996), *The Complete Book of Spells, Curses, and Magical Recipes* (1998), and *The Complete Book of Vampires* (1998). *The Complete Book of Werewolves*, to be published in 2000, will round out the series. Each book can stand on its own but the set adds up to something like an encyclopedia of the supernatural.

The sixth and seventh books in the series address the question of whether the dead survive in some fashion as ghosts or as noisy ghosts, for which we have the word *poltergeist*, borrowed from the German. Whether the spirit lives on in some fashion after the death of a human being is a question every civilization has posed. Some have answered in rather fantastic ways. In *The Complete Book of Vampires* I quoted Dr. Samuel Johnson and his remarks will bear repeating here. In 1759, in a hurry to pay the expenses of his mother's funeral (or so the story goes), Dr. Johnson of dictionary fame wrote another book which deserves to be remembered. It was the short philosophical novel *Rasselas, Prince of Abyssinia*. In it, the philosopher Imlac says:

> "That the dead are no more...I will not undertake to maintain against the concurrent and unvaried testimony of all ages, and of all nations. There is no people, rude or learned, among whom apparitions of the dead are not related and believed. This opinion, which, perhaps, prevails as far as human nature is diffused, could become universal only by its truth; those, that never heard

of one another, would not have agreed on a tale which nothing but experience can make credible. That it is doubted by single cavilers can very little weaken the general evidence, and some who deny it with their tongues confess it with their fears."

The Complete Book of Ghosts and Poltergeists looks at those age-old fears and superstitions. It must be admitted that there are far more skeptics in the twentieth century than there were even in the Age of Reason (the eighteenth century) regarding the possibility of human personality surviving the death of the body. For the skeptics, I attempt here, as in all the other books in my series, to present scholarly research in a user-friendly way to entertain as well as educate. This book is also written for the vast majority who more or less believe.

I continue to write for a popular audience. While some may think a more somber tone would be preferable, I and almost all the readers I have heard from do not. They like to be amused as well as amazed. They are challenged sometimes, as when I get into complex theological issues in *Devils and Demons* (the most difficult book in the series, but well worth careful reading), but I never pompously pose professorially—at least not on purpose!

Ancient peoples sometimes tied the feet of the dead together to prevent the ghosts from "walking," but in these pages they will walk and perhaps dance for you. In every section the material is arranged to encourage those who read in the modern style, sampling, skipping, preferring bytes. There is even a bit of MTV-style jump-cut editing. This militates against long arguments and linearity in general, but at the same time it causes frequent breaks, during which you can stop and think about the nugget you have just acquired. I encourage you to read these books that way.

I hope this book is as well received as the others have been. I do not expect everyone to share my personal views, but I do want as many as possible to share the interesting materials I have collected. The dead are a lively topic.

Why not keep this as a bedside book and dip in for a little reading before you sleep? Happy dreams.

Acknowledgements

As usual, in presenting this book to the public I have to include some boilerplate that is none the less sincere because so familiar. In it I express my debts to others. I thank uncounted and consequently unnamable authors whose works I have consulted. In the case of many of these authors I have indeed through their writings been communicating with the dead. To those authors still with us, my thanks. I am grateful to all of them. Those writers whose works I believe the reader may wish to consult I have taken care to mention (with author's name) in the text. I am equally grateful to helpful librarians at Brooklyn College of the City University of New York and at libraries elsewhere in this country and abroad. They have directed me to, or provided through interlibrary loans, many obscure volumes I might otherwise never have seen. I owe much to my publishers and to my talented editor, Sam Kellerman. Most of all I must thank the readers who have welcomed my earlier books and sometimes accepted my open invitation to write to me to commend or criticize or correct me.

The faults are my own, except for perhaps a few typographical errors the printers made when redoing a line I corrected in proof. We all make mistakes. That we can never fully in this life avoid making mistakes—or in this life make up entirely for our mistakes— seems to me to be just one more reason for hoping that we may at some other time and on some level or other be given further opportunity to come closer to perfection.

Finally, I am grateful for those who find in these studies more merits than faults. It is the reaction of my readership that has encouraged me and my publishers to offer new volumes in the series. Enjoy this latest one!

God Bless, and Blessed Be.

Summer, 2000

Mediums were often caught in frauds, and some made money by confessing to them in print. But for every exposé such as the one whose cover is pictured above, there was at least one book in defense of spiritualism.

1

The Dead Return

"People like ghosts," wrote Douglas Hill in *The History of Ghosts, Vampires, and Werewolves*. "If hardheaded rationalism won a total victory, and erased all the old superstitions from the minds of men, people would probably miss ghosts more than any."

Following this volume, *The Complete Book of Werewolves* will conclude the series. While werewolves traditionally are not revenants from the grave but living people, the great appeal of ghosts is that they suggest that life after death is possible. That is good news to many. After life's "fitful fever," some people wish for oblivion, but most people hope to go right on, in some fashion or other. Those who return to the land of the living we call ghosts or, if noisy and violent, poltergeists.

Albert Einstein said in 1930 that he could not "believe that the individual survives the death of his body, although feeble souls harbor such thoughts through fear or ridiculous egotism." As one of the greatest scientists of the twentieth century, Einstein is sure of his immortality; the rest of us can hardly be called "feeble" for hoping that we will not be extinguished by death.

To commence, here is a *pot pourri* of information on the supposed return of the dead from The Other Side, sometimes for good purposes, sometimes for ill.

A WARNING TO START

God says (if you credit *Leviticus*):

19:31. Regard not them that hath familiar spirits.

20:6. And the soul that turneth after such as have familiar spirits, and after wizards, to go a-whoring after them, I will ever set My face against that soul and will cut him off from among his people.

Yet despite the warnings of religion (which asks us to believe in supernatural creatures, of course, promising a heaven of the blessed and angels, and threatening a hell of the damned and fallen angels), even religious people love to believe in ghosts. This is not only because of the nature of modern Americans, 10 percent of whom believe they have been abducted by aliens, or think they could be. This is something rooted far deeper.

GHOSTS

Different cultures have different ideas about ghosts. Let us examine the old English tradition; it has pretty much formed our modern American views. Here is an ominous number of pointers:

- Ghosts will walk if people have not been appropriately buried.
- Ghosts usually appear at night, ideally around midnight, "the witching hour."
- Ghosts may simply be people who do not understand they are dead or are reluctant to leave the world of the living.
- Ghosts may wish to warn the living, to get revenge, to terrify, to punish, or to guard or reveal hidden treasure or secrets.
- Ghosts can appear in the shrouds in which they were buried or in the clothes they wore in life—*e.g.* in armor if militant in death.
- Ghosts may or may not speak, but if they do it is only after being questioned.
- Ghosts may be semitransparent or look as substantial as ordinary people.
- Ghosts can float, pass through walls, cause the room temperature to drop suddenly, and appear or vanish instantly.
- Ghosts may speak in a whisper or squeak and gibber (the latter seems to be out of fashion these days).
- Ghosts make fires burn blue and candles flicker.
- Ghosts can appear to one person and be unseen by those accompanying him or her.
- Ghosts can appear in your waking or dream states.
- Ghosts may be evil spirits in disguise.

ARE THE DEAD UP TO DATE?

In *Appearances of the Dead* (1984), R. C. Finucane points out that ghosts seem to be old-fashioned in their ways. Not only do they prefer haunting old buildings rather than new ones, but they cling to old beliefs:

Eighteenth century ghosts carried on many of the menial, work-day tasks that their seventeenth century predecessors had performed, apparently unaware that great changes were going on down among the living, particularly in the realm of ideas. Percipients, consequently, went on reporting to the same old motifs, depending on their Protestant or Catholic inclinations.

Old-fashioned patterns persist. The Blessed Virgin does not seem interested in delivering messages to non-Catholics, and prefers poor peasant children (of course, if you believe in the doctrine of the Assumption, she cannot be a ghost, as she is the only human being who did not die). St. John the Baptist could qualify as a ghost, but I can find no record at all of his ghost appearing to Baptists, a major American denomination. If you will regard the resurrected Jesus Christ as a ghost, then He has the distinction of being able to appear as either a baby (as to St. Anthony of Padua) or a man of thirty-something.

The dead who come to us in dreams cannot be classified as the usual ghosts. When they bring, as some people have claimed, news of death at a distance, however, they enter the world of the paranormal.

GET THIS STRAIGHT

An apparition is the appearance of a spirit.

A ghost is the apparition of a dead person.

A wraith is the apparition of a live person not physically present.

Apparitions may be of the entire figure or a part of it (a head, a hand) and may be misty and transparent or look exactly like a person. Although ghosts and wraiths are what is called ectoplasm and are not solid, they are said to be able to move solid objects.

Poltergeists throw things. Some (fraudulent) mediums claim that ghosts leave fingerprints in wax. Objects from the spirit world made manifest in our world are called apports. Some mediums say they can bring such apports; a flower may "materialize" at a séance, for instance.

APPARITIONS

The word is a trifle confusing because we can have, it is supposed, apparitions not only of the dead, but also of the living, who are at a distance, perhaps dying at that moment. And we do not have to *see* an apparition. Our other senses can detect one. We feel a sudden chill. Disembodied voices may speak or wail. We hear inexplicable noises. Doors open and close by themselves. The light or the television or radio suddenly comes on or goes off. We smell a peculiar odor. We feel a clammy hand on our shoulder. We sense someone is watching us, standing behind us. We may or may not be able to communicate with these wandering spirits.

They may appear solid as you and I, or flimsy and transparent. They may be friends, former friends, or absolute strangers. They can be luminous, bloody, even headless. You may hear them trudging up the stairs or they may silently pass through a wall. They may be seen by everyone present, one person only, or no one at all. They may come only once, or over and over, even on a schedule.

They may be ghosts who do not even realize they are dead!

If apparitions have abnormal physical strength, exhibit clairvoyance, blaspheme, float, or levitate, they may be, according to the Roman Catholic Church, demonic. Cross yourself and run for the nearest exit.

The appearance of a dead person is called a ghost but it is alleged that a living person may appear in moments of crisis far from where that person actually is. This is called a wraith, and it usually comes to deliver a message of some import. Josephine may have appeared to Napoleon in May 1821 to tell him he had but a little time to live (she had long been divorced from him and herself had died in 1814). Unlike an apparition, which takes no notice of observers, the wraith makes a spectral visit to a specific person for a specific purpose. A wraith appears when the target is awake, not dreaming, but people can see representations of such warning figures in dreams, too.

G. N. M. Tyrrell in *Apparitions* (1942): "Apparitions are the sensory expression of dramatic constructs created in regions of the personality outside the field of normal consciousness." To this psychologist, apparitions are purely human, not supernatural. American psychologists tend to follow Tyrrell's lead.

GREGORY THE GREAT

St. Gregory (usually called The Great) was born in Rome about AD 540. He rose to be *prætor*. Suddenly, about 575 he threw all honors aside and, following the invitation of Christ to sell everything, give the money to the poor, and follow Him, Gregory astounded his fellow Christians by doing just that. He retired to a monastery. One day, seeing a fair-haired slave from Britain in the market, he said the boy looked not like an Angle but an Angel, and he promptly set off to convert Britain.

The Pope, at the insistence of the Romans who did not want to lose Gregory, made him come back. On the death of Pelagius II in AD 590, Gregory was very unwillingly forced to take the papal tiara. You may know of Pope Gregory the Great because of Gregorian chant, but before he died (AD 604) he did many other things, including dispatching St. Augustine to convert those English he found so attractive. Gregory also found time to write from personal experience, and from the experiences of his wide circle of friends, a great collection of supposedly true ghost stories. Mostly they underlined the suffering (in Purgatory) of dead sinners who came back to beg the living for prayers to free them from their punishments in the afterlife.

RALPH WALDO EMERSON ON IMMORTALITY

"I notice that as soon as writers broach this question they begin to quote. I hate quotation. Tell me what you know."

SAMUEL BUTLER ON IMMORTALITY

"To himself everyone is an immortal. He may know that he is going to die, but he can never know that he is dead."

ELIE WIESEL

"Man, as long as he lives, is immortal. One minute before his death he shall be immortal. But one minute later, God wins."

JOSEPH ADDISON

It must be so—Plato, thou reason'st well!—
Else whence this pleasing hope, this found desire,
This longing after immortality?
Or whence this secret dread and inward horror
Of falling into naught? Why shrinks the soul
Back on herself and startles at destruction?
'Tis the Divinity that stirs within us,
'Tis Heaven itself that points out an hereafter,
And intimates Eternity to man.

WILLIAM FAULKNER

"I decline to accept the end of man. It is easy enough to say that man is immortal simply because he will endure; that when the last ding-dong of doom has clanged and faded from the last worthless rock hanging tidelessly in the last red and dying evening, that even then there will still be one more sound: that of his puny, inexhaustible voice, still talking. I believe that man will not merely endure; he will prevail. He is immortal, not because he alone among creatures has an inexhaustible voice, but because he has a soul, a spirit capable of compassion and sacrifice and endurance."

THE WANDERING JEW

Walking the earth as a ghost—but not a vampire—is The Wandering Jew. Having insulted Christ at the time of the Crucifixion, he is condemned to "wait until I come again." I discuss the whole story in *The Complete Book of Spells, Curses, and Magical Recipes* and summarize the plot of Eugène Sue's novel *Le Juif Errant*, a nineteenth-century bestseller.

At the height of The Wandering Jew's popularity in the last century, German poets such as Aloys Schreiber, Wilhelm Müller, Albert von Chamisso, August Wilhelm von Schlegel, and others made use of the legend's romantic charms, which Goethe once planned to do but never got around to doing. Other literary appearances of The Wandering Jew are found in:

Anonymous, *The Wandering Jew* (tract, 1870)
Sabine Baring-Gould, *Curious Myths of the Middle Ages* (1884)
Moncure Daniel Conway, *The Wandering Jew* (1881)
Gustave Doré, *The Legend of The Wandering Jew* (translated 1857)
Alexandre Dumas, *Tarry Till I Come!* (translated 1901)
David Hoffman, *Chronicles, Selected from the Originals by Cartaphilus* (3 vols., 1853)
Gen. Lew Wallace, *The Prince of India* (2 vols., 1893)

There is an annotated bibliography called *The Wandering Jew* (Avrahm Yarmolinsky, 1929) and a survey of the legend's history, also called *The Wandering Jew* (Joseph Gaer, 1961). The legend appears in such plays as:

> Andrew Franklin, *The Wandering Jew; or, Love's Masquerade* (1797)
> Isaac Goldberg, *The Stranger* (1920, from David Pinsky's Yiddish play, 1906)
> Sidney Royce Lysaght, *The Immortal Jew* (1931)
> David Mackinnon, *Ahasuerus: A Persian Play* (1920)
> E. Temple Thurston, *The Wandering Jew: A Play in Four Phases* (1920)

The Wandering Jew has been named Malchus (when assumed to be the High Priest's servant whose ear was cut off by St. Peter), Cartaphilus (when assumed to be the doorkeeper of the High Priest), Lakedion or Laquedem (from Hebrew *l'kodem*, "ancient one"), Johannes Buttadeus (Latin for "John Hit-God"), Juan Espera en Díos (Spanish for "John Trust-in-God"), Paulus, Ahasuerus, Judas, Theudas, and Melmoth (as in Charles Maturin's *Melmoth the Wanderer*).

In Jewish and Muslim versions of the tale he may be identified with the Prophet Elijah and have names such as Zerib ben Elia or Michob Ader. He can be a poor shoemaker, a rich diamond merchant, etc. He can grow ever more infirm with age or rejuvenate every 40 or 70 years. When the first millennium came, his story was especially attractive because it affirmed he would die at the Second Coming, the end of the world. As the second millennium ends, the tale may revive once more, most likely on the screen. Films thus far have included:

> Roma-America's silent version of Sue's novel (1913)
> Stoll (UK)'s silent version of Thurston's play (1923)
> Jaffa's film in Yiddish with Jacob Ben-Ami (1933)
> Twickenham (UK)'s version of Thurston's play with Conrad Veidt (c. 1935)
> Distributori Independenti's *L'Ebreo errante* with Vittorio Gassman (1948)

The version with Conrad Veidt (famous as Cesare the somnambulist in *The Cabinet of Dr. Caligari*) was regarded as Nazi anti-Semitism. The Vittorio Gassman version, however, was promoted in the US as anti-Nazi propaganda and called *The Sands of Time*.

The political significance of tales of the Undead has yet to enjoy full analysis, but it is clear that vampirism and capitalism have been connected in the minds of some. The importance of tales of the supernatural, as with science fiction, is that they are metaphors for discussing actualities—persistence, predation, politics....

Two of the modern world's greatest longings are for immortality and for non-being; blessed redemption and easeful death. The Wandering Jew's legend involves both. It has lasted a thousand years.

The Wandering Jew's story, like the vampire's, has never-ending attraction. It can be adapted to many circumstances and audiences. It oddly makes death seem less frightening, and death is the greatest fear we all have. As the hero of J. P. Donleavy's *The Ginger Man* says:

> ...Jesus, when you don't have money, the problem is food. When you have money, it's sex. When you have both, it's health.... If everything is simply jake then you're frightened of death.

ROMAN GHOSTS

The best known of these may be Shakespeare's ghost of the eponymous character in *Julius Caesar*. However, the first Roman to give a notable description of a specter was the historian Tacitus. In his taciturn way, he didn't say much.

Pliny and Pausanius and many other writers take the existence of ghosts more or less for granted. In classical times, everyone believed in them. As Dr. Johnson would say, they are in logic ridiculous and in belief inextinguishable.

It was said of Shakespeare that he was not merely of his time but for all time. Nonetheless, every artist is first if not foremost of his or her time. That's unavoidable. Whatever the dramatist Shakespeare personally believed, he knew that his audiences believed in ghosts, and he gave in to them. In *Hamlet*, Shakespeare illustrates his belief in ghosts (or his conviction that his audience will accept them). He also brings out the Theory of Correspondences, which asserts that if something happens on one level of existence it will be reflected on another level. Recall the Star of Bethlehem at the birth of Christ, or the darkening of the sky in the middle of the afternoon and the dead rising from their graves at the moment of Christ's crucifixion.

Shakespeare has a character who is supposed to be reliable say that strange things occurred on the night before the murder of Julius Caesar: a lion (representing the leader of men) was loose in Rome and "The sheeted dead did squeak and gibber in the Roman streets."

Andrew Lang, arguing that beliefs in the paranormal ought to be included in folklore studies, wrote learnedly of the heritage of classical literature:

> We possess Palæphatus, the life of Apollonius of Tyana, jests in Lucian, argument and exposition from Pliny, Porphyry, Iamblicus, Plutarch, hints from Plato, Plautus, Lucretius, from St. Augustine and other fathers [of the Roman Catholic Church]. Suetonius chronicles noises and hauntings after the death of Caligula....

BRITISH LIBRARY MANUSCRIPTS OF INTEREST

Brooklyn can boast the birth of A. E. Waite. But he went to Britain and became a leading figure of British occult circles in the last decade or so of the nineteenth century. He revised the organization and rituals of The Order of the Golden Dawn. He wrote about both unprinted and printed sources of magical rituals (some of his work is conveniently reprinted in *Chambers Dictionary of Beliefs and Religions*, 1992, and elsewhere). Regarding necromantic rituals remaining unprinted in his time he recorded:

> Sloane [MS#] 3884 includes a process of Necromancy—how to call the ghost of a dead body—the invocation of spirits into a crystal—the form for summoning spirits within the circle—and a method of exorcism in the Tuscan language—all impudently attributed to the author of the *Nullity of Magic*—that is to say Roger Bacon [1214-1292, but this MS's material is pretty clearly not of thirteenth-century origin].... Sloane [MS#] 3850 is a MS of the seventeenth-century.... [with] processes, mostly in Latin, but some in English, for the discovery of things lost, the recovery of things stolen, for the spirits of the dead who cannot rest in their graves, and for persons possessed of evil spirits....

THE BLOODY COUNTESS

The Countess Erzebet or Elizabeth Báthory of Hungary had important relatives. Therefore she more or less got away with murdering hundreds of girls and bathing in their blood. When this was discovered, her maid (with whom she had a shocking lesbian affair—shocking not because it was same-sex but because it was different class, an aristocrat with a mere servant) and others suffered death. The countess, however, was simply walled up in her castle for the rest of her life.

You can read her story in *The Complete Book of Vampires*—all that blood! She is not related to the monstrous Gilles de Rais (who murdered hundreds of boys and appears in *The Complete Book of Devils and Demons*), who perpetrated his crimes to please The Devil. The countess was seeking only to improve her appearance. The Bloody Countess really belongs here, in a discussion of ghosts and souls, for the blood to her was a matter of *spirit*. In a twisted, sad, magical way, she hoped that by bathing in the blood of maidens she would capture their youth. Some child molesters have a similar rationale for consuming the sperm of boys.

Inevitably, the countess's gruesome history has been the subject of numerous biographical and fictional accounts. A recent appearance of this monster is in an hour-long ballet, *The Countess*, choreographed and danced by Yvette Bozsik and her company from Budapest, brought to New York in June 1998. The *New York Times* called it "a stylish, often eerie portrait of a woman locked into a hermetic world in the company of the maid who becomes her lover." The review added that the ballet "did not explore very deeply into history or the psyche...."

People who believe they can capture the spirit of someone by using their blood (or blood products) do deserve to be looked into very deeply.

POLITICALLY INCORRECT

Alian, Pausanius, Strabo, Suidas—right down the alphabet, ancient historians tell and retell the legend of Ulysses at Temesa in Italy. It's a ghost story about a rapist. A man violently deflowered a local virgin and was stoned to death by the townsfolk. This annoyed him so much that he came back to haunt them.

He bothered them so much that they were driven to consult the oracle of Apollo for advice. The oracle told them that the ghost would continue to terrorize them until they built a temple in honor of the dead man and annually offered him a sacrifice. The sacrifice? One local virgin.

Being nice to rapists is not considered a good idea today. Legends of earlier times are often at variance with the beliefs and values of the modern world. We sometimes find it impossible to understand how people could placate violent ghosts—or believe in ghosts at all. There is an illustration of the Temesa tale in Beaumont's *Treatise on Spirits* (1705).

THE FEAST OF ANTHESTERIA

Of all the feasts at which folklore or religion say ghosts appear, perhaps the most interesting was the one known to Athenians, at the height of Greek culture, as the Feast of Anthesteria. Ghosts were supposed to roam the city all day. Care was taken to keep them out of public shrines (around which ropes were tied) and private houses (where pitch was put on the doors so that the ghosts would stick to them if they tried to enter). Food was left outside to keep hungry ghosts from venturing in.

At the end of the day, incantations drove the ghosts back to their resting places and their vacation in town was over.

A PARTY FOR THE ROMAN GHOST

In classical times, Romans believed not only in household gods, to whom they sacrificed, but also in annual visits by ghosts, for whom they threw a party for three days each May. Public shrines and temples were prepared to keep the ghosts out, as private homes were opened to them. The ghosts came for the food and entertainment, and in numbers.

Getting them to leave was a problem. (Maybe you have had similar problems with live guests after three days.) Here's the Roman method of getting the ghosts to go, listed as instructions to the host:

> Rise at midnight. Wash your hands. With appropriate magical gestures and the nine times repeated incantation "With these beans I redeem me and mine" toss nine black beans over your shoulder without looking where they fall. Wash your hands again and then clash bronze vessels together [as the Chinese and many other peoples say, noise bothers spirits]. Say nine times, "Go forth, paternal shades." Look behind you. The ghosts should have taken the beans and gone. If not, repeat the ceremony.

A PHILOSOPHY

Thales (640-546 BC) maintained that there was no fundamental difference between life and death. When asked why, then, he chose life instead of death, he replied, "Because there is no difference." Philosophers talk that way.

Michael Servetus (1511-1553), condemned to be burned at the stake for heresy, told his judges, "I shall burn, but this is a mere incident. We shall continue our discussion in eternity."

In a familiar papyrus, Osiris watches over the weighing of a soul against a feather. The souls of those who do not bear the weight of guilt are lighter. The feather represents truth.

Blaise Pascal (1623-1662) admitted that he did not know whether there was life after death or not, but he said it was wisest to live as if there were— just in case.

Sir Isaac Newton (1642-1727) opined that to give his opinion on the immortality of the soul would be premature. "I am an experimental philosopher," he explained. However, every believer in ghosts and every person fascinated by vampires demonstrates that all of us, skeptics or not, hope that we are not dead when we die. We welcome any shred of hope that there is something besides oblivion after the death of the body.

A modern view, unless you think all aspects of the supernatural are nonsense and parapsychology is an empty pseudo-science, might be best expressed in the view of Herbert Thurston, SJ. This Jesuit inevitably looked at the question from the religious point of view. On the subject of ghosts and poltergeists, he wrote:

> That there may be something diabolical, or at any rate evil, in them I do not deny, but, on the other hand, it is also possible that there may be natural forces involved which are so far as little known to us as the latent forces of electricity were known to the Greeks. It is possibly the complication of these two elements which forms the heart of the mystery.

MAY THIS BODY BE SAFE FROM WITCHES!

The Greeks, who were producing electricity by rubbing amber, were famously interested in science. They were also interested in superstition. (Charms against the evil eye are more than tourist trivia in Greece today; the Greeks remain superstitious). The Romans copied the Greeks in both science and superstition, as they did in so many other ways.

Here's something Roman. In Apuleius' *The Golden Ass*, young Telephron undertakes to guard a corpse overnight to prevent witches from eating off the nose and the ears. The witches cast a spell over Telephron and eat *his* nose and ears. He does not discover this until it is too late. They have given him a false nose and ears, made of wax.

For modern superstitions, see Loring Danforth's *The Death Rituals of Rural Greece* (1982).

THE RESURRECTION OF THE BODY

Some Christians believe that after the last trumpet sounds, the dead are to arise incorruptible, returning to the bodies they had in this life. Nancy Mitford wrote to Evelyn Waugh that it would probably be much like "finding your motorcar after a party."

SPEAKING WITH THE DEAD IN EARLY LITERATURE

The most famous examples occur in *Samuel* I:28 (the Witch of Endor calls up a dead person for King Saul), *The Epic of Gilgamesh* (in which the hero evokes his dead friend Enkidu), Homer's epic *The Odyssey* (Ulysses employs Tireseus), and Aeschylus' drama *The Persians* (Atosa summons the dead Darius the Great).

The early literature of cultures less familiar to us in the West, however, has similar material, especially those cultures of Asia and Egypt. In these accounts of acts of necromancy, sacrifices were sometimes offered and the ghosts were usually asked to foretell the future on earth rather than to describe the afterlife. Thus, from ancient times it was as true as now that, in the words of Sir William Empson:

> Liberal hopefulness
> Regards death as a mere border to an improving picture.

MEDIEVAL SUPERSTITIONS ABOUT APPARITIONS

It was believed in medieval times that apparitions—if not actual bodies—of the dead could be seen. It was likewise believed that apparitions were more likely to appear at certain times. Friday and Saturday nights were preferred. The Devil appeared chiefly, it was said, at the full moon. If an apparition appeared to two or more people at the same time, it was likely more genuine and less dangerous.

Naturally, medieval credence in ghosts, undead vampires, devils, demons, and other inhuman spirits was aligned with the common beliefs of the time, including the immortality of the soul, the punishments of Purgatory before one's soul could enter heaven, and many other articles of faith (or superstition).

Don't forget that all of Christendom was founded upon the cornerstone belief that a human body rose from the dead. Christ "was crucified, dead, and was buried. On the third day, He rose again...."

The Last Thing is Death by H. Beham (1500-1550)

DE MORTUIS NIL NISI BONUM

The belief that the dead can still hear us recommends that we "speak nothing but good of the dead."

The Greek actor who is the narrator of Mary Renault's *The Mask of Apollo* (1966) reminds us that even before the Romans, it was believed that "at a funeral it is proper to remember only the good; or one offends the gods below, and calls the angry ghost to vengeance."

Not criticizing the dead may well go beyond fairness (because they cannot reply) to fear (lest they can).

PET POWER

Many believe that the extraordinary hearing and sight of animals such as dogs and cats enables them to detect alien spirits, ghosts, demons, and all, when we cannot. People report animals frozen with fear all of a sudden or barking furiously or refusing to enter a room.

When I was a graduate student at Princeton my roommate and I took in a pet cat who patiently watched, then pounced upon, chased, and destroyed invisible mice. I do not believe she saw ghostly mice. I think she was playing. She certainly "said" nothing when we put her in the bathroom of a student who claimed to have turned on the light there one night and seen the ghost of a student who had hanged himself years before. Or perhaps the cat was only interested in mice.

ST. JUDE

Most people, even those who do not believe in saints, have heard of St. Jude, "The Patron of Lost Causes." According to St. Augustine, it was St. Jude who added to the *Credo* the fundamental Christian belief in "the resurrection of the dead." Is that a Lost Cause?

NORWAY

With its fjords and lakes full of *nissen* and other water sprites and its forests and farms thronged with trolls, Norway has quite a number of human ghosts as well. One of the strangest is the *deildegast*, a perturbed spirit condemned to wander because in life he moved boundary stones in order to steal land. If you meet one, help to free him by putting boundary stones back where they ought to be. If at sea you encounter the mysterious Man on Board, let him help by rowing or trimming the cargo in the hold.

STANDARDS IN JUDGING REPORTS OF GHOST ACTIVITY

Andrew Lang in *Cock Lane and Common Sense* (1894) examined the evidence for poltergeist activity in a famous case (which we take up later in this book).

In later writings, Lang complained that folklorists and anthropologists were ready to listen to reports of ghosts in rural traditions and ancient times but whenever "honorable" modern people come forward with reports of ghosts appearing, "folklore turns a deaf ear" and leaves the question to The Society for Psychical Research.

Of reports of ghosts in modern life, Lang had this to say (when he writes "ghost-story" he means not fiction but alleged true experience):

> If a 'ghost-story' be found to contain some slight discrepancy between the narration of two witnesses, it is at once rejected, both by science and commonsense, as obviously and necessarily and essentially false. Yet no story of the most normal incident in daily life, can well be told without *some* discrepancies in the relations of witnesses. None the less such stories are accepted even by juries and judges. We cannot expect human testimony suddenly to become impeccable and infallible in all details, just because a 'ghost' is concerned. Nor is it logical to demand here a degree of congruity in testimony, which daily experience of human evidence proves to be impossible, even in ordinary matters.
>
> Toward those who claim to have experienced the supernatural we must remain objective. We should investigate ghosts or any other reported phenomena as far as we can with rigorous scientific standards. We must apply ordinary rules of evidence. What does all available evidence prove, if anything?

The serious journal called *The Skeptical Inquirer* starts with the hypothesis that most or all reports of the supernatural, whether of ghosts or extraterrestrials, are fraudulent, but one can start with that or the opposite prejudice and it does not matter so long as the investigation is honest and complete. Science requires not only repeatable experiments but open minds, sensible standards, and logical procedures. There is too often, one might say almost without exception, a dearth of these desiderata on both sides of the issue.

Hold still for just one very important sentence from John Ellis' *Literature Lost* (1997): "Any empirical investigation requires a principled open-mindedness about the material to be studied, which may compel one to revise initial hypotheses and to draw unanticipated conclusions."

PSYCHOLOGY AND THE PARANORMAL

Broad, C. D. *Religion, Philosophy and Psychical Research* (1953)
Devereux, G., ed. *Psychoanalysis and the Occult* (1953)
Moore, R. Laurence. *In Search of White Crows: Spiritualism, Parapsychology and American Culture* (1977)
Myers, F. W. H. *Human Personality and Its Survival of Bodily Death* (2 vols., 1903)

Rhine, J. B. *The Reach of the Mind* (1947)
Wolman, B. B. *et al.*, eds. *Handbook of Parapsychology* (1977)

SOME SCIENTIFIC LITERATURE

Scientists have researched occult phenomena a little bit. Poltergeist activity and vampires have been studied in terms of sexual frustration and sexual aggression. Various other aspects of the dead and undead have been researched in terms of anthropology, forensic medicine, and pathology. Scientists have analyzed the mythology of vampirism in relation to porphyria and that of ghosts in relation to the psychological need for connection with deceased loved ones or the need to believe in one's own personality continuing after death. Paranormal science, however, awaits reproducible experiments. For more, see:

Robert Almeder, *Beyond Death: Evidence for Life after Death* (1987)
Sir James Frazer, *The New Golden Bough* (1959)
Andrew M. Greeley, *The Sociology of the Paranormal* (1975)
Earnest M. Jones, *On the Nightmare* (reprinted 1951)
L. J. Martin, "Ghosts and the Projection of Visual Images," *The American Journal of Psychology* 26 (7 April 1915), 251-257
Sybo A. Schouten, "A Test of Hewman's Theory on Paranormal Phenomena," in *Research in Paraphsychology* (ed. D. H. Weiner and R. L. Morris, 1987)
Richard A. Schweder, "Ghost Busters in Anthropology," in *Human Motives and Cultural Models* (ed. R. G. D'Andrade and C. Strauss, 1992)

Also interesting are such surveys as:

Richard Noll, *Vampires, Werewolves, and Demons: Twentieth Century Reports in the Psychiatric Literature* (1992)
Marie-Louise V. France, *Shadow and Evil in Fairy Tales* (revised 1995)

...AND THE PARAPSYCHOLOGISTS

Ruth Brandon, *The Spiritualists* (1984)
Ann Braude, *Radical Spirits: Spiritualism and Women's Rights in Nineteenth Century America* (1989)
Sir Arthur Conan Doyle, *History of Spiritualism* (1926, reprinted 1975)
Janet Oppenheim, *The Other World: Spiritualism and Psychical Research in England, 1850–1914* (1988)
Joseph Gaither Pratt, *Parapsychology: An Insider's View of ESP* (1964)
D. Scott Rogo, *Parapsychology: A Century of Inquiry* (1975)
Proceedings of Four Conferences of Parapsychological Studies (1957)

PSYCHIATRISTS AT WORK

If you fear ghosts and cemeteries or have related phobias, are you crazy? What if you think you have experienced a ghost? Are apparitions deceptive perceptions arising from deep and perhaps malfunctioning levels of the psyche or "dissociated parts of the self?" In a ghost story (such as one by Dickens) does the principal character's confusion in reporting his story suggest not a traumatic meeting with the supernatural but "partial insanity"? Can ordinary people be partly crazy when it comes to ghosts and poltergeists?

Theorists and therapists are debating such matters all the time. The psychologists are no less interested than the parapsychologists, and their investigations tend to be more rigorous if less well known.

Here are just a few very recent studies from the scientific literature:

Gallup, Gordon G., Jr. & Lori Marino & Timothy J. Eddy. "Anthropomorphism and the Evolution of Social Intelligence: A Comparative Study," pp. 77-91 in *Anthropomorphism, Anecdotes and Animals* (Robert W. Mitchell, ed.), 1997

Grotstein, James S. "'Internal Objects' or 'Chimerical Monsters'? The Demonic 'Third Forms' of the Intellectual World," *Journal of Intellectual Disability Research* 48:3 (1996), 227-248

Kipnis, David. "Ghosts, Taxonomies, and Social Psychology," *American Psychologist* 52:3 (1997), 205-211

Kracke, W. "Dreams, Ghosts, Tales: Parintinin [Indians of Brazil] Imagination," *Psychoanalytical Review* 84:2 (1997), 273-288

Morton, Mary. "The Story of a Ghost," *Psychoanalytic Psychotherapy* 11:1 (1997), 19-27

Tytler, Graeme. "Charles Dickens' 'The Signalman': A Case of Partial Insanity?," *History of Psychiatry* 8:31 (part 3) (1997), 421-432

PARAPSYCHOLOGICAL RESEARCH

Parapsychological research has been going on in organized fashion since the nineteenth century in Britain, where the Society for Psychical Research (SPR) was founded in late Victorian times and a Ghost Society was even earlier in operation. SPR is at 1 Adam and Eve Mews, London W8 6UG. An American SPR was founded in the nineteenth century and involved William James and other psychologists. In the twentieth century, Duke University has been a leader in parapsychological research. Also to be noted here are:

American Society for Psychical Research
5 West 73rd Street
New York, NY 10023

The Center for Scientific Anomalies Research
PO Box 1002
Ann Arbor, MI 48103

Committee for Scientific
Investigation of Claims
of the Paranormal
1203 Kensington Avenue
Buffalo, NY 14215

Department of Parapsychology
Department of Behavioral
Medicine and Psychiatry
PO Box 102, Medical Center
University of Virginia
Charlottesville, VA 22908

Graduate Parapsychology Program
Department of Holistic Studies
John F. Kennedy University
Orinda, CA 94563

Parapsychological Association, Inc.
PO Box 12236
Research Triangle Park, NC
27709

Parapsychological Foundation
228 East 72nd Street
New York, NY 10021

Parapsychological Research Group
3101 Washington Street
San Francisco, CA 94511

The International Society for the
Study of Ghosts & Apparitions
Penthouse North
29 Washington Square West
New York, NY 10011-9180

Clubs, fanzines, and the like come and go. For current information, the internet may be your best source.

ALTERNATIVES

Uncounted millions believe in reincarnation. We even have Americans called Renata and Renée, though perhaps thoughtlessly named.

Death Comes to a Sleeping Woman by H. Beham (1500-1550)

I shall not tackle reincarnation thoroughly in this book, partly because if your spirit enters another form after your death it is not exactly a matter of the ghost of the dead but a deathless spirit of the living. I do wish to pique your imagination with this question: What would have happened if your spirit was incarnated in another body than the one the God, or Nature, issued you?

Such matters pop up in pop art. I recently saw a film called *Sliding Doors* (1998). In it a young woman both manages to press into a train—and also doesn't. Her spirit then exists in two bodies and she leads parallel lives. This is presented as a comic situation. In Krzysztof Kieslowski's film *Blind Chance*, one spirit, running for a train, heads into three different states of reality.

If you believe the human spirit exists after death, do you believe that the body it happens to have lived in will have a great influence on the nature, maybe even the fate, of the ghost that leaves it?

There is another question. Do you believe that the human soul or spirit exists not only after death but before? Do spirits come to inhabit earthly bodies, or do they have no existence until they are somehow produced in the human being, as consciousness is, only by that mortal and, shall we say, mechanical being? If there is no spirit until the human being is conceived, then it may perish when that human being dies. In that case, there is no life of the soul or spirit outside the body, and none after death. Dead is dead. No ghosts at all.

A THOUGHT

Kierkegaard remarked that life has to be lived forward but can only be understood backward. Do you think that when it's over your ghost will finally see it all clearly?

SLOW FINAL CURTAIN

British short story writer Pauline Melville has a view of the afterlife that more people hold than you might imagine. The title story of Melville's *The Migration of Ghosts* (1998) has a husband who toys with ideas of reincarnation but a more sensible wife who wants her spirit after death to hang around a little, to "hover," she says, "until it just dissolves." Ghosts may be temporary beings, gradually losing strength and finally disappearing for good.

THE LIVING AND THE DEAD IN MEDIEVAL SOCIETY

Jean-Claude Schmitt does not believe in the reality of ghosts—he writes that "the dead have no existence other than that which the living imagine for them"—but he insists that to medieval people the dearly departed were important and influenced the religion, politics, and daily lives of those they left behind. The dead were prayed for in Masses, feared and revered.

From a mass of medieval texts, Schmitt (translated by Teresa Lavender Fagan as *Ghosts in the Middle Ages,* 1998) has unearthed a great deal of information about solitary specters, vengeful ghosts, pitiful revenants, etc. He explains who was said to have returned to whom and why. Make no mistake: whatever you think of ghosts, your European ancestors fully believed in them and acted accordingly.

GHOSTLY RETRIBUTION

There are many reported cases of ghosts coming for retribution, often in dreams (which might suggest that we speak of nightmares, not ghosts). Here is an example from Frank Kermode's autobiographical *Not Entitled* (1997):

> This very morning I woke out of a dream of disgrace: I had been giving a series of readings of something I'd written, aware that it was not very good, though the audience, seated round a long table, seemed patient. Then the late Graham Hough, a friend but an unsparing critic, began to chatter rudely to his neighbor.... And it seemed he had two good reasons for being rude to me. The first was that he had spent more than three years in a Japanese prison camp and I hadn't. The second was that I stayed away from his funeral.

THE FIRST SPIRITUALIST

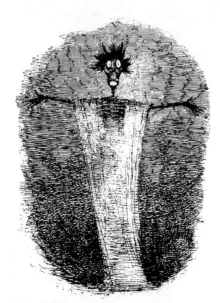

A frightful apparition.
George Cruikshank (1792-1878).

People attempted from time immemorial to communicate with the dead: it was called necromancy and was roundly condemned as a black art by various religions, including the Christian denominations (even though the Witch of Endor is reported in The Bible).

The first to claim that the dead were communicating, in the United States at least, was John D. Fox of Hydeville in Wayne County, upstate New York, who heard rapping noises. He is discussed in an earlier volume in this series, *The Complete Book of the Devil's Disciples*.

Spiritualism, one of America's own home-grown religions, is unusual in being based upon ghosts.

"SHE WAS DEAD"

Because so much of the ghost story and spiritualism and other effusions of the Victorian spirit spring from the sentimental approach to death that Dickens triumphantly exploited, here is the famous death of Little Nell, from chapter 72 of *The Old Curiosity Shop.*

It is highly characteristic of an era when funerals were filled with pomp; when people wore jewelry made of the hair of the deceased or cherished a lock of hair in a locket; when people kept in their parlors a cast of a dead hand, even a death mask; when cemeteries were filled with statues of mournful angels. The Victorian era was probably the height of sentimentalizing death.

This description of Little Nell is a *locus classicus* in Victorian literature, a literature famous for the happy ending and (as Henry James phrased it) "a distribution at the last of prizes, pensions, husbands, wives, babies, millions, appended paragraphs, and cheerful remarks," not to mention eternal joy in the afterlife, or "pie in the sky." Little Nell's demise was a scene out of which Dickens wrung every drop of pathos, bringing tears to all eyes at his dramatic readings. This was the character so beloved that when the packet arrived with the installment in which Little Nell was to perish, crowds of readers gathered at the docks in New York City and shouted to the sailors as the ship came in, asking if Little Nell was really dead.

It is only fair to add that no less a literary critic than Oscar Wilde remarked that no one who did not have a heart of stone could read these words of Dickens without laughing. You be the judge.

> Waving them off with his hand, and calling softly to her as he went, he stole into the room. They who were left behind, drew close together, and after a few whispered words—not unbroken by emotion, or easily uttered—followed him. They moved so gently, that their footsteps made no noise; but there were sobs from among the group, and sounds of grief and mourning.
>
> For she was dead. There, upon her little bed, she lay at rest. The solemn stillness was no marvel now.
>
> She was dead. No sleep so beautiful and calm, so free from trace of pain, so fair to look upon. She seemed a creature fresh from the hand of God, and waiting for the breath of life; not one who had lived and suffered death.
>
> Her couch was dressed with here and there some winter berries and green leaves, gathered in a spot she had been used to favour. "When I die, put me near something that has loved the light, and had sky above it always." Those were her words.
>
> She was dead. Dear, gentle, patient, noble Nell was dead. Her little bird—a poor slight thing the pressure of a finger would have

crushed—was stirring numbly in its cage; and the strong heart of its child mistress was mute and motionless forever.

Where were the traces of her early cares, her sufferings, and fatigues? All gone. Sorrow was dead indeed in her, but peace and perfect happiness were born, imaged in her tranquil beauty and profound repose.

And still her former self lay there, unaltered in this change. Yes. The old fireside had smiled upon that same sweet face; it had passed, like a dream, through haunts of misery and care at the door of the poor schoolmaster on the summer evening, before the furnace upon the cold wet night, at the still bedside of the dying boy, there had been the same mild lively look. So shall we know the angels in their majesty, after death.

THE POWER OF PRAYER

In 1529 Adolphus Clarebach, because of his religious opinions, was taken to the Poultry Tower in Cologne to be repeatedly and cruelly tortured and finally brutally put to death. For years this tower had been the site of fearful apparitions.

From his first night in the tower, Clarebach prayed ardently to God. After his execution, the apparitions were gone from that place for good. He went to his death at the stake—consecrated to Vulcan, as people said, which meant burned alive—calm in his soul.

"Such is the power that a pious man's fervent prayer to God has against the Devil's schemings," writes Johann Weyer in *De Præstigiis Dæmonum*, assuming that apparitions are diabolical. He writes that prayer in the name of Christ

> is the art higher than the heavens, deeper than hell, free from danger, hostile to shades, disregardful of ghosts, hating idols, needing neither incense nor wine [for its ceremonies]. It commands all specters, ghosts, and the spirits of the dead; it ignores all tombs and graves and appearances of the dead. With untroubled brow it banishes empty terrors, and nightly apparitions, and the appearance of the denizens of the underworld....

KEEPING SCORE

I have always thought that for some of my contrarian friends, the worst thing about death might be that it means joining the majority. I think I slipped and said somewhere that in the long run the living may outnumber the dead. If I did, it was a misstatement, if you will accept the politicians' term.

Anne Dillard's essay "The Wreck of Life" in *Harper's* (January, 1998) has the statistics. She quotes a letter from demographer Nathan Keyfitz

God the Father, The Holy Ghost, and the Dead Christ by El Greco

to historian Julian Kaplan: "The dead outnumber the living....Credible estimates of the number of people who have ever lived on the earth run from 70 billion to over 100 billion."

Ms. Dillard adds:

> Averaging those figures puts the total persons ever born at about 85 billion. We living people now number 5.8 billion. By these moderate figures, the dead outnumber us about fourteen to one. The dead will always outnumber the living.

THE GHOST WALKS

There are many popular expressions regarding payday—the American Army created the most vulgar, "the eagle shits." But the phrase "the ghost walks" often baffles those who hear it. It comes from the first act of *Hamlet*:

> Thou hast uphoarded in thy life
> Extorted treasure in the womb of earth.

Shakespeare's character refers the Elizabethan belief that one of the reasons ghosts would return was to direct the living to buried treasure the dead had hidden away while they were alive.

NECROMANCY

Since the term "black magic" has come to take the specialized meaning of calling the dead back for the benefit of the living, a mention must be made in a book about ghosts. However, the reader should consult an earlier book in this series about magicians and spiritualists and other practitioners of necromancy. You will there encounter some wondrously weird people and practices; you will find much of interest in *The Complete Book of the Devil's Disciples*.

POSSESSION

We all have times when we say we are "not ourselves." But are we ever possessed of a foreign spirit? Is "what's got into you?" a reasonable question?

The Bible tells us that iron can enter into your soul. It also says that demons can and do enter into your body. In *The Complete Book of Devils and Demons* there is, of course, some discussion of possession by demons, usually treated with exorcism. Elsewhere we hear of amulets used to protect against this and other evils.

There can also be, some say, possession by elementals. Some religions hold that human thoughts can take on an existence as elemental forces and that these can trouble the living. Particularly in Eastern mysticism there are methods suggested for preventing, identifying, or dealing with possession by these "thought forms" or nasty "engrams" or elementals. The West has little belief in that sort of thing.

Finally, some believe that dead human beings can take possession of the living as vampires or ghosts. Possession by ghosts is not often mentioned—unless you count those mediums or channelers who claim that the dead take them over to speak through them. Somehow spiritualists and even those who speak in tongues or manifest other religious ecstatic states shy away from talking about possession and exorcism and such. But they do insist that "something came over me."

Ask your medium, guru, or "professional" psychic if she or he thinks that actual possession ever takes hold. You may find that no one has brought this up with them before, and maybe even that your faith in them is significantly altered by what they say in reply.

OUT OF BODY EXPERIENCE

A considerable number of people claim to have had OBE (not the Order of the British Empire or Others' Bloody Efforts, but floating above one's own body and looking down on it, Out of Body Experience). If so, they may have had a taste of what being dead—we use to say "giving up the ghost"—is like. With no firm evidence, some people claim that the spirit hangs around the body and its usual haunts for some time after death, only gradually taking the hint that it is time to move on. On occasion people have claimed that a particular ghost is unaware it is dead and does not want to leave.

To be rid of those who may wish to linger, make certain the appropriate rituals for departure are performed. And when you come back from the cemetery, rearrange the furniture. Do not keep a dead person's room "exactly as they left it." Rent it out, or turn it into a sewing room or something. Make a habit of saying "Rest in peace" when the name of the dead comes up, instead of "If only____were here."

PHANTOMS AND FEMINISM

Important in the history of the emancipation of women are the saintly mystics who reported heavenly visions. So also were the witches condemned for black magic. In each case, women broke free of the constraints of the powers that were and radically declared themselves to be directly in touch with higher powers.

The church found its male hierarchy unable to challenge the visions reported; men were relegated to taking down dictation (later to censor or recast, perhaps) of what the captives of the convent had to say. Men were compelled to rely upon mediums, most of them female, to convey the messages from Beyond in spiritualism as well. If men really believed that wise women were all that wise and powerful, they must have been rather foolish to risk their ire and bring them before tribunals.

But brought to court and to confession—often via hideous tortures—and to what was called justice, they certainly were. Through the course of the witchcraft persecutions, men shifted from the traditional argument that women were silly creatures and easily duped and led astray, to denouncing them for willingly signing up with The Devil. The church could do little to combat hysterical Spanish nuns or even fraudulent New England table-rappers, but in their day they could and did condemn to the flames practitioners of witchcraft. Most of those were women, many just early devotées of what we might now call alternative medicine.

Christina Larner equated witch hunting with "woman hunting," and the misogyny in the history of magic and witchcraft has been noted by a great many recent writers in this field, including myself. The hatred of women and of the body, exhibited in the writings and tortures of the Holy Inquisition era are horrifying. The weeding out of supposed undesirables both in "the burning times" and in the Holocaust and "ethnic cleansings" of our century betrays deep-seated and terrifyingly basic human fears and flaws.

To be fair, we must admit that some other recent scholarship takes a less feminist tack. For example, Stuart Clark's magisterial book on demonology, *Thinking with Demons* (1998), argues that witches were prosecuted or persecuted not because they were women but because they operated in opposition to established authority. (He doesn't get into why women would have felt marginalized and persecuted in the Judeo-Christian culture.)

Witches literally turned widdershins, against the direction of the sun's movement, against God. Satanists turned things upside down, even the crucifixes at their Black Masses. Witches challenged and frightened both church and state, so the church excommunicated them for heresy and the state seized upon them as traitors. They were not always thought useless, for they made medicines as well as love philtres and poisons. Other villagers often turned on them solely out of greed or spite and only after years of more or less comfortable participation in the life of the community. However, they were a minority, and any minority tolerated by the majority can pretty swiftly be turned into a target.

Diane Purkiss gets these and many other points straight in her forthright and provocative attack on other scholars' ill-founded judgments of magic and witchcraft. Her book, *The Witch in History* (1998), is a must.

We need an equally erudite, equally bold book on *The Ghost in History*. In that, as in everything, it will be well to remember that women hold up half the sky and, at least until artificial wombs, cloning, or other unusual methods of reproduction render them in that essential task redundant, women make it possible for the human race to continue from one generation to the next. Continuation seems to be a good idea, even though the centuries that have gone by since "the burning time" have not seen that race become much more humane.

IT'S TEN O'CLOCK: DO YOU KNOW WHERE YOUR CHILDREN ARE?

Christ is reported to have said in no uncertain terms that "unless one is born of water and the spirit, he cannot enter into the kingdom of God" (John 3:5). So the Roman Catholic church for centuries taught that when unbaptized babies died they went not to Hell or Purgatory,

Prayers to saints (dead humans) were supposed to gain their help in protection against demons (non-humans).

which hardly seemed fair to non-sinners (or humans with Original Sin but none of their personal doing), but to Limbo. Limbo, as the name suggests, was on the edge of Heaven and Hell, not unpleasant, but not paradisical.

In 1994, in the reign of John Paul II, the Roman Catholic Catechism abolished Limbo. That left miscarried fetuses and unbaptized infants "to the mercy of God." Heaven knows where they go. They are souls, not just wasted sperm and egg. They are souls as are aborted fetuses. Limbo was never "infallibly" declared by the church, so the doctrine could be changed. Whether "there is no Limbo" is now something Roman Catholics must believe, I am not sure. I suppose those Catholics who worry about such things will just make up their own rules (as they do on sexual matters such as abortion, contraception, homosexuality, and so on—to hell with what the pope says) and say dead babies go to Heaven.

It would be nice if dead babies did go to Heaven. I don't think they do. I think Heaven has to be earned. If not, the best thing you could do for a baby is to kill it before it is baptized—or grows up to be a sinner. Send it right to Heaven. I do not countenance that, however, any more than I recommend killing fetuses. On the other hand, I recommend contraception. If you do not want a baby, do not conceive one, I say, and today there are reliable ways to avoid unwanted babies.

You do not have to worry that contraception is killing a soul or keeping souls from being born, that spirit babies are getting tired of waiting for you to do what you've been told to do: increase and multiply. The Roman Catholic Catechism asserts that the soul is created at the moment of conception; it does not exist before that. Most people are as confused about the soul before birth as they are about the soul after death. Even catechisms cannot convince us that we know what is real.

In "Storming Limbo" an anonymous writer wrote in *Spy* for August 1997:

> The Church, it seems, is trapped in a mythology in which (1) God creates a supply of souls and then instantly blows most of them into oblivion [most pregnancies terminate naturally], and (2) His Son comes down to earth and announces that the unborn, currently called Holy Innocents, cannot go to Heaven. Is this any way to run a universe?
>
> Via the new Catechism, the Church has finally admitted that the whereabouts of the vast majority of God's children— that is, the vast majority of the ever-conceived who did not result in live births and could not be baptized—is beyond Christian explanation.

There are a great many people in the world, of course, who find most things are "beyond Christian explanation" and are managing to get along pretty well nevertheless. And new problems come along all the time to shake up traditional beliefs and religious denominations. One example: what will human cloning (certain to be opposed by many religions, certain to happen nonetheless) produce—just another body (or bodies) or another body (or bodies) and another soul (or souls) identical to the first?

In connection with our interests here, we do not so far have to worry about clones or the ghosts of clones. But if Limbo no longer exists, or never did, that is one place fewer for ghosts to come from.

VENGEFUL GHOSTS

Vengeance is said to be one of the most powerful motives for the dead returning to bother the living. It is often difficult to distinguish between a vengeful ghost and a vampire. Ever since the *utukku* of the Babylonians, which I would define as a vengeful ghost rather than a vampire (which some folks consider it), ghosts up to no good are reported to be a fact of life.

IVAN VASILLI

The Russians built the steamer *Ivan Vasilli* in 1897. It turned out to be a ghost ship somewhat like the *Demeter*, the ship on which, in that same year, Bram Stoker's Dracula arrived in England from his Transylvanian castle.

Vasilli's weirdness was not immediately apparent; it was not until 1903 that news of a poltergeist onboard became common knowledge (or common belief). A phantom whose appearances were accompanied by sudden cold began to terrify and sometimes paralyze crew members, but at no time did all the crew die, as on the *Demeter*. The poltergeist appeared in a ghastly glow but did not throw many things around. Rather, he drove the crew members to distraction or desertion. Several captains committed suicide; several crew members died of inexplicable causes. The ship was eventually burned.

SOME VERY IMPORTANT GHOSTS

Some people, annoyed by séances, have pointed out that nobody really important seems to come back from the dead and nothing the dead say to the living is of any use. In response, others have said that the truly important dead have important work to do and cannot be bothered with us, or that there is some regulation that prevents the dead from unfolding the tale and giving us any real idea of The Beyond.

The most useful ghost may have been that of blind Homer, who was said to have assisted George Chapman in his translation into English of *The Iliad*, the translation that Keats found so wonderful. Keats communicates his excitement about it in the famous sonnet *On First Looking into Chapman's Homer*.

DO GHOSTS HAVE ANY MEMORY
OF THEIR HUMAN LIVES AT ALL?

Of course not, argues Terence Penelhum in *Survival and Disembodied Existence* (1970). The argument is crucial for occultists, because if neither a returning ghost nor a reincarnated soul has any sense of the past, then *who* exactly is "coming back?"

Our personalities are what we recall, what is in our minds. If one could download all the contents of a human mind into a computer, then, in a significant sense, that computer would *be* the person. Thus, the identity of a ghost with no memory of his pre-death tenure on Earth is open to question.

SATURDAY NIGHT FEVER

If you want to exhume a vampire to destroy it, do it on a Saturday. Tradition assures us that vampires are dormant on Saturdays, and Saturdays only. A ghost, however, can come any night of the week—even in the daytime.

NIGHT CALL

If in the middle of the night you are awakened by hearing your name called, never answer the first time. Better let the caller repeat the name a few times. That way you will be safe, for everyone knows that a vampire can call you in the night but is not permitted to call more than once. Ghosts are said to call sleepers repeatedly until they awake.

BORDERLAND

That was the title of an occult journal edited in the 1890's by journalist and medium W. T. Stead, born in 1849 and drowned at the sinking of the *Titanic* in 1912. It is crammed with stories from an age possibly more superstitious than our own.

One typical vampire tale was contributed by Dr. Franz Hartmann in 1895. It concerns a miller whose apprentice ate ravenously and still kept wasting away. He complained that every night around midnight, something came and sat upon his chest and drew the strength out of him. The miller decided to test the veracity of this story. He went to bed with the boy but remained vigilant and, sure enough, just about midnight, some sort of ectoplasmic thing arrived—it felt like cold gelatin—and the miller promptly seized it and threw it into the fire. The boy recovered his strength and ceased to waste away.

Wrote Dr. Hartmann: "Those who like myself have, on innumerable occasions, removed 'astral tumours,' and thereby cured physical tumours, will find the above neither 'incredible' nor 'inexplainable.'"

I myself have seen Mexican practitioners perform what they call "psychic surgery," but neither that nor what the good doctor describes in the miller's boy's bed really has anything to do with "astral tumours." And how does Dr. Hartmann equate a tumour with a vampire? He has some sort of modern version of the succubus, a medieval superstition to which religious people gave far too much credence for far too long.

GHOSTS IN BRITAIN AFTER WORLD WARS

During wars there are always stories of ghostly presences, veridical dreams, wondrous happenings, hypnopompic experiences (dreams in which you think you have awakened and seen something). In World War I the fiction of an Angel of Mons was picked up and widely and fervently believed to be fact. There were ghostly battalions, ghostly aerial battles, ghost ships, and, of course, ghosts of those killed in battle bringing the news home at the very moment of their demise.

My father claimed to have had a casual chat with an army buddy only to hear later that the fellow had been killed some time before that. His fellow soldiers quite believed that and some did not think it unusual.

After World War I, spiritualism got a boost because the British lost so many promising young men in the slaughter of stupid trench warfare. They were particularly unwilling to let go of their slaughtered dead. One war poet said they died "like cattle." Sir Arthur Conan Doyle, Sir Oliver

Lodge, and other celebrities who lost sons in the Great War lent their names to spiritualistic propaganda. Mediums flourished, even though The Society for Psychical Research, Houdini, and a number of other organizations and individuals dismissed all blatant trickery.

The British romance with haunted castles and poltergeists in the rectories was a major feature of life between the wars. After World War II, British widows welcomed novels such as Josephine Leslie's comforting ghost tale *The Ghost and Mrs. Muir*. In America, a television series based on the novel was very popular. Every village and hamlet, city and shire has its ghost tales, and these are industriously collected and published. Three examples: Terence W. Whitaker's *Lancashire's Ghosts and Legends* (1982), Jean Forman's *Haunted Royal Homes* (1987), and Harry Ludlam's *The Restless Ghosts of Ladye Place* (1967).

A GHOST STORY FROM TEXAS

From *Publications of The Folk-Lore Society of Texas* (1932, ed. J. Frank Dobie) comes this little story from Marta Emmons. It offers essential information for coping if and when you are confronted by a ghost, so work your way through the dialect carefully:

> "I knew a' ole man that alluz wo' two paiah o' draws. But when he died his wife didna' lay out but one paiah foh 'im. Well, agter de fun'el, e kep' a-comin' back an' a-comin' back. Eva night he'd come right in dat front do' o' her ouse. So se moved from dat place, but he jes' kep' a-comin' jes' the same. She moved fo' o' five times, an' he jes' kep' on a-comin' back eva night o' the worl'. Finely se taked to some o' her frien's. They asked 'er why she don' talk to 'im. She say 'cause she scared to. But they say fo 'er to say, "What in de name o' the Lawd do you want?" So dat night he come ah'in.
>
> This time she walk' right up an' met 'im an' say, "What in de name of de Lawd do you want?"
>
> He looked at 'er right study of a long time, but she nevah move, an' she jes' stan' theah; an' finely he say, "Honey, gimme 'nother apiah o' draw's please."
>
> She say, "Aw right, I'll give 'em to you"; an from dat day to this he nevah as come back no mo', she say. An' dat's de way it is: When you ask 'em what in the name o' de Lawd they want, an' then tell 'em you'll giv it to 'em, they'll go 'way an' leave you alone.

WINGS ON MY FEET

The Stepin Fetchit stereotype of the superstitious African American terrified of ghosts was long a staple of American humor. It also appeared in a Negro Minstrel song of the above title. One verse ran:

I believes in a ghost. I believes in a haint.
Good God-a-Mighty, I ain't no saint.
Ain't go no arms, ain't of no haid!
Don't stop to count them tracks I made.

A FEMINIST AVENGER FROM BEYOND THE GRAVE

Sleep tight.

Comic books have long presented superheroes and wonder women as fighters for truth, justice, and the American Way. As those ideals have been modified in modern times, the avengers have echoed new concepts.

Wonder Woman, Miss Fury, and Girl Commandos have been followed by Lady Death, Shi, and Ghost.

Ghost is the ghost of an investigative reporter of the Brenda Starr type who was murdered by Bad Guys. She is back to wreck vengeance and zap any man who commits violence towards women. She doesn't have the lesbian tendencies of Hothead Paisan or the sexual fetishness of some Japanese mod maidens of mayhem, but she is politically as well as anatomically correct!

KNOCKING

It is by rapping, some say, that the dead can communicate at séances. Rapping is also among the ways poltergeists can annoy the living. And 3 knocks on the bedstead, an old superstition says, calls the dying to their rest. When the 3 knocks are heard, the person has very little time left to live.

THE BEST RECENT POLTERGEIST BOOKS

Colin Wilson, *Poltergeist: A Study in Destructive Haunting* (1993)
Sarah Hapgood, *The World's Great Ghost and Poltergeist Stories* (1995)
John Spencer & Ann Spencer, *The Poltergeist Phenomenon: An Investigation into Psychic Disturbance*   (1997)

DEAD OF THE WORLD, UNITE!

Of all the nuttiness that came out of Russia in the nineteenth century (when even czars were crazy for the occult) the nuttiest beliefs may well be those of the Cosmist Nikolai Federovich Fedorov, on whom George M. Young has a good survey essay in *The Occult in Russian and Soviet Culture* (1997, an anthology edited by Bernice Glatzer Rosenthal).

Fedorov held firmly to the belief that all the people who had died in the long history of the world ought not to be forgotten—or wasted. He proposed to gather up their dust, reassemble them, and bring them back to life. Because that dust might now have been wafted off into space, his agenda included traveling into space and visiting other planets. He said reanimating the dead was surely a scientific possibility and also an inescapable moral duty.

How to do it? Fedorov was ready to leave that to mere technicians. He was an idea man. He likewise suggested that the weather could be controlled by magnetism, but he didn't want to get tied up on the details of that, either.

TALKING BOARD

Schlock merchants of the occult now want to sell you a Talking Board. It's a round Ouija. They claim it "enables you to communicate with non-physical entities and your own Higher Self."

I would listen to an explanation about the latter claim if anyone wants to offer one, although I think the capital letters are laughably egotistical. However, those "non-physical entities" are undemonstrable, as far as I can tell. Buy one and sue for consumer fraud damages.

The popularity of this kind of thing in catalogues of scented candles and colored "crystals" and "mystic" jewelry makes it clear that many people do, in fact, believe they can communicate with "non-physical beings" like the dead, angels and devils, gods and goddesses. Scary.

Do you really believe that the masters of the universe are interested in you and your latest partner for fornication and are ready to take time to answer questions about your "relationship"? Do you really believe divine forces are concerned about solving petty personal problems that your therapist cannot?

I respectfully suggest that you get down off that Higher Self and get real. Take rational and regular steps to make yourself a better person. Don't rely on self-appointed non-entities who assure you that you have a right to "expect a miracle."

ARE GHOSTS FROM THE DEVIL?

The literature of witchcraft contains more than one example of people selling their souls to The Devil in order to have visions of their dead children or congress with a late wife or experience some other apparitions. It is alleged that The Devil can appear in any form or dispatch demons in any form, grotesque or attractive, with this sole proviso: because God the Creator is the only source of perfection, The Devil cannot reproduce a form exactly. He can only get it almost right. There is always some flaw, some defect—which gives the ordinary human being a chance to detect evil, I suppose. Few people today recall the old "fact" known to so many medieval people, which is that if you look closely at an apparition you may see that the face is reversed, as in a mirror.

That some apparitions are from The Devil is seldom doubted by those who believe in ghosts. Here is, however, a somewhat heterodox opinion from Sir Thomas Browne (1605-1682), whose writings on urn burial and other aspects of death were influential for centuries. In his *Religio medici* (The Religion of a Physician, 1643), he goes so far as to claim that *all* "apparitions and ghosts of departed persons" are but tricks of The Evil One and

> not the wandering souls of men, but the unquiet walks of Devils, prompting and suggesting us unto mischief, blood, and villainy; instilling and stealing into our hearts that the blessed Spirits are not at rest in their graves, but wander solicitous of the affairs of the World. But that those phantasms appear often, and do frequent Cemeteries, Charnel-houses, and Churches, it is because those are the dormitories of the dead, where the Devil, like an insolent Champion, beholds with pride the spoils and Trophies of his Victory over Adam.

Certainly the orthodox religions teach that *all* attempts at communication with the dead are forbidden. (You cannot be a Roman Catholic or certain kinds of Protestant and participate at all in Spiritualism.) At the same time, these religions teach that some living persons have legitimate visions of the dead, especially of saints, and that these things are of God, not of The Devil. If you believe in angels and saints, however, you must believe in fallen angels and demons. Be careful.

Ask any apparition what you would ask any stranger: "Where are you *from?*" Note, of course, that strangers sometimes, and demonic powers always, lie.

GOODBYE!

There are a great many uncheckable instances of the newly dead coming to announce their departure to the living persons closest to them. The Society for Psychical Research (London), for example, has collected many documents in which people swear that when they were sleeping or wide awake they saw the figure of a loved one who might have been as far away as India, and therefore knew that the person represented by the figure had died. I edited two volumes of such papers in *Phantasms of the Living* years ago. I remain particularly skeptical of messages received in dreams. I have had many dreams that came true—but many more that did not. I fear that coincidence explains too much.

Some people report hearing their names called by the dying: Heinrich Mann says he was alone in the Tyrol in 1910 when he heard his sister call his name. For an instant he thought it was quite ordinary, and then he realized that no one there ever called him *Heinrich*, only *Herr Mann*. Later he discovered that his sister, far away, had committed suicide.

Only examples of such activity reported to reliable witnesses and written down *before* the news of the death arrives can, I think, compel any credence. At the same time, each and every one of us knows that there are in our lives some experiences we cannot prove to have happened but that we know did happen—and that other people would be fools to believe without proof.

SLEEPY HOLLOW

Sleepy Hollow in New York State is the site of Washington Irving's famous tale of "The Headless Horseman," who turns out to be no more a ghost than the late, lamented Mrs. de Winter in Daphne du Maurier's popular novel, *Rebecca*. The locals decided in 1996 that they liked the name Sleepy Hollow better than North Tarrytown, and petitioned to change to it. Ghosts have been named for the places where reported, but this is a case of a town being named for a place where a ghost was imagined to be seen.

Those who lie unburied are said to be the most likely not to leave the earthly plane but to linger as ghosts, probably vengeful ghosts.

SOME EARLY REPORTS ON MODERN SPIRITUALISM

E. W. Capron, *Modern Spiritualism* (1855)
Hereward Carrington, *The Physical Phenomenon of Spiritualism* (1907)
J. W. Edmonds & G. T. Dexter, *Spiritualism* (1853-1855)
R. Hare, *Experimental Investigations of the Spirit Manifestations* (1856)
A. R. Wallace, *Miracles and Modern Spiritualism* (1876)
Report of the Seybert Commission on Spiritualism (1887)

IN SUPPORT OF SPIRITUALISM

Everyone loves a lord—or even a knight or baronet—in England. And so, despite the exposure of many fraudulent mediums, spiritualism garnered some dignity because it drew the support of Sir William Crookes (president of The Royal Society), Sir Arthur Conan Doyle (knighted for some propaganda relating to the Boer War but world famous for creating Sherlock Holmes), and Sir Oliver Lodge (an eminent scientist). Each of these men had personal reasons for their involvement in spiritualism. Crookes had a torrid affair with a famous medium (Florence Cook) and Conan Doyle and Lodge lost loved ones in the Great War.

Lodge's son Raymond, a lieutenant in the South Lancashire Regiment, enlisted in September 1914 and was killed by a shell fragment in Flanders in September 1915. His early death was a great loss to his family and friends, and brought even greater motive to Lodge, who for years had studied the paranormal to see if the dead could be contacted through mediums. He defended spiritualism in *Raymond; or, Life and Death* (1916). After nearly 400 pages, he makes observations such as these:

> The body is our machine, our instrument, our vehicle of manifestation; and through it we can achieve results in the material sphere. Why seek to deny either the material or the spiritual? Both are real, both are true. In some higher mind, perhaps, they may be unified; meanwhile we do not possess this higher mind. Scientific progress is made by accepting realities and learning from them; the rest is speculation. It is not likely that we are the only intelligent beings in the Universe. There may be many higher grades, up to the Divine; just as there are lower grades, down to the amoebæ. Nor need all these grades of intelligence be clothed in matter or inhabit the surface of a planet. That is the kind of existence with which we are now familiar, truly, and anything beyond that is for the most part supersensuous; but our senses are confessedly limited, and if there is any truth in the doctrine of human immortality the existence of myriads of departed individuals must be assumed, on what has been called "the other side."
>
> But how are we to get evidence in favour of such an appar-

ently gratuitous hypothesis? Well, speaking for myself and with full and cautious responsibility, I have to state that as an outcome of my investigation into psychical matters I have at length and quite gradually become convinced, after more that thirty years of study, not only that persistent individual existence is a fact, but that occasional communication across the chasm—with difficulty and under definite conditions—is possible...it is a subject that attracts cranks and charlatans. Rash opinions are freely expressed on both sides [of the issue of the possibility of communication with the dead]. I call upon the educated of the younger generation to refrain from accepting assertions without severe scrutiny, and, above all, to keep an open mind.

Writers of Victorian Britain such as Sergeant Cox (*Mechanism of Man: What am I?*, 1879) were utterly convinced that spiritualism was a fact to which only invincible prejudice could blind one: "No physical science can array a tithe [tenth] of the mass of evidence by which psychism [spiritualism] is supported." What do you think?

HEAVEN

It is fashionable now to say that everyone goes to Heaven. New Age gurus even suggest that Hitler and others you would not expect will in fact be encountered there. St. Augustine said that only 144,000 would be saved and enjoy eternal bliss; he calculated that Heaven was not large enough to accommodate more.

Marlene Dietrich said to an interviewer who asked her about the afterlife: "You can't believe that they're all flying about up there, can you?....It must be terribly crowded with all those people flitting about up there."

DESTRUCTION OF IDENTITY

We do not like to think that our identities will be snuffed out by death. We do, however, have a long tradition not only of attempting to obliterate the names of such dead as we despise but also of trying to kill their hopes of an afterlife.

Archeologists have discovered that ancient Egyptians wrote the names of people on pottery and then smashed it to destroy them. They preserved the bodies of some dead so that the spirits could return to them occasionally, but they burned the corpses and pulled down the monuments and shrines of the dead they wished to destroy, chipping their names off stellæ and other records.

If you have ever attended a Jewish wedding you may recall that a glass (today wrapped carefully in a cloth) is stepped on and broken, the wedding couple's past being destroyed as a future for them begins. This Jewish custom, according to Theodore H. Gaster in *The Holy and the Profane* (1980), comes from that ancient Egyptian practice of smashing pottery with names on it.

WOULD YOU TAKE A CALL FROM THE CHAIRMAN OF THE BOARD?

In California it is difficult to go to your grave in any way that will make the papers. After all, the competition already includes someone who was mummified and placed in a glass case at Forest Lawn, and another who was interred in her convertible. But Frank Sinatra was buried in May 1998 with a bottle of whisky and dimes in change. After his son was kidnapped, years ago, Sinatra always carried 10 dimes in his pocket, so he would never be without change for the telephone. He was buried with 10 dimes. His heirs immediately began to squabble over the rest of his wealth.

WHAT TO DO IF YOU SEE A GHOST

Harry Price spent a well-publicized lifetime as a ghost hunter, a career reported in his many "psychist's" books and his *Confessions of a Ghost Hunter* (1936). His run-ins with poltergeists at Borley Rectory; his unsuccessful attempt to change a goat into a young man atop a German mountain; his experiences with a man on The Isle of Man who had a mongoose that could speak several languages—all that and more on this extraordinary character will be found in Paul Tabori's *Harry Price: The Biography of a Ghost Hunter* (1950) and the somewhat more debunking *Search for Harry Price* by Trevor Hall (1978).

Anyway, if you see a ghost, here are Price's instructions:

> Do not move, and on no account approach the figure. If the figure speaks, *do not approach*, but ascertain name, age, sex, origin, cause of visit, if in trouble, and possible alleviation. Ask the figure to return, suggesting exact time and place. Do not move until figure disappears. Note exact method of vanishing. If through an open doorway, quietly follow. If through a solid object (such as a wall) ascertain if still visible on the other side.

THE EASIEST WAY TO GET RID OF A GHOST

The *curanderos*, or witchdoctors, of Veracruz, Mexico, may have the easiest and cheapest method of banishing all sorts of spirits. They cut figures out of paper and tear them up. Farther south, near San Cristobal de las Casas, I have seen them draw evil spirits and diseases out of patients by passing a live chicken over them. In Europe and Asia, this is done with just an egg.

WHAT TO SAY TO A GHOST

Ghosts are reported to say many different things to people, from "Boo!" to "Revenge!" There is at least one that tells you to buzz off. That one is at Giffard Hall near Torrington in Devon. Sir Walter Giffard (d.1243) is reported to greet visitors with a blunt "Get you gone!"

If you see a ghost, be politer than that. Ask an apparition what it wants. If it will not reply to that, you can tell it "Get you gone!" You might add that it *is a ghost*, for sometimes as I said earlier dead people (we are told) don't know they are dead, which is why they don't go away.

SPELLS FOR CALLING UP GHOSTS

Suppose you *want* to contact a ghost? You could try a Ouija board, a séance, or a spell.

I did not include the spells, used by Odysseus, to call up the dead, when I wrote *The Complete Book of Spells, Curses, and Magical Recipes*, but the ancient writer Julius Africanus, in his *Kestoi* of a version of *The Odyssey*, not only gives them in full but even tells you which libraries he consulted in order to find them. Julius Africanus is an extremely obscure source, but they are there if you need them for anything. You will not find them in any modern edition of *The Odyssey*, so don't think you can get them easily.

The spell or incantation used by the biblical Witch of Endor is not recorded. Nor is the precise ritual used by "Éliphas Lévi" in the nineteenth century to call up Apollonius of Tyre. I do describe that harrowing experience in the aforementioned earlier book of mine, but not fully enough for you to try the necromancy. I wouldn't recommend anything like that.

THE SKELETON HAND

From the melodramas of the mid-nineteenth century, I have unearthed for you the "Demonical Drama" of *The Skeleton Hand; or, The Demon Statue* (with the celebrated Mr. Cony as The Statue).

There are many sensational scenes amid colorful "Leipsic Forest" and "Leipsic fair," with the usual camp of banditti, moonlit gardens, dungeon, rocky pass and waterfall, etc. Jealous of a rival for the heroine, Herman von Klishing (Mr. Reynolds) vows revenge and with a "Terrific Incantation!" endows a garden statue with life. Unfortunately, Herman thereupon becomes a statue. Then, with the "Mysterious Appearance of the Skeleton Hand" and grand tableau, Act I ends.

In Act II, The Statue "proclaims his love" for Lestelle (Mrs. Atkinson) and attacks her father. Then The Statue identifies as a murderer her lover Wolfgang (Mr. Cowle). The innocent Wolfgang is about to be executed for murder when in rushes Hans Hoodelkin and says the murderer is none other than *The Statue himself*. The Statue flees to the point of a crag, carrying Lestelle, but the soldiers fire at him. The rock is blown up, and "Lestelle is Saved!"

When The Statue is dead, Herman "staggers to front and dies... Wolfgang again saves Lestelle, and The Skeleton Hand appears, Grand Tableau." The End.

What is strange about this play is that the "skeleton hand" is totally extraneous, not connected to or needed in the story in any way, it seems. Other melodramas made extensive use of the supernatural. The Gothic had all sorts of ghosts and goblins and haunted castles and the rest. Even Shakespeare used the dug-up skull and stooped to having a statue seem to come to life. Later we had Frankenstein's monster, The Golem, The Mummy, and more.

But *The Skeleton Hand* is a remarkable example of how successful some silly attempts to scare the public with a gimmick can be. A mad teenager in a hockey mask or a madman with a chainsaw is nothing compared to something from the *grave*.

THE MECHANISTIC VIEWPOINT

Here is the mechanistic viewpoint of those who say there are and can be no such thing as a ghost, courtesy of Geoff Viney, who in *Surviving Death* (1993) does not accept this view but summarizes it fairly and succinctly:

> According to the mechanistic viewpoint we are what we appear to be, that is to say our bodies—nothing more, nothing less. Biologists tell us that we exist as a complex organism of bones, flesh, cartilage, and blood, supported by an intricate nervous system. Without these things we could experience nothing; consciousness is simply a function of the supercomputer we call the human brain. The species of Homo Sapiens may have developed through the evolutionary process to create a society wholly distinguishable from those which characterize the lower forms of life, yet like any other animal, man is subject to the same biological needs and constraints. If our vital organs fail, we die just as surely as any other organism, and for all creatures death is the inevitable end of life. We are a collection of cells and nothing more; extinguish the cells and there is nothing left. Man may have traveled to the moon and explored the furthest reaches of space through radio telescopes, built the pyramids and split the atom, written *Hamlet* and painted the Mona Lisa, yet he is really little more than an extremely clever monkey— a highly developed primate.

APPARITIONS IN BRITAIN AND AMERICA

There is something startling about the statistics produced in Britain by the census of 1890 and The Society for Psychical Research's Mass Observation Project of 1948. In Britain, apparitions of the absent living are more common than apparitions of the dead.

In the United States, things are different. Larry Danielson ("Paranormal Memorates" in Howard Kerr and Charles L. Crow's *The Occult in America*, 1983) writes (p. 704):

> The American vernacular data, in contrast, describes apparitions of the known dead in 55 percent of the cases and supernatural appearances of the living in only 6 percent. The remaining texts concern paranormal encounters with persons unknown to be dead or dying.

10 INFORMATION SOURCES ON THE SPIRITS OF THE DEAD IN PRIMITIVE RELIGION

Eliade, M., ed. *Encyclopedia of Religion* (1986)
Jensen, Adolf E. *Myth and Cult Among Primitive Peoples* (trans. M. Choldin & W. Weissleder, reprint 1963)
Lowie, Robert. *Primitive Religion* (1923)
Mbiti, John S. *Introduction to African Religion* (1992)
Parrinder, Geoffrey. *African Traditional Religion* (1976)
Puhlvel, J., ed. *Myth and Law among the Indo-Europeans* (1970)
Radin, Paul. *Primitive Religion: Its Nature and Origin* (1957)
Seltzer, R., ed. *Religions of Antiquity* (1989)
Turville-Petre, E. O. G. *Myth and Religion of the North* (reprint 1975)
Tylor, Edward Burnett. *Religion in Primitive Culture* (1956)

A SELECTION OF CREEPY NEW BOOKS FOR CHILDREN

Alyssa Capucilli, *Inside a House that is Haunted* (1998)
Bruce Coville, *The Ghost Saw Red* (1998)
Richard Dansky, *Corax* (1998)
Cynthia C. DeFelice, *The Ghost of Fossil Glen* (1998)
Kristi Holl, *Let Sleeping Ghosts Lie* (1998)
Joan Holub, *Pyjama Party* (1998)
Paul Hutchens, *The Haunted House* (1998)
Barbara M. Joosse, *Ghost Trap: A Wild Willie Mystery* (1998)
Susan Korman, *The Ghost of Camp Whispering Pines* (1998)
David Lubar, *Gloomy Ghost* (1998)
Joan L. Nixon, *The Haunting* (1998)
Christopher Pike, *Christopher Pike's Tales of Terror* (1998)
Susan Saunders, *The Creepy Camp-Out* (1998)
Ellen Steiber, *Hungry Ghosts* (1998)
R. L. Stine, *Escape of the He-Beast* (1998)
Tom B. Stone, *The Easter Egg Haunt* (1998)
Vivian Vande Velde, *A Coming Evil* (1998)

Molly Williams, *The Ghost Hunt at Trembly Towers* (1998)
Kay Winters, *The Teeny Tiny Ghost* (1998)
Betty R. Wright, *A Ghost in the Family* (1998)

Ghost stories for kids—and the likes of *I Was a Second Grade Werewolf* and *I Was a 6th Grade Zombie*—have been a major item from both large and small presses for years. Old stories such as *The Legend of Sleepy Hollow* have plenty of competition from new books and series. Many of these juvenile books are attractively illustrated and all of them are geared to capturing the young imagination and motivating young readers. The first in this list, for instance, involves rebuses and reading. The quality of the writing ranges from truly clever to carefully commercial, sometimes worse, but the kids seem to love them all.

As young people's reading levels increasingly keep them from enjoying the classics of previous centuries or even of the first half of this century, juvenile readers get simpler and simpler. Grownups who find their darlings cannot cope with Dickens or the like are glad that easy books are available—with pictures.

AT SÍGGJA Í HAMFER

This is the way in the Faroes they say "to see an apparition," and traditionally it means you are going to experience some catastrophe. As late as the 60's and 70's of the twentieth century, stories related to this old superstition circulated. Some were collected and printed by Eyoun Andreassen in *Tradijon* (*Tradition*, 1977). Here is an English translation prepared with the assistance of Ola J. Holten (with whom I have been collaborating for years on a big book on the folklore of the North):

> It happened on the island of Dimun in The Faroes. My brother and a friend had walked down to the shore. It was autumn (a time of very changeable weather) and they wanted to deal with their boat, because a storm was brewing.
>
> As they got down there by the shore they saw some men coming along towards them, perhaps six or seven. They were clad in oilskins and high boots. They went by as my brother and his friend were busy making the boat secure, so they only caught a glimpse of them.
>
> The very same night a ship sank. The crew of the ship were the men who had been (mysteriously) seen on shore.

That is a typical story because apparitions are usually of complete strangers, but here is another. In this one the teller of the story knows the people he sees:

> My uncle—he was better at seeing apparitions than my brother— once saw something when Captain Napoleon went down with the

Fiskere på vej hjem fra Nordstranden, Michael Ancher (1849-1927),
Skagens Museum.

ship *Olivia* in 1912. My uncle was out cutting turf. When he reached the shore at the end of the fjord he found that the skipper Napoleon and a dozen of his crew were walking behind him. My uncle, in fact, knew the captain well and also some of his men, those who came from his community. All of them wore sou'westers and oilskins. They went across the beach in front of him.

My uncle put down his load of turf but did not turn around lest he lose sight of them. What he saw brought sorrow to him: their oilskins were dripping water.

My uncle instantly knew that the *Olivia* had gone down. That proved to be the case. It happened off Sørlandet, but why nobody ever found out.

A NEW WORLD

Here is the pious belief of the nineteenth century as expressed in James Gates Percival's once-popular *Contemplation of Religion*. On her deathbed a religious woman's "faith sees a new world" before her:

> A few short moments over, and the prize
> Of peace eternal waits her, and the tomb
> Becomes her fondest pillow; all its gloom
> Is scattered. What a meeting there will be
> To her and all she loved here! and the bloom
> Of new life from those cheeks shall never flee:
> Theirs is the health that lasts through all eternity.

FROM THE LATIN POET MARTIAL

> Prepare the couch and call for wine.
> Rose garland with your locks entwine.
> Perfume yourself, but always know
> The gods bring death to all below.

ASSORTED STRANGE BELIEFS REGARDING THE AFTERLIFE

From a huge available corpus of astounding beliefs it is difficult to select just a few "believe it or not" examples, but try these:

> The beginning of it all (if you believe one Christian "expert") was soon after 3640 BC, the date he figured out for the Creation. Of course, tradition says the earliest people did not die nearly as soon as moderns do, so date the commencement of human afterlife from some time after 3640 BC. Human remains older than that have been found since that figure was arrived at, as you know. Mummies from Peru are older than those in Egypt, older than the

famous Ice Man found in the Alps recently, older than the most ancient mummies of China (who happen to have red hair, blue eyes, and plaid clothes).

One American football player marks his best plays by pounding his chest twice and pointing to heaven, where he believes his dead grandparents are following the game. Hundreds of thousands or millions of other Americans attempt to communicate with the dead in more articulate ways.

The Rev. Billy Graham has stated firmly that 1500 cubic miles is the size of heaven. How in hell does he know? (This differs from St. Augustine's estimate, which I prefer to accept because it is considerably smaller.)

The Chinese drive away nasty ghosts and other evil spirits with noise—gongs, drums, cymbals, firecrackers—but keeping goldfish also keeps bothersome spirits off the premises. Despite the *New Yorker* cartoon in which someone complains that the fish are "too noisy," this is a quieter way of dealing with the problem.

The strangest spirits seen in films must surely include those in *Fallen, Judge and Jury, Spirit Lost, Toothless, Jack Frost* (reincarnation as a snowman!), and *Ghost* ("It was over—or was it?"). *Ghost* featured Whoopi Goldberg as a "Spiritual Advisor" in a Brooklyn storefront: "$20 Contact the Dearly Departed $20." She produced startling results: "There is stuff going on you wouldn't believe. *I* wouldn't believe it." (I didn't believe it myself). My favorite line (from *High Spirits*) about ghosts in the movies is: "Look, you're a ghost, I'm an American. It would never work out." Another line from the same script contradicts all the West Coast reports of revenants: "No respectable ghost would live in California."

The Rev. Joanna White—a priest at the Episcopal church of St. Andrew, Richmond, Staten Island (NY)—lives in the 175-year-old rectory, in a graveyard. She claims the area is haunted by a drummer boy, and she reports:

> Now I don't do haunted, so I said, "Please, I'm not up to this tonight," and it went away.

"I don't do haunted" appears to underline Church of England more than Church of English, don't you think?

Yoruba tribesmen in Nigeria believe that wearing masks can bring back the spirits of their ancestors. Elsewhere in Africa, some people get into far more terrifying rites to produce the effect.

The places alleged to be haunted by people are innumerable, but in England the Isle of Dogs is said to be haunted by...hunting dogs. They are alleged to have perished there with a man and his wife (who do not haunt the place).

This present book has a lot more on ghosts than it does on poltergeists, and it seems that more ghostly than poltergeist activity is reported everywhere. Ernesto Bolzano, an investigator of occult experiences, looked at 532 reported hauntings and ghosts beat out poltergeists 374 to 158.

Ian Stevenson's huge work on *Cases of the Reincarnation Type*, published by the University of Virginia Press, opens with a volume on 10 cases from India and follows with 3 more volumes on cases from Sri Lanka (Ceylon), Thailand (Siam), Lebanon, and Turkey. If indeed there is a persistence of personality after the death of the body maybe you don't have to be a bodiless spirit after you die; perhaps you can get a new body to go on in.

Producer and director Blake Edwards (Mr. Julie Andrews) claims his guardian angel is gay. Since angels are traditionally sexless, could it be then that his guardian angel is not an angel but a ghost, a dead human? In the famous film *It's a Wonderful Life* the guardian angel is wimpy but clearly male. It is not clear whether he used to be a human being or not, but one might imagine he once was. Angels on many TV programs devoted to this popular topic today are of all colors and all sexes. They appear to be indistinguishable from people, or from ghosts.

Two extraordinary works on ghostly apparitions are Andrew Morton's *An Universal History of Apparitions* (3rd edn, 1738) and F.G. Lee's *The Other World; or, Glimpses of the Supernatural* (2 vols., 1875). Two striking sources of information on the poltergeist are Sacheverell Sitwell's *Poltergeist* (1940) and the collection called *New Directions on Parapsychology* (reprinted 1975) that was edited by John Beloff. Two poltergeist cases that have been done to death (in my view) are hashed over in E.U. Dingwall & K.M. Goldney & T.H. Hall's *The Haunting of Borley Rectory* (1955) and Guy Lyon Playfair's *This House is Haunted: An Investigation of the Enfield Poltergeist* (1980).

Their have been a number of weird ghosts in minor Off-Off and Off-Off-Off Broadway plays of late. To note just one, let me mention the late Aristotle Onassis' ghost in Scott Sublett's satire on the late Princess of Wales (*Die, Diana, Die*), staged (not without howls of protest) in California.

The Aztecs believed butterflies might be the spirits of the dead returning in a universe that is constantly renewing, and a snake shedding its skin to them represented rebirth, the recycling of souls.

When a Portland (OR) subway was built under a cemetery locals were distressed and one Javanesse-American complained that "life is out of balance" because of that. Lao Buddhist monks have been called in to fix things. Also, Sua Lee Cha (a Hmong shaman) has attempted to buy off aggrieved spirits with "spirit money."

One person has argued that even inanimate objects can have (as it were) their own ghosts. Adolphe d'Assier in *Posthumous Humanity* (1887) suggested that inanimate objects might possess a double, a spirit image, and he said that poltergeists propel these images.

A nineteenth-century picture by M. Byfield shows the ghost of a murdered person appearing to his murderers.

Death's Door, a drawing by William Blake for Robert Blair's famous eighteenth-century poem "The Grave," engraved by Louis Schiavonetti and not by Blake himself (much to his annoyance).

2

Ghosts in the European Tradition

A GHOST STALKS EUROPE

European culture is full of stories of benign ghosts and ghastly specters that are, as Captain Marryat would say, "as savage as a bear with a sore head." In this chapter you will hear of some of them, from classical antiquity to the present.

A CORNISH PRAYER

From ghoulies and ghosties and long-leggety beasties
And things that go bump in the night, Good Lord, deliver us!

THE DEAD WE HAVE ALWAYS WITH US

The very first humans who ventured west into what we now call Europe brought with them primitive man's fear of death and perhaps also some traditions of ancestor worship or calling upon the departed to help the living. The earliest burials yield hints that from the start Europeans thought there might be some continued existence elsewhere for those who have departed from this life. These beliefs and the fears of death have been studied by Freud and Jung and many other modern psychologists, but for ages past were simply unquestioned. The dead were not necessarily entirely gone, people said. G. N. M. Tyrrell calls this the unquenchable desire to believe in "the persistence of personality."

"To lie in cold obstruction and to rot" is not an attractive finality. Moreover, it seems sensible to live as if there is an afterlife; that way one will not wake up to a perhaps nasty accounting.

THE BLACK ART

Witchcraft in our western tradition began with attempting to raise the spirits of the dead to foretell the future. That's necromancy. That's what that witch of Endor was up to in The Bible, and that's what witches are reported to be doing by pre-Christian writers.

Aeschylus (*c.* 525-456 BC) in *The Persians*, a tragedy of 472 BC, and his only surviving play on a contemporary topic, shows us a ghost and suggests it is just the kind of foolishness that those stupid Persians would fiddle with. In the play, the widow of the Persian king Darius the Great, accompanied by a chorus of Persian nobles, uses magic to raise the ghost of her husband and to learn what she ought to do.

The word *magician* comes to us from eastern astrologer-priests—remember the Three Magi who see the star and follow it to Bethlehem in Judea to see what wonder it portends?—and one of the things mages were supposed to be able to do is precisely what the Christ was later to do: raise the dead. But Christ raised the dead Lazarus and brought him back to life. He didn't call him up temporarily, for divination, by necromancy.

Ghosts and necromancy feature in Horace (65-8 BC), Lucian (AD 35-69), Apuleius (born AD 123), Pausanias (*fl.* AD 150), and other Roman writers. Lucian and his famous uncle, Seneca, both wrote about the supernatural because their employer, Nero, was fascinated by it. The ghosts of Seneca's drama became a feature of the pseudo-Senecan drama of the Elizabethan public stage, a major trend studied by F. L. Lucas and others in modern times. The Roman writer Lucian used the same sensational material for horror effects. His witch, Erictho, raises the dead with drugs and a blood transfusion—of boiling gore! She creates a kind of golem or Frankenstein monster by this method.

Christianity, dreading devils and demons, soon forbade all such dealings.

Nowadays we speak of dealing with ghosts as a somewhat more respectable venture. We describe those who dabble not as practitioners of the black arts but as spiritualist mediums. Really, however, if they are not simple fakes they are necromantic witches.

The conventional Christian view is that we should treat ghosts as we treat temptations from The Devil: resist them, avoid them, and don't invite them by getting into what the theologians call "occasions of sin." Maybe we cannot stop sin and ghosts from coming to us, but we must not call or court them. "Lead us not into temptation, but deliver us from evil." Ghost-laying is pious; ghost-hunting for any other purpose, even science, is strictly forbidden. Burn your Ouija board. If a ghost or poltergeist actually appears, call an exorcist, not a ghost-hunter.

You may have trouble getting an exorcist. Exorcism may be popular among horror writers but it is much played down these days by the churches. A Roman Catholic exorcism (available in certain circumstances to non-Catholics as well) is now performed only by designated specialists (although every priest became an exorcist on his way to ordination) and only with the express permission of a bishop. This is because only a tiny percentage of ghostly apparitions and poltergeists are considered by ecclesiastical authorities to be demonic, and demons are the only spirits they will banish with those rites. At the same time, religion is in no position to deny the existence of the spirits of the dead. How can it condemn miraculous visions and other things the non-religious count as mere superstitions?

Religion, some aver, was invented precisely to handle our fear of death and to explain where the dead have gone. The earliest records of mankind give evidence of religious rites not only to express grief but also to assist the journey and to protect against the return of the dead. It has always and everywhere been believed that black arts might be able to manipulate the dead, perilous as that might be, or reach useful elemental spirits or create "thought forms."

THE ONLY GOOD GHOST IS A REALLY DEAD GHOST

Plato said that good, complete, and happy ghosts don't walk. He wrote:

> You know the stories about souls that, in their fear of the invisible, which is called Hades, roam about tombs and burial grounds in the neighborhood of which, as they claim, ghostly phantoms of souls have actually been seen; just the sort of apparition that souls like that might produce, souls that are not pure when they are released [by death] but still keep some of that visible density, which explains why they can be seen...it is clearly not the souls of good but those of the wicked that are compelled to wander about such places as the penalty for a wicked way of life in the past. They must continue to wander until they are once more chained up in a body.

This suggests that terrestrial life is only a passing, inferior state of the soul in time and in the body, what the poet Alexander Pope so aptly calls "this isthmus of a middle state" between two eternities. The body is seen as a prison. It is, another more modern poet says, a clumsy "heavy bear" that goes with us. Death frees the worthy man (and woman) from the prison. Some are certain that only those with inferior souls, or work left undone on earth, are condemned to hang around after the death of the corruptible part of us.

Some Eastern religions hold that the inferior person has to come back over and over, life after life, until purified enough to move on to the next plateau. Reincarnation is a punishment imposed on those of deficient spiritual quality.

In light of all this, if you see a ghost do not feel terror. Feel pity. Don't attempt to get a ghost to solve problems for you. A ghost has enough problems of its own, if only coming to grips with the fact that it is dead. Surely a ghost has more important things to do than to go "boo!" at you, or rap out silly messages on your table.

RAISING THE DEAD

The Greeks tell of apparitions of the dead as well as of gods and goddesses, but mostly the dead came to them in dreams. Plutarch says there was a cave (probably at Cumæ, where there was a sibyl) where those who wished to consult the dead went, fell asleep—perhaps drugged—and saw ghosts in dreams.

This was not really necromancy. That was much disapproved of. By the time of Heliodorus' *Æthiopica*, several centuries into the Christian era, necromancy had a very bad reputation. In this work, the witch is just an Egyptian, and when she raises her own dead son he sits up and criticizes her for it. She herself winds up dead, and good riddance.

Centuries later, in the Middle Ages, when superstition was supposedly at its height, the *Canon Episcopi*, or official handbook for bishops, made necromancy (and indeed all pagan practices and black arts) the sign of the heretic. The position of the church was somewhat contradictory. On the one hand it declared that witchcraft was a snare and a delusion; at the same time it said witchcraft was terribly dangerous, and not to try it.

THE BATTLE CONTINUES TO RAGE

It was said that the sounds of the fearful battle of the Greeks against the Persians at Marathon echoed over the field for a very long time thereafter.

A spectral army clatters through the Eberbach Valley. It was said to have appeared just before the final defeat of Germany in World War II.

WHAT EXPLAINS THE APPEARANCE OF GHOSTS?

Other than saints appearing as miracles or spirits called up by black magic, either of which demands faith or superstition and sidesteps science, what are ghosts? Maybe they are just dreamed or hallucinated, only in the mind of the one who "sees" them. Maybe they are created by psychokinesis or telepathy, issuing from the mind of the one who "sees" them. But if they exist in a less subjective manner, what could explain them? Religion (standard or spiritualist) might look on them as proof of the existence of a soul that does not die with the body. G. N. M. Tyrrell considered them proof of the existence of the persistence of personality after death, the imprints (as it were) made by once-living forces. This has been referred to by more than one investigator as "footprints in the sands of time."

A ghost in armor appears to foretell of the impending death of his son, the Duke of Buckingham.

Science has offered a theory of ghosts as records. Sir Oliver Lodge, a sincere believer in what his colleague F. W. H. Myers in The Society for Psychical Research called *Human Personality and Its Survival After Bodily Death* (a classic book reprinted 1961), suggested that it might be possible that "strong emotions could be unconsciously recorded in matter." The then novel photograph and the phonograph suggested to him that impressions made could be retained and replayed.

In *Man and the Universe*, Sir Oliver discussed

a haunted house...wherein some one room is the scene of a ghastly representation of some long past tragedy. On a psychometric hypnothesis [basis] the original tragedy has been literally photographed on its material surroundings, nay, even on the ether itself.

SIR OLIVER LODGE
After he lost his son in the first world
war, Sir Oliver's life (1851-1940)
was dominated by psychical research.
See *Raymond* (1916), his autobiography
(1931), and *My Philosophy* (1936).
A distinguished pioneer in wireless
communication (*Signaling Across Space
Without Wires*, 1897), Sir Oliver is
chiefly remembered today for trying
to communicate with the other side.

All right, I can accept that the atoms of the world are disturbed by all our passages and that it is not inconceivable that a record of some sort of that is made, if not retrievable, but why a tragedy only? Cannot intense happy experience also make an impression? And, most important of all, why is it that some people are said to be able to pick up these impressions while others are not so sensitive? If impressions are picked up, by what human mechanism is this done and how are the senses of sight and sound, etc., activated?

It seems easiest, somehow, to believe that all ghosts and such are mere hallucinations or lies, not the spirits of the dead somehow stuck on the road to a higher plane of existence. Universal beliefs of mankind, some held even longer than the expectation of afterlife, have in time been exploded. Without either unquestioning faith or unquestionable science to guide us, we must say that all these beliefs are prompted by nothing more than the understandable but basically pitiful hope that we see in the works of ghost hunters, and in authors such as Florence Marryat (*There Is No Death*, 1921). Those authors, I believe, are dead and are not coming back. Their hope has, I fear, been helpful in life, dashed in death. Too bad.

FEAR OF GHOSTS IN ROMAN BRITAIN

T. C. Lethbridge, a keeper of Anglo-Saxon antiquities, was fascinated with "the confused and difficult subject of the ancient gods of Britain." He conducted archeological digs in Cambridgeshire that turned up evidence of early Britons' fear of ghosts.

In his book *Ghost and Ghoul* (1961), Lethbridge writes of the dig at Guilden Morden in Cambridgeshire:

> We found the coins put in dead persons' mouths to pay Charon's fare across the Styx. There were bells at the ankles of children to scare away evil spirits. Lamps were found which had been left burn-

ing in the graves to light the dead through their dark passage. Shoes, which the Vikings knew as "Hell shoes", were found beside the ashes of the corpse for its spirit journey.... Food—eggs, meat and oysters—was included for the same journey. Above all there were signs that the Romano-Britons at Guilden Morden had been afraid of the return of the ghosts of the dead.... We can... be reasonably sure that the people who buried these dead had a firm belief in [the soul's] survival and in ghosts, which they dreaded.

One corpse was put into an undercut grave in the chalk and jammed in with rocks. Another—an arthritic old woman whom the author says may have therefore been "bad-tempered"—had her head cut off and placed at her feet. Another corpse's head was cut off and rested on his chest.

The Romans in Britain (who were, by the way, mostly Dacians and Thracians and not from Italy) do seem to have laid their ghosts well. Very seldom does one hear of a ghost in Roman costume stalking in Britain. There was a report, however, of an Englishman who drove by what resembled a Roman camp at night. He said to himself that it must be a film company shooting on location. Then he noticed that he could see through the people to the trees behind them. He knew that many people believe ghosts are transparent. He drove off, reported the case with protestations that he had not been driving "under the influence," and discovered that others had also claimed to have seen such a sight. Perhaps not all the Romans are now nothing but (as A. E. Housman wrote) "ashes under Uricon."

ROMAN SOLDIERS MARCH BY

So they say in York. There the cathedral and Holy Trinity Church and a number of other buildings are said to be haunted. At one place, according to the locals, Roman soldiers can be seen marching by. They are visible from the waist up only, for they are marching on the old Roman Road of Eboricum, and that lies a couple of feet lower than the level of modern York, England.

UNCONVENTIONAL CONVENTION

All the ghosts of Britain are supposed to gather on December 21st each year at the Stripers Stones. These are near Bishop's Castle in Shropshire. But Peter Underwood, president of The Ghost Club and author of *Ghosts and How to See Them* (1993), who claims to have seen numerous British ghosts, says that "I have never met anyone who has seen them, or even a few of them, at that time and place."

In December in Britain you must be content with ghosts of Anne Boleyn (Hever Castle) and Charles Dickens (Rochester Castle, more famously haunted by Lady Blanche de Warren), of a phantom monk at

Strata Florida Abbey (Wales), a phantom coach and horses at Roos Hall (Suffolk) and a carriage that crosses the frozen Loch of Skene (Scotland), a poltergeist throwing around Christmas cards at the royal residence of Sandringham (Norfolk) and, in Shropshire, the tolling of a sanctus bell from the depths of Bomere Pool. Not to mention the usual mysterious appearances for New Year's Eve of a black pig in Hampshire, and spectral hounds in Dorset.

I'm afraid the Ghost Convention is a non-starter. The ghosts seem to be too busy to take time off to get together, if we can judge by Underwood's authoritative Ghost Calendar. They are occupied from January (when every January 19th at Braddock Down in Cornwall the horses' hooves of Cromwell's cavalry have been sounding since 1643) to December (when, on the last day of the year, on The Isle of Wight, a long-vanished house, Knighton Gorges, briefly reappears, "sometimes ablaze with lights and echoing music").

MONKS AND NUNS

For some reason I have never seen addressed, monks and nuns—chiefly medieval— seem to haunt a lot of places. One would think that ghosts would come from all walks of (former) life and from all professions and occupations, but we seldom hear of a spectral TV repairman or phantom plumber—no it's always a bloody nun or a hooded monk, sometimes processions of them. Terence Whitaker's *Haunted England* (1987) is typical. Although its subtitle refers to the most popular of spooks—"Royal Spirits, Castle Ghosts, Phantom Coaches, and Wailing Ghouls"—he has whole chapters on "Ghostly Monks" and "Phantom Nuns."

Whitaker repeats what I must consider rather unreliable, unsubstantiated reports of monkish ghosts seen at Whalley Abbey (Lancashire) and two more (with nasty poltergeist proclivities) at nearby Chingle Hall, one at Bury St. Edmunds, some at Beaulieu Abbey ("because of the general peace and tranquillity of the place, it is not really surprising that some of the early inhabitants remain"), a friar at Buriton, a ghost at the former abbey at Missenden, and others at the village church at Checkley in Staffordshire, the vicarage at Elm in Cambridgeshire, the parish church at Farnham in Surrey, Lindisfarne's Holy Island, and, of course, in London churches.

Westminster Abbey houses what may be the ghost of World War I's "Unknown Soldier" and the restless spirit of John Bradshaw, haunting the deanery because he was president of the court that sent Charles I to have his head cut off. Miles Coverdale, translator of The Bible, is supposed to haunt the church of St. Magnus the Martyr, near London Bridge, though the present church was built by Sir Christopher Wren in 1676 to replace one destroyed in The Great Fire of London.

THE FEAST OF BLOOD. 829

things that had ensued regarding the after death condition of that fair girl.

The noise increased each moment, and finally there was a sudden crash.

"She comes! she comes!" gasped Ringwood.

He grasped the front of the pulpit with a frantic violence, and then slowly and solemnly there crossed his excited vision a figure all clothed in white. Yes, white flowing vestments, and he knew by their fashion that they were not worn by the living, and that it was some inhabitant of the tomb that he now looked upon.

He did not see the face. No, that for a time was hidden from him, but his heart told him who it was. Yes, it was his Clara.

It was no dream. It was no vision of a too excited fancy, for until those palpable sounds, and that most fearfully palpable form crossed his sight, he was rather inclined to go the other way, and to fancy what the sexton had reported was nothing but a delusion of his overwrought brain. Oh, that he could but for one brief moment have found himself deceived.

"Speak!" he gasped; "speak! speak!"

There was no reply.

"I conjure you, I pray you though the sound of your voice shouldhurt me to perdition—I implore you, speak."

All was silent, and the figure in white moved on slowly but surely towards the door of the church, but ere it passed out, it turned for a moment, as if for the very purpose of removing from the mind of Ringwood any lingering doubt as to its identity.

He then saw the face, oh, so well-known, ut so pale. It was Clara Crofton!

"'Tis she! 'tis she!" was all he could say.

It seemed, too, as if some crevice in the clouds had opened at the moment, in order that he should with an absolute certainty see the countenance of that solemn figure, and then all was more than usually silent again. The door closed, and the figure was gone.

He rose in the pulpit, and clasped his

A sensational moment in *Varney the Vampire:* the apparition of "that fair girl," Clara Crofton!

The chapter on ghostly nuns has more of the same. The author comments that being of the cloth, these churchly ghosts are gentle creatures. In his amusing song about *The Stately Homes of England,* Sir Noël Coward refers to the great houses as delights for psychical researchers and mentions the ghost of a "rowdy nun" who was murdered and "resented it" and "greets you in the hall."

PETER UNDERWOOD

To list his publications is to underline the steady popularity of his subject. They include:

A Gazetteer of British Ghosts (1971)
Into the Occult (1972)
Haunted London (1973)
A Gazetteer of Scottish and Irish Ghosts (1973)
A Host of Hauntings (1973)
Deeper into the Occult (1975)
The Ghosts of Borley [Rectory] (1975)
Hauntings: New Light on Ten Famous Cases (1977)
Dictionary of the Supernatural (1978)
Ghosts of North-West England (1978)
Ghosts of Wales (1978)
Ghosts of Devon (1982)
Ghosts of Cornwall (1983)
Ghosts of Hampshire and The Isle of Wight (1983)

No Common Task: The Autobiography of a Ghost Hunter (1983)
Ghosts of Kent (1984)
This Haunted Isle (1984)
Ghosts of Somerset (1985)
Gazetteer of British, Scottish, and Irish Ghosts (1985)
The Ghost Hunters (1985)
The Ghost Hunter's Guide (1986)
Westcountry Haunting (1986)
Ghosts of Dorset (1988)
Mysterious Places (1988)
Ghosts of Wiltshire (1989)
Exorcism! (1990)
Ghostly Encounters (1992)
Ghosts and How to See Them (1993)

Nowhere else will I bother you with nearly thirty titles by a single author. I list these here to demonstrate that experts not only have a tendency to write the same book over and over but that on the subject of ghosts, British publishers and the British public have an unquenchable interest and a typical provincial pride. It all adds up to a few facts worth noting: the British love ghosts; they believe any old place is distinguished by having one or more; they see the contributions superstition makes to local color and local commerce; they think the West Country is especially populated with ghosts; and they believe ghosts walk mostly at midnight (but the Man in Gray, London's chief ghost who haunts Drury Lane Theatre, plays only matinées), some all year and some few only on certain anniversaries.

They get snobbishly excited about ghosts with (former) titles and are also very interested in noisy poltergeists. With all the organizations in the UK devoted to ghosts, not even Robin Furman's "Ghostbusters UK" seems anxious to lay ghosts and be done with them. Like the Stately Homes, they are part of the Heritage—and maybe, as Sir Noël Coward suggests in that song about *The Stately Homes of England*, "We only keep them up for Americans...," tourist attractions.

THE ODDEST GHOSTS

The Man in Gray and others who walk by day are unusual. So is the old woman who haunts The Gargoyle Club in London's Soho, the oldest night-club in Europe (they say), though recently just a strip club. Odd, too, is the ghost of a pet monkey which haunts Athelhampton Hall in Dorset. There is a Green Lady (whose appearance foretells disaster), many a White Lady (see below) many a Gray Lady (I like the one at Seaton Delaval in Northumberland), and a Brown Lady at Loseley House in Surrey. There is another Brown Lady in East Anglia; near aptly named Fakenham, at Raynam Hall, someone suspected she was a fake and shot at her, but the bullet went harmlessly through her.

Rudyard Kipling haunts his house in Sussex, Bateman's. Oliver Cromwell haunts Basing House in Hampshire, with his head on, although the Cavaliers used it for a football. Later it was recovered and is buried in a secret place in Cambridgeshire. Dorothy Southworth, who died confined to a convent on The Continent, nowhere near Lancashire, still haunts her ancestral abode, Samlesbury Hall, near Liverpool. Her picture appears on the inn sign of the New Hall Tavern. It is useful to note, in passing, how many theaters and inns are supposed to be haunted in Britain. There is a shelf of books on them. Presumably having a ghost is good for business; in the United States ghosts seem to prefer bed and breakfast establishments.

It must be said that we Americans do our best though we lack royal personages and great antiquity in our history. Henry Comstock is said to haunt his Ophir Mine, and some weird stories are told of George Washington appearing on horseback to lead the 20th Maine Regiment to victory at Little Round Top at the Battle of Gettysburg. Gen. Oliver J. Hunt, when sober, swore Washington was there, helping the Union Army. How could a loyal son of Virginia fight on the side of the Damn Yankees? You expect us to believe that sort of thing?

GHOST DANCES

Among Native Americans in the nineteenth century, "Ghost Dances" were a magical ritual. They were performed in the hope that they would drive the white man from Amerindian lands and restore the buffalo and the way of life enjoyed in North America before the Europeans came. After the massacre at Wounded Knee, the Ghost Dances ceased.

But the "Ghost Dances" of Europe were those which Johann Weir writes of in his massive compendium, *De Præstigiis Dæmonum*. That influential book reached a much expanded and improved sixth edition (1583) before the learned doctor died. He writes of ghost dances of "white sibyls", by which he means "specters which were particularly hostile to women in labor and infants at the breast, still in their cradles." He adds that the spread of the gospel in Germany had by his time banished such old superstitions. Then he uses the term "demon" for these wicked personages, suggesting he may have meant "spirits," not "ghosts," in the first place.

WIVES OF HENRY VIII

I don't think many have seen the ghost of Bluff King Hal. He probably holds the record, however, for the mostly ghostly family.

Catherine of Aragon, Henry's first wife, is said to haunt the gallery of Kimbolton Castle in Huntingdonshire. The ghost of Catherine Howard is said to this day to run desperately down the gallery of Hampton Court Palace. In life she tried unsuccessfully to reach the chapel and was dragged off to execution for supposed infidelity.

Bickling Hall, in Norfolk, where Anne Boleyn spent a lot of time as a child, is just one of the places her ghost stalks, carrying the head that Henry's executioner chopped off. She drives headless, with a team of headless horses no less, at midnight along the road to Bickling Hall so some locals report.

The eldest of Henry VIII's three children, usually known as Bloody Mary, haunts Sawston Hall in Cambridgeshire. Mary inherited some of her father's talent for music (he wrote *Greensleeves*) and she occasionally renders a tune on the harpsichord.

Her younger sister, Elizabeth I, is said to haunt Windsor Castle, although in life she much preferred Richmond. The boy, who reigned briefly as Edward VI, does not have much legend attached to him, but he has been seen with a book. His sister Elizabeth was a highly educated lady who mastered half a dozen languages. She is said to be seen more frequently walking along, her nose in a book.

Henry VIII himself is said to join a clutch of other monarchs in haunting Windsor Castle.

SOME OF THE MORE ECCENTRIC BOOKS
ABOUT HAUNTED BRITAIN

Richard Baxter, *Certainty of the World of Spirits* (1691)
John Beaumont, *Historical Treatise of Spirits* (1705)
Sir Ernest Bennett, *Apparitions and Haunted Houses* (1939)
Thomas Bromhall, *Treatise of Spectres* (1658)
Aidan Chambers, *Ghosts and Hauntings* (1973)

John Graham Dalyell, *Darker Superstitions of Scotland* (1834)

R. C. Finucane, *Appearances of the Dead: A Cultural History* (1984)

C. Green, *Apparitions* (1975)

Sarah Hapgood, *500 British Ghosts and Hauntings* (1993)

W. B. Herbert, *Phantoms of the Railways* (1988)

Andrew Lang, *Cock Lane and Common Sense* (1894)

Rodney Legg, *The Ghosts of Dorset, Devon, and Cornwall* (1986)

A. MacKenzie, *Apparitions and Ghosts* (1971)

Eric Maple, *The Realm of Ghosts* (1964)

Curtis Smith, *Spirits of London* (1988)

William Grant Stewart, *The popular superstitions and festive amusements of the highlanders of Scotland* (1823)

Violet Tweedale, *Ghosts I Have Seen* (1920)

The tortures of Hell from *Le Grant Kalendrier* published in Troyes (France) in the Sixteenth Century.

SOME BLARNEY FROM IRELAND

John J. Dunne, *Haunted Ireland* (1977)
Hans Holzer, *The Lively Ghosts of Ireland* (1988)
James Reynolds, *Ghosts in Irish Houses* (1947)
Sheila St. Clair, *Psychic Phenomena in Ireland* (1972)
John D. Seymour, *Irish Witchcraft and Demonology* (1913)

BRITTANY

The ghosts of Brittany deserve a whole book of their own, but no one has ever attempted to fill the need. Still, there are many ghost stories traditionally told by the inhabitants. I was invited to walk through a reveling group of ghosts coming down a very steep cobbled street at the stroke of midnight in one of the old villages I visited in the early nineties (I happened to be there on their single appearance of the year).

Moreover, annually there is the ancient ceremony of the Pardon of the Troménie or Tour of Refuge. That takes place on the second Sunday of

July and it is widely believed that the ghosts of the dead rise to make the pilgrimage with the living.

GHOST BUSTERS

It was the United States that produced the movie *Ghostbusters*, but Britain deserves credit for earlier and determined investigation of ghostly phenomena. The Society for Psychical Research began collecting evidence of apparitions there, among other evidence of the paranormal, and many allegedly haunted houses and other places were thoroughly investigated. Harry Price, Hanz Holtzer, Peter Underwood, and many others have been busy ghostbusting in the UK.

Recent books on investigation of this sort include:

Eddie Burke, *Ghost Hunter* (1996)
James M. Deem, *Ghost Hunter* (1982)
Elizabeth Hoffman, *In Search of Ghosts* (1992)
B. Jaegers, *Ghost Hunting* (1988)
Simon Marsden, *Journal of a Ghosthunter* (1994)

In the United States such well (self-)publicized figures as Sybil Leek and Hans Holzer wrote a great deal about the occult, including the alleged occurrence of ghosts, but their work may be said without prejudice to be more connected with entertainment than with the sort of science or pseudo-science pursued by the average British investigators or by Dr. Rhine's investigations of ESP and such at Duke University. The professional practice of religious exorcists is quite another subject. Exorcism is discussed in other books in my series. Have a look at pp. 119-130 in *The Complete Book of Devils & Demons*. I provide the formula if you dare to try it yourself.

GHOST PARTIES

Some mention of these has been made already, but it should be noted that the practice is widespread. The ghosts of the dead are entertained by headhunters of the Pacific, by the Mexicans in their famous Day of the Dead, by the Armenians at the Passover of the Dead (following Easter), and so on. In some cultures, a memorial dinner is held after the burial; in Greece it comes forty days after. By that time, one assumes, the ghost has adjusted to her or his new condition and is ready to socialize a little.

In some families places are regularly set at the table for the departed. The milk and cookies left out for Santa Claus in some American households have their parallels in food and drink left in other cultures for the dead. Cold milk is especially appreciated, it cools down the fires of Purgatory or Hell. In Greece and in some parts of Italy a mere glass of water will suffice, but some kind of soul cake needs to be provided.

My grandmother kept the old English custom of making and giving away soul cakes, and kept at least one from each Halloween season to "bring good luck." I liked the ones made with a gingerbread man cookie cutter, the ones that had raisins for eyes. I make some every year in her honor, though she has been dead for most of my life and her husband, my maternal grandfather, died in 1925, before I was born.

It is not foolish to remember the dead, even if they do not come back for refreshments. They are absent friends, often benefactors. The toast "Absent Friends" should include the dead.

THE WHITE LADY

Many a ghost is so described. Many are said to be brides who died while still in their wedding dresses. Others may be nuns in white habits, persons wrapped in white shrouds for burial, persons in mourning (white was used for the purpose before we adopted black), and so on.

Also, ghosts are often said to be surrounded by a white aura. Live people have colored auras. The radiance surrounding the Risen Christ was white.

The most famous such ghost must have been the White Lady of the Hohenzollerns, the Graffin Alice of Orlemunde. She walked sorrowfully, having killed her own two children, and her appearance at the palace of Unter der Linden (whence she is also sometimes called the White Lady of Berlin) was said, like the Irish banshee or white lady, to precede a death. In her case it meant death in the dynasty of the Hohenzollerns. After World War II the palace fell into the Russian sector and was razed, so she walks no more.

The ghostly Lady in White who stalks Glamis Castle in Scotland is apparently still on the job. Pluckley (Kent)'s White Lady is not much in evidence these days. There is another at Cwn Heldeg (Wales).

Victor Hugo, fascinated with séances, at one such gathering was promised that a ghostly White Lady would return at exactly three o'clock in the morning. At precisely that ungodly hour the doorbell rang, but neither Hugo nor anyone else in his household dared to answer the door.

If you read German, see N. Rehbinder's *"Die Weisse Frau"* in *Deutsche Rundschau* 212 (September 1927), 234-241.

CREMATION

Does cremation have any effect on ghostly perambulations? Cremation is becoming increasingly popular in Britain, and in Germany there is a trend for people to be cremated and the ashes buried anonymously. The Roman Catholic Church particularly objects to this practice. Pastoral letters have been read from the pulpit to state officially that this is not only against the custom of the church but interferes with traditional mourning.

In China, where elaborate funerals have been the custom from time immemorial, the government is trying to suppress "waste" and to press for simple cremation. In America, even those who want simple cremation and little or no ceremony are sometimes buried with a certain amount of pomp and expense, with the relatives disregarding the wishes of the deceased. Cheap funerals are widely regarded as, well, cheap. Undertakers are delighted. Service Corporation International (the US leader in corpse disposal) is, however, offering a no-frills "family care" package at half the price of the usual funeral. Even half price, however, is substantial. It's the high cost of leaving.

Our *American Way of Death* has been the laughingstock of writers such as Jessica Mitford, but neither her exposé nor Evelyn Waugh's *The Loved One* sufficed to *bury* the extravagance of Forest Lawn Cemetery. There have been some reports that ghosts have returned to complain that too little or even too much has been spent on their obsequies. Choose that cardboard box (for cremation), pine box (for interment), or bronze casket (for show) carefully!

But be careful about burial or you may have a ghost on your hands, or so people have long believed. In *Popular Religion in Germany and Central Europe, 1400-1800* (1996), Rob Scribner (who edited the anthology with Trevor Johnson) writes of the hardiness of old superstitions:

> Early modern Protestantism, despite its official doctrine and practice, proved unable to eradicate the traditional popular concerns [in the Holy Roman Empire] about spirits, ghosts, and poltergeists, restless souls, and above all the untimely or "dangerous dead," those for whom the rites of separation had been imperfectly performed. Here official behalf could do no more than exercise a passive tolerance of what it could not eradicate.

You might read Paul Barber's *Vampires, Burial, and Death: Folklore and Reality* (1988) and, if you can manage German, Thomas Schürmann, *Nachzehrglauben in Mitteleuropa* (1990).

Proper burial is an important issue if the dead are to rest in peace. That is mentioned as early as Sophocles in *Antigone*. This does not mean that you have to buy an expensive funeral. Just have a ritually correct one. Whatever the request of the deceased, I do not think that cremation fulfills that requirement. But, of course, if you do, fine. It's your religion, your Loved One—and your problem.

DEATH CAN BE BAD FOR YOU

Death, if we are to credit mediums, can make a musician's style suddenly grow very poor. Music said to come from Mozart and Liszt from beyond the grave is pretty much garbage.

The *Totentanz* (dance of death) was a common medieval theme in art. Here Death leads the jester in an illustration printed in Basle as the theme continued into the Renaissance.

When (Marguerite) Radclyffe Hall's lover Mabel Batten died, a medium called Mrs. Leonard brought "John" (as Radclyffe Hall liked to be called) her Mabel's words from The Other Side. John's surviving girlfriend, Mabel's cousin Una Troubridge, said Mabel's speech after death had suddenly become notably common, even ungrammatical.

PHANTASMS OF THE LIVING

Perhaps useful to mention here in connection with ghosts are apparitions of the living. A number of people claim to have seen "in person" other living people who were at the time a distance away, perhaps on the other side of the world. Josephine may have appeared to warn Napoleon he had but a little time to live, but some living persons reportedly delivered similar messages. Apparitions of the living have also been said to warn people who thereby have escaped danger or death.

How living persons can be apparitions—or how one can tell whether an apparition is of a living person or a ghost—is unclear. Both are said to be semitransparent.

THE DEAD BOY COMES TO TELL HIS FATHER

The poet Ben Jonson's recorded conversations with his friend William Drummond of Hawthornden contain a lot of interesting details, includ-ing gossip about why Elizabeth I was the "Virgin Queen" because of a physical deformity. But the most touching story is that of the death of young Ben Jon-son, the poet's oldest son, at the tender age of seven in 1603. Jonson later said in a mournful verse that the boy had been his "best piece of poetry." The boy's ghost appeared older than his age at death and was marked with a red cross, as were the doors of houses where bodies were to be picked up by collectors in the city during the plague. This is what Drummond wrote:

Ben Jonson

> At the time the pest was in London, he [Jonson] being in the coun-try at Sir Robert Cotton's house with old [William] Camden, saw in a vision his eldest son, then a child and at London, appear unto him with the mark of a bloody cross on his forehead, as if it had been cutted with a sword; at which amazed he prayed unto God, and in the morning he came to Mr. Camden's chamber to tell him, who persuaded him it was but an apprehension of his fantasy at which he should not be dejected. In the mean time comes there letters from his wife of the death of that boy in the plague. He appeared to him (he said) of a manly shape, and of that growth that he thinks he shall be at the resurrection.

AWAY WE GO

Like it or nor, away we all go, eventually. Some say the good die younger than the rest of us. We all die peacefully in our sleep (the best way, most people think), or in an accident (killed instantly is preferred), or in some more lingering, painful way. Many people are more afraid of the final pain than the deadly blow. "I'm not afraid of death," said Woody Allen. "I just don't want to be there when it happens."

Some people kill themselves, in desperation or by bad habits. Some deaths are expected, others are called sudden. But really all of them are sudden: one moment you are there and the next you are not. People who almost passed away make much of the light at the end of the tunnel. Nobody knows for certain whether that comes from the doors of Heaven opening up or the human brain shutting down. Death remains the greatest certainty that is also a mystery. Death, as Hamlet remarked, is a journey to an unknown country from which no traveler returns. It "puzzles the will."

Some people have gloried in heroic deaths, but many have made their exits rather ludicrously: the pope who opened his mouth to pronounce an anathema only to have an insect fly in and choke him to death; the king whose horse stumbled over a molehill; and many lesser mortals who perished in ways that would have been terribly embarrassing to the victim except that they were fatal. On occasion the end is the fault of the victim, whether from a major mistake or an accident that would probably not have happened to anyone who lacked the victim's weaknesses. Think of the mountaineers who recklessly put themselves in danger of death to climb some summit just because it was there. Think of the brave adventurers who wanted to do something good for mankind, or just had courage equal to their curiosity. Think of the egotistical swanning around of Isadora Duncan, who perished when her foolishly long scarf caught in the wheels of an open car in which she was speeding along.

The reason we pause here to "look to the end" is simply to remark that the method of death, in many times and cultures, is said to govern whether the spirit rests in peace or rises to roam among the living. Lack of respect for dying persons, or dying wishes, is said to bring on ghostly revenge.

Proper funerals, with the emphasis on loss rather than cost-cutting, would seem to be the best insurance of the survivors feeling comforted—and safe. Both sensitivity and superstition always cost you more. The placing of grave goods dates back as far as the Paleolithic (Old Stone) Age and likely indicates not only equipment provided for the afterlife but going-away presents to pacify the dead. Later, if the dead have to win games to get to rest (as in the Egyptian religion), or be

Sebastian Brant, *Stultifera navis* (1497)

weighed in the balance (as in many religions) or get over a "bridge of the requiter" (Zoroastrianism), the living also have to pass the test of treating the dead with due regard. The religions of Oceania and indeed a great many others say that the dead inhabit some far-off land. The Greeks spoke of The Islands of the Blessed. From wherever they may be, it is feared, the dead may return, even to hurt the living.

Requiescat in pace may refer not only to the departed but to the worried mourners, with their denial, anger, guilt, and fear.

NERO'S GHOST

Romans loved ghost tales. One example will suffice here. I choose one of the longest-lasting ghosts in all history. It is that of Nero, among the most despised and dissolute of all the emperors, last of the glorious Julio-Claudian dynasty. He reigned from AD 54 to 68. Besides murdering his mother and (legend says) fiddling while Rome burned, he lived a life so outrageous that even Suetonius had to stretch his powers to describe it.

He made such an impression, in fact, that when he committed his long-drawn-out and melodramatic suicide— "*Qualis artifex perio*," were his dying words ("What an artist perishes in me") because he fancied himself a superb actor and poet and would not even die without a performance—some people refused to believe he had finally left the stage of the world. Tacitus reported more than one false Nero springing up in the Eastern empire.

In another way he did stubbornly refuse to make a farewell appearance. E. L. Withers in *Royal Blood* (1964) wrote that

> the terror generated by Nero had been so enormous that for a long time in his stead, there were those who cautiously continued to place flowers at his tomb [on the Pincian Hill, where the Villa Borghese is today], venerate his statues [though the 120-foot statue of him as the sun god at the Golden House disappeared], and make public his edicts. Romans found themselves unable to believe that a being so monumental in wickedness could be merely mortal, but confident that he would, like an avenging god, someday return to confound his enemies. And this aura of wickedness remained so persistently attached to his name that as much as a thousand years later, in the eleventh century at the death of the Middle Ages, his murderous spirit was still reported to haunt the summit of the Pincian Hill.

UNHAPPY GHOSTS IN HELL

The Christian Hell is for sinners, but the Norsemen said that Elvidner (Misery) was a place ruled over by the goddess Hel and received not only criminals of all kinds but any man who died a peaceful death, without the shedding of blood. Dying of disease or mere old age was considered a shame in their warlike world. That was called a "straw death," dying in your bed of straw instead of dying (as we used to say) "with your boots on." In J. C. Jones' poem *Valhalla*, about the abode where the blessed dead feast and frolic, here is the description of Hell:

Elvidner was Hela's hall,
Iron-barred, with massive wall;

Horrible that palace tall!
Hunger was her table bare;
Waste, her knife; her bed, sharp Care;
Burning Anguish spread her feast;
Bleachèd bones arrayed each guest;
Plague and Famine sang their rune;
Mingled with Despair's harsh tunes.
Misery and Agony
E'er in Hel's abode shall be!

A BOGGART

The old word *boggart* is related to *bog, bogey, bog-gard, bogeyman*, and *bug* in the sense of specter or goblin. In Lancashire they have a tradition of the boggart being a huge spectral black dog with fiery eyes and fierce appearance. Sometimes these supernatural dogs are harbingers of death; sometimes they are forms that human ghosts have assumed. Elsewhere such devil dogs are said to have huge saucer eyes and roam blasted heaths and other frightening places. Ghostly animals of all sorts are common in folklore.

A book of necromantic and other magical formulas published in Denmark in 1906.

Here is a bit from Dennis Bardens' *Ghosts and Hauntings* (1965):

Ghost dogs are connected with many sinister happenings of the past. A strange story once attached to the village of Dean Combe, Devon. A prosperous weaver, having died, was found after death to be hard at work, as usual, at his loom and shuttle. His family invoked the aid of the local parson, who in a commanding voice told the weaver, Knowles, to leave his shuttle and come down at once. This the weaver declined to do until he had worked out his quill [used all the thread on his bobbin or spool], but on response to further commands, he came down to the parson, who straight-way threw in his face a handful of consecrated earth from the churchyard. At this the ghost became immediately transformed into a black hound.

THE GHOST OF GEORGE II

After his father started the regrettable Hanoverian dynasty in Britain, George II (1683-1760) succeeded him as king and Elector of Hanover in 1727. He had few distinctions, but one was that he was the last British monarch to command armies in the field (he won at Dettingen, 1743). Another is said to be that he haunts Kensington Palace. He is said to worry a lot about weather vanes, hoping good winds will bring him good news by ship from Germany.

AFTER MIDNIGHT

'Tis now the very witching time of night,
When churchyards yawn and hell itself breathes out
Contagion to this world.

—William Shakespeare, *Hamlet*.

WILLIAM BLAKE ON GHOSTS

Alexander Gilchrist's *Life of William Blake* noted that once, at Lambeth, Blake had seen a ghost—"scaly, speckled, very awful"—and had run out of the house in terror. But Gilchrist adds of that truly imaginative genius that "he was wont to say that they [ghosts] did not appear much to imaginative men, but only to common minds, who did not see the finer spirits. A ghost was a thing seen by the gross bodily eye; a vision [was a thing seen] by the mental [eye]."

SIR WALTER SCOTT AND THE SUPPOSED GHOST OF LORD BYRON

In the famous Eleventh Edition of the *Encyclopaedia Britannica* Andrew Lang explained that

> Sir Walter Scott's vision of Byron, lately dead, proved to be a misconstruction of certain plaids and cloaks hanging in the hall at [Scott's home] Abbotsford, or so Sir Walter declared. Had he not discovered the physical basis of this illusion (which, while it lasted, was an apparition, technically speaking) he and others might have thought it was an apparition in the popular sense of the word, a ghost.

PARTING

When a person is near death, open all the locks and doors and winows of the house in order to facilitate the soul's departure. In Switzerland (as I note in *The Complete Book of Superstition, Prophecy, and Luck*) there are even little windows in houses for the escape of the soul.

Death is coming soon if you hear a *banshee* or howling animals or bells at night, or if you see circular lights or hear the rapping of the deathwatch beetle. Death at the turning of the tide is an old superstition of those who go down to the sea in ships. If the herb Robert is picked it will hasten death. Keep any bird from flying in the open window.

If the bed of the dying person stands across the run of the floorboards (*athurt planshun*, as they used to say in Cornwall), the soul's departure may be hindered. Move the person to the floor, if required. Stand in the death chamber; do not sit down while a person is *in extremis*. Do not let a cat jump over the dying person or corpse; do not let a nun cast a shadow on the person.

After death, do not let tears fall on the corpse. In old Ireland, mournful lamentations were forbidden until 3 hours after death—wails might summon the spirit back before that time. Be respectful of the dead, and back out of the room. Do not turn your back. Take with you anything you brought in. Do not leave the corpse in the dark; keep a candle burning by it while it is in the house. No one person should light more than 2 candles, or at least not 3 from one taper.

Sit up with the corpse until the funeral, which should not be so speedy as to prevent those who knew the deceased from passing by the coffin to pay their respects. In Yorkshire, where people are thrifty, those at the wake go home as soon as one candle gutters out. They must not leave earlier. Mourners must be given refreshments at the wake and after the interment. Hired mourners can also be provided if you have the money. A deaf and dumb boy in the undertaker's procession is regarded as a nice touch.

So are black trappings for the hearse and the horses, black gloves for the pallbearers (who ought to be about the same age as the deceased, if possible), black armbands, etc. Men are supposed to wear black ties to funerals and everyone should dress somberly.

Of course the corpse must be washed before being dressed in shroud or clothes. An open coffin is traditional. A white coffin may be used for children and virgins. In fact, white was traditional for British funerals (as it is still in some societies) before black became the custom, as I told you before.

Remove the body feet first from the house and, if you are very afraid of the spirit's return, take it to the funeral by a roundabout route. Arriving at the lych gate—whose name tells us it is where the priest meets the corpse arriving at the church—be sure the body goes in east to west. If necessary, carry the corpse around the church first. The coffin lid should be screwed down, not nailed, after those who wish to have kissed the corpse or put into the coffin the dead person's bible or other treasured belongings, flowers, and so on.

Do not say "If only [dead person's name] were here." Don't make any disparaging remarks about the dead. It is best not to mention the names of the dead, at least not without adding a "may he/she rest in peace" or a similar sentiment.

Carry out last wishes and provide a wake and decent funeral. Tend the grave. Some few people even pour libations over graves. Hang up near the place in church where a maiden used to sit a pair of white gloves carried by an innocent in her funeral procession. Hang up a knight's helmet,

weapons, a banner. Give the dead all respect; you do not want to have an enemy in the spirit world.

Right after the death, tell the bees of it. Some people say you must tell houseplants, too, or they will perish. Temporarily cover birdcages. Stop clocks until after the funeral. Some people leave one clock stopped permanently at the exact minute of death. This seems unwise, but if the clock stopped of its own accord do not touch it.

Too much keeping the things as the dead knew them is considered asking for trouble. Rearrange the furniture, particularly in the dead person's own room, as soon as possible after the funeral. Keeping everything "exactly as it was left" invites return by the ghost. You know that. So does setting a place for the departed at the table.

To get things back in order for the living, wash the bed linens and last clothing of the person. Do not stint on dressing the corpse in good clothes or burying the corpse with rings, watch, etc., worn in life. Under no circumstances bury a woman without her wedding ring. If you can afford it, give away to the poor all the rest of the clothes of the dead person. You can keep a lock of hair for a locket and certain momentoes. Don't be too quick to sit in the departed person's favorite place. Tie up any loose ends of the loved one's business as expeditiously as possible. You don't want a ghost coming back for any unfinished business.

Take various precautions, different in different areas, to keep death from entering the house again. Stick a steel knife in the loaf of bread, the cheese, and so on. Iron is good for keeping all spirits, good and bad, away.

Be certain that the knell (sometimes called the "passing bell" or "soul bell") is sounded without interruption by the church bells but absolutely not at the same time that clocks are striking the hour. Of course today many old customs have fallen by the wayside, what with simple cremation, churches that may not have bells to ring, and people requesting there be no ceremony. Why not put into your will right this minute all the ceremony you want—and threaten survivors who do not follow your Last Wishes?

Your baptism you are too young to enjoy. Your marriage ceremony you have to share with another. Your funeral is all yours!

These are just a few of the many British and Irish superstitions surrounding the mystery of death. Every culture has some of its own.

CORNISH PASTY-FACED RESIDENTS

Visiting allegedly haunted places in Cornwall makes a lovely holiday. I've done it on more than one occasion. John Tregeagle's ghost is said to stalk bleak Bodmin Moor. There's a Gray Lady at Llanhydrock House near Bodmin and another at Trerice, St. Newlyn East. A ghostly priest sometimes attends funerals at Poundstock Church. A friend of mine swears he has seen him. I think the stranger may just have been a passing tourist who popped in (as the British say), noticing there was a service in progress, and then slipped out quietly. I have done the same myself, attending weddings and funerals uninvited and inconspicuously, just because some church whose architecture I wanted to see happened to be in use at the time I passed along. My friend obstinately refuses even to consider my theory about the so-called phantom priest.

Another ghostly cleric wanders around the priory church at St. Michael's Mount. A mermaid sings from Pendour Cove at Zennor. And among haunted inns you can choose from The Dolphin on the quay at Penzance, The Trout at Lostwithiel, and the Manor House at Rilla Mill.

DEATHLESS PERFORMANCES

Some favorite movie stars are said to haunt us still, and not just in late-night reruns on television. The ghost of James Dean had been reported more than once, and the ghost of Maria Montez was said in 1951 to have appeared in France. Certain dead Hollywood stars are frequently asked to make a comeback at séances.

The performer who had the greatest interest in the afterlife was Harry Houdini, and he vowed he would try to communicate from The Other Side—if there was one. Some people believe he did manage to convey a message to one of the many mediums who tried to contact Houdini after his death. The message, it was said, was verified by Houdini's wife and identified as a secret code they used to use in a "mind-reading" act they played in vaudeville many years before.

Frederick W. H. Myers

No actor, loathe as actors are to make final farewell performances, has ever made a comeback as much discussed as that of F. W. H. Myers, the British parapsychological researcher. He arranged for a message (entrusted to the archbishop of Canterbury and other unimpeachable persons) to be placed in sealed envelopes. After his death mediums were invited to see if they could get the message at séances. Mrs. Verrall did, most people who have examined the evidence agree, come up with the secret message Myers had recorded, which involved Diotima (from classical times) in a garden with which Myers was familiar from his youth.

A GHOST BRINGS A MURDERER TO JUSTICE

Ghosts are said not only to haunt their murderers to bring them to confession but even to report the facts of violent deaths to others so that the murderers can be apprehended and punished. Murder, as Macbeth said, will speak with most miraculous tongue.

Robert Surtees (1779-1834) tells of an instance of that. Surtees had a whole antiquarian society named for him because he devoted so much of his life to writing a history of Durham, which was published 1816-1840. As in many of these histories, much of the material may be unreliable, but here is a ghost story he tells:

> One Walker, a yeoman [farmer] of good estate, a widower, living at Chester-le-Street, had in his service a young female relative named Alice Walker. The result of an amour which took place between them caused Walker to send away the girl under the care of one Mark Sharp, a collier, professedly that she might be taken care of as befitted her [pregnant] condition, but in reality that she might no more be troublesome to her lover. Nothing was heard of her until, one night in the ensuing winter, one Thomas Graham, coming down from the upper to the lower floor of his mill, found a woman standing there with her hair hanging about her head, on which were five bloody wounds. According to the man's evidence, she gave account of her fate; having been killed by Sharp on the moor on their journey, and thrown into a coal pit close by, while the instrument of her death, a pick, had been hid under a bank along with her clothes, which were stained with her blood. She demanded of Graham that he should expose her murder, which he hesitated to do, until she had twice reappeared to him, the last time with a threatening aspect.
>
> The body, the pick and the clothes having been found as Graham had described, Walker and Sharp were tried at Durham before Judge [Sir Humphrey] Davenport in August, 1631. The men were found guilty, condemned, and executed.

THE SCENE OF THE CRIME

Old Norse legends tell of fairy lights or will-o'-the-wisps leading people to the scene of a murder. The lights were supposed to be the souls of the murdered, who with every step on the way to the scene said "It is right" and with every step on the way back said "It is wrong."

HOLCROFTS HOAX?

Holcrofts Holt was built about 1475 and claims to be "definitely one of Oxfordshire's most haunted inns." I don't know. One of its ghosts is said to be a highwayman named Claude Duval (whom I cannot trace). However, he is alleged to have been hanged at Tyburn (London's infamous place of execution near Hyde Park) and buried in Covent Garden, so what he is doing around an Oxfordshire inn, even if he operated there, is questionable.

The proprietors have supplemented him with the ghost of a cavalier, an old woman with a small black bag, and a poltergeist who shakes beds. I think they are trying too hard and with too little reason.

I have been in a number of English inns with creaking floorboards, conversations heard through the walls, noises in the dead of night, bad electrical wiring (so that the light came on in the middle of the night), clanking (bad plumbing), and even rather startling characters flitting along the corridors. I believe Holcrofts Holt would not bother me in the least.

RISEN FROM THE GRAVE

Premature burial was a potent cause of belief in the "undead," and a number of people, history records, woke up to find themselves about to be buried or even already in the grave. Some were lucky enough to escape. The actress Rachel was being embalmed when she "woke up," but she died soon after. Graves have been opened which reveal that the deceased was buried alive and struggled vainly to escape the tomb. In St. Giles, Cripplegate (London) we can see the monument to Constance Whitney, who did eventually die and was buried there. It gives notice that on a earlier occasion she rose from the coffin and went on living.

THE BUCCANEER'S GHOST

Henry Morgan (1635-1688) was a pirate who was in and out of favor in his time but wound up respectable, knighted, and governor of Jamaica. However, spiritualists claim, that was by no means the end of Sir Henry.

They say that in 1850 Sir Henry came back as a ghost and introduced himself at a séance as John King. The famous Davenport Brothers, who used to stage shows of supposed mediumship, named him John King.

He told Jonathan Koons, another medium, that he was in fact the king of a group of 165 spirits of pre-Adamic origin, which hicks in Ohio were

ready to believe. For years he gave other stories in séances to a wide variety of the mediums of the time, including Madam Blavatsky, Agnes Guppy, Mrs. Nelson Holmes, Katy King, Eusapia Palladino, W. T. Stead, Charles Williams, and others. At a séance almost anywhere, there was a good chance John King (Henry Morgan) would drop in. No medium seemed to be able to get an exclusive. He may hold the record for appearances with the largest numbers of facilitators of the nineteenth century, although with all that he never said anything really worthwhile.

Nineteenth-century people marvel at a ghostly carriage.

Oddly, he has not been active in twentieth-century occult circles. I wonder why.

ANKOU

This is the Breton name for a ghostly figure (sometimes in a shroud, sometimes a skeleton) that arrives to warn a person of imminent death, or to escort the person to The Other Side. In Brittany they say the last person to die in the parish in the year has this gruesome job for the next year. Now and then, they claim, the *ankou* wails like a *banshee*.

THE GHOST OF THE INN

Advertising a ghost is no more uncommon among B&Bs and inns in Britain than most other places. Ghosts are good for business. There are quite a few ghosts, however, who really do not get much appreciation, so here is a little publicity for them. Ghost hunters who want to get off the well-worn path in Britain might look into the haunted rooms at:

The Aspen Hotel, Ballater, Grampian
The Manor House Hotel, Moreton-in-the-Marsh, Gloucestershire
Ye Olde Mason's Arms, Branscombe, Devonshire

If Studley Prior, Horton-cum-Studley, Oxfordshire, is not in fact haunted, it ought to be. Nathaniel Hawthorne visited Studley Priory and wrote (1855): "there are long corridors, an intricate arrangement of passages, and an up-and-down meandering of staircases, amid which it would be no marvel to encounter some forgotten guest who had gone astray a hundred years ago, and was still seeking for his bedroom while the rest of his generation were in the grave."

THE GHOST SHIP IN THE SOLWAY

There is supposed to be a ghost ship called the *Betsy Jane* which haunts The Solway. It was a slave ship trading with West Africa that sank there as it was heading back to Britain centuries ago. It is the British equivalent of the *Flying Dutchman* and, with its crew of the dead, reminds us of the ship, previously noted, on which Dracula reached Whitby in Stoker's novel. I don't know if dead slaves still haunt it. No one has been able to board the *Betsy Jane* to see.

SCOTTISH GHOST

Gen. Dalywell of the Royal Scots Guards is said to ride his white horse still on Errack Bridge's ruins and stories are told of the seventeenth-century house in which he played cards with The Devil—and beat him by cheating.

The Devil, angry as hell, threw the gaming table at the old soldier. It crashed through the window and sank in a pond. In 1878 an old table was found in the pond and everyone said it must be the one mentioned in the story. The house, in West Lothian, has four turrets, and the locals say they anchor the building lest The Devil blow it away in his wrath.

BOOKS FROM BEYOND

Many books have been claimed as dictation from the dead via the Ouija board, a device that was given a terrific boost by spiritualism's rise in the nineteenth century. Stewart Edward White's *Betty Book* (1919) can serve as an example; he said it had been given to him from The Beyond by his dead wife Betty and a group of "Invisibles."

AFTER THE MURDER AT THE RED BARN

In 1826 in England, William Corder took his fiancée, Maria Marten, to a place named for its red barn. There he murdered her and hastily buried the body under the floor. But he gave himself away by his subsequent actions and was arrested, tried, and convicted. In 1828 he was hanged outside the Bury St. Edmunds jail in the presence of an enthusiastic crowd.

The crime became famous because of a sensational melodrama called *Maria Marten; or, The Red Barn*. It was common in those days to put true crime stories on the stage. (Now they turn up in opportunistic reporting, novels, and movies made chiefly for television.) This was a trend that had produced one of the greatest hits of the previous century, George Lillo's *George Barnwell; or, The London Merchant*.

The executed criminal's cadaver was handed over to medical students for dissection, as was then the custom. His skin was tanned to bind a book about the crime. His skeleton was placed on display for teaching purposes in the medical school.

Dr. Kilner, on the staff of the teaching hospital, stole the skull as a souvenir and replaced it with one from another cadaver from the dissecting room. Soon the ghost of William Corder began to haunt Dr. Kilner's house.

Terrified, Dr. Kilner tried to give the skull away to a Mr. Hopkins, a retired prison official who had bought the old Bury St. Edmunds jail. Dr. Kilner wrote that "as you already own Corder's condemned cell, and the gallows where they hanged him, it won't harm you to look after his skull."

Neither Dr. Kilner nor Mr. Hopkins, reports Daniel Cohen in his entertaining *Encyclopedia of Ghosts* (1984, 1989), had any luck thereafter, until the skull was finally given burial in consecrated ground. Then the hauntings ceased. William Corder was at rest at last.

SOME STRANGE READING ABOUT GHOSTS IN BRITAIN

Dennis Bardens, *Ghosts and Hauntings* (1965)
W. F. Barrett, *On the Threshold of the Unseen* (1917)
Peter Haining, *Ghosts: The Illustrated History* (1974)
Charles, Viscount Halifax, *Lord Halifax's Ghost Book* (reprinted 1961)
Edward Langton, *Supernatural... from the Middle Ages until the Present Time* (1934)
Shane Leslie, *Shane Leslie's Ghost Book* (1955)
Mary L. Lewes, *The Queer Side of Things* (1923)

Death with Three Women by H. Beham (1500-1550)

Alasdair Alpin MacGregor, *The Ghost Book: Strange Hauntings in Britain* (1955)
Andrew MacKenzie, ed., *A Gallery of Ghosts* (1972)
Edgar D. Mitchell, *Psychic Exploration* (1974)
Elliott O'Donnell, *Ghostly Phenomena* (194?)
A. R. G. Owen and Victor Sims, *Science and the Spook* (1971)
William Oliver Stephens, *Unbidden Guests* (1945)
Paul Tabori, *Companions of the Unseen* (1968)
C. J. S. Thompson, *The Mystery and Lore of Apparitions* (1930)
J. Stafford Wright, *Christanity and the Occult* (1971)

PRESENT!

Corneliu Codreanu founded The Legion of the Archangel Michael and its military arm, The Iron Guard, in Bucharest in 1927. His was a Fascist organization that attempted to build a national community of living—and dead—Romanians. At its meetings, when the names of fallen comrades were called, the living shouted, "Present!"

Sketches from *A Journal kept by Richard Doyle in the year 1840*
ABOVE: An excited crowd rushes into the Royal Academy's first exhibition of Charles Maclise's painting of Macbeth alarmed at the appearance of the Ghost of Banquo.
BELOW: Schoolboys—Doyle was one at the time—stand before Maclise's painting.

IRISH GHOSTS

In *Devoted People* (1997), a scholarly study of the beliefs of the Irish in early modern times, Raymond Gillespie writes:

> Walking spirits came in many forms. First there were those who might come from heaven. The Jesuit William Good reported in the early seventeenth century [1610] that the native Irish believed that the souls of the dead were with the heroes of the past "and they say that by illusion they oftimes do see such." More logically from a Catholic perspective purgatory was likely to be the origin of the spirit. Indeed around St. Patrick's [P]urgatory in Donegal, said to be the entrance to that world, there were frequent reports of fearful walking spirits although such stories were not reflected in any of the official writings on purgatory. The function of most of these spirits, like [that of] other wonderful disturbances in the natural order, was to signify divine displeasure at a turn of events. One of the most dramatic manifestations of this sort of revenging ghost appeared at the bridge of Portadown after the drowning of a number of Protestants there in late 1641.

One witness, Elizabeth Price, said she saw there

> a vision or spirit assuming the shape of a woman waist high in the water with elevate[d] and closed hands, her hair disheveled, very white, her eyes seemed to twinkle in her head and her skin [was] as white as snow. Which spirit or vision seemed to stand straight upright in the water divulged and then repeated the word "revenge, revenge, revenge."

Twenty years later, the Rev. W. Lightbourne was repeating the story in *A Thanksgiving Sermon Preached at Christ's Church* [Dublin] *Before the Lords Justice and Commons upon 23 October 1661*.

Today Portadown is internationally infamous for the Protestant parades through Catholic neighborhoods that have incited repeated violence in that godforsaken city. Some ghosts ought to be seeking revenge for that, volubly.

RUSALKA AND SUCH

In Russian folklore, this is the ghost of a maiden who has drowned in a spring, river, pool, or waterfall and haunts the spot where she perished. Round about Pentecost each year she is said to be most in evidence. Dvořak has an opera of this title. I saw it at the Metropolitan Opera and noted the witch's recipe for the potion that turned the *ondine* (water nymph) into a human being. It contained such ingredients as bile and "the beating heart of a bird," as the Met's little caption machine informed me.

See also:

Jonas Balys, *Dvasios or žmones* (Ghosts and Men, Lithuania, 1951)

THE SEERESS OF PREVORST

Prevorst was a village in Swabia, and there in the late eighteenth century was born a seeress who later became known as Frau Friederike Hauffe. In 1826 she came to the attention of Dr. Justinus A. C. Kerner, who thought at first she might be simply hysterical (a condition blamed on female anatomy) but discovered that she had incredible powers. She could read a document placed face down on her stomach. She was in touch with the dead, even using their help to trace a document that proved the innocence of a man accused of an embezzlement to which a dead man confessed. She could foretell the future. She was (she said) constantly surrounded by spirits, including malicious poltergeists who threw things. Her mediumistic trances took much of the strength of her frail constitution and, despite Dr. Kerner's treatments, she died in 1829.

Dr. Kerner published the whole story in a book later translated into English as *The Seeress of Prevorst* (1845). The translator, Mrs. Catherine Stevens Crowe (1799?-1876), herself became one of the most popular writers on the occult in Victorian England. Her own book, *The Night Side of Nature; or Ghosts and Ghost Seers* (1848), was nearly as widely read as *The Seeress of Prevorst*. Much of the century's interest in animal magnetism, hypnotism, trance mediumship, and The Other Side in general was bolstered by the public interest in these two works.

By 1859 Mrs. Crowe was publishing her *Spiritualism, and the Age We Live In*. Her importance as a novelist was far outweighed by her writings on the supernatural and the fact that she brought to English readers the fabulous Frau Hauffe and the rather embarrassed but boldly believing Dr. Kerner.

THE WANDERING JEW IN SCANDINAVIA

There is an old Danish ballad—its age is proved by the spelling—about The Wandering Jew with the lines

> *En skomager har jeg været,*
> *boet I Jerusalem*

or, in English,

> I have been a shoemaker,
> I lived in Jerusalem

I will not reproduce and translate it here, but I offer a piece of Scandinavian oral tradition regarding The Wandering Jew. In 1921, Edvard Langset, the folklorist, took down from an informant in Meldal the folktale I render into English here:

> At the time that they were laying the foundations for the church at Meldal the builders caught sight of a grey old man who approached them and sat down and wailed by the wall of the church. One of the builders went up to him and asked what sort of fellow he was, and he replied:
>
> "Oh, I'm an outlaw. I have committed an unpardonable sin. I cannot die, and therefore I am condemned to wander for ever and ever."
>
> "What kind of sin have you committed?" asked the builder.
>
> "I once was the door guard for Pontius Pilate. And when the Lord Jesus passed by me, I beat him. That cannot be forgiven me. So I am an outlaw and cannot die. Here I am, weeping over my transgression. And I am not worthy to pass the holy wall. I must get up again and continue my endless journey."
>
> The builder asked if he would like something to eat. The outlaw answered:
>
> "I can eat, but I can also abstain."
>
> Then the builder asked him to go along with him to his home and get something to eat, but the stranger replied:
>
> "No, I cannot. I must sit here a while longer to cry over my sin."
>
> "So, you will not come with me?" the builder repeated.
>
> No, the stranger would not go along, and the builder left with his workmates. When they returned, the stranger had vanished. Later they heard that he had passed through the neighboring community of Orkdalen. There he sat down wailing over his sin of having beaten Jesus.

The Wandering Jew has appeared before in the books of this series, but it seems good to place him here, because in this particular telling of the oft-told tale—this version very few if any of my readers will have heard—we have more proof of the widespread popularity of a story of a man who was a kind of living ghost, cursed with immortality, or cursed at least until The Last Judgment.

GASTKRAM

This is the word the people in Bohusländ (in Southern Sweden) use even today to describe what we would call the "clutch" of ghosts.

Bohusländ is a coastal area, so there are many stories of drowned sailors returning as ghosts. A little to the north, in Svealand, the unruly spirit might be an unwanted child that has been murdered and cannot rest in the grave. In either case, ghosts are said to walk by night and to have to go back to their graves before sun-up. You might see such a ghost trying to get a ride on the road, standing to the side and looking forlorn. You would be well advised to refrain from picking up hitchhikers at night. Once the cock crows and the sun is up, you are safer.

In the old days, your horse would alert you to the presence of a ghost hitchhiker. The horse would balk and refuse to go on. If you did let the hitchhiking ghost have a ride in your carriage, and you managed to get the horse to pull it, as you went along the carriage would grow heavier and heavier until the horse could hardly move it. You would see the horse's difficulty. You might even have to get out and walk to get the carriage with the ghostly passenger up a hill.

To be sure you had a ghost aboard what you did was go to the front and look backward at the passenger though the upright parts of the horse's collar. For some reason the ghost passenger would find that unpleasant and would simply disappear. Of course you might have picked up a ghostly passenger without even knowing it—ghosts can, as you know, be invisible if they wish—and in that case your horse would have been showing difficulty dragging the carriage uphill and you would thereby have been alerted to the extra weight of the passenger you couldn't even see.

Everyone knows that spirits hate iron or steel. So if it was raining or for some other reason you did not want to get out of the carriage, all you had to do was draw a steel knife through your teeth three times. Everyone knows three is a magic number.

What you had to be afraid of was the *gastkram*, a terrific hug from the ghost (visible or invisible) which could crush a man's ribs or make a woman pregnant. In Sweden today the term *gastkramming* is used when an otherwise "inexplicable" pregnancy occurs, and, oddly, it is used by people who do not know the old superstition about ghostly hitchhikers.

The superstition, however, has been around for a long time. If you know Swedish you can read about it in such folklore studies as these:

Louise Hagberg, *Gengängare, spöken* (Ghosts, Spooks, 1937)
Bengt af Klintberg, *Gasten i svensk folktradition* (Ghosts in Swedish Folk Tradition, 1973)
Ebbe Schön, *Älvor, vättoer och andra väsen* (Elves, etc., 1986)

If you can't read Swedish, all you need is the guidance of Schön, a leading Nordic folklorist, who writes (I translate with the help of Ola J. Holten):

A soldier encountered a ghost in the middle of the road at night. Neither soldier nor the ghost would step aside. So the soldier ran his sword through the body of the ghost, but the ghost only said, "Take it out again and try a better stab!" The soldier, however, was certain that the sword was well and truly placed and he left it there, until daybreak. At that point the ghost vanished. On the point of his sword the soldier found just a bone from a skeleton.

MYLINGAR

Murdered children's ghosts are called *mylingar* in Sweden, *myringer* having been in ancient times the word for a murdered person. In pagan times, deformed or defective children were often killed outright. Today we are more subtle about this, and science enables us to dispose of the unwanted before they are born, or before they can be abandoned in a desolate place and left to die. (Remember Oedipus, with his feet bound together, left to die by parents who feared a curse?)

Christianity arrived in Scandinavia around the eleventh century. By the fourteenth century the practice of doing away with unwanted children had been pretty much stamped out. By the seventeenth century killing an unwanted child was a capital offense. The blow usually fell on an unmarried mother. There was no punishment for the man who had got her pregnant and refused to marry her. For one thing, paternity was harder to prove than it is today, and for another the woman was always the one to blame, they said.

If and when an unwed mother disposed of an infant and later married, the ghost of the dead child (it was believed) was likely to turn up at the marriage feast and put a damper on the festivities. The ghost might come back as a handsome young man who asked the bride to dance and then danced her to death. Or he might seize her, cry "I want my mother's milk!", bite her breast, and kill her.

ALAS, POOR FRED!

There was an amusing doggerel epitaph written when Frederick, a typically sappy Prince of Wales in the Hanoverian line, died. It began:

Alas! Poor Fred, who was alive and now is dead....

Magic squares and something resembling the sacred monogram IHS (for "Jesus Savior of Mankind") are features of this Swedish equivalent of the Amish hex signs found in the United States today. This Nordic example is from 1727. It was believed to keep trolls, ghosts, all kinds of spirits in check. I like that typically Scandinavian mixture of Christian and pagan icons. You cannot be too cautious!

I use this quotation to introduce a piece on Frederick II (1194-1250), who succeeded his grandfather, Frederick Barbarossa (Redbeard), as Holy Roman Emperor. He is germane here because Frederick II was said to have become immortal and been condemned to roam the earth until Judgment Day. Not a ghost, but more like The Wandering Jew.

The story arose from the fact that thirty-four years after Frederick II died, at Fiorentino on December 13th 1250, a number of impostors arose. The first two were easily disposed of, but the third was a madman truly convinced that he was Frederick II. For political reasons some German prelates and princes were ready to go along with the imposture. He was captured and burned at the stake by politicians on the other side, but then a rumor started that in the ashes no bones had been found and that, miraculously, Frederick II still lived. Before he was burned—a fate usually reserved only for heretics or sorcerers, and perhaps they considered the imposture both—this impostor swore he would rise again!

Not long after his death at Wetzlar, up sprang a fourth impostor, at Utrecht. They burned him at the stake also. The folk belief would not die.

In a chronicle of 1434, the charge of atheism once leveled at Frederick II is repeated. It was baseless in the first place, although it was true that it had been a little difficult to get Frederick to go on the crusade that he promised the pope as a condition of being crowned emperor. He did actually go on the crusade, and in fact made himself King of Jerusalem before he rushed back to battle the papal allies who had taken up arms during his absence.

The chronicle also gives startling information about the rumors of immortality (which it imputes to devices of The Devil) still circulating at that late date:

> From the Emperor Frederick, the heretic, a new heresy arose which some Christians still secretly cling to: they believe absolutely that the emperor Frederick is still alive and will remain alive until the end of the world, and that there had been and never shall be any other legitimate emperor....

BRIDEY MURPHY

Bridey Murphy was said to be an Irish girl who died in the first half of the nineteenth century, and subsequently more or less took over an American housewife in Colorado, brought up in Illinois in the fifties. The modern woman, Virginia Tighe, was of Irish background but claimed she knew nothing of Ireland at all. She was able, many believed, under hypnosis to prove her metapsychosis and recall her past life as Bridey Murphy, or perhaps to permit Bridey Murphy to speak through her as a medium.

Morey Bernstein, the hypnotist, wrote a bestseller, *The Search for Bridey*

Murphy (1952). It was quite a while before the American public suspected that Mrs. Tighe was being fed information or was faking a biography or autobiography on her own. What was actually going on was and remains impossible to determine with certainty. The significant thing, I suppose, is that millions of Americans were prepared to believe that the case of Bridey Murphy was proof positive of either reincarnation or the communication with a living person by a dead one.

It could not even be proved that anyone named Bridey Murphy, answering to the descriptions given, was ever born, lived, and died in the places so carefully described by Mrs. Tighe.

HOW TO BECOME A GHOST

To create a false ghost of the sort I have just been describing, all you need is a Ouija board and an imagination. To become a real ghost, of course, first you have to die. But if you think you'd like to come back to do some haunting, British folklore tells you how: put pigeon feathers under the pillow of your deathbed. That's how Catherine Earnshaw's ghost explains herself in *Wuthering Heights.*

Relative to this is the case of some friends of mine who, in the late sixties, playing with a Ouija board, allegedly got in contact with a dead Englishman who provided reams of detail about his childhood, education at a Public School, service with the East India Company under the nineteenth-century *Raj*, and long retirement in a Sussex village. He had been dead, he said, since before the twentieth century began. He was ignorant of the modern world but full of information about Victorian times and foreign climes.

When the whole story had been "received," they began to check on its many specific and lively details. Not a single one of them could be corroborated. This *person* had never existed. The whole thing had come unconsciously, one presumes, from the imaginations of people playing with the Ouija board in a basement flat on St. Leonard's Terrace in London's Chelsea during long winter evenings. I wonder if the elaborate story of Bridey Murphy came from Mrs. Tighe's imagination, or hers and Bernstein's, consciously or unconsciously. I don't know. Never will.

A MOVABLE GHOST

After the death of Sir Noël Coward, two of his former lovers had him buried at the spot where they all used to sit and have drinks in the evening, looking out at the Spanish Main from Coward's house in Jamaica.

Graham Payne writes in *My Life with Noël Coward* (1994):

There was one final incident which sounds like an episode from *Blithe Spirit* [a Coward play with a ghost in it]. Each day, Coley

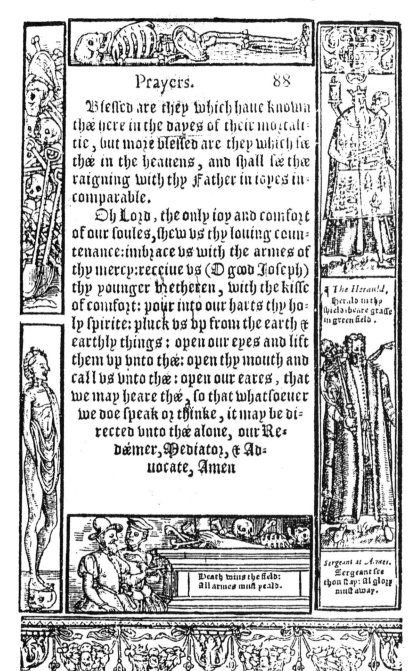

Prayers. 88

Blessed are they which haue known
thee here in the dayes of their mortali=
tie, but more blessed are they which see
thee in the heauens, and shall see thee
raigning with thy Father in ioyes in=
comparable.

Oh Lord, the only ioy and comfort
of our soules, shew vs thy louing coun=
tenance: imbrace vs with the armes of
thy mercy: receiue vs (O good Ioseph)
thy younger bretheren, with the kisse
of comfort: pour into our harts thy ho=
ly spirite: pluck vs vp from the earth &
earthly things: open our eyes and lift
them vp vnto thee: open thy mouth and
call vs vnto thee: open our eares, that
we may heare thee, so that whatsoeuer
we doe speak or thinke, it may be di=
rected vnto thee alone, our Re=
dæmer, Mediator, & Ad=
uocate, Amen

¶ The Herauld.
Herald in thy
shield, beare grasse
in greenfield.

Sergeant at Armes.
Sergeant see
thou say: Al glory
must away.

Death wins the field:
All armes must yeald.

[Cole Lesley] and I would sit by the grave for a little while, as if maintaining the habit would give us something to hang on to. One day, we quite suddenly looked at each other and said together: "He's gone!" Strange as it may sound, the vibrations that we felt so strongly abruptly vanished.

My thought was that he's gone back to Europe or...I don't know where. I don't think we're *supposed* to know. Sure enough, when we got back to [Coward's house in] Switzerland, the vibrations were there. You may say that's what we *wanted* to think, but friends who came to the house confirmed our feelings by remarking on the happy atmosphere. Even today, though I live there alone, that feeling of Noël's presence is as strong as ever. That's why I'm never lonely.

If true, this is a notable example of a ghost changing residences. Ghosts are popularly said to be stuck with the place where they died, sometimes even lurking there because they have nowhere else to go. However, they can move around. As I reported in another book, Fulke Greville, Lord Brooke made the mistake of reading his will to a valet who, much disappointed in his own prospects, promptly murdered him. This occurred in London, but Brooke's ghost, according to some, prefers to haunt a comfortable country castle where he gets many visits from tourists.

FINNISH GHOSTS AND SHAMANISM

In Finland people use "death sand" (graveyard dust) and even bits of corpses (a dead finger is favored) to break up marriages. They do not call on ghosts except through especially gifted persons called shamans. Only shamans, they say, can reach the spirit world, in trance. Finns are not sure whether the dead who appear in dreams and trances are ghosts or not.

I mention the Finns here because they are the most familiar shamanists to us, despite the fact that the aboriginal peoples of America brought shamanism with them from Asia and continue to practice it (more or less unnoticed) in the United States and Canada. It is a basic part of their Native American religions. Shamanism is a worldwide fact, and for some odd reason we in the United States tend to be interested in shamans among the peoples in distant cultures and not in our own. The Amerindian shamans deserve more attention. Moreover, they deserve more credit than they have been given for the founding of another American religion, spiritualism—Amerindian shamans were the first American mediums.

NO HAUNTING SPANISH PLACES

Reviewing Javier Marías's novel, as translated by Margaret Jull Costa under the title *Tomorrow in the Battle Think on Me*, Michael Kerrigan wrote in *TLS* for November 15th 1996:

There is no Spanish word for "haunt," Victor Francés, the narrator in Javier María's dazzling new novel, reminds us. Ghosts may prosaically "appear in" or "walk through" particular settings; they may, more dramatically, "torment" or "persecute" living individuals. But they don't habitually haunt as they do in English—frequenting, informing, laying claim.

Marías's hero has the shades of his past surrounding him, as does Richard III on the night before the fatal battle of Bosworth Field. That's where the title of the novel comes from. He is haunted. But in Spanish, places are not haunted.

Detail of *The Interment of Count Orgaz* by El Greco

I select the Spanish language as it is better known to many of my readers, but I stress that all cultures have their own languages and in those the concept of *haunting*, as well as many others we speak of in English, may well be missing or different. In considering as widespread an idea as the dead returning, we must be aware that not everyone thinks as we do. In fact, nobody who does not speak English thinks the same way those who speak English do. Did you ever think of that?

THE TAPESTRIED CHAMBER

This tale by Sir Walter Scott (1771-1832) first appeared in *The Keepsake* (1829), was soon translated into French (1829) and Spanish, and appeared in anthologies in various languages since then, including my own *Tales of Mystery and Melodrama* (1977). It exhibits the leisurely pace of Scott's period, perhaps exaggerated by a man who, when his publishers went bankrupt, was said to write 50 pages a day before breakfast. If you in modern impatience wish to "cut to the chase," start at the point where the general says at last: "I will proceed with my story as well as I can...." That's about halfway through.

> The following narrative is given from the pen, so far as memory permits, in the same character in which it was presented to the author's ear. He has claim to neither further praise nor deeper censure than corresponds to the good or bad judgment which he has

employed in selecting his materials. He has studiously avoided any attempt at ornament which might interfere with the simplicity of the tale.

At the same time it must be admitted that the particular class of stories which turns on the marvelous possesses a stronger influence when told than when committed to print. The volume taken up at noonday, though rehearsing the same incidents, conveys a much more feeble impression than is achieved by the voice of the speaker on a circle of fireside auditors, who hang upon the narrative as the narrator details the minute incidents which serve to give it authenticity, and lowers his voice with an affectation of mystery while he approaches the fearful and wonderful part. It was with such advantages that the present writer heard the following events related, more than twenty years ago, by the celebrated Miss Seward of Litchfield, who to her numerous accomplishments added in a remarkable degree the power of narrative in private conversation.

In its present form the tale must necessarily lose all the interest which was attached to it, by the flexible voice and intelligent features of the gifted narrator. Yet still, read aloud to an undoubting audience by the doubtful light of the closing evening, or in silence, by a decaying taper, amidst the solitude of a half-lighted apartment, it may redeem its character as a good ghost story. Miss Seward always affirmed that she had derived her information from an authentic source, although she suppressed the names of the two persons chiefly concerned. I will not avail myself of any particulars I may have since received concerning the localities of the detail, but suffer them to rest under the same general description in which they were first related to me. For the same reason, I will not add to or diminish the narrative by any circumstance, whether more or less material, but simply rehearse, as I heard it, a story of supernatural terror.

About the end of the American War, the officers of Lord Cornwallis's army, which surrendered at Yorktown, and others who had been made prisoners during the impolitic and ill-fated controversy were returning to their own country to relate their adventures and repose themselves after their fatigues. There was amongst them a general officer to whom Miss S. gave the name of Browne, but merely, as I understood, to same the inconvenience of introducing a nameless agent in the narrative. He was an officer of merit, as well as a gentleman of high consideration for family and attainments.

Business had carried General Browne upon a tour through the Western counties when, in the conclusion of a morning stage, he found himself in the vicinity of a small country town which presented a scene of uncommon beauty, and of a character peculiarly English.

The little town, with its stately old church whose tower bore testimony to the devotion of ages long past, lay amidst pastures and cornfields of small extent, but bounded and divided with hedgerow timber of great age and size. There were few marks of modern improvement. The environs of the place intimated neither the solitude of decay, nor the bustle of novelty; the houses were old but in good repair and the beautiful little river murmured freely on its way to the left of the town, neither restrained by a dam nor bordered by a towing-path.

Upon a gentle eminence, nearly a mile southward of the town, amongst many venerable oaks and tangled thickets, the turrets of a castle were seen. It was a place as old as the wars of York and Lancaster, but seemed to have received important alterations during the age of Elizabeth and her successor. It had not been a place of great size, but whatever accommodation it formerly afforded was, it must be supposed, still to be obtained within its walls. At least such was the inference which General Browne drew from observing the smoke arise merrily from several of the ancient wreathed and carved chimney-stalks. The wall of the park ran alongside the highway for two or three hundred yards; and through the different points by which the eye found glimpses into the woodland scenery, it seemed to be well stocked. Other points of view opened in succession; now a full one, of the front of the old castle, and now a side glimpse at its particular towers; the former rich in all the bizarrerie of the Elizabethan school, while the simple and solid strength of other parts of the building seemed to show that they had been raised more for defense than ostentation.

Delighted with the partial glimpses he obtained of the castle through the woods and glades by which this ancient feudal fortress was surrounded, our military traveler was determined to inquire whether it might not deserve a nearer view, and whether it contained family pictures or other objects of curiosity worthy of a stranger's visit. Leaving the vicinity of the park, he rolled through a clean and well-paved street, and stopped at the door of a well-frequented inn.

Before ordering horses to proceed on his journey, General Browne made inquiries concerning the proprietor of the château which had so attracted his admiration. He was equally surprised and pleased at hearing in reply the name of a nobleman, whom we shall call Lord Woodville. How fortunate! Many of Browne's early recollections, both at school and at college, had been connected with young Woodville, who, by a few questions, he now ascertained was the same person as the owner of his fair domain.

Lord Woodville had been raised to the peerage by the decease of his father a few months before, and, as the General learned from the landlord, the term of mourning being ended, he was now taking possession of his paternal estate in the jovial season of merry autumn. He was accompanied by a select party of friends to enjoy the sport of a country famous for game.

This was delightful news to our traveler. Frank Woodville had been Richard Browne's fag [servant] at Eton [school], and his chosen intimate at Christ Church [university]; their pleasures and their tasks had been the same; and the honest soldier's heart warmed to find his early friend in possession of so delightful a residence, and of an estate, as the landlord assured him with a nod and a wink, fully adequate to maintain and add to his dignity. Nothing was more natural than that the traveler should suspend a journey, which there was nothing to render hurried, to pay a visit to an old friend under such agreeable circumstances.

The fresh horses, therefore, had only the brief task of conveying the General's traveling carriage to Woodville Castle. A porter admitted them at a modern Gothic lodge, built in that style to correspond with the castle itself, and at the same time rang a bell to give warning of the approach of visitors. Apparently the sound of the bell had suspended the separation of the company, bent on the various amusements of the morning; for, on entering the court of the château, several young men were lounging about in their sporting dresses, looking at and criticizing the dogs which the keepers held in readiness to attend their pastime. As General Browne alighted, the young lord came to the gate of the hall and for an instant gazed as at a stranger upon the countenance of his friend, on which war, with its fatigues and its wounds, had made a great alteration.

But the uncertainty lasted no longer than till the visitor had spoken, and the hearty greeting which followed was such as can only be exchanged betwixt those who have passed together the merry days of careless boyhood or early youth.

"If I could have formed a wish, my dear Browne," said Lord Woodville, "it would have been to have you here, of all men, upon this occasion, which my friends are good enough to hold as a sort of holiday. Do not think you have been unwatched during the years you have been absent from us. I have traced you through your dangers, your triumphs, your misfortunes, and was delighted to see that, whether in victory or defeat, the name of my old friend was always distinguished with applause."

The General made a suitable reply, and congratulated his friend on his new dignities, and the possession of a place and domain so beautiful.

"Nay, you have seen nothing of it as yet," said Lord Woodville, "and I trust you do not mean to leave us till you are better acquainted with it. It is true, I confess, that my present party is pretty large, and the old house, like other places of the kind, does not possess so much accommodation as the extent of the outward walls appears to promise. But we can give you a comfortable old-fashioned room, and I venture to suppose that your campaigns have taught you to be glad of worse quarters."

The General shrugged his shoulders, and laughed. "I presume," he said, "the worst apartment in your château is considerably superior to the old tobacco-cask in which I was fain to take up my night's lodging when I was in the Bush, as the Virginians call it, with the light corps. There I lay, like Diogenes himself, so delighted with my covering from the elements that I made a vain attempt to have it rolled on to my next quarters; but my commander for the time would give way to no such luxurious provision, and I took farewell of my beloved cask with tears in my eyes."

"Well, then, since you do not fear your quarters," said Lord Woodville, "you will stay with me a week at least. Of guns, dogs, fishing-rods, flies, and means of sport by sea and land, we have enough and to spare: you cannot pitch on an amusement but we will find the means of pursuing it. But if you prefer the gun and pointers [dogs], I will go with you myself, and see whether you have mended your shooting since you have been amongst the Indians of the back settlements."

The General gladly accepted his friendly host's proposal in all its points. After a morning of manly exercise, the company met at dinner, where it was the delight of Lord Woodville to conduce to the display of the high properties of his recovered friend, so as to recommend him to his guests, most of whom were persons of distinction. He led General Browne to speak of the scenes he had witnessed; and as every word marked alike the brave officer and the sensible man, who retained possession of his cool judgment under the most imminent dangers, the company looked upon the soldier with general respect, as on one who had proved himself possessed of an uncommon portion of personal courage; that attribute, of all others, of which everybody desires to be thought possessed.

The day at Woodville Castle ended as days usually do at such mansions. The hospitality stopped within the limits of good order; music, in which the young lord was proficient, succeeded to the circulation of the bottle. Cards and billiards, for those who preferred such amusements, were in readiness. But the exercise of the morning required early hours, and not long after eleven o'clock the guests began to retire to their several apartments.

The young lord himself conducted his friend, General Browne, to the chamber destined for him, which answered the description he had given of it, being comfortable but old-fashioned. The bed was of the massive form used in the end of the seventeenth century, and the curtains of faded silk, heavily trimmed with tarnished gold. The sheets, pillows, and blankets looked delightful to the campaigner when he thought of his "mansion, the cask." There was an air of gloom in the tapestry hangings, with their worn-out graces curtaining the walls of the little chamber, gently undulating as the autumnal breeze found its way through the ancient lattice-window, which pattered and whistled as the air gained entrance. The toilet, too, with its mirror, turbaned after the manner of the beginning of the century, and a coiffure of murrey-coloured silk, and its hundred strange-shaped boxes, providing for arrangements which had been obsolete for more than fifty years, had an antique and melancholy aspect. But nothing could blaze more brightly and cheerfully than the two large wax candles; if aught could rival them, it was the flaming, bickering fagots in the chimney, that sent at once their gleam and their warmth through the snug apartment. Notwithstanding the general antiquity of its appearance, the apartment was not wanting in the least convenience that modern habits rendered either necessary or desirable.

"This is an old-fashioned sleeping apartment, General," said the young lord, "but I hope you find nothing that makes you envy your old tobacco-cask."

"I am not particular respecting my lodgings," replied the General, "yet were I to make any choice, I would prefer this chamber by many degrees to the gayer and more modern rooms of your mansion. Believe me, that when I unite its modern air of comfort with its venerable antiquity, and recollect that it is your lordship's property, I shall feel in better quarters here than if I were in the best hotel London could afford."

"I trust—I have no doubt—that you will find yourself as comfortable as I wish you, my dear General," said the young nobleman. Once more bidding his guest good-night, he shook him by the hand and withdrew.

The General once more looked round him, and internally congratulating himself on his return to peaceful life, the comforts of which were endeared by the recollection of the hardships and dangers he had lately sustained, undressed himself, and prepared for a luxurious night's rest.

Here, contrary to the custom of this species of tale, we leave the General in possession of his apartment until the next morning.

The company assembled for breakfast at an early hour, but without the appearance of General Browne, who seemed the guest that Lord Woodville was desirous of honouring above all whom his hospitality had assembled around him. He more than once expressed himself surprised at the General's absence, and at length sent a servant to make inquiry after him. The man brought back information that General Browne had been walking abroad since an early hour of the morning, in defiance of the weather, which was misty and ungenial.

"The custom of a soldier," said the young nobleman to his friends. "Many of them acquire habitual vigilance, and cannot sleep after the early hour at which their duty usually commands them to be alert."

Yet the explanation which Lord Woodville thus offered to the company seemed hardly satisfactory to his own mind, and it was in a fit of silence that he awaited the return of the General. It took place near an hour after the breakfast bell had rung. He looked fatigued and feverish. His hair, the powdering and arrangement of which was at this time one of the most important occupations of a man's whole day, and marked his fashion as much as, in the present time, the tying of a cravat, or the want of one, was dishevelled, uncurled, void of powder, and dank with dew. His clothes were huddled on with a careless negligence, remarkable in a military man, whose real or supposed duties are usually held to include some attention to the toilet; and his looks were haggard and ghastly in a peculiar degree.

"So you have stolen a march upon us this morning, my dear General," said Lord Woodville; "or you have not found your bed so much to your mind as I had hoped and you seemed to expect. How did you rest last night?"

"Oh, excellently well! Remarkably well! Never better in my life," said General Browne rapidly, and yet with an air of embarrassment which was obvious to his friend. He then hastily swallowed a cup of tea, and neglecting or refusing whatever else was offered seemed to fall into a fit of abstraction.

"You will take the gun to-day, General?" said his friend and host, but had to repeat the question twice ere he received the abrupt answer, "No, my lord; I am sorry I cannot have the opportunity of spending another day with your lordship: my post horses are ordered, and will be here directly."

All who were present showed surprise, and Lord Woodville immediately replied, "Post horses, my good friend! What can you possibly want with them, when you promised to stay with me quietly for at least a week?"

"I believe," said the General, obviously much embarrassed, "that I might, in the pleasure of my first meeting with your lordship, have said something about stopping here a few days; but I have since found it altogether impossible."

"That is very extraordinary," answered the young nobleman. "You seemed quite disengaged yesterday, and you cannot have had a summons to-day; for our post has not come up from the town and therefore you cannot have received any letters."

General Browne, without giving any further explanation, muttered something about indispensable business, and insisted on the absolute necessity of his departure in a manner which silenced all opposition of the part of his host, who saw that his resolution was taken, and forbore all further importunity.

"At least, however," Lord Woodville said, "permit me, my dear Browne, since go you will or must, to show you the view from the terrace, which the mist, that is now rising, will soon display."

He threw open a sash-window and stepped down upon the terrace as he spoke. The General followed him mechanically, but seemed little to attend to what his host was saying as, looking across an extended and rich prospect, he pointed out the different objects worthy of observation. Thus they moved on till Lord Woodville had attained his purpose of drawing his guest entirely apart from the rest of the company, when, turning round upon him with an air of great solemnity, he addressed him thus:

"Richard Browne, my old and very dear friend, we are now alone. Let me conjure you to answer me, upon the word of a friend, and the honour of a soldier. How did you in reality rest during last night?"

"Most wretchedly indeed, my lord," answered the General, in the same tone of solemnity; "so miserably that I would not run the risk of such a second night, not only for all the lands belonging to this castle, but for all the country which I see from this elevated point of view."

"This is most extraordinary; then there must be something in the reports concerning that apartment," said the young lord, as if speaking to himself. Again turning to the General, he said, "For God's sake, my dear friend, be candid with me. Let me know the disagreeable particulars which have befallen you under a roof where, with consent of the owner, you should have met nothing save comfort."

The General seemed distressed by this appeal, and paused a moment before he replied. "My dear lord," he at length said, "what happened to me last night is of a nature so peculiar and so unpleasant, that I could hardly bring myself to detail it even to your lordship, were it not that, independent of my wish to gratify any request of yours, I think that sincerity on my part may lead to some explanation about a circumstance equally painful and mysterious. To others, the communication I am about to make might place me in the light of a weak-minded, superstitious fool, who suffered his own imagination to delude and bewilder him; but you have known me in childhood and youth, and will not suspect me of having adopted in manhood the feelings and frailties from which my early years were free." Here he paused.

Lord Woodville replied: "Do not doubt my perfect confidence in the truth of your communication, however strange it may be. I know your firmness of disposition too well to suspect you could be made the object of imposition, and am aware that your honour and your friendship will equally deter you from exaggerating whatever you may have witnessed."

"Well, then," said the General, "I will proceed with my story as well as I can, relying upon your candour; and yet distinctly feeling that I would rather face a battery than recall to my mind the odious recollections of last night."

He paused a second time, and then perceiving that Lord Woodville remained silent and in an attitude of attention, he commenced, though not without obvious reluctance, the history of his night adventures in the Tapestried Chamber.

"I undressed and went to bed, so soon as your lordship left me yesterday evening; but the wood in the chimney, which nearly fronted my bed, blazed brightly and cheerfully, and, aided by a hundred exciting recollections of my childhood and youth, which had been recalled by the unexpected pleasure of meeting your lordship, prevented me from falling immediately asleep. I ought, however, to say that these reflections were all of a pleasant and agreeable kind, grounded on a sense of having for a time exchanged the labour, fatigues, and dangers of my profession for the enjoyments of a peaceful life, and the reunion of those friendly and affectionate ties, which I had torn asunder at the rude summons of war.

"While such pleasing reflections were stealing over my mind, and gradually lulling me to slumber, I was suddenly aroused by a sound like that of the rustling of a silken gown, and the tapping of a pair of high heeled shoes, as if a woman were walking in the apartment. Ere I could draw the curtain to see what the matter was, the figure of a little woman passed between the bed and the fire. The back of this form was turned to me, and I could observe, from the shoulders and neck, it was that of an old woman, whose dress was an old-fashioned gown, which, I think, ladies call a sacque; that is, a sort of robe completely loose in the body, but gathered into broad plaits upon the neck and shoulders, which fall down to the ground and terminate in a species of train.

"I thought the intrusion singular enough, but never harboured for a moment the idea that what I saw was anything more than the mortal form of some old woman about the establishment, who had a fancy to dress like her grandmother, and who, having perhaps (as your lordship mentioned that you were rather straitened for room) been dislodged from her chamber for my accommodation, had forgotten the circumstance, and returned by twelve to her old haunt. Under this persuasion I moved myself in bed and coughed a little, to make the intruder sensible of my being in possession of the premises.

"She turned slowly round, but, gracious heaven! My lord, what a countenance did she display to me! There was no longer any question what she was, or any thought of her being a living being. Upon a face which wore the fixed features of a corpse, were imprinted the traces of the vilest and most hideous passions which had animated her while she lived. The body of some atrocious criminal seemed to have been given up from the grave, and the soul restored from the penal fire, in order to form, for a space, a union with the ancient accomplice of its guilt. I started up in bed, and sat upright, supporting my self on my palms, as I gazed on this horrible spectre.

"The hag made, as it seemed, a single and swift stride to the bed where I lay, and squatted herself down upon it, in precisely the same attitude which I had assumed in the extremity of horror, advancing her diabolical countenance within half a yard of mine, with a grin which seemed to intimate the malice and derision of an incarnate fiend."

Here General Browne stopped, and wiped from his brow the cold perspiration with which the recollection of his horrible vision had covered it.

"My lord," he said, "I am no coward. I have been in all the mortal dangers incidental to my profession, and I may truly boast that no man ever knew Richard Browne to dishonour the sword he wears; but in these horrible circumstances, under the eyes, and as it seemed, almost in the grasp of an incarnation of an evil spirit, all firmness forsook me, all manhood melted from me like wax in the furnace, and I felt my hair individually bristle. The current of my life-blood ceased to flow, and I sank back in a swoon, as very a victim to panic terror as ever was a village girl, or a child of ten years old. How long I lay in this condition I cannot pretend to guess.

"But I was roused by the castle clock striking one, so loud that it seemed as if it were in the very room. It was some time before I dared open my eyes, lest they should again encounter the horrible spectacle. When, however, I summoned courage to look up, she was no longer visible. My first idea was to pull my bell, wake the servants, and remove to a garret or a hay-loft, to be ensured against a second visitation. Nay, I will confess the truth, that my resolution was altered, not by the shame of exposing myself, but by the fear that, as the bell-cord hung by the chimney, I might, in making my way to it, be again crossed by the fiendish hag, who, I figured to myself, might be still lurking about some corner of the apartment.

"I will not pretend to describe what hot and cold fever-fits tormented me for the rest of the night, through broken sleep, weary vigils, and that dubious state which forms the neutral ground between them. An hundred terrible objects appeared to haunt me; but there was the great difference betwixt the vision which I have described, and those which followed, that I knew the last to be deceptions of my own fancy and over-excited nerves.

"Day at last appeared, and I rose from my bed ill in health, and humiliated in mind. I was ashamed of myself as a man and a soldier, and still more so, at feeling my own extreme desire to escape from the haunted apartment, which, however, conquered all other considerations; so that, huddling on my clothes with the most careless haste, I made my escape from your lordship's mansion, to seek in the open air some relief to my nervous system, shaken as it was by this horrible encounter with a visitant, for such I believe her, from the other world.

"Your lordship has now heard the cause of my discomposure, and of my sudden desire to leave your hospitable castle. In other places I trust we may often meet; but God protect me from ever spending a second night under that roof!"

Strange as the General's tale was, he spoke with such a deep air of conviction that it cut short all the usual commentaries which are made on such stories. Lord Woodville never once asked him if he was sure he did not dream of the apparition, or suggested any of the possibilities by which it is fashionable to explain supernatural appearances; as wild vagaries of the fancy, or deceptions of the optic nerves. On the contrary, he seemed deeply impressed with the truth and reality of what he had heard; and, after a considerable pause, regretted, with much appearance of sincerity, that his early friend should in his house have suffered so severely.

"I am the more sorry for your pain, my dear Browne," he continued, "that it is the unhappy, though most unexpected, result of an experiment of my own. You must know that for my father and grandfather's time, at least, the apartment which was assigned to you last night had been shut on account of reports that it was disturbed by supernatural sights and noises. When I came, a few weeks since, into possession of the estate, I thought the accommodation, which the castle afforded for my friends, was not extensive enough to permit the inhabitants of the invisible world to retain possession of a comfortable sleeping apartment. I therefore caused the Tapestried Chamber, as we call it, to be opened; and without destroying its air of antiquity. I had such new articles of furniture placed in it as became the modern times. Yet as the opinion that the room was haunted very strongly prevailed among the domestics, as was also known in the neighborhood and to many of my friends, I feared some prejudice might be entertained by the first occupant of the Tapestried Chamber, which might tend to revive the evil report which it had laboured under, and so disappoint my purpose of rendering it an useful part of the house.

"I must confess, my dear Browne, that your arrival yesterday, agreeable to me for a thousand reasons besides, seemed the most favourable opportunity of removing the unpleasant rumours which attached to the room, since your courage was indubitable, and your mind free of any pre-occupation on the subject. I could not, therefore, have chosen a more fitting subject for my experiment."

"Upon my life," said General Browne, somewhat hastily, "I am infinitely obliged to your lordship—very particularly indebted indeed. I am likely to remember for some time the consequences of the experiment, as your lordship is pleased to call it."

"Nay, now you are unjust, my dear friend," said Lord Woodville. "You have only to reflect for a single moment, in order to be convinced that I could not augur the possibility of the pain to which you have been so unhappily exposed. I was yesterday morning a complete skeptic on the subject of supernatural appearances. Nay, I am sure that had I told you what was said about that room, those very reports would have induced you, by your own choice, to select it for your accommodation. It was my misfortune, perhaps my error, but really cannot be termed my fault, that you have been afflicted so strangely."

"Strangely indeed!" said the General, resuming his good temper; "and I acknowledge that I have no right to be offended with your lordship for treating me like what I used to think myself—a man of some firmness and courage. But I see my post horses are arrived, and I must not detain your lordship from your amusement."

"Nay, my old friend," said Lord Woodville, "since you cannot stay with us another day, which, indeed, I can no longer urge, give me at least half an hour more. You used to love pictures, and I have a gallery of portraits, some of them by Vandyke, representing ancestry to whom this property and castle formerly belonged. I think that several of them will strike you as possessing merit."

General Browne accepted the invitation, though somewhat unwillingly. It was evident he was not to breathe freely or at ease till he left Woodville Castle far behind him. He could not refuse his friend's invitation, however; and the less so, that he was a little ashamed of the peevishness which he had displayed towards his well-meaning entertainer.

The General, therefore, followed Lord Woodville through several rooms, into a long gallery hung with pictures, which the latter pointed out to his guest, telling the names, and giving some account of the personages whose portraits presented themselves in progression. General Browne was but little interested in the details which these accounts conveyed to him. They were, indeed, of the kind which are usually found in an old family gallery. Here was a cavalier who had ruined the estate in the royal cause; there, a fine lady who had reinstated it by contracting a match with a wealthy Roundhead. There hung a gallant who had been in danger for corresponding with the exiled Court at Saint Germain's; here, one who had taken arms for William at the Revolution; and there, a third that had thrown his weight alternately into the scale of whig and tory.

While Lord Woodville was cramming these words into his guest's ear, they gained the middle of the gallery, when he beheld General Browne suddenly start, and assume an attitude of the utmost surprise, not unmixed with fear, as his eyes were caught and suddenly riveted by a portrait of an old lady in a sacque, the fashionable dress of the end of the seventeenth century.

"There she is!" he exclaimed. "There she is, in form and features, though inferior in demoniac expression to the accursed hag who visited me last night!"

"If that be the case," said the young nobleman, "there can remain no longer any doubt of the horrible reality of your apparition. That is the picture of a wretched ancestress of mine, of whose crimes a black and fearful catalogue is recorded in a family history in my charter-chest. The recital of them would be too horrible; it is enough to say that in yon fatal apartment incest and unnatural murder were committed. I will restore it to the solitude to which the better judgment of those who preceded me had consigned it;

and never shall anyone, so long as I can prevent it, be exposed to a repetition of the supernatural horrors which could shake such courage as yours."

Thus the friends, who had met with such glee, parted in a very different mood; Lord Woodville to command the Tapestried Chamber to be unmantled, and the door built up; and General Browne to seek in some less beautiful country, and with some less dignified friend, forgetfulness of the painful night which he had passed in Woodville Castle.

3

Ghosts in the American Tradition

GHOSTS OF THE NEW WORLD

Some of the ghost tales of the New World came from the Old, but even in pre-Columbian times the peoples of the Americas believed in ghosts not only of humans but of other animals. Hugo Meynell, in his xenophobia, said of England that "foreigners are fools," but Americans, North, Central, and South, hold tenaciously to the same beliefs (or superstitions) that we may deplore elsewhere.

It was in the United States that a whole new religion, Spiritualism, was based on communicating with the spirits. As we shall see in later chapters, the United States may possibly contribute more than any other modern nation, in terms of literature and films and in other ways, to popular ideas about ghosts.

A DEFINITION

G. N. M. Tyrrell in *Apparitions* (1942):

> "Apparitions are the sensory expression of dramatic constructs created in regions of the personality outside the field of normal consciousness."

To this psychologist, apparitions are purely human, not supernatural. American psychologists tend to follow Tyrrell's lead.

A MOTIVE

Perhaps the most famous American writings about death are by two Britons, Nancy Mitford and Evelyn Waugh, who were outraged by the greed and

Posada, one of whose best known woodblock images (Catarina) is shown here, is one of many folk artists who have contributed to the Mexican cult of the dead. Once a year, graves are decorated, parties for the living and the dead are held in cemeteries, and children are given toy skeletons, candies in the shape of skulls, etc.

tastelessness of the funeral industry here. Americans do not like to think about death, which is one reason that funerals are put into the hands of professionals and too much money is spent at the time of need.

The information superhighway, however, has brought hearses as well as jalopies and speedsters out, so inevitably death is a topic. On http://www.islandnet.com/deathnet you can reach a site which said:

> There has to be another dimension out there, where souls of the dead are sometimes suspended, not quite at peace, not quite ready to give up what they had begun during their mortal lives. Thus, these restive spirits return to make themselves known to those who still dwell in places they [the ghosts] once knew. They come to leave a message, to finish a task, to give a warning, or to watch over a once loved location. Some of them are more restless than others.... perhaps, with some, a crime has not been avenged.... In extreme cases, so that both these restless souls and the mortals that they torment can rest peacefully, a blessing or exorcism may be necessary.

Having received neither blessing nor exorcism, apparently, San Antonio, Texas' public buildings, hotels and restaurants, haunted houses, and military posts, the internet tells us, are full of restless souls, some cheerful and some not so nice.

VADE MECUM

There is a vast library of occult books, many of them junk, but if you search hard enough you will find something interesting and perhaps useful on every aspect, including "Summoning the Dead" in popular books such as Paul Hudson's *Mastering Witchcraft* on esoteric *grimoires*, J. H. Breenan's *Reincarnation* and Judy Boss's *In Silence They Return* (automatic writing), Carla Ruekert's *The Channeling Handbook* and J. Donald Walters' *How to be a Channel*, books on spiritualism and mediumship, and so on.

The number of writers who treat death as a mere transition and who give instructions on how to contact those who have made that career move is immense. Ask yourself in each and every case, How does the writer who claims this or that to be true *know* what she or he says they know? Question authority! (Better, question pseudo-authorities!)

DEATH/TALK

Frank speaking about death is necessary. But most of us live in a culture that denies death in different ways, and very few of us actually have the opportunity to explore our thoughts, feelings and fears about death. It is a taboo.

As they explore their emotions and exchange gripes and chitchat about death, the 600 participants who have registered for a Death/Talk Conference are contemplating The End more than most Americans do. The subject, except to necrophiliacs and other death-obsessed people (for whom there is a dreadful guide I mention in *The Complete Book of the Devil's Disciples*), does not appeal, although the conference brochure calling death "the ultimate taboo" shows a lack of understanding of the real no-no's in America, which concern the power plays of race and sex.

Why, then, the undoubted American fascination with ghosts, annoying poltergeists, scary vampires? They appeal even when they appall because fundamentally they tell us: Death is Not The End. That may not be true. But, like many things that are not true, it is a very comforting thought to entertain. The whole world likes its assurance.

THERE IS NO DEATH

A comforting message from Christian Science: you're not dead, you just think you're dead. Roger Rosenblatt in "Dig, Must We?" in *Time* writes that "Mary Baker Eddy, founder of the Christian Science Church...was said to have been interred with a telephone in her crypt in case she needed to phone long distance."

Says Wendy Kaminer in "The Latest Fashion in Irrationality," from the *Atlantic Monthly*, July 1996, James Redfield's *The Celestine Prophecy* assured us that what we imagine as death is a happy transition to a higher spiritual plane: a new Eden awaits us in the next millennium. Books about near-death experiences describe the brief sojourns in heaven of people who died but were sent back to earth by God to complete their missions or simply to spread the word: there is no death.

SPIRITUALISM

As a religion it can be said to have begun in Hydesville, New York, about 150 years ago. In a simple house there, raps on the table supposedly communicated that a thirty-one-year-old had been murdered and buried in the basement. His ghost was purportedly contacted. After that it was asserted that anyone dead could be contacted by a medium. Spiritualism became a religion.

Mediums such as the Fox Sisters and the Davenport Brothers (Ira and William) took the show on the road. They were a welcome source of stage entertainment in the latter part of the nineteenth century. Later another entertainer, Houdini, exposed fraudulent mediums like these. In the end at least one of the Fox sisters confessed she had faked things. Spiritualists said she was drunk, and kept right on believing. Ira Davenport, Anna Eva Fay, and others showed Houdini how their effects had been obtained. But people said the effects they themselves produced or defended were not tricks. No matter how many mediums were exposed by investigative newspaper reporters and societies of psychical research trying to police the field and sort out questionable practices, some people only believed more strongly that they could talk with the dead. Although exposure of fraud was rife, the spiritualist vogue could not be stopped. And it still continues.

There have been exposés by reformed spiritualists such as the stories of the frauds of Camp Chesterfield, a psychic establishment, from M. Lamarr Keene. Appropriately, he had a ghostwriter, Allen Spraggett. The book is *The Psychic Mafia* (1976). Unfortunately, there has been not nearly enough hardheaded examination in the last twenty years of the claims of psychics, channelers, and others who are defrauding the public, while faded singing stars and aging movie stars are touting channeling and similar things to a wide and credulous audience.

The churches have always said this sort of thing is evil, of The Devil. Nevertheless, people holding all sorts of religious convictions, or none at all, insist that they will believe what they choose. Ordinary people, increasingly regarding dogma as a menu, insist on Spiritualism. Consumer fraud is about the only way left to attack cheaters of the gullible, and even there some people sincerely believe that it is despicable in the name of reason to snatch candy from intellectual infants.

"Séances bring so much comfort to people," one of my best friends argues.

"So do 'recreational' drugs," I counter, "but I'm opposed to their use, too." Who can handle the problems they bring, greater than any problems they solve?

SÉANCE

The word, obviously, is from the French, and for the best example of a clever man taken in by spiritualist mediums I choose the leading French poet and novelist of the nineteenth century, Victor Hugo. (Asked who the best French poet was, André Gide is supposed to have replied the equivalent of "Victor Hugo, alas!" Jean Cocteau declared that "Victor Hugo was a madman who thought he was Victor Hugo.")

Having claimed he talked with the living God, it wasn't strange that Hugo believed his medium, Delphine de Giradin, could talk with the dead. Hugo had, like Sir Arthur Conan Doyle, Sir Oliver Lodge, and many other Englishmen, not to mention all the Americans who made table-rapping a huge fad, personal reasons to want to chat with loved ones on The Other Side. These needs pushed rationality and religious taboos aside.

MEDIUMS

The medium claims to be the mediator between The Other Side and this world. All history has recorded individuals of one sort or another who claimed the power to make the linkage. F. W. H. Myers suggested instead we say "automatist," because he thought all mediums who were not conscious fakes were nothing more than subconsciously expressing something from within themselves, and nothing from Out There. Others have suggested that mediums consciously or unconsciously get their information by telepathy from those before whom they perform, not through their spirit guides at all. The spirit guides have been rabbis and little girls, Amerindians and Indians from India, all sorts, always colorful, some even allegedly angelic.

In any case, *medium* is used today to describe the interlocutor or channel at a séance, so the first modern mediums (or pretended mediums) were the table-rapping Fox Sisters (1848). This led to a great deal of debate about the powers of all who followed in this line. Many organizations were set up to investigate or advance mediumship, an art which some said one was born with and others were sure one could learn from adepts—or even could have transferred by the touch of the gifted.

Other famous U.S. mediums of the early days were the Rev. Stainton Moses, Andrew Jackson Davis, the Davenport Brothers, J. R. M. Squire,

Edgar Cayce, and Mrs. John H. Curran of St. Louis, Missouri, who gave us "Patience Worth." Elsewhere the stars of old included Eusapia Palladino, Stefan Ossowiecki, "Hélène Smith" (with news from the court of Marie Antoinette and from Mars), and especially Daniel Dunglas Home (1833-1886), who spent some time in the United States but was best known in Europe. Harry Houdini was one American who helped expose a number of fake mediums, including the notorious "Margery."

Here are fifteen books from those interested in the people who claim to channel (as we say today) ghosts. Reprinting is proof of continued popularity:

Emma Hardinge [Britten], *Modern American Spiritualism* (1870, 1970)
Michael F. Brown, *The Channeling Zone* (1997)
Hereward Carrington, *Eusapia Palladino and Her Phenomena* (1909)
Robert Galen Chaney, *Mediums and the Development of Mediumship* (1946, 1972)

Mrs. Leonora Piper flourished as a medium 1885-1915. She died in 1930. She has not been heard from since.

Eileen J. Garrett, *My Life as a Search for the Meaning of Mediumship* (1939, 1975)
Daniel Dunglas Home, *Incidents in My Life* (1863, 1973)
Ernest Isaacs, "The Fox Sisters and American Spiritualism," pp. 70-110 in *The Occult in America: New Historical Perspectives* (Howard Kerr and C. L. Crow, eds., 1983)
Gladys Osborne Leonard, *My Life in Two Worlds* (1931)
Kenneth G. Pimple, "Ghosts, Spirits and Scholars: The Origins of Modern Spiritualism," pp. 75-89 in *Out of the Ordinary: Folklore and the Supernatural* (ed. B. Walker, 1995)
Alta Piper, *The Life and Work of Mrs. [Lenore F.] Piper* (1929)
Frank Podmore, *Mediums of the Nineteenth Century* (1902, 2 vols., revised title 1963)
Allen Spraggett and William V. Rauscher, *Arthur Ford, The Man who Talked with the Dead* (1973)
Roy Stemman, *Medium Rare: The Psychic Life of Ena Twigg* (1971)
Thomas R. Tietze, *Margery* [Mina Stinson Crandon] (1973)
E. W. and M. H. Wallis, *A Guide to Mediumship and Spiritual Unfoldment* (1903)

WOMEN AND SPIRITUALISM

Just as Spanish nuns announcing they had experienced heavenly visions challenged the hierarchy of the church and disturbed many, so the Fox Sisters launching Spiritualism and the preponderance of female mediums caused some men to look askance at the new religious movement. There were also some women's efforts to use it to advance recognition of women's capabilities and civil rights. Spiritualism may have been the most significant religious movement in which women took the lead here since Mother Anne Lee came to America and announced she was the Messiah. For women and spiritualism see:

> Ann Braude, *Radical Spirits: Spiritualism and Women's Rights in Nineteenth-Century America* (1989)
>
> Susan Steinberg Danielson, *Alternative Therapies: Spiritualism and Women's Rights in Mary Lyndon; or, Revelations of a Life* (University of Oregon dissertation, 1990)
>
> Nancy Rita Kelly, *Sarah Orne Jewett and Spiritualism* (University of Massachusetts dissertation, 1991)

GEORGE M. COHAN

For *Beware Familiar Spirits* (1938), John Mulholland asked famous men for personal experiences. Here is what was written to him by the "Yankee Doodle Dandy," George M. Cohan (1878-1942):

> Late one night I got up from the desk in my den and walked down the hall to go to the kitchen for a glass of milk. I had been working on a play—hadn't had much sleep in several days and was awfully tired. Down at the end of the long hall I turned on the light right by the door. The door had a glass its whole length. Looking at the glass in the door I saw my father. That didn't seem at all surprising but I wondered, how did I happen to think that I was my son. That did bother me. I turned out the light for a moment and then turned it on again. Once more I was myself. After the glass of milk when I started back up the hall again, I found myself peering up the hall to see if I was sitting at my desk. Of course I was tired and all that but it was a very real experience.
>
> My father definitely felt that he had talked with spirits. I remember one story he told me about waking up one night and finding three old cronies in his room. These men had been doctors in the Civil War with my father when he was just a young doctor's orderly. This visit happened when my father was about sixty-five years old and the doctors, who were much older than Father, had been dead for years. Father said that he did not feel any surprise at their being there and drew up chairs and had them sit down. He recalled telling them a story about the incident when he was a boy celebrating after a battle and by accident shot off his thumb. He did not recall anything that they had said and did not remember their leaving nor his going back to bed. When he awoke

the next morning he found the chairs drawn up just as he had recalled he had placed them.

LINCOLN'S GHOST

A lot of legends have grown up around Abraham Lincoln, from a premonition of his assassination to his stalking the White House after death. Lots of people (including Wilhelmina, the queen of Holland who was forced off the throne for her pro-Nazi sentiments) claim to have seen Lincoln's ghost. You'd think he would appear at Ford's Theater, where he was shot, or nearby, where he died.

TALKING WITH/TO THE DEAD

It is well known that people visit graves to commune with the dead. They not only pick weeds or leave flowers, they chat. Jews have a custom of placing a pebble on the headstone. Whether this is done to show they were there, or as a token of the ancient practice of adding to the pile of stones that kept jackals from digging up corpses in the desert ages ago, I do not know. Some people regularly hold conversations with their departed loved ones in the rooms in which they lived (which are sometimes kept just as they left them).

The death of Diana, Princess of Wales produced many messages *to* her written in vast books of remembrance. More books of messages were created and deposited by classes of schoolchildren and others, and some $50 million worth of flowers were accompanied by hundreds of thousands of personal notes, cards, and other messages for the dead Diana to read. Ross McKibbin, after this great outpouring of love for the princess, pointed out in *London Review of Books* that the messages were in "the graveyard style which is, if anything, mid-nineteenth century," the twentieth century having failed to devise a modern style for such sentimental and superstitious notes of well-wishing and *bon voyage* to the dear departed.

ONE WAY TO GET A BOYFRIEND

Tina McElroy Ansa contributes mightily to African-American literature that incorporates old folklore and new insights in *The Hand I Fan With* (1996). In this novel Lena McPherson is the woman in the little town of Mulberry, Georgia, on whom everyone depends to get things done. When she needs a lover she finds a friend to conjure up a man. She gets a 100-year-old ghost, and for what happens next you'll just have to read the book.

DO YOU KNOW WHERE YOU'RE GOING?

Ever optimistic, 90 percent of Americans believe in Heaven but only a little over 70 percent believe in Hell. Only about two-thirds of Americans believe in The Devil.

FEEDING THE DEAD

Ghosts may come back, it is thought, because they are angry, but they can also return if they are hungry. Vampires are said to feed off their own flesh and blood before rising from the grave to seek nourishment from the living. From very early times mankind buried food (along with other useful things for the journey in the Land of the Dead) with corpses. Mummies of ancient Egyptians have been found with bread and wine, figs, and many other foodstuffs.

One odd custom involved pouring wine over graves occasionally. This may have been meant as a sacrifice, or maybe it was just the delivery of a drink to the departed. I have seen a variety of ancient tombs with holes for this purpose. I poured a glass of wine into one in Turkey.

In many places there are ritual feasts to commemorate the dead. The departed are supposed to take the essence of the food and the mourners eat and drink the rest. Once in Mexico, when I was attending a joyful party in a cemetery on the Day of the Dead, I was encouraged to eat as much as I possibly could. "You can't put on weight with this food," I was assured, "because the dead have taken the good out of it."

When Russians visit the graves of their dead, they often have a few shots of vodka to mark the occasion and toast the memory. Relatives and friends leave a little in the bottom of each glass when they toss off these shots and pour the remainder on the grave. Is this a kind of sacrifice—as when the ancients poured wine on the ground as offerings to their gods—or just an attempt to put more meaning into the words *dead drunk*?

LAURA EDMONDS

She was the daughter of the president of the New York State Senate. One day in 1905, a Greek-speaker named Evangelides got involved in a séance with Judge Edmonds and his daughter. Serving as a medium, Laura got in contact with a spirit guide named Botzaris, a dead Greek-speaking friend of Mr. Evangelides. In Greek, a language which no one present besides Mr. Evangelides spoke, a message was conveyed from the dead friend: Mr. Evangelides' son, back in Greece, had just died and the news had not yet reached America.

It was argued that because Laura Edmonds could not speak Greek except in this trance, she must be in contact with the intelligence of the dead Botzaris. Equally well, however, it could be argued that she was speaking nonsense and only Mr. Evangelides, who for his own reasons pretended it was Greek, knew that. Or, if you like, Laura Edmonds was reading the mind of the only speaker of Greek present, Mr. Evangelides.

The question can never be answered, for there is no record of what went on at the séance except that proffered by those present, and no way to determine the extent to which they were speaking the truth. Though such a spectacular event might completely convince the participants, it can only leave the rest of us doubting.

SÉANCE SCENARIOS

From Felix E. Planer, *Superstition* (1988):

One of the mischievous consequences of the belief in an afterlife, it is proposed, is its extension into spiritualism. Relying on the doctrine that human spirits exist as distinct from organic matter, spiritualism is concerned with the communication of the living with the spirits of the departed, and with various manifestations by these spirits, especially in the course of spiritualistic seances.... Spirits in general, but especially frequent visitors to earth, such as Napoleon, Alexander the Great, Shakespeare and like personages, display a definite preference for the gloomy atmosphere of the séance room...[and] the room in which it is about to take place is plunged into darkness, relieved only by the glow of a dim red light. There is a constant background of recorded music, and often the sitters are encouraged to talk or sing. For the spirits are said to like noise.

I have yet to see a medium who will perform in full light—or explain convincingly why darkness is necessary—or who will transmit messages from the dead who speak languages other than those known by the medium. This, to me, looks suspicious. Worse, the messages delivered in my experience are, as Planer strongly puts it, "of a staggering banality."

Mediums claim to have received from Beyond autobiographies, novels, poetry, and music. The quality is always poor and only goes to prove that in at least one sense the cynical Gore Vidal, commenting on a certain writer's sudden death, was wrong to call it "a good career move."

CHANNEL SURFING

Lily Andrews, *A Guide to Channeling* (1990)
Val Biryukov, *Crystal Channeling* (1996)
J. Bjorling, *Channeling: A Bibliography* (1992)
Marcy Foley, *Akanthos* (1991)
Robert Gordon, *Changing Channels* (1990)
K. Hadlock, *Dead Men Do Tell Tales* (1993)

Eric Klein, *The Crystal Stair* (1994)
Henry Reed, *Edgar Cayce on Channeling* (1989)
C. Rueckert, *A Channeling Handbook* (1987)
David Spangler, *Channeling in the New Age* (1988)

SPIRITUALISM IN LITERATURE

Thomas E. Berry, "Mediums and Spiritualism in Russian Literature during the Reign of Alexander II [1855-1881] in *The Supernatural in Slavic and Baltic Literature* (ed. Mandelker and Reeder,1988), 128-144

Thomas Blanding, "Rapping with the Thoreaus," *Concord* [Maine] *Saunterer* 17 (March 1984), 1-5

Philip Elliott, "Tennyson and Spiritualism," *TRB* [Tennyson Research Bulletin] 3 (November 1979), 89-100

Russell M. Goldfarb and Claire R. Goldfarb, *Spiritualism and Nineteenth-Century Letters* (1978)

Alan Gribbin, "'When Other Amusements Fail': Mark Twain and the Occult," in *The Haunted Dusk: American Supernatural Fiction, 1820-1920* (ed. H. Kerr *et al.*, 1983)

Ricardo Gullon, *"Espiritismo y modernismo"* [Spiritualism and Modernism], in *Nuevos Asedios al Modernismo* (I. A. Schulman, ed., 1987), 86-107

James Mulvihill, "A Source for [Thomas Love] Peacock's Satire of Spiritualism in *Gryll Grange,"* *Notes and Queries* 32 (232) (December 1987), 491-492

Michel Pierssens, *"Proust et la planchette magique"* [Marcel Proust and the Ouija Board] *Critique* 44 (April 1988), 320-335

HEMINGWAY'S OUT-OF-BODY EXPERIENCE

Related to ghosts are spirits out of bodies only temporarily. Let a novelist famous for his straightforward style describe the out-of-body experience less dramatically than those who boast of extensive astral projection. Ernest Hemingway was, as a teenager, wounded in battle in World War I. He experienced his "soul or something" leaving his body for a short time. He described it as being "as if a silk handkerchief had been gently pulled from a pocket by one corner."

GHOSTS AND RELIGION

This is a topic for a book, not a paragraph. Every religion has a position on the dead and most speak of some sort of afterlife. Here, let us note just one very American religion that has a particularly close connection with dead people: The Church of Jesus Christ of Latter Day Saints, which we usually call the Mormon Church.

Christianity claims to be based on revelations from God to the evangelists. Islam's *Koran* consists of heavenly revelations to The Prophet Mohammed. Mormonism is based on revelations to Joseph Smith, principally from an angel (Moroni), from God (God the Father and Jesus Christ also appeared to Smith), and the following ghosts: dead people named John the Baptist, Peter, James, and John. Mormons also have created the world's largest genealogical bank—said to be the equivalent of seven million books of 300 pages each—because living Mormons can be baptized in the name of dead ancestors who were unfortunate enough to live before Smith published *The Book of Mormon* (1830).

At the present rate of growth of their religion, in considerably less than a century living Mormons will, worldwide, outnumber the present population of the United States. Dead Mormons, with their baptismal arrangements, are going to be incalculably great in number.

THE DEAD IN ARGENTINA

Though not qualifying as ghosts, certain dead persons in Argentina have exerted great influence. You know about the preservation and veneration of the corpse of Eva Perón. Maybe you have not heard of the miracles attributed to the strangely preserved corpse of little Miguel Angel of Villa Union. He died as an infant in 1966 but has become, a local priest has gone on record as saying, a kind of "unofficial saint."

He has been credited with more cures and other miracles than American curiosities such as the Maine woman who, as a little girl, went into a permanent coma as a result of falling into a swimming pool and ever since has been visited by the faithful who want miracles from her. Last I heard, the family was thinking of erecting a chapel in their backyard in Worcester.

Little Miguel Angel and such other venerated corpses, however, have the advantage of being not in a coma but actually dead and therefore, in the minds of some, they have better heavenly connections.

IMMORTALITY

"Even longevity—as the postponement of the inevitable—is not enough," wrote Vico. "The stake must be changed entirely." Unreasonable human desire *not to die* is the explanation of all the superstition and hopes regarding life after this life. When we talk of vampires and other undead, ghosts and angels and such, we are comforting ourselves with promises of a supernatural solution to the human problem of natural death. We are dealing with some of mankind's wildest hopes and greatest fears. The book that you hold in your hand is more serious than you imagine. For one thing, the author hopes by writing it to influence the world in some small way even after his voice is silenced by death. The desire of writers *not to die* may be vain and pitiful, but it is real.

A STORY FROM THE SIOUX

Leonard Crow Dog has told this traditional tale of the Sioux. It concerns a man whose wife died but came back, as a ghost, to live with him and the children she had left behind. She was somewhat mysterious in her ways but otherwise a perfect wife until the husband got it into his head that he was entitled to another woman. His first wife, after all, had died. When another woman came into the house, the ghost wife returned to the land of the dead— and, the legend has it, she took her husband and children along with her.

For the Ghost dances of the Sioux, see Robert Marshall Utley's *The Last Days of the Sioux Nation* (1963). For the Ghost Dances of the Shoshone, see Judith Vander's *Shoshone Ghost Dance Religion* (1997). They resemble those of the Sioux.

"HARRY HOUDINI"

Taking a stage name that honored a French magician, Erich Weiss (1874-1923) became the most famous of all escapologists. A biographer (William Lindsay Gresham) wrote that:

> he hurled at the universe a challenge to bind, fetter, or confine him so that he, in turn, could break free. He triumphed over manacles and prison cells, the wet-sheet packs of insane asylums, webs of fishnet, iron boxes bolted shut—anything and everything human ingenuity could provide in an attempt to hold him prisoner. His skill and daring finally fused deeply with the unconscious wish of Everyman; to escape from chains and leg irons, gibbets and coffins... by magic.

Everyman also wanted to escape from death. Mediums said Everyman could, but Houdini doubted it. He said that when he died if it were possible to come back, he would make that escape too. Meanwhile, he contented himself with exposing fraudulent mediums. When he died, some say he did escape. I don't think so. Here are half a dozen of the spate of books on this complex, colorful character, whose reputation (at least) has not died:

J. C. Cannell, *The Secrets of Houdini* (1989)
William Lindsay Gresham, *Houdini: A Magician among the Spirits* (1972)
Milbourne Christopher, *Houdini: The Untold Story* (1969)
Gordon Stein, *The Sorcerer of Kings* (1993)
Thomas R. Tietz, *Margery* (1973)

BLACKFACE

The superstitions of Negroes (as they were then called if not described in less polite terms), though these superstitions were largely shared with whites, were the subject of much minstrel-show and vaudeville comedy. This spilled over into the early movies. The frightened black, saying something like "Feets, do your stuff!" and running off, was a stereotype.

An example of an "Ethiopian burlesque" is the anonymous *The Ghost of Bone Squash* (1888). Some people will recall Steppin Fetchitt in the movies, bug-eyed with the fear of ghosts. Whether African-Americans (because of African traditions brought here) were, or are, more or less superstitious than other Americans is a topic that requires more expert investigation that I have given it. In any case, I do not see that race relations would be improved by publicizing the scientific facts, whatever they might turn out to be.

RAISING A GHOST

In earlier books of mine I speak of legends regarding, and rituals promising, the raising of the dead. You may wish to read about these things in my earlier books, particularly *The Complete Book of Spells, Curses, and Magical Recipes* (1997) or in really serious *grimoires* (handbooks of magic). As I describe in detail in *The Complete Book of Devils and Demons* (1996), the greatest ritual magician of the nineteenth century—he called himself "Éliphas Lévi"—claimed to have performed the feat of raising the dead. He supposedly called up Apollonius of Tyana, but to very little effect.

If I were you, I wouldn't try it. Let the dead rest in peace. Once I shuffle off this mortal coil, I might like to come back for visits (if possible), but I would want to be in charge of my appearances. I would want caller ID if messages could reach me and would want to screen my messages with some sort of answering machine or e[ctoplasm]-mail twit filter. Wouldn't you? The idea of being at the beck and call of every idiot with a formula or stupid question, in my view, is truly what someone has called "one of the new terrors of death."

WHO'S THERE?

Any evidence such as a pool of salt water, a real rose "left behind," and so on, is supposed to counteract the disbelief in apparitions and objectively establish the existence of ghosts. Some people want to explain everything away. Others want to prove that supernatural things are not simply the delusions of those who report them. Are ghosts playing tricks, or is the mind playing tricks?

We all know how the mind can fasten on a trifle and elaborate it. We're sure we see a friend across the street very clearly but on getting closer realize we saw only a hat or coat like our friend's. We supplied the face. We walk into a dark room and think we see a mysterious figure in white rush out the window, only to realize later that in the dark our minds played with the flash of movement as a curtain blew into the room. We believe we see a shadowy figure coming right at us down a strange, dark hallway only to discover on closer inspection that there is a big mirror at the end of the hall. We have all, at one time or another, seen things that are not there. It is even vaguely possible that we may have seen supernatural beings and not noticed at all that they were anything out of the ordinary. People who believe that God Himself looks like us have little difficulty, I assume, in accepting a theory that all spiritual beings can look like ordinary mortals.

Seventy percent of Americans believe in angels. Some claim to have seen them. They say they look more or less human. A great many people, sane and otherwise, have been visited, awake or asleep, by apparitions, or truly believe they have. If we see apparitions, are they there, outside us, real? Are they created by imagination, telepathy, magic, or natural or supernatural forces we do not understand?

WHO'S WHERE?

You cannot be a ghost while you are still alive but you can perhaps get your spirit temporarily out of your body or at least produce the illusion that it has left. The spirit, some say, may possibly be able to travel great distances and appear to others to warn them of disasters and such.

Astral projection, as it is called, does not take you to the stars but it does have many adherents here on earth, particularly in the United States. Here you will find Carol Eby's *Astral Odyssey: Exploring Out-of Body Experience* (1996), likewise a video (with hypnosis sessions) on how to *Learn Astral Projection*, and many other guides for those not inclined to try St. Francis Xavier's spiritual exercises or the techniques of Tibetan lamas. Baker, Leadbeater, Muldoon, Richards, Scott, Yram and others have written popular books in this field. There are half a dozen fairly recent books:

> J. H. Brennan, *Astral Projection Workbook*
> William Buhlman, *Adventures Beyond the Body*
> Robert Crookall, *Case Book of Astral Projection*
> Robert Monroe, *Journeys out of the Body*
> Keith Morgan, *Easy Astral Projection*
> "Ophiel," *The Art and Practice of Astral Projection*

My personal advice is not to try to get out of the body but to get into the mind. You can safely explore your inner depths with The Tarot, the *I Ching*, runes, cards, *Chakra* and other sorts of mediation, or dream analysis (with expensive psychoanalysts or cheap little dream books). All of these are (in my view) ways to reach the unconscious, not supernatural powers. Despite what I describe in books such as *The Complete Book of Magic and Witchcraft*, *The Complete Book of Devils and Demons*, *The Complete Book of the Devil's Disciples* and even *The Complete book of Spells, Curses, and Magical Recipes*, I strongly recommend you do not dabble in the age-old black arts or even in the recently constructed systems of Wicca, Druidism, and the rest, whether they claim to be black or white magic. I reiterate that no magic is permitted you by most established religions you are likely to have been brought up in, and that transgression is always expensive. Transgression, rather than freeing most people from oppression, instead condemns them to the bonds of guilt.

I would advise staying clear of books on the *Mayan Oracle* (Donna Kiddie), and Pleiadians (*Pleiadian Agenda*, Barbara Hand and Clow) and other alleged extraterrestrials. Avoid seeking guidance from angels (*Sacred Magic of the Angels*, David Goddard) and saints and other spirits outside the confines of traditional religions. The millennium will unfortunately produce a whole lot of reports of extremely strange events and even suicides, as those in a hurry seek to get to The Next Plane of Existence. Stay calm. There is, unless computers throw us into chaos, nothing special about the year 2000. Or, better, 2001. Keep that fact ever before you as some people around you get kookier.

There's even a book by C. Bennett on *Practical Time Travel*. You are traveling through time right now. Make the most of it. Try to understand and profit from *this* experience.

Miss Cassell's corpse is unceremoniously if apprehensively dragged out of the grave by medical students in Indianapolis. Nineteenth-century engraving.

BURIAL AND GHOSTS

The Egyptians were neither the first nor the last to say that the dead body must be preserved so that the soul (which they called *ka*) can visit it. On the other hand, many civilizations have held the belief that if the body does not disintegrate the soul cannot be released—and may lurk as a ghost.

The remains of ancient women and men have been found by scientists in Africa and the Alps and elsewhere and studied in the name of science. Scientists, of course, do not wish to bury these specimens. In the United States a skeleton 10,675 years old was found in an Idaho quarry in 1989. It was turned over to the Shoshone-Bannock tribe for burial after a few years of research. Political pressures produced the Native American Graves Protection and Repatriation Act. That will hamper both unearthing and keeping for study ancient bones here.

Since then Amerindians have agitated for the return of all human remains held in ethnographical and other institutions, that may possibly be of their ancestors. There is a demand to bury the skeleton of a 9,300 year old man discovered in 1996 on the banks of the Columbia in Kennewick, Washington. This skeleton of a man who may have crossed the land bridge that is said to have spanned the Bering Straits in the Ice Age is apparently Caucasian, but five different Amerindian tribes want it returned to the earth and scientists do not.

Is burial necessary to free the spirit? What about the first-class relics of saints (actual bits of them) in every Roman Catholic altar and, despite the destruction of many reliquaries as papist superstition in the Reformation, the unburied bodies or parts of bodies of saints? What about head-hunters and the horrific collections of the scalps or ears of enemies as convenient substitutes for heads? What about bodies willed to science, or organ donations and even autopsies, and MIAs and the victims of accidents whose bodies were never buried? All roaming uneasily as perturbed spirits forever?

How much of a person has to be buried to free the spirit? In these days of frightful carnage in war, abortions, explosions, airplane crashes, and other large-scale disasters, is the world filling up with spirits doomed to have no rest?

JUST VISITING

Some ghosts appear to want simply to spend a little time with friends or relatives; they bring no messages; they ask no favors. In Victorian times, particularly, people collected testimonies to the appearances of such non-threatening ghosts. Typical is the story of a traveling salesman who was in his hotel room in St. Joseph, Missouri, one evening in 1876 when his sister, who had died young of cholera in 1867, appeared to him. She said nothing and soon vanished, but he reported that she looked perfectly healthy and happy. There was just one thing. On her cheek was a thin red line.

When the salesman told the story to his parents, his mother burst into tears. "She exclaimed that I had indeed seen my sister," records Sir Ernest Bennett in *Apparitions and Haunted Houses*, "as no living mortal but herself was aware of that scratch, which she had accidentally made when adjusting something about her head in the casket." His mother had touched up the scrape with powder and had never mentioned it to any living soul. This very American story has many counterparts the world over.

MAKING A FASHIONABLE APPEARANCE

European ghosts walk, it is said, in the costumes of their times. Most are knights in armor, nuns in habits, and so on. In Britain, the ghosts often appear in Elizabethan ruffs or Restoration finery. "Old Tanner," the ghost of the churchyard at Hampstead Norris, struts in knee breeches, and the local custom of horsewhipping his grave or cutting a turf from it and placing it under the altar in the church for four days just hasn't worked on him. He still walks, though his clothes are sadly out of fashion.

American ghosts are most often seen in nineteenth or twentieth century garb, the clothes in which they were buried. Even those buried naked and wrapped in a sheet do wear clothes, according to those who report seeing them. A friend of mine with a very old house in Upstate New York says his resident ghost is often seen in a smoking jacket and sometimes a nightdress, but always in the style of the last century.

Apparitions in other countries appear in appropriate national costume. Hamlet's father appears in full armor, which could not have been his garb when he was "sleeping killed," poison (he says) having been poured in his ear while he was taking a nap in his orchard. It seems that some ghosts are entitled to choose the costume in which they appear.

Occasionally ghosts appear bearing signs of the manner of their death. Banquo's ghost in *Macbeth* (which may be just the product of Macbeth's guilty conscience, for no one else sees the apparition) is drenched in blood; he has "gory locks" from a head wound. Anne Boleyn's ghost and some other decapitation victims appear carrying their heads, or without a head at all. (That accounts for the credibility of a "headless horseman" in a Washington Irving tale). Some ghosts will exhibit the murder weapon. A famous New Orleans ghost who in life had drowned, maybe suicidally, haunted a bridge, dripping slime. Some other ghosts of the drowned appear in dripping clothes and even leave puddles of salt water! In a ghost story by M. R. James, a boy reports seeing a mysterious man at night who is "wet all over" and adds, "I'm not at all sure he was alive."

The early Church Fathers such as Ireneus, Tertullian, and St. Augustine argued over whether in the next life we have bodies and souls or just souls. They decided we have bodies and souls, and also that on the Last Day we shall all arise "incorruptible" and "with the same bodies as we had in this life" (so keep up your gym schedule and don't get pierced, tattooed, or otherwise disfigured). Christians of today are more heretical. Only about a quarter of believing Christians say they think we shall have bodies at all in the afterlife, and on the subject of resurrection of the body what they say in their creeds and what they believe in their hearts are at odds. Contrariwise, more than three-quarters of all those polled in early 1997 (according to *Time*) are certain they will meet relatives and friends in heaven, presumably in recognizable human form.

NEAR-DEPTH EXPERIENCE

Channeling is the sort of pastime that some people turn to (as Mark Twain said of spiritualism) when other entertainment's pall. It is now a fad. I am afraid it tells us more about the follies of the living than the messages of the dead.

This supposed contact with the dead, extraterrestrials, people from the past and future, angels, and other entities is especially popular in America. Aging movie stars have recommended it. Some entrepreneurs support themselves handsomely with it. It has been politely studied as a somewhat weird middle-class activity by Michael F. Brown in *The Channeling Zone* (1970). He is much nicer to these kooks than the creator of the *Doonesbury* comic strip has been. In the comics, Gary Trudeau features a foolish female who channels Hunk-Ra, a 21,000-year-old warrior. This character is based on J. Z. Knight, the housewife who (according to *The Chronicle of Higher Education*) "became a channeling celebrity—and a millionaire—after a revelation that someone named 'Ramtha' was trying to speak through her." Ramtha was one of the exotic, terribly macho males that lady channelers seem to attract. Attila the Haunt.

The other books on the subject I have read are ludicrous. Most are on a par with the garbage about angelic interventions that is usually penned by some apparently bleached-blonde lady, preferably in the West, well-coifed, and so, so sincere but utterly unconvincing. To me. For those desperate to believe, anything goes.

"ANGELS AND MINISTERS OF GRACE DEFEND US"

It was inevitable that those entertainment entrepreneurs who like to keep a finger on the public pulse and purse would satisfy the public's need for close encounters with amiable aliens, angels, and ghosts.

Every Christmas you encounter on television the unfledged angel who assures us *It's a Wonderful Life* (a classic since 1946). Michael Landon played an apprentice angel on TV in *Highway to Heaven* (1967-1970) and there followed more heavenly visitors on TV and the big screen.

Not being born into sin, we have no need of salvation, and no need of a messiah to redeem our sinful souls. Neither heaven nor hell is our destination in the afterlife; we have our own various arrangements with our own various deities. The Bible is not our story; we have our own stories to tell, and they are many and diverse. Learn lots more by reading up on comparative religions and their histories in your local Library.

A comic book format presents the arguments of *The Other People*. In it Peter "Pathfinder" Davis and "Oberon Zell" say modern pagans have a religion at least as legitimate as the Judeo–Christian tradition. Pathfinder Press, ATC, PO Box 57, Index, WA 98256.

Today the air is thick with angels, as the medieval world believed. We have, as a pop play put it, *Angels in America*. I have recently seen such oldies but goodies as *Private Lives* on-stage and *Topper* on film, and we have TV's *Touched by an Angel*. A spin-off (*Promised Land*) and a rip-off (*The Travel Agency*) are in the offing. In these and other such shows, angels intervene in human affairs. In Nora Ephron's film *Michael*, John Travolta is an angel with overalls and wings who brings a dead dog back to life and aids the course of true love (also noted in *Ghost* and other films). Leslie Moonve (president of CBS) promises less of a religious tone in his hit show *Touched*, and "additional angels who will cover different demographic groups." Maybe they will have to add shows called *Triple A* (African American Angel) and revive an old pop song title you may recall, *Teen Angel*.

In *The Sixth Man*, Kadeem Hardison is a ghost who spurs his basketball team on to victory. Whether angels are spiritual beings who have never been human but are sent to help us, or ghosts who have departed this life but still care about humanity, the belief in angels is a sign these days of how deeply religious, or desperately superstitious, we Americans have become.

CUSTOM OF THE ABRUZZI

Some of the ancient, pagan customs of the Mediterranean are still to be found here and there in America. These customs were brought by immigrants in the nineteenth century and now are dying out. One, from the Abruzzi, a province to which many Italian-Americans owe their origin, is the custom of setting a table with dishes but no food and no wine, only a glass of water. This is done on Halloween after the family's dinner is cleared away. The table is dominated by a candle which burns all night. Some whose grandparents taught them the old ways also put a lit candle or two in the window to show the dead the way back home. The dead are supposed to come yearly to this repast so lacking in the usual *abbondanza*, and the departed are said to enjoy it.

SEX WITH GHOSTS

Strange Universe claims to be one of TV's family shows, but it seeks the sensational. Subject matter ranges from conspiracy theories about mind-control of the killer of John Lennon to sex with ghosts, which is the way they handled the Tantric craze, one of the Eastern religion fads of the West Coast (and elsewhere). It is just another of those mad magazines of the air that make one despair of the general public's intelligence.

The program defined sex with ghosts as "just another level of consciousness" and presented snippets of interviews with some rather odd characters who claim to do it with the dead. *Strange Universe* warns that "without proper training, sex with ghosts can be just as dangerous as sex with any other stranger," but they suggest it is neither impossible nor unpleasant. They did admit that "it may even sound a bit unhinged." Yes.

THE BROTHERHOOD OF THE ROSE CROSS

Whatever they tell you, the several modern American Rosicrucian societies, the most prominent of which is AMORC (Ancient Mystical Order *Rosæ Crucis*, which may be mystical but is certainly not ancient, founded in California in the twentieth century), do not go back to Egyptian mysteries. They do not even go back to "Christian Rosenkreutz" (said in the once-famous tract *Fama Fraternitatis*, 1614, to be the German head of a Rosicrucian Order so secret there is no historical record of it). The Rosicrucian society established in Pennsylvania, which claimed Benjamin Franklin as a member, no longer exists.

The oldest surviving Rosicrucian society in the United States dates from the nineteenth century (1868). Christopher McIntosh's *The Rosy Cross Unveiled* (1989) is out of print, and so is Dame Frances Yates' *The Rosicrucian Enlightenment* (1972). Hargrove Jennings' *The Rosicrucians* (1907, reprinted by Ayer and I believe now out of print) promises to reveal the group's "rites and mysteries" but is incomplete and occasionally incorrect, perhaps deliberately.

Rosicrucian belief asserts that though all human beings are in a sense one, the individual personality survives the physical body and has some of the characteristics traditionally attributed to souls—or ghosts.

Rites to call up the dead are not properly Rosicrucian.

THE CHURCH OF THE NEW JERUSALEM

Communication with the dead is part of the society with the above name, founded in Britain and copied in America as The New Church before the end of the eighteenth century. It was all based on the visions of Emmanuel Swedenborg (1688-1772), who himself did not found a religious denomination. He did, however, adopt the Neoplatonic idea of a soul separate from and surviving the body and was in a way responsible not only for Swedenborgianism in America but in the long run for the American religion of Spiritualism. Swedenborg's *The True Christian Religion* was translated by J. Ager in America in 1907. The General Church of the New Jerusalem (Athyn, Pennsylvania) and other Swedenborgian societies have published more of his difficult works and studies of his life and influence. Swedenborg offers startling descriptions of the afterlife.

RELIGIONS OF THE NEW AGE

As we approach the millennium (assuming that Jehovah's Witnesses are wrong and that it has not happened more or less unnoticed already), New Age spirituality is one of the movements concerned with the afterlife and talking with the dead and those on "other planes" of existence. See Michael D'Antonio's survey *Heaven on Earth* (1992) and the burgeoning New Age sections in popular bookstores. Some reading suggestions:

Terry K. Basford, *Near-Death Experiences: A Bibliography* (1990)
Martin Gardner, *The New Age* (1991)
Jon Klimo, *Channeling* (1988)
J. Gordon Melton, *The New Age Encyclopedia* (1990)

"PAPA DOC" - "JACMEL - HAITI"

The Same African-Haitian-American Deep South Spiritual Voodoo Hoodoo Mysteries Of The Devil Island-Haiti's King Papa Doc Houngan Bokor Sorcerer Voodoo Root Doctor Of All Secret Deep South Mysteries and African Haitian Voodoo and Heodoo - Who Works With Spirits of The Living and The Dead. Who Will Remove and Reverse All of Your Evil Cursed Spells and Crossed Conditions Away From You and Bring You Right Into Good Luck Money and Financial Success and Prosperity and Definitely Return Your Loved Ones Back To You Where They Belong With You.

1-914-667-   **9AM-9PM**

WARNING BE SERIOUSLY PREPARED AND COME DIRECT TO "PAPA DOC" WITH YOUR PROBLEM AND TELL HIM EXACTLY WHAT YOU WANT - BECAUSE YOU ARE GUARANTEED TO GET WHAT YOU WANT, SEEK AND DESIRE

ReVerse That Evil Curse!

Cure Yourself of All Strange Evil Unnatural Incurable Diseases

Now! Before It Is Too Late!

"Papa Doc" - The Root Doctor

1-914-667-   **9 AM-9 PM**

Just Above The Bronx No. 2 Train and 241st Street

REINCARNATION OF THE DEAD

The dead reincarnated are, of course, not ghosts. It may be useful here, however, to remind you again that such names as *René(e)* and *Renata* reflect the beliefs in certain cultures that involve more than mere remembrance. Among the Lapps, according to E. J. Jessen in *Finnorum Lapponumque Norwegicorum Religione Pagana* (The Pagan Religion of the Norwegian Finns and Lapps, 1767), a *jabmack* (dead relative) will appear in a pregnant woman's dreams to tell her what dead person wishes to be reborn in her child, who is to be named accordingly. Absent any direction in dreams, the information could be obtained from a shaman.

It may also be noted that Orthodox Jews prefer to name children after dead relatives, but will not do so in the case of living relatives lest they

thereby shorten the life of the older bearer of the name. The magical implications of names I treat in *What's in a Name?* and other writings. Reincarnation is not part of orthodox Judeo-Christian belief.

"Allan Kardec" (L.-H.-D. Rivail) in nineteenth-century France pro-
mulgated a doctrine of successive reincarnations with intervals of spirit
life during which these intelligences can possibly be contacted through
mediumship.

RAPTURE

On the basis of *I Thessalonians* 4:17, a number of modern and self-defined
select Americans are preparing to be swept up live into the clouds, "to meet
the Lord in the air." More than 100 million Americans expect the Second
Coming sometime soon, and therefore death in the usual sense—and
becoming disembodied spirits and ghosts—does not apply, they are confident, to them. See Paul Boyer's *When Death Shall Be No More* (1992).

CHRISTIANS AND GHOSTS

The only ghost an orthodox Christian can really have much to do with is
the Holy Ghost. Speaking of our strange ideas about death, *The Economist*,
not usually a source of Christian doctrine but in this case impeccable, states
in its "The Business of Bereavement" in the 24 January 1997 issue:

> Few of those who consider themselves Christians are aware of the
> gulf between popular belief and what Christian doctrine actually
> says. There is scanty support in the Bible, for instance, or in the
> writings of divines like St. Augustine, for the idea that the soul,
> on leaving the body [the Temple of the Holy Ghost], moves on
> promptly to a rose-tinted (or flame-red) afterlife; this view owes
> more to classical mythology [crossing the River Styx to the "other
> side"] and, latterly, spiritualism [completely condemned, for
> instance, by the Roman Catholic Church]. On a strict interpreta-
> tion of scripture, nothing happens to the soul until the end of the
> world, when it will be recombined with the body [see the Nicæan
> Creed] to await the Last Judgment. Heaven—or Hell—comes next.

However, most Christians seem to believe the dead are in Heaven or
Hell right now. (Purgatory and Limbo seem to have disappeared.) They
also believe in ghosts, which is part and parcel of the current trend of selecting attractive or convenient beliefs from the traditions and, if necessary,
holding heretical views while continuing to regard oneself as on the right
path.

"Orthodoxy is my doxy, heterodoxy is your doxy."

It is not only in Judaism that you can be orthodox, conservative,
reformed, or "non-observant." Today even staunch Roman Catholics defy the

pope on sexual matters. It goes along with wanting to have both security and freedom, leather jackets and vegetarianism.

GHOSTS AMONG THE AMERINDIANS

Every one of the aboriginal peoples had some belief in ghosts. Robert H. Lowie began to study the Crow people in 1907, and in 1935 the first edition of his *The Crow Indians* appeared. Of ghosts, he writes:

> In contrast to the spirits who live in a camp apart [from the living] are the ghosts who haunt the grave, hoot like owls, and appear as whirlwinds.... A ghost may make people insane by putting a tooth or a lock of hair from his body into the victim's.... However, ghosts are not uniformly evil. They sometimes blessed people in visions,— especially, it seems, with the power to find lost persons or property.... One of them, Gun, would invite people, darken her room, make everyone sing and then listen. Some supernatural [person] would be heard speaking, and though the visitors could not make out the meaning Gun would interpret the sounds and prophesy as to the future.

The Native American contribution to the American ideas of Spiritualism has yet to be fully investigated and appreciated.

There are many different ghost dances and ceremonies of which we have record. Among the Kwakiutl of British Columbia, for instance, there is the *Hamatsa* dance, a winter ceremony for a society dedicated to a ferocious bird that feasts on men's brains and eyeballs. This predator is called The Man-Eater at the North End of the World. The society in its name, wearing grotesquely carved masks, takes initiates on a spiritual journey to the land of ghosts, often entered through a hole in the floor of the ceremonial hut. A hollow tube made of kelp carries the voices of the dead, who speak in sepulchral tones to the initiates.

Familiar to most is the Amerindian concept of an afterlife in a serene Happy Hunting Ground, where good people go when they die. These ghosts are to be left in peace. It is dangerous to call upon them, disturbing their contentment with worries of those still living. Bad people are more likely to appear as ghosts without being summoned—restless, tortured, up to no good.

The most famous Native American ghosts, you know, are those raised by the Ghost Dance, performed in the nineteenth century in a effort to drive the white man off Indian lands and keep him from killing off all the buffalo, on whom the Indians depended for food, clothing, even the skins to make their teepees. The eradication of the natives sprang from the American republic's so-called Manifest Destiny and the sort of sentiment that the *New York Herald* printed in 1879: "The continent is getting too crowded."

Folklore knows also tragic Indian maidens who haunted cliffs off which they threw themselves in love's despair. A number of early American place names refer to these lovers' leaps.

MORE AMERINDIAN GHOSTS

The aboriginal peoples of America seem to have brought from Asia (across a land bridge over the Bering Strait in prehistoric times and by sea from China in the Shang dynasty) many superstitions regarding the dead. To these, over time, more were added. On the whole, Amerindians were wary of the dead.

The Inuit (The People), formerly called Eskimos, have always had elaborate systems of taboo, and some of these are connected to fear of ghosts. The old and infirm, it said, drifted away to die, or perhaps were driven off. Death was feared. Shamans were called upon to defend the living. The Tlingit sent their dead off on the journey to the next world with food and clothing and by burning them on cedar pyres and then reverently collecting the bones. These they saved in beautifully carved boxes. It was considered unwise to make enemies among the departed. As an old children's verse in the United States used to say, "the bogeyman will get you if you don't watch out," and childish people everywhere tend to agree.

For some aboriginal people, such as the Navajo, no amount of respect could win the dead over; all ghosts were considered *childe*, evil spirits of Earth Surface People. Even if a person was pleasant during life, death made all ghosts bad-tempered and dangerous. People were taken out of the hogans to die lest their death in the home attach them too closely to it in the afterlife. If a person did die in a hogan, a hole was made in the wall, on the north side (from which all evil came), and the body removed in that way.

Like some Europeans, Amerindians took various precautions to insure that the dead would not be able to find their way back to the world of the living. Many believed, as Europeans did, that there was a period after death in which spirits might tarry too close to the living, unaware they were dead or unwilling to accept that they must move on. Shamans were called upon to protect the living against malicious and lingering ghosts and the illness and misfortunes they could bring.

DIFFICULT PREPARATION OF AN INUIT SHAMAN

You have to become a ghost, to start with. You must be drowned and eaten by sea monsters. Then you can return in spirit and bring to your people the secrets of the world of the dead.

RESURRECTED

Amerindians had many old stories about return from the land of the dead. In early Virginia, Englishmen first heard these stories. One concerned a bad man who was allowed to return from the dead so as to warn his tribe of the punishments in the afterlife of those who transgressed while alive. Another story said that a good man was given a glimpse of a pleasant afterlife and of his dead father in that paradise and then was returned alive to his tribe "to show his friends what good they were to do and the pleasures of that place."

DO MORE AMERINDIAN GHOSTS WALK THAN WHITE MAN'S GHOSTS?

Chief Seattle wrote in a letter (1854) to President Franklin Pierce: "The white man's dead forget the country of their birth when they go to walk among the stars. Our dead never forget this beautiful earth for it is the mother of the red man."

DEATH SONG OF THE LUISEÑO INDIANS

When I discovered death was coming,
When I feared death was on the way,
I was much surprised, and sad to leave my home.

I have looked far and sent my spirit out,
North, south, east, and west, to escape death,
But there is nothing to be done, no way to avoid it.

GHOSTS AMONG THE OMAHA

The fact that Amerindian peoples made strong connections between the physical and spiritual worlds can be illustrated in many ways, but the beliefs concerning ghosts among the Omaha serves as an example.

The Omaha believed that both animals and humans, as creations of the Great Spirit, had spirits that could persist after death. When hunting the buffalo, the Omaha followed rituals designed to apologize to the animals for taking their lives—done out of need and not greed, as one source says—and to make sure that the spirits would return in new animals on which the tribe could depend for food, clothing, tipis, and more.

J. O. Dorsey in a report of the United States Bureau of Ethnology (1884) recounts how the Omaha dealt with the ghosts of murdered men and women. The murderer might be put to death or a blood price might be agreed upon and a life saved. If so, however, the murderer had to atone in various ways and for as long as four years lest the angry ghost of the murdered person return to cause trouble for the whole tribe. The murderer had to walk barefoot and wrap himself tightly in his robe, walk humbly and eat and camp apart from the others, not comb his hair or assert himself in any way until the family of the murdered person was certain the ghost was satisfied, after which they said: "It is enough. Be gone, and walk among the crowd. Put on moccasins and wear a good robe."

HAUNTED CANADA

Some people may believe that Canadians are too conservative and sober-minded, if not too sober, to report a lot of occult activity, but Quebec and Ontario can be examined in a little detail to give us an idea of what's going on in The True North.

There are reports of UFOs, mysterious substances falling from the skies (including frogs and fire) as well as black rain and other marvels, phantom ships and animals, and equivalents of the Loch Ness monster and Sasquatch, among other phenomena. Sir Arthur Conan Doyle and other foreigners passed through and noted Canadian stories of the paranormal, See:

Dwight Boyer, *Ghost Ships of the Great Lakes* (1968)
Blodwen Davies, *Romantic Quebec* (1932)
Sheila Hervey, *Some Canadian Ghosts* (1973)
R. S. Lambert, *Exploring the Supernatural* (1955)
Daniel Merkur, *Powers Which We Do Not Know* (Inuit, 1991)
Robert-Lionel Séguin. *La Sorcellerie au Québec du XVIIe au XIXe siècle* (1971)
Eileen Sonin, *More Canadian Ghosts* (1974)

In Quebec we have reports of poltergeists at Acton Vale (1969), Claredon (1889), Hudson (1880), a knot-tying poltergeist on rue Ste.-Famille in Montreal (1929), a poltergeist connected with Mère Catherine de St.-Augustine (1661-1667) in Quebec City and many accounts of religious persons encountering the spirit world since then. There is a long list of ghost reports, from phantom ships on the Saguenay to a crisis apparition in Verdun, a part of greater Montreal.

Some leading examples: ghosts at Beauport (1977); the Queen Elizabeth Hotel in Montreal (1961); a phantom at the Hôtel Dieu hospital and nunnery in Montreal (1694); a crisis apparition in Quebec City (1779) and a ghost at Nôtre-Dame-de-Grace (1967); a phantom "handsome dancer" at Routhierville (reported in *Time*, 24 November 1952); and "aerial phantom" at St.-Basile and a "religious apparition" at St.-Bruno-de-Chambly (both 1968); a "haunt" of Polly Westman at Sherbrooke in the twenties; a ghost appearing to Mrs. F. Thornley at Verdun in the sixties; and much more. Paul Sauvé was noted for exorcisms at St. Augustine of Canterbury church in Montreal in the early seventies, but all demonic possession cases are irrelevant to our interests here. The aboriginal belief in humanoid creatures in the forests was succeeded by Christian belief in all sorts of ghosts and demons.

Ontario has a famous flying cat and more than one ghost dog, not to mention a ghostly light on Lake Simcoe and a host of UFO sightings. Also: poltergeists at Burgessville (1935), Etobiocoke (1968), Keswick (1963), in Queen Street in Picton (1939), in Church Street in St. Catherines (1970), at Swastika (1952), on Silverwood Avenue in Toronto (1947), at Wellesley (1880), a "UFO poltergeist" as "invisible beings invade Canadian home" at Wooler (1968). Eberhart (details below) also mentions a poltergeist at Thorah Island (1891) and another at Black Lake (1935).

A rare book describes the poltergeist events of *The Belledoon Mysteries: Weird and Startling Events*, published by the author, Neil Macdonald, at Wallaceburg, Ontario in 1871.

Add for Ontario: ghosts at Bancroft (1951); on the Ticonderoga Reserve near Belleville in the sixties; at St. Luke's Anglican Church at Brantford (1942); at Alban's point near Brockville (1931); at Buttonville (1965); at Cherry Valley in the thirties; at Dundas in the forties; at Gormley (1968); several ghosts at Hamilton since 1929; an Indian River ghost (no date in George M. Eberhart's extensive *Geo-Bibliography of Anomalies*, 1980, to which I am very indebted for his tireless research); a "haunt" at Inglewood in the sixties; the ghost of Prime Minister William Lyon Mackenzie King (who communed with his dead mother in his latter years) at Kingsmere (1954); the "haunt" at 33 Cambridge Street in Lindsay in the sixties; the crisis apparition at London, Ontario's Elldon House about 1844; a haunting at Harland Road in Milton in 1972 (described by Brad Steiger in *Beyond Reality* 4 as "a bumper year for hauntings"); ghosts at Mississauga on several occasions in the seventies; a crisis apparition at Mt. Forest discussed by Sonin (31, 164), a haunting at Waterfalls Lodge in Nipissing 1933-1937, a couple of North York ghosts noted by Sonin (25-26, 50-51) and one discussed by Hervey (11-14), an "aerial phantom" in *Nouvelle France* (1640) reported in *Jesuit Relations and Allied Documents* (1898), a ghost in Ottawa in the sixties, a haunting at Alma College in St. Thomas in the twenties, a haunting of Laurence Avenue East in Scarborough (1970), a haunting on the Six Nations Reserve reported in the *Hamilton Spectator* on 22 October 1958, but occurring in the 1880s, a ghost at Stratford in the thirties, a haunting in Streetsville in the seventies, a crisis apparition in Sudbury (1910), "a healer haunts her old home" at Thornhill (1973), a long list of ghosts in Toronto (including Duke at Sherbourne Sts. 1830s, University College 1860s, Humber Road 1930s, Chisholm Avenue 1944, Sunnyside 1944, Walmer Road *c.* 1964, Mackenzie King's house on Bond Street 1960-1966, Walmer Road *c.* 1964, the Old City Hall 1965-1968, the Mynah Bird Club in Yorkville 1965-1968, Wellesley Street 1967-1970, Sumach Street 1968-1970, Bleeker Street *c.* 1968, Colborne Lodge 1969-1970, Avenue Road 1972, etc.).

A rare book describes the "aerial phantom" and *A Wonderful Phenom-*

enon, published by the author, Eli Curtis, in New York 1850 but dealing with events in Warwick, Ontario, on 3 October 1843.

Similar lists could be compiled for all the Canadian provinces and territories and everything brought up to date since Eberhart. I believe that the most promising and neglected stories are those involving Newfoundland (where a lot of attention has been paid to the Giant Squid but not to recording ghost stories) and to Prince Edward Island (where Irish immigrants brought a lot of their superstitions and developed a folklore that deserves far more attention than it has received). It was a Mrs. Pennée of the provincial capital, Charlottetown, whom F. W. H. Myers singled out to write about in "On Recognized Apparitions Occurring More than a Year after Death," *Proceedings of the Society for Psychical Research 6* (1899), 13, 60-63.

The most publicized Canadian occult poltergeist story is that of the Cox house at Princess and Church streets in Amherst, Nova Scotia, with what J. Lewis Toole in *Fate* 5 (January 1952), 77-84, called "The Possession of Esther Cox," though it appears not to have been a demonic possession at all. See Walter Hubbell's *The Great Amherst Mystery* (1916). The Amherst poltergeist you will hear about in our next chapter here. There are better tales still untold, particularly the land versions of the likes of Roland H. Sherwood's *The Phantom Ship of Northumberland Strait* [Nova Scotia], (1975).

Sir Arthur Conan Doyle's *Our Second American Adventure* (1923) has a chapter called "Across Canada...." He writes of a Montreal poltergeist that built "houses" with children's toy bricks but also was malicious, like a small child. This piece was reprinted in *Light* 44 (8 March 1924): 156-157.

GHOSTS ALONG THE MISSISSIPPI

The "great river" has some great ghost stories, and they are all presented in a series of books by Bruce Carlson (all 1988): *Ghosts of the Mississippi River from Dubuque to Keokuk*, *Ghosts of the Mississippi River from Keokuk to St. Louis*, and *Ghosts of the Mississippi River from Minneapolis to Dubuque*.

SCHOLARS OF PUERTO RICAN SPIRITISM

Vivian Eloise Fernandez, *The Effects of Belief in Spiritism and/or Santería on Psychiatric Diagnoses of Puerto Ricans in New York City* (Adelphi University dissertation, 1986)

José E. Figueroa, *The Cultural Dynamic of Puerto Rican Spiritism* (in "a Brooklyn Ghetto," CUNY dissertation, 1982)

Mario A. Nuñez-Molina, *Desarrollo del medium: The Process of Becoming a Healer in Puerto Rican Espiritismo* (Harvard University dissertation, 1987)

A "PROFESSIONAL" GHOST HUNTER

Bevy Jaegers claims to be the head of the world-famous United States PSI Squad, which "works in a professional capacity as police consultants for law enforcement agencies nationwide." She adds: "Our group has also for years done a yearly show on KMOX here in St. Louis."

She wrote the fifty-six page pamphlet *"Ghost Hunting: Professional Haunted House Investigation"* (1988) with the assistance of her husband, Ray Jaegers, whose spelling and other elements of style appear to be no better than hers. The pamphlet doesn't look or sound very professional, but if you want to set yourself up as a "professional" ghost hunter as, she says, "a hobby or vocation," you may find it encouraging to see how much fun others have had with few or no qualifications. Encouraging also is this: "We have never found a ghost that could physically harm anyone."

Mrs. Jaegers' basic belief is that ghosts simply are dead people who need "release" and that just about anyone can lead them to a happier and quieter afterlife. She leaves exorcism to priests. She does not approve of trances or séances. In fact, she seems to suggest, as of course many others have done, that séances are a bad idea in general, setting in motion forces with which we would rather not contend.

Mrs. Jaegers, a lady I have never met, is in my view a sincere representative of the many individuals who declare themselves to be "sensitives" and try to help people who say they have experienced occult phenomena. She does not seem to be one of the outrageously self-promoting band of which Hanz Holzer and Sybil Leek were imminent examples. Nor, however, does she have the scholarship of Peter Underwood or any reliable Society for Psychical Research methods at hand for convincing us that the psychic "imprints" and ghostly "intelligences" she says she had seen and dealt with ever were there at all.

If all this truly amateur and uncheckable so-called professional research into the occult leads the participants into useful social work and a deepened religious sense, it is all to the good. It seems to comfort all with its putative proof that at least now and then an entity "retained his personality and his feelings after death." That quotation comes from an incident described in which a ghost demanded an apology before it would vacate the premises! On the other hand, I am not encouraged by the suggestion that death fails to bring peace and that some people will remain just as cantankerous and despicable after their demise as they were in this life.

We still need a compelling answer to this question: Can it be proved by irrefutable hard evidence rather than subjective statements that ghosts have been documented—fraud, error, hallucination, and other such factors completely ruled out?

By the way, infra-red film, part of the paraphernalia of some ghostbusters, is just a case of boys with toys. Because ghosts do not give off heat, heat-sensitive devices will not produce images of them.

A CHILL RAN DOWN MY SPINE

Ever since Anglo-Saxon times, if not before, we have in our culture associated cold with evil. Witches even said that The Devil's semen was ice cold. Terrible things we find "chilling."

The argument offered for the sudden drop in temperature that is supposed to accompany the appearance of a ghost is that manifestation takes energy and that drawing this energy from the atmosphere, an apparition lowers the temperature of the surrounding air. Ghost hunters now go around with devices to measure sudden drops in the temperature. American high-tech is being brought to ghostbusting. My late friend Guy Lambert, CB, was a pioneer in measuring temperature drops in relation to subjects of physical research.

HAUNTED HOUSE

Any big old house that stands lonely or neglected can start rumors about ghostly presences. Take for example the house that William Jenkins bought in 1924 on Wilshire Boulevard at Crenshaw in what was then downtown Los Angeles.

Jenkins paid $250,000 for 25 vast rooms and two acres of land, but a year later he returned to Mexico, where he had been a US consul. His house was left empty. By the time J. Paul Getty bought it, the price was somewhat affected by the fact that everyone called it "The Phantom House."

Down south, an owner whose name had best not be disclosed here, revels in his house being rumored to be haunted. He boasts that it has not been painted "in 75 years." Maybe you know someone who takes pride in having ghosts in his/her residence.

Some people don't mind buying a phantom or two with the property, while others would be too uncomfortable. Today realtors and buyers fuss over whether a reputation of being a haunted house has to be disclosed to the buyer.

Would you like to live in a haunted house? Not poltergeists, mind you, just ghosts?

GHOSTS IN FILM COMEDY

Not all the ghosts of the cinema are frightening. Some are in comedies, as *Topper* and *The Canterville Ghost* attest. Monsters appeared in the likes of *Mickey Mouse Meets Dracula*, ghosts appeared in films with the Dead End Kids in the forties (*The Ghost Creeps*, *Spooks Run Wild*, and *Ghosts on the Loose*), with Mickey Rooney and Francis the Mule (*Francis in the*

Haunted House), in the film versions of TV hits such as *The Addams Family*, parodies of horror films (*Saturday the 14th* followed *Friday the 13th*), and so on.

TOPPER

In 1926, Thorne Smith (1892-1934) published the comic novel *Topper*. In it a mild mannered bank manager is not only bothered by his wife but also by the ghosts of the Kerbys, a playboy client and his wife. Smith wrote it again for the movies, for which he also created *Turnabout* (granddaddy of all those films in which the spirit of one person enters that of another) and *I Married a Witch* (an early riff on the theme of the *Bewitched* television series).

Films such as this, as well as the cartoonish *Casper, the Friendly Ghost*—who eventually starred in his own movie—demonstrate that audiences do not always think of ghosts as scary.

CARTOON GHOSTS

Casper, The Friendly Ghost is not the only non-threatening or amusing cartoon specter. In the movies we have had the likes of:

Alice's Spooky Adventure (1924). Walt Disney.
Buster Spooks (1929). A 2-reeler in the Buster Brown series.
Scaredy Cat (1948). Porky Pig and the sputtering cat named Sylvester.

Do such entertainments make children less afraid of ghosts and bogeymen?

HAUNTED SCHOOL

There are a number of colleges and universities, especially in our Northeast, where stories are told of ghostly apparitions of students who committed suicide or faculty members who have taken the word *tenure* far too seriously. For our example of a haunted school, however, let us go to the other side of the country and notice a public school in Gorman, California.

This school was brought to my attention in the eighties by articles in the West Coast papers such as: Steve Padilla, "The Incredible Shrinking School," *Los Angeles Times*, 21 June 1989, II, 3, and Bob Poole, "Harriet Gets High Grades as School Ghost," *Los Angeles Times*, 1 November 1989, B 3.

The school may have been the smallest in its district but it was distinguished, people said, by the ghost of a little girl called Harriet. She had, they said, been a student at the school who was accidentally killed crossing the street. The students were sure they saw her walking the corridors of the building.

Now, youngsters are famously imaginative and invisible friends and monsters in the closet are often parts of their world, but it is also worth raising the question of whether young people may have special powers to detect ghostly presences—or just unusual frankness in talking about them. Was "Harriet" a special perception or a silly put-on?

When we hear about The Devil's Backbone (a feature between Wimberley and Blanco in Texas) being haunted (as reported by Bert Wall in the *Houston Chronicle*, 17 April 1994, TM 8), are we more or less skeptical than when we hear of an otherwise ordinary public school on the other side of the country or a house on the other side of town having a ghost? Are we more likely to believe local legends, little children, or self-credentialed "psychics?"

NEWS FROM BEYOND FOR AFRICAN-AMERICANS

The early spiritualists (mostly women) in America were radical in a number of their beliefs. Not only did they assert that tappings on a table constituted a new kind of telegraphy from beyond the grave and that messages for the living could thereby be received, but also they tended to find in those messages support for such ideas as women's suffrage and the abolition of slavery.

One message, however, may be regarded as very politically incorrect by the standards of today. In discussing the Fox Sisters (whose frauds when discovered did not prove, as one book of the time hopefully put it, *The Death-Blow to Spiritualism*), Matthew Collins' program *Telegrams from the Dead* on television (in the popular American Experience series), let slip one of the pieces of information the Fox Sisters allegedly obtained from The Other Side:

THE SOULS OF NEGROES ARE A BEAUTIFUL WHITE IN HEAVEN.

BROOKLYN'S STRANGEST GHOST

I live in Brooklyn, which is reported to have more and better ghosts than any other borough of New York City, and I decided to do the research to bring you the oddest of all Brooklyn ghosts. In the long run, I have selected Topsy, a ghost who appeared some six months after her death at age thirty-six in 1903, and maybe twice. By the way, Topsy was an elephant.

Topsy had, it was rumored, killed a couple of circus trainers in Texas, and certainly had crushed one Thomas Blount to death in New York when he stupidly fed her a lit cigarette, but she was pretty docile at Luna Park, Coney Island, where it had become something of a tradition to retire, more or less, such dangerous animals.

Topsy got along well, dragging heavy timber and doing similar odd jobs at Coney Island, until the day the only *mahout* she would obey, Willy Alt, lost his temper at some Italian workmen and sicced Topsy on them. She charged them and they ran away, terrified but unhurt, but the news got out and it was decided that Topsy had to go. Poison her? Shoot her? Too slow, too cruel. Thomas Edison had a suggestion: what about thinking of all the electricity which had turned Luna Park into a fairyland of lights—and electrocuting her?

On a Sunday in 1903, on a little island in Luna Park, huge crowds turned out to see Topsy step onto metal plates and suffer a fatal shock. She fried, she fell, it was over. There were conflicting stories about what happened to the meat and the hide and the tusks, but Topsy was gone.

Until September 1903. An elephant named Columbo, who had killed a trainer in a circus in New Jersey, was in residence at the elephant barn at Luna Park when suddenly, according to her keeper, the ghost of Topsy materialized to warn Columbo that he was not in friendly territory. She advised him to get out of there fast.

According to Columbo's keeper, a twelve-year-old boy named Frank Gummis, the ghost of Topsy appeared and told in perfectly clear English how she had been electrocuted. She warned Columbo to get right out of Coney Island. The press had a field day with the story of the ghost of an elephant. Both Gummis and Topsy were widely quoted.

According to John Doyle in an interesting article on elephants in Brooklyn (*Brooklyn Bridge*, October 1997):

> In July of the following year [1904], another elephant, named Fanny, no doubt also having heard through the grapevine about Topsy's grisly fate, escaped from Luna Park and swam from Coney Island Beach to Staten Island, lumbering ashore in the town of Clifton.

Did the ghost of Topsy appear twice at Coney Island and communicate with elephants? Don't you think that must be the most unusual ghostly apparition in the history of Brooklyn? The ghosts who walk what used to be Ebbett's Field or what still is Greenwood Cemetery just cannot top Topsy.

GHOST TOURISM

Conducting gullible tourists around the allegedly haunted places in town, whether it be the French Quarter in New Orleans or some other tourist destination such as Washington, DC or New York City, is in the American entrepreneurial spirit. For the commercial tours of Washington, DC, see Steve Bates, "Doing a Spiritual Business," *Washington Post*, 26 October 1991, B1. Donna Gable's "Check Out Some Old Haunts...," *USA Today*, 12 September 1991, E11, gives a brief list of haunted houses you can visit on your own.

Ghost walking tours may have originated in London, which still has plenty of people willing to conduct them for you for a fee. The most haunted city in Britain, however, is not London, experts say. It is supposed to be York, and in 1994 the three competing guides to haunted places got together to try to keep other self-anointed experts from horning in on their Good Thing. Martin Wainwright wrote all about it in "Ghost Wars Haunt York" in *The Guardian* 2 August 1994, I5.

In the United States, in 1990 an editorial in the *New York Times* ("Boo!," 4 November 1990, 18) commented on the statistic that 43 percent of Connecticut residents believe in ghosts. They ought to have noted New Hampshire, where only a third of the population is ready to say there are no ghosts.

As I often remark, ghosts do not seem to like malls and cineplexes; they prefer older venues, such as mansions and theaters. Want to see some mansions? There are many, including the Lemp (St. Louis), the Toutorsky (Washington, DC), and the Octagon House (Fond du Lac, Wisconsin), or the former governor's mansion in Milledgeville, Georgia. Theaters? Try The Belasco (New York City, if it is still standing in the renovation of The Deuce, which I do not want to check since Disney has taken over), The Calumet (Houghton, Michigan), and many older movie palaces of New England. You can have a look at haunted houses which their (former) inhabitants got into the newspapers. Skip Amityville; try West Pittstown, Pennsylvania. It would be best to skip all the publicity-seekers at inns and bed-and-breakfast locations. At supposedly haunted hotels (as in Robin Mead's *Haunted Hotels*), inns (like the one in Norwich, Vermont), and B&Bs (everywhere), if you are told you might have to share with a ghost, do not act impressed, but demand the shared room be half price.

Why not ignore all these ghosts supposedly connected to the tourist industry and go for a specialty like haunted restaurants? I suggest you begin off the beaten track with the Spur of the Moment Restaurant & Bar (Larkspur, Colorado) or the Lost in the Fifties Roadhouse Restaurant (Angelina Co., Texas). Steer clear of bars such as The White Horse (New York City). We do not in the United States have *Haunted Royal Homes* (the subject of a book by Joan Forman and works by many other English commentators) but we do have, or say we have, Real Americana! We also have a host of occult experts, Yours Truly and David J. Skal (*Guide to Everything Undead*) among them, and even purported "ghostbusters."

Because so many people are killed in such places, battlefields are reputed to be seriously haunted. Could be. Try battlefields of our gory Civil War (such as Manassas, Virginia) and places where we clashed with the Amerindians such as Little Big Horn (Montana). Regarding the latter, see Jim Robbins' "Ghostly Tales form Custer's Last Stand," *The Boston Globe*, 31 October 1989, 3, and listen to local legends if you happen to live on some blood-soaked piece of America.

DON'T BUY A HAUNTED HOUSE

Real estate agents should have a chat with their lawyers about their responsibilities to warn prospective buyers that houses may be haunted. New York courts have decided officially that houses can indeed be haunted and that a prospective buyer learning of a "ghoulish reputation" of a house is entitled to back out and get his or her money back. You may even be able to get a refund or settlement if you buy a house *because* it is haunted (in the hope of making money on that) and discover it is not (sufficiently) haunted! One Jeffrey Stambovsky in 1991 got a New York court to declare him entitled to a refund on a house he heard was haunted. In Britain, Chingle Hall was long famous for being haunted. Even the Prince of Wales was interested in its spooky reputation. Trevor Kirkham and his wife Judy bought the manor just because of that reputation and paid £420,000 for it. When it wasn't haunted as they hoped, the valuation was only £235,000, and they went to court and collected £71,000 from the seller, John Bruce.

A COLLEGE FOUNDED BY A GHOST

This is alleged to be the case of Quimby College of Alamogordo (New Mexico), set up to grant bachelors' or masters' degrees in spiritual studies. There you can have your auras "balanced" and study the thoughts of Phineas T. Quimby, who died in 1866. (Quimby appears elsewhere in this series on the occult as the teacher and inspirer of Mary Baker Eddy, founder of Christian Science.)

Quimby is supposed to have been contacted by a medium in Alamogordo. I do not know her name. The college, unaccredited, seems to have been disbanded after some local complaint.

BOO-TIFUL LIST OF SOME RECENT NEWSPAPER SOURCES

Camizarro, Steve. "Arabi Alive with Tales of a Houseful of Ghosts," *New Orleans Times-Picayune* (31 October 1994, AB1 [Louisiana town sees The Noltings move out of a house that may be haunted]).

Darnton, John, "A Blessed Haunted Plot, This England," *New York Times* (21 April 1994, C8 [Night porter reports seeing ghost at London's Naval and Military Club]).

Davis, William A. "Haunting Providence," *The Boston Globe* (1 November 1992, B1 [Poe and Lovecraft are said to haunt College Hill in the Rhode Island capital]).

Donovan, Dianne. "Bedtime Stories...," *Chicago Tribune* (15 March 1992, 12, 14 [visiting American and ghost of Renvyle House, Co. Connemara, in Ireland]).

Foster, Mary. "Big Easy Ghosts Find Many Places to Hang Around," *New Orleans Times-Picayune* (28 October, 1989, RE1 [New Orleans residents may be annoyed by spooks]).

Gallingen, John & Jon Haber. "Blithe Spirits," *The Boston Globe* (21 May 1995, 69 [ghosts on video are the couch potato's friends]).

Grandjean, Pat. "House Where Things go Bump in the Night," *New York Times* (27 October 1991, CN, 13 [haunted house in Connecticut]).

Greenwood, Tom. "Michigan's Most Haunted," *Detroit News* (28 September 1992, A1 [Marion Kuclo's *Michigan Haunts and Hauntings* and forty MI ghost stories]).

Jimenez, Ralph. "Colby-Sawer Folks Wonder: Are Haunts in the Hallways?," *The Boston Globe* (25 October 1992, NH [New London college reports a dead principal stalks the place]).

Kronke, David. "Hollywood Boo-levard," *Los Angeles Times* (29 October 1995, 3 [the entertainment capital's lively ghosts]).

Lipkin, Lisa. "Gasp! City's Ghosts Evoked," *New York Times* (30 October 1994 CY19 [the ghosts of The Big Apple and the reactions of New Yorkers]).

Marshall, Thom. "Author Haunted by Ghostly Story," *Houston Chronicle* (24 March 1996, A37 [Jim Henderson wrote *The People in the Attic* with Doretta Johnson]).

Moore, Terence. "Fabled Ghosts of Notre Dame...," *Atlanta Journal Constitution* (3 October 1992, D2 [stadium ghost assists team to win football game]).

Niemela, Kathryn. "Double Occupancy...," *The Boston Globe* (28 January 1995, 89 [Mary Walker still walks in Norwich, Vermont, people say]).

Osinski, Bill. "Apparition Events Called a 'Nuisance,'" *Atlanta Constitution* (8 March 1993, B4 [Rockdale Co., GA, calls appearances of The Blessed Virgin a nuisance!]).

Sinclair, Aboila. "Beware the Ghost of Fripp Island [Georgia]," *Amsterdam News* (2 November 1996, 26 [one of this writer's African-American ghost legend reports]).

HOW TO GET SOMEONE'S GHOST

Michael Paterniti: "Even today, the Asmat of Irian Jaya believe that to consume a brain is to gain the mystical essence of another person." Our Amerindians are famous (or infamous) for consuming the hearts of brave enemies in order to gain their courage. We take Holy Communion.

THE SPIRIT WORLD

The whole subject of the Other Side, whether it is very much like an improved version of the world we know (as in the Roman Hades or the Amerindian Happy Hunting Ground or the paradise of Islam) or peace in the obliteration of all personality (as in the *nirvana* of Buddhism), lets us toy with speculations about What's Next.

As we worry and wonder about the future, let us all hope and trust that it will be more promising than what the cartoonist Jack Ziegler suggested when he drew a man gazing at a railroad timetable that read:

ARRIVALS		DEPARTURES	
Pestilence	4:02	Good Taste	3:32
Famine	4:15	Sleigh Rides	3:49
Martial Law	4:21	All-Beef Burgers	4:25
Triple Locks	5:00	Happiness	5:11
Unemployment	5:20	Security	5:15
Inflation	5:32	Friendly Loan Companies	5:58
Shorter Summers	5:43	Warm Blankets	6:10
Longer Zip Codes	5:46	Hardwood floors	6:15
Plastic Silverware	6:01	Homemade Ice Cream	6:31

GHOST TOWNS

There are ghost towns—once lively, now deserted—in many countries, but the ones in the American West are well known. See T. Lindsay Baker, *Ghost Towns of Texas*; James E. Sherman and Barbara H. Sherman, *Ghost Towns and Mining Camps of New Mexico*; and John W. Morris, *Ghost Towns of Oklahoma*. These are not exactly germane to our subject—unless everyone has left *except the ghosts*.

THE OCCULT MARKET

It is completely wrong to think of the so-called Occult Explosion of recent times as just a kooky or underground countercultural activity. Especially in the United States, it is also part of the very bourgeois Alternative Movement, which is damn near a MOR (middle-of-the-road) cultural fact. Many factors, from AIDS to apocalypticism in light of the millennium, have made the average American willing to toy with the mysterious and join Alternative Movements (AMs) of some sort, many of which are available in our increasingly fractured (or multicultural) society.

AMs seek practical personal advantage in Alternative Medicine and New Age religions, for instance. This can get connected to some very weird people, or the make-a-buck exploiters of very weird people, but it need not be Way Out, just offered as a way out. It appeals to the disaffected and the inexperienced. It doesn't have to be radical or youth-centered. It can also be extremely conservative and self-defined as more reasonable and more rewarding than either tradition or the traditionally Other (in the extreme, Satanist).

It's the middle-class people who unabashedly consult psychics, believe in horoscopes, fortune telling, and above all luck, and are tired of established religions which seem to them to place more of an emphasis on rules than on rewards. These people don't like the idea of spiritual awareness through discipline. They don't like discipline. They want quick results, not work plans. Having failed to find a royal road to *nirvana* through drugs, they would like a simple fix that is more legal and less lethal.

These are the people who believe in ghosts and angels and maybe aliens. They want to improve themselves, get on Another Plane, to which Self-Help and Self-Fulfillment courses, Transcendental Meditation, Tantric Yoga, jogging, or a vegan diet have not thus far raised them. These are the people who sincerely believe that the government is keeping the facts from us regarding aliens who basically want to assist us. These are the people who trust that UFOs will bring us "close encounters of the third kind," some kind of personal satisfaction and success without us having to do anything to attain or even deserve it.

Even the desperate underclass, which Edward Gibbon (describing another empire's *Decline and Fall*) skewered as "careless of futurity," are starting to think about the future—but they want help from someone, the living or the dead. They look for aliens arriving to give assistance to those who cannot or will not help themselves, or just to provide a fractured world society with a unifying common enemy.

Absent that, let us believe in ghosts and other supernatural beings.

A NEW ORLEANS JAIL

An old jail in New Orleans had a poltergeist, people claimed, whose presence was marked by the smell of cigar smoke. It flung objects at the jailers. "Once at about 3 A.M." says Bernhardt J. Hurwood in *Ghosts, Ghouls & Other Horrors* (1971), "he nearly strangled a desk sergeant, flinging him to the floor and leaving ugly bruises on his throat."

Or were prisoners getting away with something?

DESTREHAN PLANTATION

There's a haunted plantation in the swamps near New Orleans. Destrehan Plantation tour guide, Madeline Levatino, author of *Past Masters: The History and Hauntings of Destrehan Plantation* says she has all the facts (or all the legends) at her fingertips. Destrehan has a great deal of competition, even nearby.

In that part of the country, it's an unusual tourist house that does not boast a ghost, whether on an obscure plantation (Chretien Point, Louisiana), in the hustling French Quarter (such as the Hermann-Grima House), out in St. Bernard Parish (a cottage at 2039 Bayou Road), in an old manor (such as Loyd's Hall, 1820), in an old town such as St. Francisville (we mention The Myrtles elsewhere), off in the bayous, or along The

Mississippi. With Louisiana's fabled cemeteries and ages-thick legends, Destrehan Plantation is just one more spooky attraction.

In 1995, Pat DiPrima, Terri McLaughlin, and LeeAnn Atwood Sanders advertised that they wanted to create a kind of *Boo Who* or inventory of spooks in their McHenry Co., Illinois, area. Such a book for Louisiana would be much larger—and more fascinating. Maybe my friend who lives in Destrehan will compile one. He would need to correct the alleged reference guides. The National Ghost Register claimed there were 450 haunted places in the United States in the mid–nineties (Virginia led the states with 69), but at the same time the head of the Ghost Research Society in Chicago (Dale Kaczmarek) claimed that city alone had between 7,000 and 8,000 recorded ghosts.

I have, as I said, an old friend who lives in Destrehan, that swampy location outside of New Orleans (and writes stories of the occult), so I am especially interested in the 200-year-old plantation house at Destrehan. It is "swarming with spirits," reports Patti Nickell in "Destrehan Plantation," *New Orleans Times-Picayune*, 23 November 1990, 22. Angel Thompson in "Haunted House?....," *New Orleans Times-Picayune*, 3 November 1991, OTR, 1, introduces the caretaker and ghosts guide. I see no evidence at all that Destrehan is any more haunted than any other plantations of the Deep South.

PATIENCE WORTH

Not only are places such as Destrehan falsely touted. People are too. Patience Worth said she was born on a farm in Dorset in the seventeenth century, that she emigrated to America, and that she was killed here by Indians. On 8 July 1913, it is claimed, she was contacted by Mrs. John H. Curran of St. Louis (Missouri), who was playing with an Ouija board. Walter Franklin Prince of the Boston Society for Psychical Research wrote a whole book about *The Case of Patience Worth* (1927), for this ghost by then had been the author of *A Sorry Tale* (a novel set in the time of Christ and couched in a pseudo-biblical style), *Tekla* (a novel of the Middle Ages, written in a supposed medieval dialect), *Hope Trueblood* (set in the nineteenth century), and a lot more fiction, poetry, proverbs ("It taketh a wise man to be good fool"), prayers, conversations, and more. All of this Mrs. Curran "took down" from dictation by the ghost of Patience Worth, who, if she ever existed, might be considered among the most prolific seventeenth-century American authors.

Whether automatic writing and communications employing Ouija boards involve the trickery or the unconscious of the living humans or even the words of he dead is, naturally, much debated. G. N. M. Tyrrell's *The Personality of Man* (1946) is a discussion of Patience Worth and other supernatural experiences by a believer in psychical research. Those who do not believe have picked on errors in Patience Worth's "reports," as they have on those of the later "voice from an earlier time" whom I discussed earlier as Bridey Murphy, as well as many others.

I THINK SOME PEOPLE ARE GETTING CHEATED

The South is colorful enough without ridiculous stories of ghostly visitations. These are usually used by commercial establishments that desperately want business or by little towns which have no real distinction.

Guntown (Mississippi) is where John Wilkes Booth (according to Lynne Grisard Fullman in *The Southern Traveler* for September/October 1998, p. 20) lies in "an unmarked grave near where he lived his final days in seclusion." The actor Booth (1839-1865) jumped onto the stage at Ford's Theater in Washington, DC, on 14 April 1865, right after shooting President Lincoln. In the jump he broke a bone. (To have been able in the moment to deliver a line in Latin, "*Sic semper tyrannis!*", "Ever thus for traitors!", to me suggests immense stage presence). He limped off, grabbed a horse, and escaped to Virginia. There he was tracked down on 26 April and shot. Not much time to live out his life in seclusion after the assassination.

Now Ms. Fullman thinks Booth is a ghost: "Some say that if you listen closely you will hear his limping footsteps..." Really? Who are these "some"?

Maybe the same as in "Some say a ghost of the owner still lurks" in Longwood in Natchez (Mississippi). The building of this mansion was interrupted during the Civil War—the family lived in the basement while the outside of the upper structure was completed—and building was not resumed after the war. Presumably the late owner is unhappy.

Writers such as Ms. Fullman are fed stories by bed-and-breakfast proprietors such as Louis Cornay at Chretien Point Plantation near Lafayette (Louisiana) or the Pastor family of T'Frère (Little Brother) House in Lafayette. First, her husband Milton Fullman snaps a photo. Then the publicity appears in magazine articles and in books such as Ms. Fullman's *Haints, Ghosts, and Boogers: Chillbump Stories from Alabama after Dark*. Places get publicity and the Fullman's sell books.

In New Orleans a guide adds a pinch of Cajun spice to his cemetery tour in Metairie: the ghost of a brothel keeper is seen around her aboveground tomb.

In Vicksburg, the Garden Room restaurant and B&B gets on the map with a tale of Willie Sherman, a teenager, said to haunt the premises, who was killed in a hunting accident. Willie turns the TV on and off.

In Cheneyville, at Loyd Hall (built 1820), customers get a whole passel of ghosts: cooking smells from the kitchen when it is unused, mysterious footsteps in the corridors, a phantom suicide who jumped out of the window, Loyd himself stalking (hanged for a wartime crime), a slave nanny

(Sally Boston) who floats by knocking candles off mantels, a red-bearded Union soldier (Harry Henry) shot on the stairs (who plays a violin on the balcony on occasion), and—in time, I hope, but I wish them long life— Anne and Frank Fitzgerald and daughter Melinda, who run what Ms. Fullman calls this "menagerie of ghosts" at their B&B.

If there is an edge to my comment it comes from annoyance at the very possible exploitation of simple souls who want to add some excitement to visiting, eating in, or staying in old mansions. Many mansions are quaint and even beautiful. Enjoy them for that. Do not try to people them with haints and boogers. That is, as my Southern friends say, way tacky. Finally, if you pay for ghosts and you personally do not see any, demand a refund forthwith. Your word that you did not see any is at least as good as theirs that there are some. No tickee, no washee. No manifestation, no moolah. "Some say" may suit some. Don't you be satisfied with that sort of thing, I say.

A PSYCHIC IN NEW JERSEY GOES AFTER GHOSTS

Jane Doherty is now in her fifties and president of the New Jersey Society of Parapsychology (based in Morristown, New Jersey). Like many who feel they have a psychic gift, she at first resisted using her powers. Now she answers a couple of telephoned complaints a day from people who say they are troubled by ghosts. About once a month she launches a personal investigation.

She claims to have learned from a séance in Lizzie Borden's house in Fall River, Massachusetts, that the famous ax-murderer of her parents was innocent, and an abused child at that. She found "definite spirit activity in that house."

At the request of the owner of Sea Holly Inn in Cape May, New Jersey, she detected ghostly activity closer to home in 1993. The inn, she says, was haunted by a "shadowy figure" of a previous owner and by the ghost of a chambermaid. She talked the late, previous owner "into the light" and he ceased activities, but she left the chambermaid in residence. The chambermaid is a "warm presence," friendly, and presumably good for business.

PSYCHICS AND THE GOVERNMENT

Television these days is plagued by advertisements for psychics, and one company claims to be guaranteed "professional" by the United States Government. I wonder if the government consults them about presidential impeachment possibilities, stockmarket crashes, and other important matters. It doesn't look like it.

There was a time when the British government actually feared mediums. Helen Duncan was jailed for nine months during World War II because she claimed to have called up the spirit of a sailor who went down with the HMS *Barham*. The old anti-witchcraft law of 1735 was invoked to put her out of circulation for a while. After all, if she could announce the sinking of a ship whose loss was a state secret at the time, perhaps she would foresee and blab about the upcoming D-Day invasion of France.

Helen Duncan died at age 86. Years later there was discussion of a posthumous pardon for her, the last witch incarcerated in Britain. I am afraid she did not get the pardon

Believers argue that the United States Government has employed psychics in intelligence and law-enforcement capacities. That, for me, proves nothing. The United States government employs and has always employed a small percentage of utterly worthless and totally unqualified people.

THE MYRTLES

St. Francisville is a sleepy old town in the section of Louisiana where English settlers lived. There may be only a few people around the gas station by the road and seemingly no one at home in any of the beautiful preserved houses or the church by the iron-fenced graveyard. But at an old plantation house called The Myrtles, the ghosts are many and busy, or so people claim.

The Myrtles was built for David Bradford, a general of the Revolutionary War, in 1796. It was erected, folks say, on sacred ground of the Tunica Indians and so may have been cursed from the start.

General Bradford left it to his daughter Sarah Mathilde, and she married Judge Clarke Woodruffe. The judge was an irritable man, and one day when he caught a slave named Chloe eavesdropping on one of his private conversations, the judge cut one of her ears off. That brought more trouble than any curse.

Chloe retaliated by baking a birthday cake laced with poisonous oleander juice. Sarah and her two daughters died from eating it. The other slaves were so outraged that they lynched Chloe and threw her corpse into The Mississippi. Now she comes back regularly to haunt The Myrtles.

But that's not all. The Myrtles is also supposed to be haunted by half a dozen men. One is a young man stabbed in a quarrel over gambling. There are three Union soldiers killed in the Civil War. There is a lawyer who was murdered on the premises, and there is a nasty overseer who was stabbed to death as recently as 1927.

It's a poor Southern plantation indeed that doesn't have some kind of ghostly figure stalking its corridors, but The Myrtles can stand here for not only one of the most lovely, and untouristy, great old houses along the great river but also as very likely the one said to be the most tenanted by ghosts of the past, both black and white.

WAKING DREAMS

Ghosts like to walk at night, adhering to the sun-god tradition that darkness is evil. So they arrive at the dead of night and must be gone as the cock's crow heralds sunrise. These nocturnal habits guarantee that many ghosts will be abroad when people are asleep.

People say they woke up and saw a ghost. A cold hand gripped them. A shadowy figure appeared in their bedroom. They snapped out of a deep sleep to see—Something!

These are waking dreams. If you have an hallucination just as you are falling asleep, it is called by the fancy term hypnogogic. If you have one as you are waking up, it is called hypnopompic. If you have one when you are asleep, it is called dreaming.

My favorite story of a half-awake ghost experience came from my late friend Ra Cantú. He was eventually murdered in California, but long before that he had a number of extraordinary experiences. One he liked to tell about was the time he staggered, still a bit drunk, only half awake, stark naked from bed to bathroom. As he stood at the toilet, eyes mostly shut, suddenly an icy hand struck him in the center of his back. His eyes popped open and there, right beside him, looking him in the face was a figure whose features, in the dark, he could not make out. He was terrified.

"I woke up and sobered up instantly," he reported. "I turned on the light. No one there but me. *It* had vanished. I eventually pieced the events together. It was four a.m. and the heat of my loft was off. What struck me on my naked back was the ice-cold knob of the door, which swung shut after me. The shadowy face I saw was my own reflection in the mirrored door of the cabinet, which had swung open, over the sink. For an instant, though, it was the most frightening moment of my life."

Until the moment of his murder, presumably. Perhaps poor Ra is a ghost himself now, haunting the deserted canyon where his body, tied up in a mattress, was thrown after he had been killed. It is said that the young man who accidentally came upon the gruesome discovery went insane, but you know how the public likes to embroider tales... .

TERRIFIED FAMILY CLAIMS: GHOST KILLED OUR PETS

If you have glanced at the supermarket check-out rags, you will have some idea of the liveliest British-inspired tabloid journalism of today. It is likely to offer the paranormal often. The headline above is from one of Britain's best-loved tabloids, *The Sun*. It appeared on 13 May 1980, and every year since the headlines have become more outrageous. How about this:

A GHOST TAUGHT ME HOW EXTRAMARITAL SEX
COULD CURE MY PROSTATE CANCER.

THE PRINCE OF THE TORAH

Spiritualism is nothing but necromancy (if it isn't fraud), but calling up angels is magic. Rabbis before the tenth century called up *Sar-Torah* (The Prince of the Torah), as we see from Michael D. Swartz's *Scholastic Magic* (1996), but if that angel arrived he was not a ghost. You have to have been a human being to become a ghost, and angels are not human, though they are said to take human shape on occasion. For instance, take the angel who wrestled with Jacob in the Old Testament or Gabriel at the Annunciation in the New Testament.

THE AZTEC AFTERLIFE

Almost every culture has its own concept of an afterlife, which affects its attitude toward revenants. Here is an unfamiliar one, the Aztec view from the 1997 editors (Frances F. Berdan & Patricia Rieff Anawalt) of the sixteenth-century *Codex Mendoza*:

> It was believed that the great majority of people spent their afterlife in Mictlan, a realm of dark emptiness. The underworld was composed of nine layers through which the deceased had to travel. He or she was assisted by a little dog and protected from the chill winds and hazardous rivers of the underworld by his or her material possessions, all providently cremated with the body [some people were buried with their possessions—women who died in childbirth or those who died unusually, such as being drowned or struck by lightning]. The journey through Mictlan was, of course, far more difficult for the poor, because they had fewer possessions and less food buried (or, presumably, cremated) with them.
>
> Nobles and those who had lived an exemplary life were given proper funerals and had relatively easy travels through the land of the dead. However, people who had lived a decadent or criminal life could look forward to a very painful journey in the afterlife.

Infants went easily to a comfortable heaven called Xochitlapán. There milk dripped into their eager mouths from an udder tree under which they lay. Warriors, killed in battle or sacrificed, and mothers dead in childbirth went to a "House of the Sun." Daily the dead warriors carried the sun to its zenith and the dead mothers carried it to its setting.

SOLDIERS SACRIFICED BY THE AZTECS DID NOT GO TO THE LAND OF THE DEAD

From the *Florentine Codex* (c. 1500):

> They called the hearts of the captives precious eagle-cactus fruit.

They lifted them up to the sun, the Prince of Turquoise, the Soaring Eagle. They offered [sacrifices] to him; they nourished him with them. This they called the sending up of the Eagle Man, because the man who died in war went to the presence of the Sun; he went to and rested in the presence [of the Sun].. That is to say he did not go to the Land of the Dead. In this way the valor of the captive would not perish in vain; in this manner the captive gained his renown.

GHOSTLY WITCHES

The Aztecs said that noblewomen who died in childbirth might return as ghostly witches. A *civitateo*, they said, returned from the land of the dead with face whitened with chalk and dressed in hideous garments decorated with symbols of death. Flying by night like witches on their way to the *sabbat*, this horrid creature was vampire-like and drew the strength out of children, who then just wasted away. Groups of these terrible beings were said to meet at crossroads, so the Aztecs assiduously avoided those at night and by day placed there offerings of food in attempts to placate the monsters.

HAINTS AND BOOGERS

These are (as you already know) the "haunts" (ghosts) and bogeymen of American—often African-American—folklore. *Boogers*, for instance, are part of black superstition as reported both in high culture (think of Eugene O'Neill's *The Emperor Jones*) and in popular culture. The fact is that a lot of prejudice is even clearer in American folklore. There blacks, especially rural blacks, are stereotyped as ignorant and superstitious. I do not think blacks are more superstitious than whites

Undoubtedly spirits from partly-forgotten African religions (spirits who play a part in Voodoo, *Santaría*, and other faiths that mingle pagan and Christian beliefs) are still in the consciousness of many Americans of African descent. However, to say African-Americans or even all Southerners are more superstitious than the rest of us is hardly helpful and may not be correct. It might even be argued that, to the extent that the church is the heart of many black communities, black congregations have more than the usual American awareness of the supernatural. It must be noted that Hispanics and in fact evangelicals of all sorts are equally likely to feel close to another world, a world of spirits, both good and bad. Many Hispanic churches and pious practices in the home stress placating or even communicating with these spirits. *Bodegas* sell the means.

There are whites who burn the candles and put the herbs in their bath water and otherwise adopt *bodega* ways, too. Some of the practices of African religions, also, appear to have crept into white culture along with titillating stories of hexes and amulets, zombies and root doctors and voodoo priestesses. The use of graveyard dirt in many magical recipes of the folk— see *The Complete Book of Spells, Curses, and Magical Recipes*—may be a fine example of the crossover of cultures. Ghosts are not confined to believers of any one color. Magical formulæ for dealing with them are borrowed back and forth between cultures.

DRESSED TO DIE FOR

In an earlier volume in this series we noted a booklet by a New Orleans woman who suggests you break into vaults, open coffins, and spend the night with the dead.

If you need fashion items, try Necromancer, a Los Angeles boutique listed in the guide *L. A. Bizarro* (1998) as a boutique for necrophiles.

If ghosts really are hanging around, are they not outraged by such things?

RECENT BOOKS ON HAUNTED AMERICA

Your town is Nowheresville (East Jesus, The Boondocks) if you don't have a book or at least a pamphlet about its ghosts or a good tale featured in some survey. Witness a few recent samples from (as I write) the last couple of years—and remember that every year there are scads more.

Burnett, C. *Haunted Long Beach* (1996)
Hauck, Dennis. *Haunted Places* (1996)
Holzer, Hans. *The Haunt Hunter's Guide* (1998)
McNutt, Randy. *Ghosts* (1996)
Myers, Arthur. *Ghostly American Places* (1995)
Norman, Michael. *Historic Haunted America* (1996)
Scott, Beth. *Haunted America* (1995)
Taylor, Troy. *Ghosts of Springfield* (1997)
Wlodarski, R. *Haunted Catalina* (1996)
Wood, Ted. *Ghosts of the Southwest* (1997)
Woodyard, C. *Haunted Ohio* (1997)

Whether it's specialized (such as Andrew Green's *Haunted Inns and Taverns*, 1995) or a survey of one state (such as Charles Price's *Haunted Tennessee*, 1995) or city (such as Troy Taylor's *Haunted Decatur* or Brooks Preik's *Haunted Wilmington*, both 1995) or area (such as The Great Lakes in F. Stonehouse's *Haunted Lakes*, 1997) or (as they say in California) whatever, the average American book of this sort is full of stories that few would believe for a minute. Nonetheless someone always claims the story is absolutely true and some tales have been long repeated and sworn to by many.

I'm still waiting for a really good American ghost story that is so attractive that I will get up and go there to see for myself. The Europeans seem to have it all over us with their older, spookier buildings. We have a drowned ghost in Louisiana wreathed in seaweed but the Europeans have several who leave *puddles*. True, kids are offered all sorts of *My Best Friend is Invisible* books—that's by R. L. Stine, 1997—and some American houses do look as if they *ought* to be haunted, but I'm afraid there's nothing to be afraid of. Holzer and other ghostbusters' efforts at producing chills leave me cold.

If you want a really "awful thing in the attic," read fiction. (Brad Steiger has a 1995 novel of that title). America has a lot of good ghost *stories*.

SO THE BOAT SANK—GET USED TO IT

Heiress Peggy Guggenheim had some peculiar ideas about modern art (which she collected, eventually in her museum in Venice) and even about artists. She was convinced that American painter William Congdon was the reincarnation of her father, who went down with the *Titanic*. Congdon was born the very night of that disaster—whether a little after it or a little before, however, I am not certain.

REINCARNATED BUDDHISTS

Everyone knows that the Dalai Lama and certain other Buddhist priests are thought to be reincarnated generation after generation. But perhaps you do not know that action-movie star Steven Seagal has been officially declared a *tulku* (reincarnated lama) by His Holiness Penor Rinpoche, the leader of the Nyingama Buddhists. There has been some commotion about the possible selling of high titles such as *tulku*, but unquestionably this American holds that title.

FANGS VERY MUCH

In January 1998, when WB's *Buffy the Vampire Slayer* debuted in a new time slot, UPN offered *Interviews with Real Vampires*. The guide *Time Out* said that in preempting its usual comedy programs for this UPN "has sunk pretty low."

"Real vampires," in my experience, turn out to be psychos or club kids playing around. They belong in insane asylums or grungy nightspots and are not to be encouraged. They are not interesting except as minor symptoms of sickness in the society.

Scary, Life-Size
MONSTER GHOST
Obeys Your Commands!
OVER 7 FEET TALL
7' ghost darts and hovers its eyes glowing eerily in the dark. Remotely controlled up to 50 feet so you can hide and watch
MT 101 .... $1.25

People interested in ghosts, however, represent much more of a mainstream and among them you will find individuals of extremely impressive qualifications. Still, you can be a Harvard professor and still believe in UFO's. Each case of an alleged ghost has to be taken on its own and examined with as much objectivity as possible. Alleged paranormal activity deserves better treatment than it receives in *Strange Universe* and *X-Files* and similar very popular but really trashy television series.

MARY RONDEL WANTS TO TALK

Julian, son of the nineteenth-century master Nathaniel Hawthorne, reports events he recalled from time spent with the family at the Villa Contauto, just outside Florence, in 1858. His story can stand as a good example of the belief in what is called automatic writing, a form of spiritualism in which the hand of the medium is said to be guided by a spirit from Beyond and the dead write, not speak.

At that time the Hawthornes had as near neighbors in their Italian retreat the famous poetic pair of Robert Browning and Elizabeth Barrett Browning, who, like many fashionable people at the time, were fascinated by spiritualism and attended séances. The Brownings were interested in the fact that the Hawthornes' governess for their children could do automatic writing. On occasion she was invited to demonstrate her abilities as a medium.

Let Julian Hawthorne take over the story.

> One day, in the midst of some heavenly-minded disquisition from the dead mother of one of the onlookers, the medium's hand seemed to be suddenly arrested, as by a violent though invisible grasp, and, after a few vague dashes of the pencil, the name of "Mary Rondel" was written across the paper in large, bold characters.

Mary Rondel, through the medium, told the onlookers that she had died in Boston a century or so earlier and had some connection with the Hathornes (as the family spelled its name in those days).

> From this time forth, Mary Rondel, violent, headstrong, often ungrammatical, and uniformly eccentric in her spelling, was the chief figure among the communicants from the other world. She would descend upon the circle like a whirlwind, at the most unexpected moments, put all the other spirits unceremoniously to flight, and insist upon regaling her audience with a greater or less number of her hurried, confused, and often obscure utterances. But the burden of them all was that, at last, after her century of weary wandering, she was to find some relief and consolation in the sympathy of Nathaniel Hawthorne.

After a while the Hawthornes gave up these séances, moved to Rome and later to England (1859), then returned to America, where Nathaniel Hawthorne died in 1864.

After his father's death Julian Hawthorne found among his effects a large leather-bound folio of an early edition of Sir Philip Sidney's *Arcadia*. It had belonged long before to Maj. William Hathorne, whose name was in it. So were marginalia written by Daniel Hathorne, long dead, pointing out passages in love poems with "Pray mistris read this" and similar scribbles. In the book were written the names of Daniel Hathorne— and Mary Rondel.

From relatives in Salem (Massachusetts), where an ancestor of Nathaniel Hawthorne had been a judge in the infamous seventeenth-century witchcraft persecutions, came information on the eighteenth-century Daniel and Mary. Without telling his relatives about the automatic writing in Italy, Julian Hawthorne records that he discovered that about the middle of the eighteenth century, in America, Daniel Hathorne fell in love with a young Boston woman named Mary Rondel. They were never married and what happened is unclear, but Mary Rondel died soon after the end of what turned out to be an unhappy love affair.

What you might wish to consider are answers to these questions which now can never be answered definitively. Had the governess heard in Hawthorne's family or secretly read in Hawthorne's private papers about Nathaniel Hawthorne's relative Daniel and his lost Mary Rondel? Or did she have some psychic ability to read Hawthorne's mind? (He knew the story of Mary Rondel and perhaps had never told it to anyone.) The governess might have done this mindreading consciously or even unconsciously if indeed she was not being fraudulent. Or did the ghost of Mary Rondel, for some reason of her own, wander silently in the world of the dead for a hundred years and actually manifest herself far from Boston, in Italy in 1858, through automatic writing?

Occam's Razor is a principle that directs that when you are offered more than one explanation for a puzzle, you should choose the simplest one. Does that help in this case? What do you think?

THE SADDEST GHOST STORY OF ALL

Despite all the legends of restless spirits doomed to wander aimlessly in eternity and return to earth from time to time to repent their sins or perform mindless repetitions of empty actions, consider that the saddest ghost story of all time may be the one in the hit film *Close Encounters of the Third Kind*.

You will recall that this thrilling saga combines the appeals of both the UFOs and ghosts: a spaceship arrives on earth, and among the extraterrestrials are luminous figures of certain dead celebrities. Among them appears to be Amelia Earhart, a woman pilot who, outrageously overambitious and woefully underprepared, undertook an historic flight and crashed, into the far Pacific, never to be seen again.

In *Close Encounters of the Third Kind,* meaning direct contact with extraterrestrials, the incompetent Ms. Earhart, famous for failure or at best bad luck, is among their companions who come, presumably to save mankind. That our future is in any way in the hands of such losers as Ms. Earhart, frightfully brave and driven but setting off undertrained and even unable to operate her own radio, is really awfully defeatist. Or am I taking entertainment too seriously?

SARAH WINCHESTER'S BUILDING CONSULTANTS

A tourist site in San Jose (California) today is Sarah Winchester's rambling house. She communed with spirits, whom she often entertained at dinner parties where the servants said they saw no one but Ms. Winchester herself, and spirits advised her in the construction of her house. Over and over. It grew and grew, and in a confused manner. She was, apparently, one of those persons who do not like to finish anything for fear that completion means death. The spirits wanted room after room added, alteration after alteration. Sarah Winchester had the money to give them their way.

The spirits liked the number thirteen. Chandeliers had to be especially made to have thirteen lights. Flights of stairs (sometimes leading nowhere) had to have thirteen steps. Windows and doors opened onto blank walls. There were thirteen bathrooms. How many rooms? It is hard to count them. Some were added only to be sealed up.

POLITENESS TOWARD GHOSTS

Renovators of the Lott House, one of the few remaining Dutch farmhouses in Brooklyn (New York), have had troubles with light bulbs burning out quickly, doors slamming (though the windows are boarded up), and other manifestations which they seem to attribute to the late owner, Ella Suydam. She died there at age 92 in 1989.

Reports the *Village Voice* (11 August 1998, 27): "We ring the bell now when we come to the house," says archaeologist Alyssa Loorya. "We say hello to Ella."

COMPANIONSHIP

After those two regrettable women, here is a lovely one.

I have a friend who lives alone, with her dead husband. You have to know her well before she will confide in you that she believes he is still in the apartment on Central Park West, although she saw him buried in the cemetery. "There was something horrible about how the machinery, whatever it was, worked so smoothly and silently," she says, "and I sobbed at that, but nobody knew what broke me up at that point when I had got through the rest of the funeral with just a few tears."

Now when she feels his presence she talks to him, "just as you would if he were somewhere behind you, out of sight, in the room." She adds, "I stop when I feel he's gone, you know. I think old people who talk to themselves are pitiful."

On occasion a light switch goes on or off in the next room, there is a sound of someone making a cup of tea in the kitchen, or the television in the den goes on unattended, she says.

"Are you sure it's not you, being a bit forgetful?"

"Yes, I'm sure," she says with great conviction.

Once, when I came through the front door of the apartment with her, a door slammed shut down the long hall.

"George has gone into his study. He doesn't want to see anyone today."

I suggested that the air pressure affected by opening the front door might well have blown shut the door down the hall.

"Nonsense," she said. "He'll be in the kitchen in a few minutes to make himself something. It's nearly four."

She and I sat in the livingroom. I enjoyed the view of treetops in fall. George's favorite, she reminded me. After a while there were slight noises in the kitchen.

"There," she said, I thought a little triumphantly.

"There's someone in the kitchen," I said. "The maid?"

"Not today," she said.

"Do you mind if I look?" I said, and didn't wait for a reply.

As I entered the kitchen, a cup and saucer came at me. The cup missed and broke on the wall. The saucer struck me and fell to the floor. It clattered, but it did not break.

I returned to the living room, holding the saucer, which I had picked up.

"How do you do that?" I asked.

"Aching need," she replied.

It seemed best for us never to discuss the matter again. One other time, after we met to see a film at the Museum of Natural History, and went back to the apartment for a cup of coffee, a magazine on a table near me opened and pages of it began to turn.

"Must be a window open somewhere," I observed.

"Oh, sure," she said, and smiled.

I still cannot really believe there is anyone else but her in that apartment, and we have tacitly agreed not to debate the topic. If I could prove to her there isn't a presence besides her in that apartment, I wouldn't.

PERISH AND PUBLISH

Some ghosts may hang around not simply to be companionable but to accomplish some work. Back to Nathaniel Hawthorne. From Nathaniel Hawthorne's *The Old Manse* (1846):

Houses of any antiquity in New England are so invariably possessed with spirits that the matter seems hardly worth alluding to. Our ghost used to heave deep sighs in a particular corner of the parlour, and sometimes rustled paper, as if he were turning over a sermon['s pages] in the long upper entry.... Not improbably he wished me to edit and publish a selection from a chest full of manuscript discourses that stood in the garret.

The Fox Sisters (Leah, Kate, and Margaret), whose table-rapping in a farmhouse in upstate New York sparked modern spiritualism. These days when pop singers and such are on US postage stamps, the Fox Sisters, frauds or not, ought to be likewise hailed as famous Americans.

"YOU ARE ALL POWERFUL SPIRITUAL BEINGS"

This cheerful impression dawned on Dannion Brinkley, a rather unpleasant young man who was transformed into a more loving one after being struck by lightning in a small town in South Carolina one day in 1975. He was dead for twenty-eight minutes. He was resuscitated with "a great deal of damage to his nervous system." He also had a memory of typical near-death experience (out-of-body sensation, moving down a tunnel toward the light, encountering dead friends and relatives, seeing the powerful and benevolent God looking like a Halloween ghost in a sheet—the works).

He had terrific ESP on recovery. He could foretell the future. He made notes on the forthcoming collapse of communism, the election of an actor as president—R.R. must mean "Robert Redford," he said—and the disaster at Chernobyl, as well as nasty things happening to people all around him. He could win at the races and the casinos.

He became involved with Dr. Raymond Moody, author of *Life after Life*, who wanted to believe in the afterlife, wanted to understand the psychology of "millions" of death survivors, and wanted people not to be afraid of death but to look on it positively. Dr. Moody's determination to define death as a reward makes me think of an article on gobbledygook I wrote many years ago in which I noted that Madison Avenue would try to see death itself as "Nature's way of telling you to slow down."

Danny helped the good doctor preach the gospel of love and hope. He devoted himself to spreading the good news that "you're goin' home, back to a place you've forgotten about." He confidently promised a place where there is "no fear, no pain, no heartache, only love."

Danny himself died again, briefly, on the operating table, recovered, and finally passed away a third time, of a heart fatally weakened by infection from a broken hand. He had punched a wall. Having ESP and seeing that "somethin' terrible, terrible is gonna happen" to various strangers you encounter is not pleasant. Equally bad or worse is losing your wife because you neglected her to go on the lecture circuit. But he won over many others. He passed on believing that, as Dr. Moody stated, there is "another dimension of existence through which the soul passes after death." It is cheering to think that it's "not just blackness." When people objected that Danny had no M.D. or Ph.D., he stressed personal experience. He was a D.O.A.

Danny Brinkley's story was made into a movie called *Saved by the Light*. Its message was that the dead are happy, reunited with loved ones. It asserted that in the afterlife we all get "another chance." Very comforting.

A woman at one of the lectures said that when God chose Danny as a prophet "He scraped the bottom of the barrel."

"Yes, ma'am, you're right," replied Danny, nonchalantly. He knew what he knew. You can look forward, he was convinced, to being a ghost.

People are always saying, "If something should ever happen to me...." Be assured. *Something* will. Whether you become a ghost when you die— and it's *when*, not *if*—I don't know. Do you? Does anyone?

HAUNTING ADDS PUBLICITY

I don't know everything about the alleged fact that "a man was murdered in a shower with his clothes on" in Lafayette, New Jersey, but if that is true it is far from the weirdest violence in that strange state. What is certain is that the fact (true or not) is used to publicize the Ideal Farm and Garden Center (Route 5), which seasonally offers "Haunted Barn and Pumpkin Picking" to tourists. I mention this somewhat unremarkable roadside attraction simply to emphasize the point that the public is drawn to any place that is alleged to be haunted and that ghosts, real or manufactured, are of considerable business value—except perhaps in the case of a house you might want to buy to live in.

Anyone can declare that some premises are haunted, whether they can produce manifestations for paying customers or not. This both feeds on the general belief in ghosts and at the same times makes one wonder if they are not simply invented by people who want personal publicity.

I've said it before and I say it again: If you pay money to see some allegedly haunted place and do not see a ghost yourself, demand your money back. Or at least ask for free pumpkins.

GHOSTS OF GOTHAM

Besides those claimed by Hans Holzer, whose *Ghosts I've Met* and *Ghost Hunters* reports I beg leave to disbelieve, lots of ghosts have been said to have been spied in New York City. There has been a ghostly dog at Howard Beach in Brooklyn. Those who conduct ghost tours, however, would never draw a group to Howard Beach, so they content themselves with walking tours of Greenwich Village and other fashionable tourist places.

Among ghosts reported in The Village are Eleanor Roosevelt (who I think belongs farther uptown, if not at Hyde Park) and Dylan Thomas. The latter used to haunt various New York bars while alive and is (I think foolishly) alleged to haunt the White Horse Tavern after death. I see no good reasons for believing in any of the ghosts included in these tours, which are only local attempts to copy those of London and New Orleans and other places with better claims regarding apparitions.

If The Village does have a ghost, why not Aaron Burr? Or "Professor Seagull"? Or Thomas Paine; he might like the singalongs in the gay bar that occupies his old residence near Sheridan Square. Or "Marsha," the drag queen, mysteriously drowned in the Hudson at the Christopher Street pier?

What I distrust about haunted houses is commercialization and what I worry about in connection with UFO abductions is that they are never reported about anyone rich and famous. What I distrust about reports of ghosts is just the opposite—they are always of celebrities. It's the same thing as remembering previous lives. Nobody is interested in plain, ordinary people. They all want to talk about George Washington or Cleopatra.

CIVIL WAR GHOSTS

The Civil War, the bloodiest conflict our nation has suffered so far, left a legacy that includes many ghost stories. Ghosts are reported in Jonesboro (Georgia) and at many other southern sites of clashes. Ghosts are also reported, though less often, in the North.

The most famous battle of the war may be the terrible confrontation at Gettysburg, and that battlefield and the surroundings may have the most reports of ghostly activities. See Denice M. Santangelo's "Battlefield Full of Ghost Stories," *St. Louis Post-Dispatch*, 12 March 1995, T3.

America is full of Civil War buffs, the more so since Ken Burns's Civil War television series in the nineties, and many are fascinated with the ghost stories that go along with the war stories.

"A LOT OF PEOPLE DON'T WANT TO DIE"

So says Mr. Woodin of Alcor, a "life extension" company in Arizona, which for $120,000 will deep-freeze your body until science finds a way to bring the dead back again. If you wish, you can have your corpse decapitated and for $50,000 put just your head in liquid nitrogen.

Not everyone can afford this, and only a few people have had it done. (Walt Disney was not among them, despite all the rumors. He was cremated and his ashes are at Forest Lawn.) The reluctance to give up the ghost, however, is remarkable.

TALKING TO ANGELS

Michael Howard, *Finding Your Guardian Angel* (1997)
Barbara Mark, ***Hablando con su angêl*** (Talking with Your Angel, 1997)
Jennifer Martin, *The Angels Speak* (1995)

TALKING TO THE DEAD

This can range from praying to saints to the likes of a character in the film *Star Maps* (1997) who communes with the spirit of Mexican comedian Cantinflas. Please remember that the Florida schoolteacher who scared her little charges by talking to the spirits of the dead (and then managed to offend even Floridians, by changing her name to God) and your local channeler are both *crazy*. If not, they are crazy like a fox and well aware that they are on to a good scam, given the astonishing foolishness of superstitious Americans.

If Shirley Maclaine really thinks she can channel the dead, she is off her present rocker, I say, and I'll continue to say that until someone—anyone—demonstrates that talking with the dead is possible, fact not fraud.

Let's not let hope get in the way of reality. It's amazing that so many people still cling to séance and channeling and such and yet claim to be Christians, say, or Jews. Christians are not—repeat, *not*—permitted to contact the dead; check this with any really Christian Group. (New Age religions are another thing entirely, like the Church of Elvis the King or feel-good surfer spiritualists). Jews who are serious about Judaism believe that when you are dead you are dead. Period. As the ads for *Cats* say, "Now and Forever."

It's just very seductive to think about life after death, a second chance, a promotion, a place where the good really are rewarded and the bad really are punished—unlike the world we live in. I wish it *were* true that we could chat with the departed, that, as Tom Stoppard has a character say in *Rosencrantz & Guildenstern are Dead*, "every exit is an entrance somewhere else."

Add this from the same play: "Eternity's a terrible thing. I mean, where's it all going to end?" Not with endless table rapping and speaking in phony voices through floating trumpets, I'm sure. Not with mediums who claim they can call up the most talented of the dead, even read the future, and can't make a killing on the local lottery and quit seeing foolish "clients." Mediums make even astrologers look sensible!

Ask those people and their pseudo-psychic sidekicks what they have learned from their "gifts" and from talking with the dead—and why they can't make money on the stock market. And don't count on a channel to the dead to answer the burning questions you yourself have, the ones "Dan Leno" in the old music halls used to chat about almost a hundred years ago. He put in his own words questions that mankind has been worried about ever since our time began:

> What is man? Wherefore does he why? Whence did he whence? Wither is he withering?

THE GHOST TAKES OVER

Bridey Murphy (here again!) is well known when it comes to past-life memories. That case, however, is now regarded as one in which, in the kindest way of looking at it, the so-called memories were unconsciously created by the modern woman if not put into her head by the amateur hypnotist who worked on her. One way or another, Bridey Murphy was not a ghost. There is not a shred of evidence that she was a real person who lived and died in nineteenth-century Ireland, nor compelling proof that she returned among the living in the United States in the twentieth century.

For allegedly more convincing evidence of the survival of human personality after death, you have to go back to the rather obscure story of Mary Vennum of Watseka, Illinois, and the year 1877.

On 11 July 1877, Mary Vennum fell into a fit and was in a trancelike state for hours. The fit was repeated daily for some time. The thirteen-year-old said she saw angels and other spirits and eventually proclaimed that she was possessed not by a demon but by the ghost of Katrina Hogan, a rather strange local woman who had died in 1876. A doctor was called in to deal with the little girl's depression and fears, and by hypnosis he seemed to banish the ghost of Mrs. Hogan.

The next day young Mary had a new visitor: she claimed to be possessed by the ghost of little Mary Roff, a girl of twelve who had been dead a dozen years by that time. If Mrs. Hogan had been regarded as unusual, Mary Roff had been seen as something of a sensation in the whole area, because Mary Roff when alive could read while blindfolded and exhibited to many witnesses other supposedly paranormal powers.

The possession of little Mary Vennum by little Mary Roff attracted the psychical researcher Richard Hodgson who, though usually concluding that mediums he examined were frauds, in this case said it was clearly if inexplicably a genuine case of paranormal activity, "the clearest example of genuine possession that could reasonably be imagined." Geoff Viney in *Surviving Death* (1993) comments on the case:

A hundred years later that verdict has not changed. No alternative explanation has been found that goes any way to account for the plethora of correct assertions which characterized Mary Vennum's descriptions of her earlier life as Mary Roff.

Of course, a hundred years later this story cannot be checked. But it is not true to say that no alternative explanations can be offered now, or should have been offered then. Some might believe that Mary Vennum could have been reading the minds of little Mary Roff's parents when she told them of private events of which they knew. Or some people could have been lying. These are but two of the possible and equally probable, perhaps more acceptable, explanations of what was going on in the small town in Illinois.

One may wish to ask why nonentities such as Bridey Murphy and Mary Roff are the kind of dead people who are said to appear to strange females such as little Mary Vennum. If they can do these things, why don't the dead with more useful and impressive things to say contact us through more credible living persons? If the dead can really possess the bodies of the living, why does this allegedly happen so infrequently, and to so little purpose?

It is worth questioning what the dead are alleged to have said in séances or possessions. If personality indeed survives death, I for one would like to know all about the Next World in great detail. Instead I am offered by mediums and the possessed little factoids designed to establish the credibility of the speaker.

"This must be little Mary herself because she can tell us exactly what color the dress was on the doll she"—let's say—"lost on a summer afternoon years ago."

"This must be Uncle Max because he calls one of the sitters at a séance by a nickname the sitter has not heard since his youth."

And on and on. OK, let us suppose these voices do come from the Next World. Let us stop all this chitchat of the sort little kids write from summer camp ("Hi I am fine how are you?") or even dialogues between dead and living philosophers of the kind any good common room accommodates ("It must be—because the medium is not as erudite as these conversations!") and ask pertinent questions and get definite answers about the afterlife, if there are any.

Will someone explain to me why whole shelves of books devoted to verbatim accounts of conversations with those who have "passed over" contain nothing really interesting? Why are dead writers not communicating to us the conclusions of their books or Schubert finishing the Unfinished Symphony? Why doesn't someone corner William Shakespeare's shade and settle the authorship question, get the author to state the order in which he wrote whatever he did write, and establish reliable texts? If you can get to Uncle Max, you can get to Goethe. I have questions for Goethe. Put him on! There are more important messages to receive than that Aunt Minnie is happy where she is. Aunt Minnie was once happy in Boca Raton. By the way, Aunt Minnie, where *is* that place where you are now? Is it some kind of Supernatural Sun City? Do you still need a walker? Still deaf and very inattentive? Am I getting through to you?

THERE'S NO REST FOR THE EERIE

Americans, full of suspicions that authorities are keeping from them the truth about UFOs, Big Foot and Sasquatch, crop circles and mysterious lights and noises, and all sorts of X-files stuff, have made something of a hobby of publicizing supposed sightings of the Blessed Virgin Mary. Her Son is reported to make the occasional weird appearance—in trees in Liflord, Connecticut, and in Fairfield, Maine, on a rock in Medway, Massachusetts, etc. However, she is said to appear in person and to mark buildings and objects with her image quite frequently. Her statues speak, cry, bleed, and otherwise bring out the reporters.

Dennis William Hauck has a *National Directory of Haunted Sites*, but The Blessed Virgin cannot be said to be a ghost; as mentioned elsewhere, she is credited with being the only fully human person never to die. Her appearances are supernatural, but not ghostly. Still, they are often a piece with general American superstition.

She has notably appeared elsewhere, of course (Lourdes in France, Fatima in Portugal, Guadelupe in Mexico, Mejugorja in Bosnia, Cittavecchia in Italy,

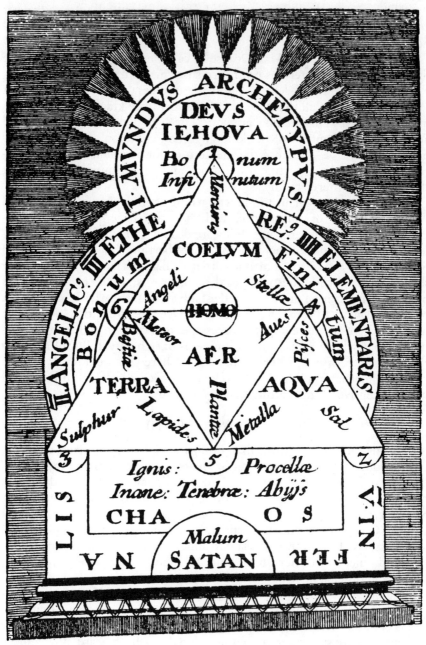

The God Jehova, "Infinite Good," at the top, Satan, "Evil," at the bottom, and Man at the center of it all.

in a slum in The Philippines, and in a monastery sixty miles southeast of Nicosia in Cyprus, to cite some modern examples). In the United States, just to mention some events of the nineties, she had gathered crowds, sometimes in the tens of thousands and weekly, in California (Colfax every Thanksgiving, Inglewood, and Watsonville); in Colorado (Mother Cabrini Shrine in Douglas County, not too far from Denver); Florida (Clearwater and elsewhere); Georgia (Convers was turned upside down by the crowds and Rockdale County experienced terrible traffic problems); Illinois (Our Lady of Snows Church, Belleville, and St. John of God Church in Chicago, also in Hillside's cemetery and as an image on a piece of particle board that carpenter George Papajohn picked up in Chicago); Kentucky (Cold Spring and elsewhere); Louisiana (which reports more miracles than any other state, at tiny Tickfaw, at Our Lady of Perpetual Help Church in the New Orleans suburb of Kenner, and in New Orleans itself); in Michigan (Livonia and St. Claire Shores); New Jersey (Marlboro Township and other towns, too); Ohio (Wadsworth, for instance); Texas (Houston and elsewhere); Virginia (notably at St. Elizabeth Ann Seton Church, Lake Ridge); and in Greek Orthodox churches as well as Roman Catholic ones.

We New York Anglicans have not had an official visit, so far as I hear tell, despite the fact that we have in Manhattan a church named St. Mary the Virgin that is so "high" with incense that it is affectionately known as "Smoky Mary's." In San Francisco and New Orleans and elsewhere there have been conferences held to discuss Marian appearances and their messages.

Icons bursting into tears (in St. Columbia Church in Virginia), in Queens, New York, (where a valuable icon of St. Irene was stolen) and stigmata and the liquefying of the blood of the long-dead saints and all kinds of other manifestations of the supernatural tend rather to embarrass than excite the church authorities. They like to play them down. Each and every one of these sightings and marvels expresses and reinforces the belief in the supernatural which makes ghosts and much else totally credible, even expectable. You can cynically remark that many a church with a mortgage due was pulled out of financial difficulties by a timely visit of the BVM, or just the full-length statue of Christ crucified closing It's eyes at the preacher's mention of His suffering, but you would have to, in fairness, add that many a soul declared for Jesus and many a life was changed for the better as the result of undergoing a transforming experience, believing one has seen a miraculous apparition.

The faithful do report they see things, whether ghosts of The Blessed Mother or not. Believing is seeing, you might say.

POPULAR THEORY FROM THE POPULAR PRESS

From Jim Knipfel's always interesting column in *New York Press*, this theory in the 9-15 July 1998 issue:

When she showed up, first thing she did was tell me all about the client of hers who had died about a week earlier...out of the blue she says, "But she's not gone yet. She hasn't passed over."
Oh dear.
"I was talking to her mother the other night, and she told me that she went into her daughter's room, and it was freezing cold. Even the bedspread is freezing cold."
Oh dear.
"She wasn't ready to go yet. That's where ghosts come from. People who die before they're ready."

HEADLESS GHOSTS

Many British readers will know the comic song about the ghost of Anne Boleyn. This queen, wife of Henry VIII and mother of Elizabeth I but, unfortunately for Anne, not mother of a male heir, is said to wander the drafty corridors of a British castle "with 'er 'ead tucked underneath 'er harm." American readers will know of Washington Irving's famous *Headless Horseman* (which turned out not to be a ghost after all). Maybe few of you know of the case of a headless ghost that haunted a house in Hamburg and in 1953 drove the frightened occupants out. One occult encyclopedia adds "in spite of a cruel housing shortage." I am astounded that some New York City landlords have not cleared out rent-controlled tenants with apparitions.

The clutching hand is a cliché of ghost movies. This one is in *The Old Dark House* (1932)

THE GHOST TRAIN

There are many stories of ghostly trains, some running regularly on lines which have long since disappeared, but Americans have a special one: the train that carried the body of the "martyred" Pres. Abraham Lincoln to its last resting place (where he lies buried with a lot of concrete on top to protect his grave from body snatchers, by the way). Everywhere people stood by the tracks to watch the black-draped car go by. It is said that every April the funeral train runs again in upstate New York, and that you can hear the strains of the military band that turned out to play as it went by. Others say the band is on the train and that you can see them but cannot hear the music.

HAUNTED PLACES IN THE USA

As this book goes to press there are well over 500 books already in print that deal with ghosts, mostly recycling short stories or retelling the folklore of this or that state or city or country. Every locality, it seems, has a haunted hill (that of the Seneca Indians I called Gehaine) or a big, haunted house, or a supposedly haunted landmark (Baldpate Inn in Colorado, for example), or a legend about dead teenagers who return, or some other ghost legend, such as a trainman who was killed and haunts a bridge. It may be said that not only are ghost stories a popular folklore and general literary genre but writing about hauntings is a popular journalistic occupation.

Abroad, Britain and Ireland figure prominently but there are similar books about most countries. There is a long shelf of books here such as Arthur Myers' *Ghostly American Places: A Ghostly Guide to America's Most Fascinating Haunted Landmarks*. I offer a representative selection of fifty-five books currently available. Please note that many of the best books in this line are out of print, so check your local libraries and the standard bibliographies. In addition, check the latest sources for new books of the type. As you can see from Nancy Roberts and Keith Windham (whom I represent with more than one title though this list has to be limited) this is a growth industry easily exploited.

I do not expect anyone to read a lot of these books. I offer one of the widest selections anywhere simply so you can find a book that deals specifically with a place you live or may visit or would just like to read about.

Baker, B. *Great Ghost Stories of the Old West* (1968)
Balliet, B. *The Ghosts of Nantucket* (1984)
Bierce, A. *Ghost and Horror Stories of Ambrose Bierce* (ed. E. F. Bleiler)
Bolick, J. S. *The Return of the Gray Man* (NC, 1961)
Bradley, N. *Gold Rush Ghosts* (1990)
Byrne, R. *Spirits of San Antonio* (1992)
Caldwell, G. W. *Ghost Stories of the California Missions...*(1939)
Carlson, B. *Ghosts of the Iowa Great Lakes* (1989)
Carrico, R. *San Diego's Spirits* (1991)
Crites, S. *Confederate Ghosts* (1994)
"   " *Union Ghosts* (1993)
DeBolt, M. W. *Savannah Ghosts* (1984)
Dunlap, J. *Slitherin' 'Round Texas* (1993)
Erickson, L. *Ghosts of the Amana Colonies* (1988)
Fiedel, D. *Haunted Lancaster County Pennsylvania* (1994)
Harden, J. W. *Tar Heel Ghosts* (1954)
Holzer, H. *America's Restless Ghosts* (1993)
Hubbell, W. *The Great Amherst Mystery* (1992)
Huntsinger, E. *Ghosts of Georgetown* (1995)

Jacobson, L. *Hollywood Haunted* (1994)
Jonas, S. *Ghosts of the Klondike* (1993)
Karl, R. *Amityville* (1991)
Lee, M. D. *Virginia Ghosts* (1966)
Martin, M. *Charleston Ghosts* (1973)
McSherry, Frank D., Jr., et al. *New England Ghosts* (1990)
"   " *Western Ghosts* (1990)
Morpurgo, M. *Ghostly Haunts* (1995)
Munn, D. *Big Sky Ghosts* (1993)
Musick, R. A. *The Telltale Lilac Bush and Other West Virginia Ghost
    Stories* (1965)
Myers, A. *The Ghostly Register* (1986)
Nesbitt, M. *Ghosts of Gettysburg* (1991)
Rhyne, N. *Coastal Ghosts* (1989)
Rider, G. *Ghosts of Door County, Wisconsin* (1992)
Roberts, N. *America's Most Haunted Places* (1987)
"   " *Ghosts of the Carolinas* (1988)
"   " *North Carolina Ghosts* (1991)
"   " *Southern Ghosts* (1987)
"   " *This Haunted Southland* (1988)
Scott, B. *Haunted Heartland* (1988)
Smith, S. *Prominent American Ghosts* (1967)
Taylor, L. *Ghosts of Virginia* (1995)
Verde, T. *Maine Ghosts and Legends* (1989)
Vollers, M. *Ghosts of the Mississippi* (1988)
Viviano, C. *Haunted Louisiana* (1992)
Waugh, C. *Haunted New England* (1988)
Welch, T. *Ghosts of Polk County* (1988)
Wells, D. *The Ghosts of Rowan Oak* (1980)
Williams, D. *Ghosts along the Texas Coast* (1994)
Windham, K. *Thirteen Alabama Ghosts* (1987)
"   " *Thirteen Georgia Ghosts* (1987)
"   " *Thirteen Mississippi Ghosts* (1987)
"   " *Thirteen Tennessee Ghosts* (1987)
Woodyard, C. *Haunted Ohio* (vol. 3, 1994)

For classroom teachers there are videos such as the filmstrip/cassette combo called *America's Most Haunted Places* (1976) and other more modern ways of capturing the kiddies' attention.

SÉANCE CAPITAL OF AMERICA

Cassadaga (Florida) may be the séance capital of America, the country which, as Sir Arthur Conan Doyle asserts in his *History of Spiritualism*

(1926), popularized if it did not invent Spiritualism, "by far the most important thing that America has given to the commonwealth of the world."

In Cassadaga, founded by a spiritualist in 1894, the whole town is full of seers, mediums and psychics. Or people who claim to be. Each clique says the others are fakes. I believe them.

SOME MORE HAUNTED PLACES

One of the sites being considered for a new baseball stadium in Denver, it was suggested, ought to be ruled out because the place is haunted.

The Jefferson Davis Hospital in Houston, said to have been erected over Confederate soldiers' graves, has been reported to be haunted.

Likewise occupied by the lingering dead as well as by the living are a community center in Los Angeles, a public library in Elmhurst (Illinois), a fire station here and there, and innumerable old houses. In fact, so many houses in such places as New Orleans as to warrant those ghost tours for visitors that you heard about.

If it gives you a thrill to think you may see a ghost (and you are sure you won't be disappointed if you don't), I suppose there is no harm in your going out of your way to some enterprising bed-and-bogeyman establishment, or trooping through old neighborhoods in a gaggle of sightseers. You may pick up some history, too, although it might be unreliable. In my experience, the most worthless Ghost Tours are offered in New York City and in San Francisco, but in both places the living are colorful enough.

LIFE AFTER DEATH IN OUR CONSUMER WORLD

You can have cremains made into jewelry (one up on bracelets of hair, beloved by the Victorians, or memorial rings worn by Elizabethans) or customized "granite slabs" (Relict Memorials of Mill Valley, California), your cadaver (or just the head, as I said) deep frozen for possible future resuscitation, DNA kept for future use, perpetual care for your website, even a "bibliocadaver" (books with blank or printed pages on paper made with cremains, from Timothy Hawley Books).

Another idea is to have your tomb made oddly enough to constitute a tourist destination. I think I would like to be buried under a church floor in Britain with a medieval-like brass on top. People could come and rub the brass for a fee and the money could go to the upkeep of the church. Also, it would be pleasant to have my tummy rubbed, even in death.

WORST MESSAGE FROM A SÉANCE

Whole books have allegedly been received through mediums. But the average message at a séance, I repeat, seems to me to resemble a silly postcard: "having wonderful time" but usually without the "wish you were here."

Choosing the most self-serving and most unlikely message from Beyond is difficult. I must, however, give that a try. I select director Gus Van Sant's claim that at a séance, Alfred Hitchcock from the grave gave Van Sant the go-ahead for a remake of the classic horror movie, *Psycho*. The remake was generally regarded as an unfortunate move.

NIGHT THOUGHTS

Woody Allen proffers wisdom. He says he doesn't want to gain immortality by his work; he yearns to achieve it "by not dying." There are many other philosophers and even a few theologians who might be quoted here regarding death and immortality, but few I can think of more profound than Allen. As for the afterlife, he is not certain but says he is bringing along a change of underwear, just in case.

Oiwa's Ghost. Detail of a woodcut by Hokusai.

4

Ghosts in the Rest of the World

GHOSTS WORLDWIDE

A concern with the dead makes the whole world kin. Everywhere and in every age people have tried to cope with the dead. They have left many records of ghosts in their written and oral traditions and still practice old customs related to the dead. A thorough book of Chinese ghost stories would be many times the size of this book; a similar tome on Japanese ghosts might be even larger. Ghosts are an important part of the life of every African village. In some other cultures people keep the bones of the dead in their houses and on occasion throw parties for the departed.

In this brief chapter we can only suggest the vast extent of beliefs about ghosts in what are to us exotic places and strange religions. I think of a statement by the Latin poet Martial:

> *Sunt bona, sunt quæsam mediocria, sunt mala plura Quæ legis hic;*
> *aloter non fit, Avite, liber.*

which means:

> *There are good things, there are mediocre things, there are more bad things*
> *that you read here. That, Avitus, is how a book is made.*

Here are some things you will think *bona*, I trust, about ghosts in far-off places. Every country and culture has produced enough material on ghosts and poltergeists to warrant a whole book; here we can have a sampling.

LIFE AMONG THE DEAD

Ever since primitive man buried goods and weapons with his dear departed, with the idea the dead might have need of such things, there has been interest in providing for a life after death. In ancient China they put household objects and even armies of soldier figurines into graves. Originally they may have slaughtered servants and buried them with their masters. In the Tang Dynasty, for instance, they put large and terrifying statues of figures like Lokhapala into the tombs in order to guard the households of the dead.

The Egyptians had a fascination with the dead. In the pre-dynastic period (up to about 3000 years before Christ) they buried their dead crouching in pits, but by the II Dynasty the dead got something like little buildings in which to "live" after death.

By the III Dynasty royalty was mummified and provided with stone "houses." Soon after, lesser mortals were interred in wooden coffins with hieroglyphic prayers for food and drink for consumption in the afterworld. Ancient Egyptian tombs may have mostly been stripped of their treasures (which included furniture, boats, and many other useful objects) by grave robbers, but those robbers left for us to find the beer and wine and bread buried with the departed. Archeologists can distinguish what food was buried with the dead from the leftovers from the lunches of grave robbers also found in tombs.

Egyptian religion held that the *ka* (spirit) had to return to the body from time to time in death to get sustenance. Elaborate efforts were made to preserve the mummified body for this purpose but, in case the mummy should be destroyed, the mummy case (made to resemble the deceased) or a statue of the deceased (seated calmly or in some other posture comfortable to assume for eternity) might serve in place of the actual remains. The anthropoid mummy case seems to have been well established by the XII Dynasty, though at first it was used only for royalty and the highest officials. In the New Kingdom (XVII-XX Dynasties) the dead person was often depicted on the

Egyptians entombed with the mummies have all the necessities for the life after death. Here food for the dead is being brought.

mummy case not as a dead person but as alive, and later (XXI-XXV Dynasties) the mummy cases got quite elaborate in their portrayal of the afterlife, especially the business of the soul being weighed in scales against the *ma'at* (feather representing truth).

There was always an interest in keeping the dead happy. If they were not happy, they might return (it was feared) and do harm to the living. All sorts of amulets and magical inscriptions were buried with the dead to assist them on their way. Likewise, all sorts of magical means were used to protect the living from the return of the dead.

From the earliest times heaps of stones were piled on graves. This not only prevented wild animals from digging up corpses; it also (it was hoped) helped to keep the dead from rising again.

THE BOOK OF THE DEAD, GILGAMESH, AND *ATHARVA-VEDA*

Three of the most interesting examples of very ancient literary compilations are the Egyptian *Book of the Dead*, the epic of *Gilgamesh*, and the encyclopedic text of the *Atharva-Veda*.

Everyone knows of the Egyptian fascination with immortality. The book about "the dawning of day" called *The Book of the Dead* is a collection, still seriously read by many, of all kinds of religious and superstitious topics connected with death and the afterlife and preserved on 2000 papyrus scrolls which date all the way from 4200 BC to 2000 BC. The Egyptian ghost stories are the oldest we have in any written form.

Gilgamesh (*c.* 200 BC) comes to us in fragments from the Assyrians and Babylonians and we have bits in Akkadian, Babylonian, and Sumerian. Recently it has been put together well and superbly translated. In the library of the great King Ashurbanipal, whom you may have seen depicted in huge bas reliefs dragged off to the British museum, the hero, Gilgamesh, talks to the ghost of his sometime rival, sometime friend Enkidu, who describes the afterlife.

The world of the spirits is also described in the *vedas* ("books of knowledge") of Indian literature. One of these is the *Atharva-Veda*, whose title translates to "Book of Spells." It includes information on incantations, magic and witchcraft, and—to note here—contacts with that other world. It can stand as another example of an ancient, pre-Christian culture's interest in life other than the terrestrial. The Indian beliefs in ghosts and demons of the early Vedic period continue in the so-called Sanskrit period (beginning about two centuries before Christ). It comes right up to our own day.

FEASTS OF THE DEAD

Many religions trace much of their appeal to their offering an answer to the question of what happens to us after we die, and many religions honor the dead not only with solemn burials but with annual festivals. These need not be dreary. In some cultures the dead are treated to parties. Their skulls may even be offered food and drink. *Sköll!*

Christianity has All Souls' Day, to which All Hallows Eve (now Halloween) is attached. Those kids arriving at your door for trick or treat are to recall the need, as I say elsewhere, for grateful ghosts.

Ancient Greeks celebrated the yearly return of the dead in the eighth month of their calendar (Anthesterion), which occupied part of our February and part of our March. The Anthesteria, which was mentioned earlier, lasted several days. Joyous festivities marked the return of the dead and, though we lack details, probably celebrated the resurrection of Dionysus. Later the resurrection of Christ was to be celebrated in Spring, at Easter, connected to the vernal equinox.

For Christians, the big black-and-white party comes at the end of the world: the trumpet shall sound, the dead shall rise, incorruptible, and (as is often the case) the greatest pleasure of those rejoicing at the party (in Heaven) shall be that a great many people did not get invitations and cannot crash the event (being sent to Hell).

In some cultures the dead are kept in or around the house and feted on important occasions as members of the family. I go only as far as portraits of ancestors on the walls.

THE SOUL

Christians believe in the duality of soul and body; at death the soul, which is immortal, leaves the body. We have located the soul at various times in the pupil of the eye, the crown of the head, the nape of the neck, the blood, a bone in the chest, etc. The spirit is supposed to be able to leave the body under certain conditions and return (as in sleep), to be in danger of being drawn out by black magic or taken over by demons, and finally to be expelled with the last breath. This is called "giving up the ghost," or releasing the spirit.

As Sir James Frazer notes, Dutch anthropologists reported that "in Celebes they sometimes fashion fish-hooks to a sick man's nose, navel, and feet, so that if his soul should try to escape it may be hooked and held fast." The soul of Aristeas of Proconnesus was said to have issued from his mouth "in the shape of a raven," and this reminds us that the Holy Spirit also descended in the shape of a bird, a white dove. One supposes that bird imagery suggests flight.

In Melanesia, people believe the soul is dual; at death it breaks up into *aunga* (good) and *adaro* (evil) parts. The *adaro* elements can be dangerous until they eventually perish, but they do die, unlike demons, who were never human. The *aunga* elements live on forever. These good spirits of the dead are worshipped by, and watch over, the living.

If you want to steal someone's soul there are many methods recorded by superstition. Here is that used among the Malays, whom Sir James Frazer credits with being the best at stealing souls, for whatever purposes. This method is for use with a sexual partner:

> When the moon, just risen, looks red above the eastern horizon, go out, and standing in the moonlight, with the big toe of your right foot on the big toe of your left [forming some sort of circuit of energy], make a speaking-trumpet of your right hand and recite through it the following words.

> OM [a sacred syllable, as used in Buddhist meditation]. I loose my shaft, I loose it and the sun is extinguished.
> I loose it, and the stars burn dim.
> But it is not the sun, moon, and stars that I shoot at.
> It is the stalk of the heart of that child of the congregation, [victim's name].
> Cluck! Cluck! [Equivalent to calling an animal] soul of [victim's name], come and walk with me.
> Come and sit with me,
> Come and sleep and share my pillow.
> Cluck! Cluck! Soul.

Repeat this thrice and after every repetition blow through your fist.

The person who comes to you as a result of soul stealing is not, however, a ghost, any more than a zombie (or a person whose soul has been subdued by poisoning, vulgarly assumed to be a corpse reanimated) is a ghost. The recipe for making zombies, we may note in passing, along with many others you are decidedly not encouraged to try, is in *The Complete Book of Spells, Curses, and Magical Recipes* (1997).

MODERN TECHNOLOGY

How's this for weird: D. Scott Rogo and Raymond Bayless's book *Phone Calls from the Dead* (1979)? If readers would like to send me news of their equally uncheckable experiences, perhaps I can enter the lists with *E-Mail from the Dead* and *Weird and Wired: The Uncanny Online*. Keep those cards and letters coming in! I have in my time received a few letters from the dead, but the letters were written before the correspondent checked out. It's nice now and then to get mail you don't have to bother to answer. Or should it be answered, somehow?

SPEAKING OF THE DEPARTED

Speak nothing but good of the dead, or they may return to harm you. Arabic speakers call the dead *al-marhüm* (the one to whom mercy has been shown) or *al-maghfūr* (the one who has been forgiven); not to do so is thought to invite a ghost coming to haunt you.

SPIRITS AMONG THE ARABIC SPEAKERS

A *jinn* (which we call a "genie") is a spirit but not human and therefore not a ghost. Demons are not ghosts. Neither is a *gûl* (which we call a "ghoul"): it's a supernatural monster that eats the dead. What we'd call a real ghost Arabic calls an *ifrit*. It is mentioned in the Koran, which also features a devil and demons. In one of the 1001 tales in *The Arabian Nights*, the ghost of a woman returns to save her widower from drowning. She is described as *ifrítah* or *junníyah*. The world of Islam is said to be filled with demons and other supernatural creatures. Islamic believers live in a world of wonders. Actually, I think we all do, but we are used to sunrise and Spring.

GHOSTS OF THE ASHANTI

In this African tribe or nation, a suicide is often said to come back as a ghost and may even be reincarnated to live another life with a bad end. Executed criminals are feared: they may return for revenge. Corpses may be buried with charms so as to prevent their return, or marked so that the dead can be recognized if they come back.

"Some of the dead," writes the eminent Africanist Geoffrey Parrinder, "had their heads shaved and painted red, white, and black so that they would be recognized if they walked as ghosts."

HOLMAN

This is a guy you won't want to meet on a dark night. (His principal activities take place at sunset, midnight, and dawn, so he is around a lot). If he catches you walking through a cemetery in Sinhala, he will grab you from behind by the shoulders. You will be found dead of fright. It is not clear whether the *holman* is a ghost or a monster. In either case, avoid him. If you don't know where Sinhala is, so much the better.

OF THE ASIAN PERSUASION

Lately the Hong Kong movie industry seems to have gone off the ghost kick somewhat, but in the eighties ghosts were all the rage there. Have you seen *Rouge* or *Crazy Spirit* or *Zu: Warriors of the Magic Mountain*? Ghosts have always been popular in Asian films.

Asian literature is chock full of ghosts. It is only our western lack of familiarity with the languages and literatures of the East that keeps us from knowing just how widespread is the lore of ghosts there.

JAPANESE GHOSTS

In addition to human ghosts, the Japanese have ghost gods.

Some of these can be awful and malicious. In Aoyama Cemetery (Yokyo) they put up a tombstone for Oiwa, a seventeenth-century woman, that is several feet higher than any of the others. This was an attempt to get on her very vengeful ghost's good side. Japan has a long tradition of ghost tales, and ghosts enter into a great deal of Japanese pictorial art, many festivals, *kabuki* plays, films, etc.

Many of the 3,500 or 3,600 new religions in America contain something old, something new, something borrowed, and something Buddhist. But reincarnation doesn't fit very well with the Judeo-Christian or Protestant-Pragmatic trends, so it tends to be neglected. Still, the Next Life promised by Christianity has some lasting appeal, even if today some people such as the Heaven's Gate lot believe the Next Life will be on other planets of our solar system where we shall be not so much reincarnated as reconstituted. Beam us up, Scotty!

We must have at least one example of reincarnation in modern American art, and I choose a play by Yuko Hamada and Yukihiro Saji called *The Flower of Water* and subtitled *Awakening From Two Beings*. It opened on New York City's Theater Row in mid-June 1997. The two beings are Japanese women: Murasaki, a prostitute under Japan's strict class system in the Edo period (1600-1867) who commits suicide not only to get out of a bad life but in hopes of a better life, and Aya, her reincarnation, who is in the "sex industry" in Japan in the modern period.

As exotic to most European as the Japanese is the Russian. The Ha-Bimah Jewish theater in Moscow poster here proclaims the final performance of *The Dybbuk* on January 18, 1925. The play has continued to be a staple of the Yiddish theater repertoire, but not in our time.

GHOSTS IN THE KABUKI THEATER

In the catalogue of an exhibition at the Spencer Museum of Art (University of Kansas), *Japanese Ghosts and Demons* (1985), the editor (Stephen

Addiss) and James L. Secor write:

> In the nineteenth century, ghosts, spirits, demons, ogres, and ani-
> mal transformations crowded into the world of art, in part reflect-
> ing the disturbed social conditions of the time [the Edo Period].
> The same supernatural infusion had already occurred in kabuki the-
> ater, the entertainment par excellence of the common people. In
> theatrical representations, ghosts were the most prominent
> among otherworldly subjects, perhaps because they provided
> opportunities for spectacular dramatic effects. Spectral themes were
> well-accepted by audiences, since the belief in possession and
> hauntings was still extremely prominent.
>
> Popular tales were put on the stage, and in return the stage
> influenced popular fiction and art. Printmakers such as Utagawa
> Kunisada (1797-1861) came after the highpoint of *kabuki* but
> immortalized many of its scenes and actors, both male and trans-
> vestite (*onagata*, "woman's way or shape" actors). The ghosts of the
> murdered and suicides were common in *kabuki*'s sensational sto-
> ries, but effects such as "flying heads...and accounts of atrocities
> or manners of vicious women" were censored by the government.

A scene from Rokujuen's novel *The Story of the Craftsman of Hida* (1808). The priest
Funanushi is visited by the ghost of his daughter.

The government also banned contemporary references, so plays were set in the past although redolent of their era. An example is *Sakura-hime azuma bunshō* (The Cherry Blossom Princess of Edo). In it, superstition, politics and romance are intertwined (the form called *naimaze*), and the setting is moved back to the Kamakura Era (1185-1392). The princess is born with a fist tightly closed. Growing up unwanted because of this deformity, she decides to become a nun. The monk Seigen, however, opens her fist and in it discovers a small incense case with his own name inscribed on it (in Chinese characters).

Seigen had given this same case to his homosexual lover, Shiragiku, many years before. Shiragiku threw himself off a cliff, mad for love, expressing the wish that he might be reborn as a woman so that he could marry Seigen. Seigen believes Sakura to be his lost love. Their relationship is, to say the least, rocky. In the long run, Seigen, after many misfortunes, dies and comes back (accompanied by special lighting effects and an insistent *doro-doro* drumbeat that is as effective as its emotion-heightened imitation in Eugene O'Neill's *The Emperor Jones*) to haunt Sakura, who has to live the life of a prostitute.

The female *yurei* (ghosts) is often less fierce in appearance than the male, but no less dangerous and relentless. "Hell hath no fury like a woman scorned," an English poet wrote; the Japanese female ghosts demonstrate the truth of this fully in fiction and drama. The ghost tales might be based on real events, such as *Yotsuya kaidan* (Yotsuya Ghost Story, 1825), or entirely made up. In *Yotsuya Ghost Story*, the draw is particularly in the Oiwa episodes, in which her vengeful ghost pursues the murderer Iyemon. Iyemon's guilty terrors remind us of those of the murderer in Leopold Lewis' *The Bells*, an all-stops-out British melodrama in which Sir Henry Irving gave his greatest performances.

A BUTTERFLY

An ancient Japanese tale tells of an old man who lay dying and a white butterfly that hovered around his bed. Fearing the butterfly might be an evil spirit, a member of the family chases it away and follows the butterfly to a nearby cemetery. It lights on the grave of one Akiko, who had died, the tombstone said, fifty years before at the age of eighteen. The grave was well tended and there was a bunch of fresh flowers reverently placed there. The butterfly had landed on that bouquet.

Returning to the house of the old man, the family member was told he had died peacefully. And that Akiko? She was a girl he had loved. When death took her from him fifty years before, he had moved to this house by the cemetery so that every day he could visit her grave and bring fresh flowers. The butterfly? It must have been the ghost of Akiko, which came to escort the old man to the land of the dead.

TWO MORE JAPANESE GHOST STORIES

Briefly, in one ghost story a character says she is terrified that she might come back as one of the common figures of Japanese stories, the "hungry ghost." She is asked, "If you had a choice, would you rather be a ghost, even a hungry ghost, or just dead?"

In Buddhist doctrine, there are various levels of existence, and besides the hells and the dwellings of humans and demigods and animal spirits and malignant spirits, there is the land of the "hungry ghosts." A ghost, if sufficiently motivated, can enter our plane of existence. Those that do, it seems, are mostly women who have been badly treated in this life. One would not want to be one of them, or to encounter one of them.

In Ueda Akinari's (1734-1809) brilliant *Ugetsu monogatari* (Tales of Moonlight and Rain) female ghosts abound. In one tale, a merchant goes to the capital (Kyoto) to sell silk. He promises his anxious wife he will return by the next fall. War breaks out and his return is years delayed. When he gets back home he finds his neighborhood mostly derelict but his own house in good condition and his old wife happy to see him. They share their stories of separation and their joys at being reunited and go to sleep together. The next morning the merchant wakes alone; he discovers his wife has vanished. In fact, she had died years before. He has to pray at her grave to put her long-departed soul to rest. He has slept with a ghost.

THE *UPANISHADS* AND THE CHRISTIAN SCRIPTURES

The *Upanishads* are ancient documents from India which concentrate on the attainment of mystical experience to be gained by (as the name says) "sitting near" a master. They are relevant here because they seek the very meaning of life and death. The scholars of these scriptures ask, "What is that which, being known, everything is known?"

Christianity, according to St. Paul, promises that after we are dead we shall see truth "face to face" and meanwhile we see only "as in a glass, darkly" at best. Think of death as a learning experience.

NO IFS, ANDS, OR *BHUTS*

Bhuts are angry ghosts in India. Unhappy in the spirit world, they come along to bother the living. One variety of these creatures (vampire-like except that they are dead) is called *airi*. Those are ghosts of men killed while out hunting, and they are accompanied by vicious ghostly dogs. To see them can be fatal.

If attacked by one of these creatures, lie down flat on the ground (they hate that). Or burn tumeric, a spice familiar in curry powder (they hate the smell).

FISHER'S GHOST CREEK

On a small bridge over what is now called Fisher's Ghost Creek in Australia, people claimed they saw the ghost of a man who pointed to direct their gaze downwards. After a number of reports of this apparition, people dug and found the bones of Fred Fisher, who had been murdered in 1826.

THE STRANGER AS A GHOST

One reason the *conquistadores* who landed near Vera Cruz and destroyed the empire of the Aztecs were not immediately wiped out: they happened to land on exactly the day that had been foretold as the day of the return of the great Quetzalcoatl (Plumed Serpent). Cortés was taken by many to be the dead hero of Mexicans.

When after World War II Australia was given the rather thankless task of civilizing Papua New Guinea, where for 40,000 years isolated savages had intermittently battled each other, the white *kiaps* were taken by the natives to be ghosts. Automobiles were called their mothers, because the white "ghosts" got "inside them and were carried around."

AFRICAN GHOSTS

Every nation and tribe of Africa has its ghost superstitions. After all, doesn't everyone have ancestors? Do not the dead hover around, sometimes helping, sometimes hurting? Early in his career, Jomo Kenyatta in *Facing Mount Kenya* (1936) wrote about the beliefs of his native people, the Kikuyu. In Time-Life's *The Mysterious World* we read:

> Although the Kikuyu use a wide variety of herbal cures for common ailments, those remedies were considered powerless against certain diseases attributed to an evil spirit of one of the victim's ancestors, which only a magician could locate. By communing with the supreme council of all ancestral spirits, he could drive the tormentor away from the victim, using a combination of magic powders, incantations, and ritual enactments. It was not work that could support a charlatan; payment for a magician's services came only after a sick person got well.

Since Kenyatta's time, Christianity has taken perhaps a firmer hold in some parts of the Dark Continent and some Africans for other reasons have turned on their magicians. There have been horrendous reports of numerous people being barbarously assaulted as suspected witches and even witch doctors. But the Time-Life editors say: "In the last decades of the twentieth century, the practices Kenyatta described in his book remain an accepted part of many Kikuyu lives."

SENDING A MESSAGE

There is much discussion of the dead sending us messages through mediums at séances and by other means, but perhaps you would like to know how you can send *them* messages.

Sir Richard Burton (1821-1890) tells of the method used in Dahomey by the king there in 1863. Wishing to send a message to his ancestors, he simply told the message to a servant and then cut off the servant's head, which sent him on his way to the land of the dead.

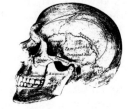

Side view of the skull. (Cryer.)

ADUÎ RÁT PÍRAN DÁ VÊLDÁ

That translates as "midnight is the time for saints" (coming back from the dead and revealing themselves to observers either dreaming or awake). Richard Carnac Temple quotes it as occurring frequently in the literature of India. It refers to the coming of dead heroes, saints, and ghosts. Examining the ancient, sacred literature (which he called *Legends of the Punjab* in three volumes published 1884-1900), Temple analyzed the supernatural elements in fifty-nine "legends" of ancient bards, touching on the central belief in the immortality of both divine and human persons.

Under "Immortality" he lists reappearances, saints, ghosts, spirits, gods, godlings, *birs* or warriors, demons and devils, and discusses exorcism. He found just one exorcism: "a Hindu *jogi* cures a Muhammadan family of goblins and spirits by medicines and herbs; and it is to be observed that in the passage in question the goblins were Musalman (*jinn*) and the spirits were Hindu (*bhut*)."

A STORY FROM THE CONGO

From Jan Knappert's *African Mythology* (1995):

> A hunter walked through the forest with his three dogs... Ntuntu, Mbwa, and Kapakala. Well-trained dogs they were, loyal and faithful. They stayed an antelope so the hunter could shoot it with an arrow. They headed for home, but it was late and darkness was spreading rapidly. The hunter saw an old house and decided to spend the night there. The house belonged to a ghost, but the hunter did not know that. The ghost came home late that night and found the hunter asleep surrounded by his dogs, and a big dead antelope hanging from the ceiling. (These ghosts love antelope's meat but they love man's meat even more. For the purpose of carving man-meat, ghosts have a huge thumbnail, looking like an ax

such as butchers use to cut animal bones). In order to prepare this thumbnail for rapidly cutting through human bones, the ghost held it in the fire until it was glowing red. The pungent odour woke the dogs, who growled so that the hunter woke up. Seeing his host with a large red-hot nail on his left thumb, the hunter suspected witchcraft and asked: "What do you want?" "I only wanted to carve a piece of this delicious antelope," answered the ghost, disappointed but looking innocent. The hunter pretended to go back to sleep, knowing that he would be carved up if he did fall asleep. Before dawn, the ghost wanted to disappear with the antelope, but the dogs would not let him. They tore him to pieces, discovering that a ghost is nothing but bones—which dogs love to gnaw. Thus they saved their master.

The hunter was lucky he did not go mad, as most people do who see ghosts in the Congo, but he could easily have rid himself of the ghost by simply pricking his thumb, because it is believed there that ghosts flee at the sight of human blood. At the same time, ghosts are popularly believed to eat human flesh to make up for the flesh they, mere white skeletons, have lost. The *mizimi* (ancestral ghosts) of the Bantu go out at night to look for blood. *Matebo* (outcast dwarf ghosts of Angola and Zaïre) eat human beings.

Everywhere in Africa, ghosts are feared and placated with offerings of food, of which they consume only the spirit.

Dale Kellet Fitzgerald's dissertation (*Spirit Mediumship and Séance Performance among the Ga of Southern Ghana*, 1977) ought to be published. Indeed the whole subject of mediumship in African religion and superstition deserves more such serious study, although most outside investigators have been moved to mention this aspect of African life.

HEADHUNTERS OF BORNEO

Like headhunters in many places, the headhunters of Borneo thought that the head contained what they called the *toh* (or ghost) of a person after death. It was therefore thought magical and to it were ascribed powers to fertilize the soil, promote crops, and bring prosperity to the community that preserved and honored the head. Capturing a head was believed to bring not simply honor but good luck to the headhunter.

TULPAS

In Tibet, people believe they can create "thought forms," which is to say that sheer intense concentration could make your imaginary friend take on corporeality. Think a spirit into human form. Alexandra David-Neel said she did but that he became a nuisance.

HONOR YOUR ANCESTORS

Many Chinese still believe that failing to honor one's ancestors, particularly by moving their graves, will cause ghosts to rise and wreak havoc with descendants. Many stories are told of retaliation by disturbed ghosts.

Traditionally, the Chinese believe that the spirits of ancestors enter into sacred tablets. The living place these in shrines and honor them with special ceremonies. The living even present gifts and food to these spirits. In return, the spirits of the dead help the living and interceded with the gods on behalf of pious descendants.

CURSES!

The living sometimes suggest that if we do not follow their wishes we may expect bad news from The Other Side. Shakespeare's bones rest surprisingly undisturbed, perhaps because he caused a curse to be put on his tomb against those who would move the bones.

At Hieropolis (Pamukkale or "Cotton Fortress" in Turkey) among the ruins are elaborate tombs, at least one of which bears a long inscription. It calls for unauthorized persons not to take over the tomb, sets fines and articulates curses for those who would invade the dead man's privacy, and seems to suggest that if you don't watch out he will come back and exact vengeance on you. All over the world, people are afraid of the curses of the dead. Many are the stories of how the dead came back to punish transgressors and, of course, one of the world's most famous plays, *Hamlet*, is about a father's ghost coming back not to kill his murderer but to urge his son to do so.

THE GHOSTS OF BURMA

Like other countries of the East, Burma has a long tradition of ghosts which are said to be people punished for bad lives, improperly buried, not respected, back for revenge, and so on.

Many Buddhists believe that when you die you may have a variety of possible fates. You could go into a kind of suspension until you are reincarnated, or you could live an active life among the dead. You could become a demon or another kind of inhabitant of hell. You could be reincarnated as a person (this is considered unlikely and is ranked among what are called the "five rarities") or as an animal. Or you could wander as a ghost. Ghosts are invariably restless and unhappy. You'd be better off dead!

Melford E. Spiro's *Buddhism and Society* (2nd edition, 1982) is one of the best books on the fascinating people of Burma and their astonishing beliefs.

ANCIENT BELIEFS

Every civilization has entertained theories about the dead, but few have been so concerned with them as the Egyptians of the time of the pharaohs.

The matter is complicated, but briefly it can be said that the ancient Egyptians believed in three human spirits, *ba*, *ka*, and *akh*, and that the last of these somewhat resembles our ghost. This spirit required that the dead body be preserved. The mummification of corpses and magical protections on the cartonnage are well known. Egyptians used to bury with their dead a board game called *sennet*. The spirit was supposed to have to win this game against those who would prevent the spirit from entering the life of the underworld.

The Chinese of the Han Dynasty said that at death the corpse (*hsing*) was left by the life force (*p'o*) and *hun* might stay united, perhaps as a ghost to perform some deed (such as avenging murder). Freed of earthly things, the *hun* struggles to reach heavenly blessedness. (A cosmological map may be provided for the complex and hazardous journey after death). The *p'o* hangs around the corpse for 3 years, longer if proper funeral arrangements are made. Pieces of jade—for the exceptionally wealthy a whole suit of jade pieces connected with gold wire—keep the *p'o* in the corpse.

A jade mask was found on the face of a ruler buried at Palenque in Mexico, a country whose ancient connections with Asia are only now coming to light.

To assist the *p'o* in Yellow Springs (not Ohio, but the Chinese purgatory), money, domestic furniture, even family and servants were buried with the important dead. Later these were represented by models of people, as in Egypt, but in China some of the retainers might be life-size. One corpse has been disinterred with a whole *standing* army. Today paper models of necessary equipment for the new life, even automobiles and cellular telephones, are burned at traditional Chinese funerals, along with Hell Money to spend there. Firecrackers are set off to drive demons away from the funeral. They detest a racket.

A ceramic of the Tang Dynasty (AD 618-907) in the Brooklyn Museum depicts a tomb guardian (Lokhapala, standing on a bull symbolic of strength) of ancient China. But people everywhere have sought from time to time protection from the dead as well as for the dead. Ghosts have often been feared.

Without a successful funeral the dead Chinese person might well become a ghost (*kuei*) and terrorize the living.

In his readable and reliable encyclopedia of myth and legend, *Chinese Mythology* (1992), Derek Walters tells how a *p'o* not properly released could be a vampire:

Li Chiu, a pedlar of Hou San, finding no lodging was obliged to spend the night in a temple. During his sleep, Wei-t'o [a *deva* or god who, armed with a great sword, guards a manifestation of The Buddha as a goddess of mercy in Buddhist temples or, because of a confusion of names, accompanies Ti-tsang Wang, King of the Earth's Womb, in Taoist temples], the Protector of Temples, appeared to him in a dream, warned him of impending danger, and told him to hide behind his statue. Li Chiu woke up in time to see a coffin open and a vampire emerge. Following the advice given in his dream, he jumped behind the statue of Wei-t'o just as the vampire sunk its teeth into it. Most Chinese ghosts are not vampiristic but many can be dangerous in other ways.

CHINESE GHOSTS

In China the ghost story has from time immemorial been a major art form. Chinese ghosts can be good or bad or mixed. Because the Chinese believe in three aspects of the soul (the higher, the lower, and the part that inhabits and is honored at the altar of ancestors) a dead person can appear in several places at once. As is common in Asia, some Chinese ghosts are ludicrous clowns and others are vengeful and hateful.

FROM THE ANALECTS OF CONFUCIUS

Tzu-lu asked how we should serve ghosts and spirits. The Master responded, "Until you have learned how to serve men, how can you serve the ghosts of men?" Tzu-lu then ventured to ask about the dead. The Master said, "Until you know the living, how can you know the dead?"

GOLDEN LOTUS

This a Chinese story about a young man haunted by the ghost of a dead girl named Fu Shu-fang. He seeks help from a Mr. Wei. We join the story in progress.

The young fellow told Mr. Wei the whole story and received from him two powerful amulets, one to hang at his door, one to hang over his bed. These kept the dead girl from returning to him. She came no more nights.

More than a month went by. The young fellow went out carousing with a friend who lived by the Bridge of the Embroidered Robes and forgot Mr. Wei's warning to stay away from the area of the temple where Fu Shu-fang was buried. As he passed by, Golden Lotus met him and said that her mistress worried much why he had been neglecting her. The young fellow allowed himself to be conducted into the temple, where he met with the beautiful young girl. She berated him for neglecting her, dismissed the warnings of Mr. Wei, and led him to lie down with her—in her tomb!

Sometime later, the young fellow's next-door neighbor, wondering where his friend had disappeared to, went to the temple and found the tomb. He noted that the tassel of the young man's gown was hanging out of the closed tomb. When he alerted the monks and they opened the tomb, in it they found the young man dead and decomposing but the girl, no longer a skeleton, looked as beautiful as if she were just sleeping.

The monks were astonished and explained that Fu Shu-fang had been buried there twelve years ago but that the family had moved away and nothing more was heard of them. In all the interval the monks had no knowledge of any ghostly activity. Not until now.

The coffin was taken and buried with both corpses in it at a crossroads at the west gate of the city. There, on certain stormy nights, the ghosts of the couple could be seen walking hand in hand, preceded by Golden Lotus carrying her double-peony lantern. Anyone who saw the apparition fell ill, and only the virtuous survived the chills and fever. Those who were not virtuous soon died.

The people in their fear turned to Mr. Wei, but he said his powers were not strong enough to deal with a haunting like this. He recommended that they consult the Taoist hermit Iron Hat, who lived on the Mountain of Four-fold Clarity.

Without delay a whole crowd of people from the city went to that mountain and with great difficulty climbed to the top. There they found Iron Hat sitting at a table watching his servant boy play with a crane, a symbol of longevity. They begged the old man to help them with the hauntings and deaths.

The hermit said that he had withdrawn from the world and for sixty years had lived apart from society, but he took pity on the people and, with his servant boy, painfully made his way down the mountain and into the city.

At the west gate he caused an altar about six feet square to be erected and, kneeling before it on a little mat, he wrote a magic formula on a piece of paper and burned it. Out of the smoke appeared a small army of tall soldiers all in brocade gowns and glittering armor, holding halberds. They stood at attention, awaiting orders.

The old hermit berated them for allowing the ghosts to wander around dangerously and commanded them to bring the girl's, Golden Lotus', and the young man's ghosts before him.

This was soon accomplished. The three ghosts were brought before the hermit in the wooden yokes of criminals. They were whipped and forced to confess their crimes. The young man pleaded that the death of his wife had left him without a woman and that he had fallen prey to the beautiful shade, as had Chêng in the well-known story of the fox woman. He did not know how to express his shame and repentance. Fu Shu-fang pleaded that she had died young and before having connection with any man. Her lustful urges led her to seduce the living, and she did not know how she could cease her evil ways or make restitution for what she already had done.

The servant girl Golden Lotus wept and told how she lost her virginity, bore a child, was buried in a funeral mound, and how she came to be a wandering ghost. Someone had taken clay from the funeral mound and made a figurine of it. Giving it a name, they had breathed life into it, and Golden Lotus was therefore condemned to wander as a spirit.

The confessions were recorded and the hermit wrote his verdict with bold strikes of the brush:

> In the days of old, when the emperor Yü cast the Nine Tripods as symbols of the world, no ghost could control its shape. When Wei Ch'iao lowered his lantern of rhinoceros horn into the abyss, the palaces of the waterworld, where live the dragons, were compelled to exhibit their true forms. The dead and the living inhabit different worlds. When by magic or deceit they cross, disasters come to human beings. That is why, as old tales record, the Duke Ching of Chin died when he met the ghost of Tai-li and also why Duke Hsaing of Ch'lu died when he met a ghostly wild boar. Anyone who conjures evil becomes a ghost when he dies. He who creates suffering while he lives suffers in the afterlife. That is why the messengers of heaven are there to destroy the ghosts and why courts in the underworld sit to punish evildoers after their death. Dragons and ghosts and man-eating demons cannot be allowed to roam free to terrify mankind.
>
> Since that time, order and righteousness, peace and contentment have been established. Still, evil spirits take the form of plants. On stormy nights or in the gray dawn when the moon and stars are growing dim, they walk abroad, though invisible to human eyes. Like a cloud of flies, like a pack of pariah dogs, rapacious as wolves, they whirl around and rage like an inferno.
>
> The young man from the Ch'iao family did not realize this when he was alive but deserves no pity in death. The young woman from the family of Fu was lustful in death as in life. Golden Lotus deceitfully used that funerary figurine to lead men astray. They have all three broken the laws, willfully and maliciously. They can expect no mercy. The danger to mankind must be removed, the temptations that lead mankind astray must cease.
>
> The double-peony lantern is to be burned. The evil ones are to be cast into the lowest dungeons of Hell.

He had scarcely pronounced the sentence before it was executed. The three miscreants were dragged away howling and vanished with the magical army.

Shaking his sleeves with a gesture of freeing himself from the memory of evil, the hermit walked off to his mountain retreat. The next day, when the people went to thank him, he had vanished. His simple hut was untenanted. When the people saw this and went to see Mr. Wei to explain it all, they found that he had been struck dumb. He could not speak a word.

—Adapted from Ch'ü (1341?-1427)

FROM THE GREAT CHINESE POET, LI PO

The swift river runs into the sea
And nevermore returns.
Don't you see on the high tower
A white-haired person
Looking sorrowfully into his bright mirror?
In the morning of life his locks
Were like black strands of silk.
In the evening of life they are like snow.
Let us, therefore, while we may,
Taste of all this world's delights.
Do not leave the golden cask of wine
Standing alone by the light of the moon....
I want only the long ecstasy of wine.
I do not desire to awaken....

TAO TE CHING

From Lao Tzu, sixth century BC:

If you learn to handle people
By letting them alone,
Ghosts will not return to haunt you.
Which is not to say there are no ghosts
But that their influence on the living
Has to be regarded as good.
And just taken for granted.
Actually, there is no difference at all
Between the living and the dead.
We are all part of one life force.

BLOODSUCKING GHOSTS OF INDIA

These may properly belong in *The Complete Book of Vampires*, but the Indians say they are ghosts. In any case they are believed to "live" after death by sucking the blood of the living. They are angry because they died violently, by murder or suicide, or were not given proper burial.

YORUBA DEFENSE AGAINST GHOSTS

In Africa, among the Yoruba, if one of a pair of newborn twins dies the mother carries around with her a wooden figure designed to represent the dead child. This not only keeps the living child company but gives the dead one a "body" to inhabit so it will not trouble the living.

Preserving the corpse so that the spirit can visit it is in a number of African cultures a major concern. The spirit without a body can become a ghost.

MONSTERS BREEDING

Non-Western cultures often suggest that certain kinds of supernatural creatures cannot breed, with their own kind or with humans. In the West, however, debates once raged among theologians over whether it was possible for The Devil or demons to breed with humans. Martin Luther, many people already know, was once claimed by the Roman Catholic Church to be the product of sex with The Devil. Seldom or never does anyone suggest that ghosts and humans can breed, or that ghosts enjoy a sex life of their own. The Muslim paradise seems to promise sex after death—Byron dismissed it as "dark eyes and lemonade"—but many other religions do not. Modern movies do feature some lovers returned from the dead.

THE BANANA OR THE MOON?

In Madagascar the folk tell of how our original parents, whom we in The West call Adam and Eve, were asked by God if they wanted to be like the banana or like the moon. The banana tree grows and bears fruit and dies; shoots spring from it so that more banana trees are created. The moon disappears from time to time but always comes back. It does not reproduce, but it never perishes.

Our human parents chose the banana, not the moon. So our lives are brief, but we can bear fruit. From one tree come many trees over time. Death comes to each of us, but we are not cold and sterile like the moon.

AN AFRICAN FOLK TALE

That previous story was from Barbara Stanford's collection in *Myths and Modern Man* (1972). Here is another, this one from the Hottentots. This is the way she tells it, with the comas as quoted and the confusion of *hare* and *rabbit*, but with a powerful message for us all about life after death:

> In the olden days, the moon sent a message to man that "As I die and dying live, so you shall also die and dying live." She asked an insect to carry the message to mankind for her.
>
> The insect started taking the message, but on the way, the hare

caught up with her and asked where she was going. The insect replied that she had a very important message for man.

"You are so slow. Let me take the message," said the hare.

Ancient Greek funeral chorus.

"All right," said the insect.

So the hare ran on to man. But when he arrived, he delivered the message in this way. He said, "The moon has sent this message. When I die, I perish, and when you die, you will also perish altogether."

When the moon found out what the rabbit had done, she hit the rabbit in the nose with a stick. To this day, rabbits have a slit nose, and man believes that when he dies he will perish.

THE ISLANDS OF THE BLESSED

The Happy Hunting Grounds of the Amerindians and the Valhalla of the Scandinavians are known to many today, but the Islands of the Blessed are not so familiar. They also are places where mythology said people went after death, although they are unusual in that few if any spirits were said to bother coming back once they arrived there.

In Greek myth the islands where the dead live in peace and some luxury are first mentioned by Hesiod. He located them well beyond the Pillars of Hercules, way out in The Atlantic, into which, so far as we know, the Greeks never ventured until hundreds of years after Hesiod. It was not until Kolaios of Samos went through the Strait of Gibralta about 620 BC that the Greeks got into that ocean. Even then they did not go far westward.

The Europeans did not reach "beyond the sunset, and the baths of all the western stars" (as Tennyson's Ulysses puts it) until an Irish monk we call St. Brendan sailed westward in the sixth century AD. He is reported to have visited Newfoundland, after which he explored the eastern shores of what is now the United States, finding there a single old Irish monk, like himself, stranded on this continent as a result of an even earlier Celtic adventure on the high seas. Could the Amerindians have picked up the Happy Hunting Grounds from Irish monks who sailed to the west? Or did American aborigines bring those myths eastward, having arrived in North America by crossing from Asia?

St. Brendan is also said to have given Scandinavians impetus for sailing westward. Norsemen made a temporary home in Vineland or what is now Nova Scotia. It was no Happy Hunting Ground or Island of the Blessed, so they did not stay long. Even Iceland or Greenland seemed more hospitable in some ways.

Those places sailors discovered more or less by being blown off course. It may be that they were blown off course on other voyages and struck The Azores or even went all the way to North America. We in the United States today may live in what some people used to think of as lands of the dead, happy hunting grounds, permanent refuges of the heroes of long ago.

REINCARNATION AND ANIMALS

When Mad Cow Disease struck Britain, many cattle had to be destroyed, but there were no religious repercussions, just financial ones. However, Buddhists react differently. When 1.3 million chickens had to be destroyed in Hong Kong in 1998 because of an avian influenza scare, Buddhist monks and nuns offered a week of prayer and meditation. Yong Sing, abbot of the Western Monastery, warned: "Hong Kong will suffer retribution. People and chickens may look different, but they are both alive, and we shouldn't kill things." Are you going to Hell because of your oven roasted chicken?

RATS

Theories of reincarnation suggest that human souls come back in the guise of various animals, even rats. There is a temple in Rajastan (India) of Karni Mata, a woman who lived some 600 years ago and whose clan, it is believed, is reincarnated in rats.

Therefore the temple is full of rats, fed and celebrated by the believers.

BUDDHIST DILEMMA

It takes a scientist like Stephen Chu, who shared the Nobel Prize for physics, to identify the problem he calls "conservation of souls," when it comes to reincarnation.

More and more people are being born, especially in Asia, and if souls are recycled as in Buddhist belief, where are these extra souls to come from?

A DIP IN THE GANGES

Some Hindus believe that a dip in the sacred river Ganges at the time of the *kumbh mela* festival will do you a lot of good. You will be released from the cycle of reincarnation and go to rest after you die. But you must take your dip at Hardwar, Allahabad, Nasik, or Ujjain only. A dip then and there is considered to be worth 18 million dips taken at other times and places.

AVOIDING REINCARNATION

The *Tibetan Book of the Dead* tells you what to do on the 49 levels of consciousness of the *bardo* plane after you die. The separation of the spirit on the *bardo* plane from the corpse takes several days, even if it is facilitated by a *hpho-bo* (extractor of consciousness). Burial then follows, the exact time being determined by an astrologer. The body is trussed up in the fetal position, because the spirit will go on to be reborn into this world. Actually, what deluded humans think of as reality is only illusion, say Tibetans. Life is nothing but an illusion from which we all must escape at last. Some people, however, must go through many incarnations before they become sufficiently detached to reach the stability of paradise.

The religion very much stresses detachment and not worrying about the result of actions. It preaches acceptance and humility, but if you really want to take matters in hand the *Tibetan Book of the Dead* also explains how to avoid rebirth. This useful information is in a section on what may be translated as "the closing of the door of the place and time for rebirth." Some are unwise or unlucky in this, others not.

The southern continent is the only one of the four the religion recognizes that is recommended, but, as you know, people are born elsewhere as well. Of the classes of beings available, *devas* (rather like angels) are best, but if you have to take a human form you are advised to try to be a Brahmin, a priest, and so on. Whenever you enter into human life again you will be given both a task and an opportunity.

If you flunk, you repeat the course.

REVIVING THE CORPSE IN TIBET

This is ill-advised, according to the experts. Tibetan sorcerers attempt this and, it is said, sometimes succeed, but if the corpse is brought back to life and made to do a frantic dance, the sorcerer must bite off its tongue. If he fails to do that the corpse kills the sorcerer.

As in the necromancy of many cultures, bringing back the dead is a very risky business.

WHAT ARE THEY SAYING?

All ghosts speak the same language, and it isn't yours. So says Emmanuel Swedenborg in *The True Christian Religion*:

> There is a universal language, proper to all angels and spirits, which has nothing in common with any language spoken in the world. Every man [and woman], after death, uses this language, for it is implanted in everyone from creation; and therefore throughout the whole spiritual world all can understand one another.

Another of Swedenborg's many odd beliefs is that we are gifted with merely apparent life, all creation is dead, and only God lives. Maybe we all ought to be speaking that one language of the dead right now!

A TALE OF SAVITRI

The Hindus tell the story of Savitri, a princess in India who was the most beautiful and intelligent woman on earth. Indeed, people thought she might

There was a time when kings and anyone else who could afford philanthropy thought to improve their chances of felicity in the afterlife by building charities in this life or endowing charities in their last testaments. Do this in your will, just in case it can help.

be, in her perfection, a goddess. To find a husband suitable for his daughter the king had no small task and, admiring her judgment, he turned to her and said, "You must find a husband for yourself."

So Savitri set out to find a mate and soon returned with Satyavan, a kind man whom she found looking after his blind father.

"You have made a wise choice," the sage Narada told the princess. "The father of Satyavan is a king from whom his enemies have taken both his kingdom and his sight, but he rejoices in his wonderful son. Unfortunately," the sage added, "Satyavan is destined to die exactly one year from today."

But Savitri said she would rather be married to Satyavan for one year than to anyone else for a long lifetime, so they were wed, and they lived happily together for a year.

On the day on which the prophecy said Satyavan was to die, Savitri took him to the very forest where she had first found him. As they walked through the forest, Satyavan suddenly felt faint and fell down. Savitri cradled his head in her lap and began to pray.

Soon Yama, the god of death, appeared. Yama extracted the soul of Satyavan from his body and went off to take it to the Land of the Dead. Savitri followed, but soon Yama spied her and to her he said: "Do not attempt to follow me to the Land of the Dead. It is for you to go back to the living and there to arrange the burial of the corpse of Satyavan."

"I will not leave my husband," she replied. "That dead body back there is not my husband. You have the soul of my husband with you, so I shall stay with you."

"You are a brave and wise woman," Yama replied, "and I am moved to give you anything you like with one single exception: I shall not give you back the life of your husband."

"Please give Satyavan's father back his sight, then," said Savitri.

Yama replied, "I shall grant your wish, but I wish you would stop following me."

"Oh, no," replied Savitri, "for I have always been told to keep the best company possible and you are surely the best company because in the end everyone goes with you."

Yama was flattered by this remark, and he offered Savitri another wish, any wish but that her husband live again.

"My father the king," she said, "loves me but has always longed for a son and heir, so I wish you would give him a son."

"I am the god of death and not of life," said Yama, "but I promised you your wish and you shall have it and your father shall have a son. He shall have many sons, if you will please stop following me."

"But there is so much I can learn from you who has seen so much," replied Savitri.

"Where among mortals could I learn what so powerful a god must know?"

Flattered once more, Yama offered her still another wish. Any wish but the return to life of Satyavan.

"In that case, I myself would like to have many sons."

"Then so you shall," said Yama. "Now stop following me. You bother me, although I must confess you are the boldest and most faithful wife I have ever encountered."

"Indeed I am the most faithful wife, and I will lie with no other man except my husband. Now remember that you promised me many sons, and if I do not bear them for Satyavan, I ask you: For whom shall I bear them? How can you make your promise good?"

"I give up," said Yama, smiling as a god of death seldom smiles. "In all my work I have never returned to the living a soul I have taken for the Land of the Dead, but you compel me to give you back your husband, or go back on my solemn promise."

And so Yama released the soul of Satyavan, and Satyavan and his shrewd and steadfast wife Savitri lived happily together again. And she bore him many sons, creating much life with the man she had brought back from the dead.

MORE ON SPEAKING OF THE DEAD

Sir James Frazer in *The Golden Bough* speaks of the taboo regarding the use of the names of the dead in Africa and Australia, Armenia, the Americas, India and among the Ainus of Japan and many other peoples. The taboo was almost universal among the Amerindians here. Circumlocutions such as "that one" or references involving relatives and so on substitute for the name of the deceased. But the strangest way thought to avoid attracting a ghost may be that found among the natives of the Lower Murray River by G. F. Angas (*Savage Life and Scenes in Australia and New Zealand*, 1847). The natives there carefully avoid mentioning the name of a dead person "but if they are compelled to do so, they pronounce it in a very low whisper, so faint that they imagine the spirit cannot hear their voice."

GOSES: A PERSON WHO CANNOT GIVE UP THE GHOST

From Jonathan Rosen, "The Talmud and the Internet," in *The American Scholar* (Spring 1998, 49), a tale of the virtue of letting the dead depart:

> The Talmud tells a story about a great Rabbi who is dying. He has become a *goses*, but he cannot die because outside his hut all his students are praying for him to live, and this is distracting his soul. A woman climbs to the roof of the Rabbi's hut and hurls a clay vessel to the ground. The sound diverts the students, who stop praying. In that moment, the Rabbi dies and his soul goes to heaven.

The woman too, says the Talmud, has guaranteed her place in the world to come.

A GHOST STORY FROM SOUTH AFRICA

Jesse Adelaide Middleton had such success with her first book that she turned out another, and from the second, *Another Grey Ghost Book*, here is a tale, much briefer that her "Wynyard Ghost Story." She says she heard it from a lady who knew the "well-known commissioner" of the tale and heard it from him and his wife. Ms. Middleton called it "At a Boer Farm." It is the kind of ghost story that, though it stands or falls on the uncorroborated testimony of a single person, people like to believe and repeat. Lots of people say, "I saw a ghost." Can you believe them? Do you believe this story that follows? Why? Or why not?

Going on his rounds, a well-known commissioner in South Africa stopped his horse at the gate of a farm at which he had often stayed before.

He had become very friendly with Johan Schmidt, the Boer farmer who owned the farm, and they often had long talks together over their pipes in the cool of the evening.

The farmer was not at all happy in his domestic affairs. His wife often left him, but each time he took her back and they lived together as before. She was, however, a perpetual worry to him. The commissioner was aware of this fact and so, indeed, was everybody in the neighborhood.

When the Englishman arrived there was nobody at home but,

An old woodcut shows witches digging up the corpse of a dead baby to make devilish potions. Parts of dead humans and animals (presumably with some idea they still contained some spirit) were frequently used in magical recipes.

being on a friendly footing, and having his native servant with him, he entered the house and made himself at home. The servant attended to him, and he sat down in the veranda and smoked while waiting for somebody to return.

Presently the farmer came in, evidently much perturbed, and, after greeting him, said, "Have you seen my wife? Is she here? She has gone off again."

"I have not seen anybody," said the commissioner, "but I knew you would not mind my making myself at home."

"Oh no, certainly not," said the farmer; "do, please, make yourself quite comfortable."

They talked for a little while, and then Schmidt said he must go and look for his wife. He went out, and the commissioner stayed all night alone at the farm, and in the morning got on his horse and rode away.

He next called at a little hotel some miles off and stopped there for refreshment. While having lunch, as he knew the people who kept it very well and knew that they were aware of the state of domestic affairs at the farm, he said to his host and hostess—

"Schmidt is in great trouble again; his wife has gone off once more. Have you, by any chance, seen anything of her?"

"*Schmidt!*" they exclaimed. "Why, he died last week and was buried!"

"But I stayed last night at the farm, and saw him and talked with him," said the commissioner, quite aghast.

Thereupon they gave him all details, and the affair so shocked him that he never really got over it. The farmer, it seems, had been worrying greatly about his wife, who had gone off again at the time of his death, and his spirit had returned to the house to seek her.

WORLDWIDE

Foreign books on our subject are almost as numerous as the ones we note in English. Here are a few in foreign language and English to compare and contrast.

> Giorgio Batini, *Italia a mezzanotte* (Italy at Midnight, ghost lore, 1968)
> Jonas Balys, *Dvasios ir zmonès* (Ghosts and Men, Lithuania 1951)
> Charles F. Emmons, *Chinese Ghosts and ESP* (1982)
> Hermann Hilde, *Geistersagen und Geisterglauben im Saarland* (ghost lore in a part of Germany)
> Amiyakumára Cakrabartí, *Alaukika galpera sankalana* (Bengali ghost stories, 1965)
> James Noël McHugh, *Hantu Hantu* (ghosts in Malaysia, 1959)
> Yoshie Ogasa, *Nihon no yokai densetsu* (Japanese ghost stories, 1966)
> Francis Thompson, *The Ghosts, Spirits, and Spectres of Scotland* (1973)

THE EGYPTIAN BOOK OF THE DEAD

This book, quite popular in the sixties and afterwards in certain hippie as well as more formal circles, despite having almost 200 chapters of very obscure directions, gives rituals not only for sending the dead happily on their way but also suggests that actions may be necessary to prevent them from coming back. It tells you what to do.

Egyptians, as you will recall, went to extraordinary lengths to preserve dead bodies so that the *ka* (or we might say ghost) of the person could come back to visit its former residence. Properly prepared, successful in passing the judgment after death, the dead Egyptian soul was rewarded by Ra and, each of his limbs and parts becoming one with a god of the Egyptian Pantheon, at last was himself incorporated into Ra himself.

From Sir E. A. Wallis Budge's translation of *The Book of the Dead* here is a speech of Ra in *Egyptian Religion* (1899): "Thou shalt come forth into heaven, thou shalt pass over the sky, thou shalt be joined unto the starry deities." This had little or nothing to do with anything "Seth" thought up lately or Beat riffs on *The Book of the Dead*.

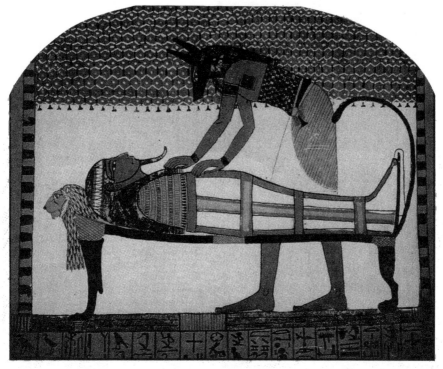

Anubis, or a priest wearing a mask to call on that god's powers, ministers to an Egyptian mummy. The body has been preserved so that the soul may revisit it.

An early nineteenth-century engraving of the house in Cock Lane which all London was talking about in 1762.

5

The Poltergeist

NOISY GHOSTS

To this point we have encountered noisy ghosts, or "things that go bump in the night." But there is a special class of noisy ghosts which we call poltergeists. They are not content simply to be apparitions and scare people—they are determined to throw things around and generally cause a ruckus. They have been of special interest to the general public because of their rambunctious nature. They have, with their knockings, been the foundation of Spiritualism, and they fascinate psychologists because they seem somehow to be connected to the energies surrounding teenage girls.

This chapter is devoted to them. You will also hear of them in connection with the cinema; they are naturals (supernaturals?) for movie effects.

THE BELL WITCH

Perhaps the only monument to a poltergeist anywhere, certainly the only official historical marker to a witch in the United States, is to be found on a Tennessee highway. It reads:

BELL WITCH

To the north was the farm of
John Bell, an early, prominent
settler from North Carolina.
According to legend, his family

was harried during the early
nineteenth century by the
famous Bell Witch. She kept the
household in turmoil, assaulted
Bell, and drove off Bettery Bell's
suitor. Even Andrew Jackson
who came to investigate,
retreated to Nashville after
his coach wheels stopped
mysteriously. Many visitors
to the house saw the furniture
crash about them and heard
her shriek, sing, and curse.

The witch (named Kate Batts) carried on for four years, then announced she would be back after seven more. Her visit in 1828, however, was short. John Bell's eldest son said the witch had threatened to haunt his descendants in 107 years, but in 1935 no such activity took place. Today the witch's cave, on a bluff over the Red River, can still be visited. The poltergeist, who expressed such sentiments as "I can't stand the smell of a nigger," was not only dangerous but politically incorrect, and more sensational stories since have made the Bell Witch otherwise passé. There are several books on the Bell Witch, the old one by M. V. Ingram (1894) being probably the best but now hard to find.

Since 1846 members of the Bell clan have been riding this hobbyhorse. Charles Bailey Bell published his version of The Bell Witch, *A Mysterious Spirit*, in 1934 (reprinted 1972). As poltergeist stories go, it is not really remarkable, but it is authentic Americana. Moreover, it is better documented than most cases, among the earliest of which was one in 1682 of a "stone-throwing devil" investigated by the Secretary of the Province of New Hampshire, Richard Chamberlain (says Joe Nickell in *Entities*, 1995) or the Newberry "Daemon" in Massachusetts reported by the Rev. Increase Mather in *An Essay for the Recording of Illustrious Providences* (1684), which Nickell treats with admirable judiciousness.

Also, the Bell Witch never had a confession of trickery, as did the Fox Sisters' disturbances (Margaret Fox later explained it was "to terrify our dear mother"), those in Atlanta, Georgia in 1883 by Lulu Hurst (who had a career on the stage talking about her life), students torturing a teacher in Stark County, North Dakota in 1944, little Joyce Saunders in Louisville, Kentucky in 1951, and many, many others, in America as well as elsewhere.

Joe Nickell points out that the lie-detector test, or just the threat of one, seems to be even more effective than exorcism; it is the new way to make poltergeist complaints stop abruptly. It looks as if most, if not all, cases of poltergeist action can be traced, as Frank Podmore said way back in Victorian times, to disturbed or mischievous children, not ghosts, not demons.

THE NOISIEST GHOSTS

It was presumably spirits that old Kate Batt used to torture John Bell and his family and throw their furniture around. We call these disturbed and disturbing spirits by the German name, *Poltergeist* ("rattling ghost"). *Polter* in German is related to noisy wedding–evening celebrations, our chivaree, sort of. The ghosts who make a lot of noise and bother generally do their mischief in houses where there are adolescents, usually young girls, and some psychic experts claim that the adolescents act as lightning rods to attract these spirits, becoming some sort of mediums to them. Poltergeists are likewise attracted to anyone who is undergoing puberty, is sexually frustrated, or is in a state of sex-starved transcendence, like saints and nuns.

The Freudians say that sex explains these odd goings-on. It's all very human. Poltergeists differ from devils and demons in that they are ghosts of human beings, but when—as the movies tell us—they enter into toys and dolls and other objects to terrorize, it is difficult to tell whether they are diabolical or ghostly. In any case, the effect is the same.

Poltergeist activity has produced some of the oddest theories in the whole strange literature of superstition. One example from the useful *Encyclopedia of Occultism and Parapsychology* (3rd ed., 1991):

> To explain the crashing noises without physical source, such as the sounds of breaking crockery afterwards found intact, Adolphe d'Assier put forward an extraordinary theory in his book *Posthumous Humanity* (1887). He suggested that inanimate objects also possess a double, phantasmal image[,] and that it is this duplicate which is flung by the poltergeist.

Some parapsychologists assert that poltergeist activity requires telekinetic forces be unleashed by both a dead spirit and a living one, working together, even if this is unknown to the living person.

ANGRY GHOSTS

Modern parapsychologists worry about whether the mind can influence things outside the body. They bring that consideration into the discussion of poltergeists, but maybe ghosts get angry simply because they are being disturbed. Poltergeists are known for their bad tempers and deliberate lies and scorn for human beings. In this they resemble traditional demons, imps, and occasional trolls.

Heliodorus may have given us some explanation as early as the third or fourth century AD. Perhaps following the lead of first-century Lucian,

Heliodorus said that ghosts absolutely hate to be disturbed! *R.I.P.*

Ghosts that do physical harm are somewhat akin to destructive poltergeists. There's a ghost of a boy in Jon Stephen Fink's *If He Lived* (1997) that's a nasty piece of work. Reviewing the novel in *TLS* (21 February 1997, 22), Stephen Poole writes that "it will be a strong-minded reader who, reading alone in the early hours of the morning, does not pay slightly more nervous attention than usual to every creak of the timber, every rattle of the window pane." Vicious ghosts frighten us, but people love thrills and eagerly seek them out in popular entertainments.

THEOPHRASTUS BOMBASTUS VON HOHENHEIM'S THEORY

Somehow this German scientist, who called himself "Paracelsus" to boast he was the equal of the great Greek Physician, Celsus, keeps getting into these books of mine. People do, however, like to see his name. This time we cite him in relation to what he called *pulsatio mortuorum*, mysterious rappings which he took as signs of someone's imminent death.

FRANÇOIS PERRAULT

This Frenchman told a tale of "The Devil in Mascon" appearing to him, with mysterious rappings. He told it to the Irish scientist Robert Boyle, youngest "son to the earl of Cork and father of modern chemistry." Boyle, always interested in the curious, persuaded Perrault to publish. Thus we acquired one of the earliest detailed reports of alleged poltergeist activity. There are passing references in classical literature but this French seventeenth-century writer really deserves a prime place in the popular imagination.

THE SCOTTISH VERDICT

In the famous Eleventh Edition of the *Encyclopaedia Britannica*, the entry on "Poltergeist" contains this passage:

> On the theory that there exist "mysterious agencies" which now and then produce the [poltergeist] phenomena, we may ask what these agencies can possibly be? But no answer worthy of consideration has ever been given to this question. The usual reply is that some unknown but intelligent force is disengaged from the personality of the apparent medium. This apparent medium need not be present; he or she may be far away. The Highlanders attribute many poltergeist phenomena, inexplicable noises, sounds of viewless [invisible] feet that pass, and so forth to *tàradh*, and influence exerted unconsciously by unduly strong wishes on the part of a person at a distance. The phrase *falbh air farsaing* ("going uncontrolled") is also used. [Campbell, *Witchcraft and Second Sight in the*

Scottish Highlands, 1902, pp. 144-147]. The present writer [Andrew Lang, author of *The Book of Dreams and Ghosts* and famous collections of fairy tales] is well acquainted with cases attributed to *tàradh*, in a house where he has often been a guest. They excite no alarm, their cause being well understood. We may call this kind of thing *telethorby*, a racket produced from a distance... . It may be worthwhile to note that the phenomena are often regarded as death-warning.

In Scandinavia this will-at-a-distance superstition has also been found. August Strindberg has one of his characters believing that he may have been guilty of another person's death by willing it, and Strindberg himself appears to have held this belief. This connects the theory more with malevolent witchcraft than the death warnings of the banshee, because the death is willed, not simply announced. Note that the *tàradh* can be not a ghost but the errant spirit of a living human being. Lang believed that "many a so-called 'ghost' may be merely the *tàradh* of a living person."

LILITH

This, according to tradition, was the name of the first wife of Adam. She was an evil, rapacious creature. The name *Lilith*, which is sometimes employed in vampire stories, is one of those Babylonian things (in this case *Lilátu*) that the Jews took over to create their own demonology. In *Isaiah*, Lilith is a bloodthirsty predator of the night. Even the Hebrew word for "demon" (*shéd*) is a borrowing from the Babylonians, where Hebrews also got the idea of wings on angels and many other concepts of good and evil. With post-exilic Judaism came the concept of Satan ("The Adversary") as head of all the evil spirits, later Sammael.

HOLY HELP

Cyprian's hagiography of St. Cæsarius of Arles claims that in AD 530 the saint drove off a poltergeist with holy water. This is a remedy still tried.

The deacon Helpidius, physician to Theodoric, king of the Ostrogoths, complained of showers of stones—inside his house. St. Cæsarius solved his problem. Whether the problem was a demon or a poltergeist is unclear. Father Thurston in *Ghosts and Poltergeists* (1953) comments that at that period "all upsetting disturbances were ascribed to satanic agency." See *Monumenta Germaniæ historia: Scriptores rerum Merovingicarum* (Monuments of the History of the Germans: Writings about Merovingian Matters) III:473.

In *Bibliotheca rerum Germanicarum* (Library of German Matters) VI:29, we find in the life of St. Willibrord by Alcuin (735-804) the following story. It seems to involve a demon, not a poltergeist. It certainly is designed to increase faith in holy water's efficacy.

A certain father of a family and his household suffered grievous trials from a mocking demon.... On a sudden he used to carry off food, clothing, and other necessary things and throw them into the fire. He even took a little child while it was lying in bed between the father and the mother, they being fast asleep, and threw it into the fire. But the parents, being aroused by the infant's wailing, were able to rescue it, though only just in time. The outrages which the family endured from this horrible spirit took many forms. Neither could it be driven out by any of the priests, until the holy bishop at the father's request sent him some water which he himself had blessed. He directed that all the household gear should be taken out of their dwelling and sprinkled with this water, for he foresaw in spirit that the house itself was about to perish in flames. These injunctions having been complied with, a fire, which broke out in the place where the bed had stood, attacked the empty building and entirely consumed it. When, however, another house was built on the same site and blessed with holy water, there was no recurrence of the trouble previously experienced.

WHERE TO TURN FOR HELP

In Britain, Harry Price was one of the leading poltergeist investigators, but not an academic. In America we have Professor Daniel Baer, Boston College, who investigates the phenomena. He is profiled by Joseph P. Kahn in "Professor Poltergeist," (*Boston Globe*, 31 October 1991, 81). Every Halloween there is a glut of stories about experts and pseudo-experts on the occult. This one seems to know his business.

What you want to avoid are ignorant, so-called experts. Ours is a world in which one can write a book and instantly become in a wider sense "the guy who wrote the book" on any subject. There is in my local newspaper an advertisement for telephone psychics. The ad promises anyone can earn hundreds of dollars a week at this and offers to give you the few hours' training they say you will need.

One ghostbuster I happen to know used to work in a gas station.

An astrologer I know bought a paperback on "sun signs" and changed her name for business and soon was able to support herself and leave her husband.

And a much-employed psychic investigator I know turned to this work with no experience except in a custom frame shop and subsequently in a federal prison, where he served a fairly brief sentence for child molesting.

If you think you have angry spirits throwing heavy objects, you need competent help. Even the church may not offer exorcism; their specialty is demons and possessions, and poltergeists are not demons nor the victims possessed. For free I'll give you this helpful hint: move all teenagers (especially the girls) out of your house. Send them to camp or to visit relatives. See what happens to disturbances in your home. Actually, even if you do not experience poltergeist activity, you may want to do this from time to time anyway.

BATTLES LONG AGO

It may be that the noisiest ghosts are those which fight great battles of the past over and over in the skies. The ghost of an earl of Stafford is said to have appeared to Charles I the night before the defeat at Naseby and warned him to avoid the battle. Charles fought it and lost, and the troops of ghosts are reported to have fought Naseby over and over thereafter.

The noisiest on record is the poltergeist show which repeated the Battle of Edgehill in the English Civil War. Charles I sent investigators to the scene, but I can find no record of their report.

THE CURÉ OF CIDEVILLE

It was 1849 and the French were beginning to take a renewed interest in spirits. *La Gazette des Tribuneaux* (Gazette of the Courts) reported three weeks of flying projectiles that demolished a house near the rue des Grès in Paris. The provinces were not to be left out of the headlines, as we see from a case from Seine Inferieur. The parish

The couple on the left are reacting to their servant, Adolphine Benoît, creating poltergeist activity in nineteenth-century France.

priest of a small French village there was taken to court in 1849 by a shepherd named Thorel for having denounced Thorel as a sorcerer. The curé replied that Thorel was a notorious sorcerer and had confessed as much to him.

Thorel was certainly the follower of a sorcerer whom the curé prevented from treating one of the parishioners. That sorcerer had been sent to jail, vowing vengeance. It was less that clear that Thorel was responsible for the poltergeist in the abbey. Two little boys testified that Thorel had placed a hand on their heads and muttered strange words, after which, when they went back to the abbey, malicious poltergeist hauntings broke out. It seemed that the smoke and fires of hell had been loosed and spirits were conversing by means of rappings. When the little boys left the abbey in 1851, all disturbances ceased. All that came of the trial was that Thorel was pretty much established as the sorcerer the curé had said he was, though Thorel blamed the sorcerer (who was then in jail) for the events.

SCREAMING SKULLS

There are many stories in England of eccentrics who demanded that their heads be detached from their bodies and kept in the front hall or some other prominent place in the house as a (grisly) relic. Any attempt to put them out of sight led to fearsome screaming. The head of Theophilus Brome has been kept in a cabinet in the hall of Higher Chilton Farm, in Somerset, for a couple of hundred years. Around Lake Windemere the Phillipsons used to have two skulls, the Calgath Skulls, which refused to be destroyed, but they and their legend seem to have disappeared now. "They were thrown out, burned, and even ground to powder," writes one enthusiast, "but they always returned to the niche in the staircase."

Removing any of these screaming skulls from their houses was supposed to start a run of poltergeist activity and bring about general bad luck.

THE DRUMMER OF TEDWORTH

If you have ever been driven near to distraction by a small child with a drum or other noisy toy you can appreciate the problems of John Mompesson.

His seventeenth-century house was infested for a couple of years with a demon drummer, a poltergeist of some sort, ghost or devil. Joseph Glanvill (1636-1680) told the story with all seriousness in his philosophical defense of belief in witchcraft, *Sadducismus triumphatus* (1666). In this case, the phantom drummer was trying to attain at least one of the two most frequent goals of poltergeist activity, attention and revenge.

It was 1661 and Mompesson, a magistrate, was bothered by persistent drumming in the street of the village of Ludgershall (Wiltshire). The cause was a vagrant named William Drury, who was begging with false papers. Mompesson ordered him held for trial and took away his drum. Drury escaped (or was let go by the constable and told to move on) but Mompesson had the drum, and when it arrived at Mompesson's house in Tedworth all hell broke loose. There were loud and repeated knockings, drumbeats, scratching and other noises, a sulfurous smell, destruction of property, and injury to horses. Dr. Glanvill investigated. He was amazed.

Then in 1663 William Drury appeared again, arrested for stealing a pig in Gloucester. He was questioned about the poltergeist at Tedworth and admitted that he had "plagued" Mompesson and said Mompesson would never have a moment's peace until Drury got back his drum.

Tried for witchcraft on the basis of this statement, Drury stated he had studied magic in some "Gallant Books." The court at Salisbury convicted him. After the exposure of "The Witch-Finder General" Matthew Hopkins a couple of decades before, people were wary of burning people at the stake for witchcraft in England. So Drury was sentenced to transportation, which meant simply that he was shipped out of the country. Once Drury was out of the country, the poltergeist activity ceased. But he returned, and it resumed. The phantom drumming became one of the most talked about events of its time.

POLTERGEISTS IN POPULAR CULTURE

A blockbuster novel, as a hit movie, and as fodder for television, Stephen King's *The Shining* brought an army of poltergeists in scary makeup to wide public attention. Overlook the improbabilities of the snowbound Overlook Hotel in Colorado, the scene of the frightening action. It is a deserted resort with magnificent antique furniture, modern television, but no telephone to call 911. It burns down because the Good Guys decide to flee rather than turn off the boiler, but the author assures us, to coin a phrase, "all's well that ends well." The Colorado Phoenix Co. will rebuild. Need we fear a sequel?

SWISS FUSS

In 1860-1862, so terrific and persistent were the poltergeist manifestations in the ancestral home of the Holler family at Staus that the husband and wife and their seven children became the targets of the curiosity of hundreds of people. Theirs must rank as one of the best reported poltergeist cases of all time. When an investigation committee removed the family from the house for almost a week and checked the house with great care, no activity was observed; when the family moved back in the whole business started up again. In the end, the Holler family had to leave the house for good. Who was pleased with that result, and why? These things were never determined.

All that is clear is that if one or more of the children were responsible, they were extremely clever and determined. There may be in this case some interesting evidence regarding the power of suggestion or mass delusion. The works of L. L. Vasiliev on telepathy and suggestion are useful.

However, we have to be careful that we do not dismiss a case more readily because there is a great deal of testimony from witnesses.

Doubting an unsubstantiated personal report is one thing. Calling into question what hundreds of people say they have experienced in groups of different sizes on different occasions is another. Likewise we must remember that more than one person can be involved in fakery. In Windsor, in a case Hereward Carrington details in *Personal Experiences in Spiritualism* (1928), and which he proved to be fakery, a large number of people decided to "play a prank on an old judge." But the judge still clung to his conviction that the Windsor Poltergeist was real!

What I find most interesting of all about parapsychology is that reports that some people dismiss as obvious fraud can make true believers even stronger in their convictions. On both sides there seems to be a great deal of resistance to reaching conclusions that everyone must accept. One hears so often the very British phrase, "I don't want to know." Or the American cliché: "Don't confuse me with the facts; my mind is made up."

POLTERGEIST IN BRAZIL

Don Cid de Ulhoa Centro and his family were pestered by a poltergeist in São Paulo in 1959 to the extent that they had to call in an exorcist. A Roman Catholic priest conducted three exorcisms, but the strange phenomena continued unabated. At one point an egg which had been placed in the refrigerator suddenly dropped—slowly floated, really—to the floor. When picked up it was uncracked, and still cool.

After forty days the phenomena suddenly stopped. They remain totally unexplained. David C. Knight includes the story in his *The Moving Coffins* (1983). I think I have the explanation of the much noted Caribbean moving coffins. I think water got into the tomb and they floated around. But the floating egg leaves me baffled.

THE RAPPING NUN

People often assume that spirits allegedly communicating by rapping first were heard of when the Fox Sisters jump-started Spiritualism by cracking their joints secretly, as it turned out. But many stories of spirits rapping were told long before that, and even in rural upstate New York the Fox Sisters may have heard of this phenomenon. They may also have heard how much publicity these things generated.

A sixteenth-century case involved a nun called Alix de Telieux, who went bad and ran off with stolen jewels from the convent of St. Peter in Lyon. She died, in poverty and misery, in 1524. That same year another nun in that convent, Antoinette, woke up thinking she had just been blessed and kissed by someone. Another time she was swept up into the air.

Authorities were called in. The almoner to François I, Adrien de Montalembert, undertook to speak with the spirit and by a code of raps learned from it where Alix had been buried, that she wanted to be exhumed and buried in the convent graveyard (which was done), and that she knew all sorts of secrets about sister Antoinette and Montalembert himself. Montalembert had an eyewitness account of the matter and Cardinal Tencin looked into the case. The Church did not deny strange things were going on, but neither could it stop them.

Eventually Sister Alix manifested herself as a ghost to Sister Antoinette and announced she was departing. She was never seen or heard of again.

Elsewhere in this series I have had occasion to cast some doubt on the veracity of nuns reporting supernatural experiences in this period. A number of them made accusations of demonic possession which caused uproars in France, particularly when sexual scandals surfaced. In this case, Andrew Lang, who recounts the story in *Cock Lane and Common Sense* (1894), asserts that the report has "an agreeable air of good faith." While, as with most ghost and poltergeist stories, we are left with very little explanation not only of how the ghost was raised but what, if anything, it wished to accomplish by frightening and sometimes torturing a victim, this report was in its day not at all doubted and still may command belief in some people.

What do we learn about the afterlife from this episode? For one thing, maybe personality persists after death, which many people yearn to be true. For another, those who committed crimes in life may rest uneasily in death and may even come back to atone for their sins. Still more, ghosts seem to be worried about how and where they are buried; a botched funeral may produce a walking spirit. Finally, ghosts can be visible or invisible to the living and can communicate with them by raps or even by speech, or so some people report.

POLTERGEISTS CAN SPEAK FINNISH

Finnish is in the Finno-Ugric group of Uralic languages, the Ugric part signifying that Hungarian joins with Finnish in constituting something outside the general run of European languages. There are more than five million speakers of Finnish, most of them, naturally, in Finland, though there are expatriate Finns in the United States, Canada, Australia, and elsewhere, and even some speakers of the closely-related language Karelian in the former Soviet Union. Among the strangest speakers of Finnish are the Finnish poltergeists reported to have spoken in Kylmänoja, c.1850, in Hemmilä in 1873, and in Raisio in 1883.

Most poltergeists in Finland or elsewhere do not communicate much but content themselves with throwing things and, common in Finland among these angry spirits, burning down buildings.

Finnish poltergeists are also reported to have made other auditory demonstrations, not only the traditional knocking in answer to questions but whistling, imitating musical instruments, mimicking the sawing of wood, the clinking of coins, the sounds of brooms sweeping floors, and so on.

If you happen to be able to command Finnish, you can read all about such disturbances in these and other sources:

Herman Arola, *Lehtimäen asukkaita* (1965)
Martti Haavio, *Suomalaiset kodinhaltitat* (1942)
Pekka Laakspnen, *Parkanon seuden kertomusperinnettä* (1971)
Samuli Paulaharju, *Lapin muisteluksia* (1922)
Mirjami Pihlaja, *Isojoen pitäjän kirja* (1984)
Jaakko Tamminen, *Luksanniemen pirusta, joka ihmeellisella tavalta kujeili* (1887)

THE POLTERGEIST OF THE SAVANNAH

Montague Summers in *The Vampire in Europe* (1929) tells a tale about a mysterious force that was neither a vampire nor in Europe, but an American poltergeist. The story was first reported in the *San Francisco Examiner* (Summers says) for 29 November 1891.

The Walsingham family was at dinner in their house beside the Savannah river (in Oakville, Summers says) when blood began to drip onto the table from the ceiling. The family had endured the mysterious ringing of bells and throwing around of furniture ever since they moved into the house, but this was too much—especially when they examined the room above and, taking up the carpet, found a thin film of dust on an absolutely dry floor.

The Walsinghams promptly decamped. A young man who braved a stay one night in the haunted house had his lamp and fire put out and was severely beaten up by invisible hands.

Summers suspected "a phantom of the vampire family" because the young man was thereafter for quite a while in a very weakened condition, as if he had lost a lot of blood. But there were no marks of fangs, so I call it a poltergeist manifestation.

POLTERGEISTS IN AFRICA

Unruly and angry spirits who cause commotions and damage are not at all uncommon in the world of African superstition. Many peoples have their individual tales of the poltergeist. He (it is usually a he) is said to be riled up about an unpleasant end of some sort, an inadequate burial, or being ignored by his survivors.

He can have sex with his former spouse—which is fatal to her—or he can content himself with throwing around kitchen utensils, dulling the edges of weapons, and (among the Ila of Zambia, for instance) knocking women's bundles off their heads. Some African poltergeists act silly. Others are very dangerous.

Poltergeists are comparatively common, if reports are to be credited, all over sub-Saharan Africa. They appear to be more bloodthirsty than poltergeists reported in the works of European writers such as Raymond Bayless (1967). For the politer British variety, see J. Hayward's "Knock! Knock! Who's There!" in *The Spectator* 165 (12 July 1940), 33.

It is sometimes difficult to distinguish between the ravaging poltergeist of Africa and the evil demons and plagues called up by witch doctors. Any poltergeist should once have been a live human being.

AN EARLY POLTERGEIST IN GERMANY

Hrabanus Maurus, who was not German, and other German writers of the ninth century may be more important, not to mention French ones such as Nithard, or Anglo-Saxon chroniclers, but in the obscure reports of the German writer Siegebert there is a good poltergeist story. It goes like this, in my translation:

> This year [AD 858] there appeared in the diocese of Mentez a spirit which initially showed itself by throwing things and beating against the walls of houses as if with a huge hammer. Then it undertook to speak up and divulge secrets and exposed the perpetrators of several thefts and other crimes likely to disturb the neighborhood. In the end it vented its hatred against one particular person and incessantly persecuted him, denouncing him to his neighbors as the cause of God's anger against the whole town. The spirit never ceased to assail this unfortunate, tormenting him without pause, burning all the grain in his barns, setting fire to any place he happened to go. The clergy undertook to banish the spirit through exorcism, incantations, holy water—to which the spirit responded with rains of stones that wounded several of the priests. They having fled, the spirit was heard to say that he had once been compelled to hide in the cowl of a priest who had assaulted the daughter of one of the leading men in the town. The spirit behaved in this disruptive way for three years altogether and before it was done every house in the town had been set on fire.

THE ROSENHEIM CASE

One Anna S. was the focal point of a mysterious case in 1967. It involved flashing lights, ringing telephones, rotating pictures, and other supposed poltergeist activity in a business office in Rosenheim, in Bavaria. Hans Bender of the *Institut für Grenzgebeiete der Psychologie* reports the story in *Proceedings of the Parapsychological Association* 5 (1968) 31-33, and F. Karger and G. Zicha also commented on the case, 33-35. At one point the unattended telephone was dialing numbers faster than any human could—and calling for the time announcement forty or fifty times in a row.

LOOK UP, LOOK OUT

Poltergeist activity is said to begin sometimes with water or oil inexplicably dripping from the ceiling. Then things begin to fly around and get broken and the activity spreads from one room to the other.

GREMLINS

This was the name the Royal Air Force gave in World War II to alleged malicious and invisible little creatures who, like poltergeists, make things malfunction, get lost, and seem to attack the user.

WHERE POLTERGEISTS LIVE

In Germany, of course, where their very name came from. One of the earliest reports of a poltergeist is in *Annalesa Fuldenses* and describes an attack on a farmer at Bingen am Rhine. In France, disgraced nun Alix de Telieux, in 1524 was the first to communicate from The Other Side by a system of raps, as you have heard. Italy, and Spain, to a lesser extent, also began to report poltergeists. In Britain (which cherishes its ghosts) and in the United States (whose media loves to feed on sensational events) gradually they entered the public imagination. Now everyone has heard of poltergeist movies.

But sober Swedes and calm Canadians also have reported the common hails of stones, dragging of heavy objects, rattling of chains, and flying household objects associated with rowdy spirits, and even the breaking of dishes, the popping of corks, the destruction of books, and the heavy tread of invisible beings. These troublemakers also like to throw open windows, play with electricity and other utilities, overturn tables, and slam doors.

There is a good side to a place having the reputation of being haunted, even infested with a poltergeist. In John Ashbery and James Schuyler's *A Nest of Ninnies* (1969), a character says, "My house in Vermont was cheap partly because there is supposed to be a ghost in it—that of a virgin who likes to emit hair-raising groans. But I told the agent, 'You do not frighten one nurtured on Descartes and Auguste Comte.'"

If you can stand the noise, you may be able to pick up real estate inexpensively if you don't mind sharing the premises with a poltergeist. So long as it doesn't break expensive furniture, a poltergeist, like any resident or visiting spirit, guarantees a bargain.

POSSIBLE POLTERGEISTS IN PURITAN NEW ENGLAND

Increase Mather (1639-1723), clergyman, prolific writer, and president of Harvard, wrote "Concerning Things Preternatural Which Have Happened in New England" in the fifth chapter of his immensely influential *Essay for the Recording of Illustrious Providences:*

> Inasmuch as things which are preternatural, and not accomplished without diabolical operation, do more rarely happen, it is pity but that they should be observed. Several accidents of that kind have happened in New England, which I shall here faithfully relate, so far as I have been able to come unto the knowledge of them....
>
> As there have been several persons vexed with evil spirits, so diverse houses have been woefully haunted by them. In the year 1679, the house of William Morse, in Newberry in New England, was strangely disquieted by a demon. After those troubles began, he did, by the advice of friends, write down the particulars of those unusual accidents. And the account which he giveth thereof is as followeth:—
>
> ON DECEMBER 3, in the night time, he and his wife heard a noise upon the roof of their house, as if sticks and stones had been thrown against it with great violence; whereupon he rose out of his bed, but could see nothing. Locking the doors fast, he returned to bed again. About midnight they heard a hog making a great noise in the house, so that the man rose again, and found a great hog in the house; the door being shut, but upon the opening of the door it ran out.
>
> ON DECEMBER 8, in the morning, there were five great stones and bricks by an invisible hand thrown in at the west end of the house while the man's wife was making the bed; the bedstead was lifted up from the floor, and the bedstaff flung out of the window, and a cat was hurled at her; a long staff danced up and down the chimney; a burnt brick, and a piece of a weather-board, were thrown in at the window....
>
> At another time an iron crook that was hanged on a nail, violently blew up and down; also a chair flew about, and at last lighted on the table where victuals stood ready for them to eat, and was likely to spoil all, only by a nimble catching they saved some of their meal with the loss of the rest and the overturning of their table.
>
> People were sometimes barricado'd out of doors, when as yet there was nobody to do it; and a chest was removed from place to place, no hand touching it. Their keys being tied together, one was taken from the rest, and the remaining two would fly about mak-

ing a loud noise by knocking against each other. But the greatest part of this devil's feats were his mischievous ones, wherein indeed he was sometimes antic enough too, and therein the chief sufferers were, the man and his wife, and his grandson. The man especially had his share in these diabolical molestations. For one while they could not eat their suppers quietly, but had the ashes on the hearth before their eyes thrown into their victuals, yea, and upon their heads and clothes, insomuch that they were forced up into their chamber, and yet they had no rest there; for one of the man's shoes being left below, it was filled with ashes and coals, and thrown up after them. Their light was beaten out, and, they being laid in their bed with their little boy between them, a great stone (from the floor of the loft) weighing above three pounds was thrown upon the man's stomach, and he turning it down upon the floor, it was once more thrown upon him. A box and a board were likewise thrown upon them all; and a bag of hops was taken out of their chest, therewith they were beaten, till some of the hops were scattered on the floor, where the bag was then laid and left....

ON JANUARY 23, (in particular), the man had an iron pin twice thrown at him, and his inkhorn was taken away from him while he was writing; and when by all his seeking it he could not find it, at last he saw it drop out of the air, down by the fire. A piece of leather was twice thrown at him; and a shoe was laid upon his shoulder, which he catching at, was suddenly rapt from him. A handful of ashes was thrown at his face, and upon his clothes; and the shoe was then clapt upon his head, and upon it he clapt his hand, holding it so fast, that somewhat unseen pulled him with it backward on the floor... .

FEBRUARY 2. While he and his boy were eating of cheese, the pieces which he cut were wrested from them, but they were afterwards found upon the table, under an apron and a pair of breeches; and also from the fire arose little sticks and ashes, which flying upon the man and his boy, brought them into an uncomfortable pickle. But as for the boy, which the last passage spoke of, there remains much to be said concerning him as a principal sufferer in these afflictions: for on the 18th of December, he sitting by his grandfather, was hurried into great motions, and the man thereupon took him, and made him stand between his legs; but the chair danced up and down, and had like to have cast both man and boy into the fire; and the child was afterwards flung about in such a manner, as that they feared that his brains would have been beaten out; and in the evening he was tossed as afore, and the man tried the project of holding him, but ineffectually. The lad was soon put to bed, and they presently heard a huge noise, and demanded what was the matter? and he answered, that his bedstead leaped up and down; and they [the man and his wife] went up, and at first found all quiet, but before they had been there long, they saw the board by his bed trembling by him, and the bedclothes flying off him; the latter they laid on immediately, but they were no sooner on than off; so they took him out of his bed for quietness.

DECEMBER 29. The boy was violently thrown to and fro, only they carried him to the house of a doctor in the town, and there he was free from disturbances; but returning home at night, his former trouble began, and the man taking him by the hand, they were both of them almost tript into the fire. They put him to bed and he was attended with the same iterated loss of his clothes, shaking of his bedboard, and noises that he had in his last conflict; they took him up, designing to sit by the fire, but the doors clattered, and the chair was thrown at him; wherefore they carried him to the doctor's house, and so for that night all was well....

All this while the devil did not use to appear in any visible shape, only they would think they had hold of the hand that sometimes scratched them; but it would give them the slip. And once the man was discernibly beaten by a fist, and a hand got hold of his wrist, which he saw but could not catch; and the likeness of a blackamoor child did appear from under the rug and blanket, where the man lay, and it would rise up, fall down, nod, and slip under the clothes, when they endeavored to clasp it, never speaking anything.

Neither were there many words spoken by Satan all this time; only once, having put out their light, they heard a scraping on the boards, and then a piping and drumming on them, which was followed with a voice, singing, "Revenge! Revenge! Sweet is revenge!" And they being well terrified with it, called upon God; the issue of which was, that suddenly, with a mournful note, there were six times over uttered such expressions as "Alas! Me knock no more! Me knock no more!" and now all ceased.

The man does, moreover, affirm that a seaman (being a mate of a ship) coming often to visit him told him, that they wronged his wife who suspected her to be guilty of witchcraft; and that the boy (his grandchild) was the cause of this trouble and that if he would let him have the boy one day, he would warrant him his house should be no more troubled as it had been. To which motion he consented. The mate came the next day betimes, and the boy was with him until night; since which time his house, he saith, has not been molested with evil spirits.

Thus far is the relation concerning the demon at William Morse his house in Newberry. The true reason of these strange disturbances is as yet not certainly known: some (as has been hinted) did suspect Morse's wife to be guilty of witchcraft.... Others were apt to think that a seaman, by some suspected to be a conjurer, set the devil on work thus to disquiet Morse's family; or, it may be, some other thing, as yet kept hid in the secrets of Providence, might be the true original of all this trouble.

AN IRISH POLTERGEIST

Montague Summers in *The Vampire* tells this tale, and seems to believe it is true:

> Major C. G. MacGregor of Donaghadee, County Down, Ireland, gives an account of a house in the north of Scotland which was haunted by an old lady, who resided there for very many years and died shortly after the beginning of the nineteenth century. Several persons who slept in the room [where she died] were sensibly pushed and even smartly slapped upon the face. He himself on feeling a blow upon the left shoulder in the middle of the night turned quickly and reaching out grasped a human hand, warm, soft, and plump. Holding it tight he felt the wrist and arm which appeared clothed in a sleeve and lace cuff. At the elbow all trace ceased, and in his astonishment he released the hand. When a light was struck nobody [else] could be seen in the room.

Uncheckable stories such as this suggest to me that reporters may well have dreamed of attack. On waking up, of course, they found no one else was there. I am very suspicious of ghostly visitations in the  middle of the night. How can we be certain the person alleging supernatural events took place was not asleep when the marvelous thing supposedly occurred?

It makes you wonder why ghosts and poltergeists are loathe to manifest themselves in broad daylight. I have no desire to sit in on séances where the medium insists that the lights all be turned off, either. Why can't the spirits arrive in a normally lit room and before people who are vigilant and wide awake? I myself have learned how to fake some impressive séance effects performable with the lights fully on. Why cannot mediums produce results under like circumstances?

THE COCK LANE GHOST

London has many famous ghosts, but the prize must go to the eighteenth-century ghost of Cock Lane, if only because it was the subject of so much comment in its time and so many studies thereafter. The best-known book on it is Andrew Lang's *Cock Lane and Common Sense*, (1894).

The poltergeist started its activities in November 1759 in the house of Richard Parsons, clerk of the church of St. Sepulcher in the Smithfield market section of London. A pregnant woman, Fanny Lynnes, was lodging in Parson's house while her common-law husband was away. He was common-law because he couldn't marry her, she being his deceased wife's sister, an English legal quiddity that Sir W. S. Gilbert made fun of well over a century later. In her man's absence, for companionship Fanny Lynnes slept with Parson's 10-year-old daughter, Elizabeth. They began to hear funny noises behind the wainscoting.

Parsons said it was just the cobbler next door. The noises grew louder. Fanny, six months pregnant, died of smallpox. Then the rappings became more persistent. Parsons had the wainscoting ripped out, but nothing untoward was found. The noises continued. Little Elizabeth went into convulsions. The neighbors were all horrified. They started to spread rumors.

Parsons called in clergy in the person of a curate from St. Sepulcher's. The clergyman (Rev. John Moore), in a Protestant spirit of sharing rather than sacraments,instead of attempting to exorcize a demon set up a system of raps to communicate with the ghost. And what the spirit revealed was astonishing.

The spirit identified herself as Fanny Lynnes. Now, why the noises had begun before Fanny died needs some explanation, but they may have been the work of her dead sister. Fanny said her common-law husband (William Kent) had poisoned with arsenic both his wives, her sister Elizabeth Lynnes and herself!

This was not unattractive news to Richard Parsons, who owed William Kent money and was not repaying it on the schedule upon which they had agreed. It was a shock to William Kent, who sought out the Rev. Mr. Moore, and was stunned when the clergyman communicated with Fanny's ghost (that system of raps). To his face the ghost accused Kent of murdering her.

Cock Lane became a sensation. A committee was set up to examine Elizabeth Parsons, and Dr. Samuel Johnson, "Ursa Major" himself, was a part of it. Dr. Johnson, with his usual air of complete certainty, but on the firm and unshakable basis of ignorance, declared the whole thing a fraud. For the committee, the ghost would not signal at all.

But young Elizabeth Parsons, though moved from one house to another to avoid curious crowds, was increasingly pestered by the ghost. The problem was chiefly that the ghost would no longer manifest itself when others were around. Put to the test, Elizabeth thought she must fake the noises. But she was caught in that deception and the whole story was declared what Dr. Johnson had harrumphed it was, an utter fraud. Cock Lane became synonymous with imposture.

Colin Wilson writes in *Poltergeist!*:

On 25 February 1762, there appeared a pamphlet entitled *The Mystery Revealed: Containing a Series of Transactions and Authentic Testimonials respecting the supposed Cock Lane Ghost, which have been concealed from the Public*—the author was probably Johnson's friend

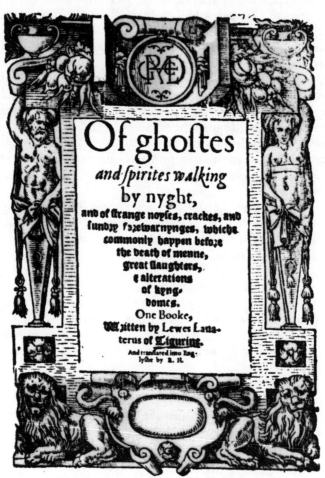

Of ghoftes
and *spirites walking*
by nyght,
and of ftrange noyfes, crackes, and
fundry fozewarnynges, whiche
commonly happen befoze
the death of menne,
great flaughters,
¢ alterations
of kyng·
domes.
One Booke,
Written by Lewes Lana·
terus of Tigurine.
And tranflated into Eng·
lyfhe by R. H.

Printed at London by Henry Benneyman
for Richard VVatkyns, 1572.

Oliver Goldsmith. A satirical play called *The Drummer;* or, the *Haunted House* was presented at Covent Garden. And William Kent began legal proceedings against Richard Parsons. In July 1762, Mr. and Mrs. Parsons and a woman called Mary Frazer—who had often acted as "questioner" to the ghost—appeared before the magistrates in the Guildhall. Parsons was charged with trying to take away the life of William Kent by charging him with murder. The judges remained unconvinced by the evidence of neighbors who had heard raps resounding from all over the room, and were certain that Elizabeth [Parsons] could not have made them. And finally, Parsons was sentenced to two years in prison, and to stand three times in the pillory; his wife was sentenced to one year, and Mary Frazer to six months. The Reverend Moore and one of his associates had to pay out £588 in damages to Kent. There was universal sympathy for Parsons, and when he stood in the pillory, the mob took up a collection for him—an unusual gesture for a period in which malefactors were often badly injured in the pillory. (Later in the year a man convicted of sodomy was stoned to death in the same pillory.)

Wilson was convinced that the Cock Lane ghost was a poltergeist, not an impostor. If so, the Cock Lane ghost can be called the most famous British poltergeist, because the shenanigans at Borley Rectory, repeated by occult faddists and journalists alike, are basically very boring and more than a little open to doubt, what with batty English clergymen, unreliable or unsubstantiated witnesses, and at the center of it all the dubious researcher Harry Price. Call Borley Rectory (which burned down years ago) the Most Hyped House in Britain, not the Most Haunted House in Britain. There were instances of poltergeist behavior of far more interest in considerably more downmarket places in England, such as London's less-than-fashionable suburbs of East Acton, Battersea, and Enfield. There were hair-raising stories in backwaters less sophisticated than London where the tabloids did not reach but the locals were more inclined to believe. If you must know all the details of Borley Rectory, read *The Haunting of Borley Rectory* (1956), a full report for The Society for Psychical Research by E. J. Dingwall and others.

You would enjoy Douglas Grant's *The Cock Lane Ghost* (1965). If someone wants to make a movie of the story, I'd love to write the script. It's a more interesting tale than *The Crucible.*

PSYCHOKINESIS

This (usually PK) is mind over matter. Poltergeist activity, many argue, is unconscious use of PK by a person, nothing supernatural by a ghost. Because J. B. Rhine's experiments, though flawed and questioned, have established that there is in fact such a thing as PK, this makes for a theory attractive to scientists that is a little more acceptable somehow than Carl Jung's idea of "exteriorization" of personal energies. Those are essentially sexual energies somewhat resembling the energies in the theories of Wilhelm Reich. All this is on the fringe of Establishment science.

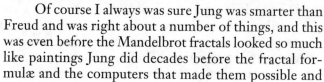

Of course I always was sure Jung was smarter than Freud and was right about a number of things, and this was even before the Mandelbrot fractals looked so much like paintings Jung did decades before the fractal formulæ and the computers that made them possible and displayable as stunning mandalas were invented. I think Jung's explanations may bring us closer to accepting and comprehending PK than do the theories advanced by other scientists.

If in Russia one Nina Kulagma could move small objects around a table by concentration of mind, then presumably some others can move objects through the air the way poltergeists are said to do. People may indeed be able to produce table rappings without resorting to the tricks that made the Fox Sisters and their nonexistent "Mr. Splitfoot" first famous and later notorious.

CANADIAN CAPERS

At Amherst (Nova Scotia) there was in 1878 "'the great Amherst mystery,' which lasted exactly a year," says Peter Underwood in *Ghosts and How to See Them* (1993). He is correct in his description of the "threats to kill written on the walls, movement of objects, inexplicable fires and sounds like thunderclaps," but he is wrong to describe Nova Scotia as "USA."

In a tiny, two-story dwelling in Amherst lived shoemaker Daniel Teed, his wife, their two sons, his brother, and his brother-in-law and two sisters-in-law. The poltergeist activity centered around the somewhat neurotic spinster sister of Teed's wife, a dumpy girl in her early twenties named Esther Cox. People were afraid she was crazy enough to set fire to the house, a danger to everyone in the village of timber houses built close together. In fact, in the long run she deliberately set fire to someone's barn and went to jail over it. After that there was no more trouble.

When Esther got a job in John White's restaurant in town, she seemed to bring the poltergeist disturbances right along with her. When she was out of Daniel Teed's house, there was no further disturbance there, but for a while things were pretty spectacular, and Walter Hubbell, a stage magician who saw a book in the incidents and boarded with Teed long enough to collect evidence for his little masterpiece, got lots of good copy.

The psychic researcher Hereward Carrington looked into the story and collected evidence, but it was 1907 then and he may not have got the right spin on things. Moreover, he refused to pay Esther (a bitter old married lady by that time) the hundred dollars she wanted for an interview so he did not have her side of the case at all. In 1919 Walter Franklin Prince wrote up the story, as well as he could piece it together, in *Proceedings of the American Society for Psychical Research*. This is further testimony to the fact that a juicy poltergeist story has a lot of mileage in it, often more than it really deserves.

Today, looking at Prince's report, we see that he was on to something that is now even more popular, Multiple Personality Syndrome. Nowadays people are boasting (or suffering) not two faces of Eve or several sides of Sybil but dozens of "people" inside them, some of them rather distasteful creatures. They are suing their psychiatrists and denouncing on television all the dangers of brainwashing and misdiagnosis and medical mismanagement and much more. Remarkably, juries are making them rich.

But Esther never got rich, nor well adjusted. Apparently, if she was not a conscious fraud, Esther was a psychological mess, partly due to unpleasant sexual relations with her boyfriend, and the bad side of her, unconsciously, was looking for attention or revenge. They should have cottoned onto this as soon as Esther in trance delivered the poltergeist's denunciation of her no-good boyfriend, Bob MacNeal. But no one put two and two (or the two sides of Esther) together.

ELEANORA ZUGUN

The story looks suspicious because it involved Harry Price, and the more we have learned of him over the last half century or so the less we have come to trust him. But it is an interesting story nonetheless, and one that raises interesting scientific questions.

A Hungarian girl just reaching puberty, Eleanora Zugun, was convinced by her 105-year-old grandmother that she, Eleanora, was possessed by The Devil. Then poltergeist activity struck: hails of stones and other violence followed Eleanora wherever she was sent. She wound up in a church institution and then in an insane asylum. She was taken in by the Countess Zoë Wassilko-Szerecki, and though the devil inside her punched and slapped and insulted her, and caused havoc wherever she was, young Eleanora enjoyed her new life and became something of a celebrity. She was taken to Vienna and tested and then to Berlin, but by 1927 her brief moment of fame was over. The poltergeist activity ceased. Eleanora departed for Romania, to become a hairdresser.

The enthusiasm followed by skepticism that marked her case is a rather common pattern in connection with celebrities of this sort. Also, it is often argued that no one would inflict wounds on himself, but undoubtedly this is contradicted by self-abuse by the insane and by the mortification of the flesh by nuns and others in the quest for purity, not to mention some doubtful cases of the stigmata. It seems likely that certain people have much greater needs than others for attention and, in some cases, actual powers over their own bodies that other people do not have or cannot use effectively. The ability of the mind miraculously to open as well as to heal wounds has been amply demonstrated, and miracles are said to occur when a person is able to heal another instantly by some power of mind, often transferred by simple gestures or the laying on of hands. Our minds have more power than we realize. I assume that when the twenty-first century ends mankind will be amazed at how little of this we understood in the twentieth century.

AMERICAN POLTERGEISTS

Unfortunately, the most famous stories are either wholly fictional (particularly in the movies) or completely or mostly faked (as with the otherwise undistinguished house in Amityville, New York). Insofar as the Amityville story reached a wide audience in the cinema as *The Amityville Horror*, interest in poltergeists was strengthened in America. Insofar as the Amityville business was eventually discounted as fakery, belief in poltergeists has been weakened in America.

AT THE TRIAL OF BRIDGET BISHOP, SALEM, 1692

Cotton Mather helped very much to energize the witchcraft persecutions in Massachusetts with his interviewing of people and his authorship of *The Wonders of the Invisible World*. Rushing into print with the sensational news from Salem, he reported in great detail the trials of the unfortunates who were caught up in this puritan frenzy. It is only fair to remark, however, that some of the people were at least trying to dabble in witchcraft, and that God's people used witchcraft to fight back at them!

Bridget Bishop may have had a lot of unfounded allegations heaped upon her but the tradition of calling eccentric old women witches was a long one, and the Puritans had brought it with them as surely as they brought their bibles from England. Almost everyone believed implicitly in witches. At her trial, John Bly and William Bly testified that "being employed by Bridget Bishop to help take down the cellar-wall of the old house where she formerly lived, they did in holes of the said old wall find several poppets, made up of rags and hogs-brussels [bristles] with headless pins in them, the points being outward." Bridget Bishop couldn't explain these magical dolls. On the other hand they do seem to have belonged to some earlier tenant of the house, not to her. In any case, whether Bridget Bishop was a witch or not, *someone* was practicing witchcraft in Salem, or attempting to do so.

At her trial (2 June 1692), she pleaded not guilty to witchcraft. Witnesses testified to various poltergeist activities and apparitions. Witnesses swore her apparition did "oftentimes very grievously pinch them, choke them, bite them, and afflict them" and on occasion tear their clothes, wreck a wagon, frighten them in the night, and so on. They also said they had complained to her and she had denied being a witch but that in person she actually tortured them with her evil eye.

John Cook testified:

> that about five or six years ago, one morning, about sunrise, he was in his chamber assaulted by the shape of this prisoner; which looked on him, grinned at him, and very much hurt him with a blow on the side of his head; and that on the same day, about noon, the same shape walked in the room where he was, and an apple strangely flew out of his hand, into the lap of his mother, six or eight foot from him.

Others swore that they had been "overlooked" (bewitched) by Bridget Bishop. They said on oath that her wraith had appeared to them, a sow and an infant child died because of her witchcraft, a young boy was for years driven to insane activities after she consorted with him, and when her wraith appeared people who saw it were rendered speechless and could not move to flee or defend themselves. Several deaths, people suspected, were caused by her, and all the witnesses—and the Rev. Mr. Mather says there could have been many more testifying against her, "but there was no need of them"—caused all others present to look on the old woman as in league with The Devil.

Cotton Mather ends his report of this trial with a sensational touch:

> There was one very strange thing more, with which the court was newly entertained. As this woman was under a guard, passing by the great and spacious meeting-house of Salem, she gave a look towards the house: and immediately a demon invisibly entered the meeting-house, tore down a part of it: so that tho' there was no person to be seen there, yet the people, at the noise, running in, found a board, which was strongly fastened with several nails, transported unto another quarter of the house.

There are many such testimonies to witchcraft in the early annals of New England, but this one can serve as a good example of a sort of poltergeist activity claimed to involve people still living (appearing as wraiths, not ghosts, and in person) and imagined to be employing demons or some preternatural powers to create the effects of poltergeists. These stories allege that poltergeist activity need not be the evidence of spirits but that Satan gives to certain human beings who write their name in his book miraculous powers to do evil and cause suffering and dismay.

THE BOYS IN THE BASEMENT

In 1810 in the village of Sampford Peverell in Devon, John Chaves and his family moved into a house they rented from a Mr. Talley, a house that was soon found to be extremely uncomfortable. There were mysterious noises, footsteps, banging sounds. Objects were thrown around. The servants claimed they had been punched by invisible fists. A bible and a sword went flying through the air. Eyewitnesses were astonished. Chaves complained bitterly to his landlord.

The landlord, Talley, retaliated by accusing Chaves himself of faking poltergeist activity and Chaves was driven out of town by enraged locals. The explanation of it all that at least some people gave was that there was no poltergeist but that the local boys were using the cellars for smuggling and when Chaves got too close to finding out what they were up to they undertook to scare him out. Failing that, they had Talley and his friends drive him out.

This would not be the first nor the last time that criminal activity was protected by stories of supernatural goings on. This is another promising plot for an exciting film.

THE POLTERGEIST AT STOW-ON-THE-WOLD

This picturesque English village is often in the papers as a tourist attraction, but in 1963 it made headlines because of a poltergeist that ripped off wallpaper, threw things around, and generally created havoc in a family's previously quiet home. When the family gave up and went off on a holiday, the poltergeist went with them. Eventually they got in touch with it somehow and ascertained that it was the spirit of a workman who had been accidentally killed on the building site a few years earlier. After that, peace came again to the household and attention could be diverted to repairing broken furniture.

"BAD TRIP AT WOODSTOCK"

That is the title of the third of these tales of British poltergeists all related by Quentin Cooper & Paul Sullivan in lighthearted UK Radio 5 features and collected in *Maypoles, Martyrs & Mayhem* (1994). These authors brought together a number of British tales, including tales of the supernatural, and old customs and quirks with which most students of Britain are at least to some degree familiar.

The following story commences with Oliver Cromwell's men taking over the manor at Woodstock in the Civil War in 1649 and chopping down the King's Oak in the park. On 16 October, a "devil" appeared (in the form of a black dog) and poltergeist activity began. Let Cooper and Sullivan tell it:

Before you could say "poltergeist" the firewood was scattered, the beds were jigging about, assorted household objects were flying willy-nilly, candles were being snuffed, glass was shattering, and occupants were being doused with ditch water.

Matters came to a head when one of the Commissioners saw a disembodied hoof kicking a candle. He struck at the hoof with a sword, but his weapon was snatched from him. No mean feat for a hoof. The man was pummeled senseless, and the other Parliamentarians immediately fled, keen to keep their Roundheads round. The haunted Manor house was deemed a no-go zone for humans, and it was knocked down soon afterwards. A stone marking the site of the house can be seen at Blenheim Palace park, Oxfordshire.

The whole business beginning with the disturbing of the firewood gathered from the destruction of the King's Oak suggests to me a political rather than poltergeist motive behind all this. I think it not impossible that the Roundheads were being subjected to some knavery by local Royalists, outraged by the loss of the tree and by the whole Puritan crew that had moved into the manor. How this cavalier crew managed their tricks, if tricks they were, of course I cannot say. But whatever the forces were that wanted the Parliament men out, the eviction was effected. The destruction of the manor house soon after suggests to me frustration or revenge on the part of Cromwell's men.

ANOTHER BELL WITCH

We began this section of poltergeists with the famous Bell Witch and here is a lady named Maxine Bell, when last I heard living near Los Angeles, who might be called a witch but probably would prefer to be called a channeler, healer, astrologer, or psychic.

Among her abilities is getting music by dictation from dead composers. Her symphony given her by Beethoven from beyond the grave was performed in Los Angeles in the forties, but I can find no one who heard it. In the seventies, according to Nat Freedland's *The Occult Explosion*, Ms. Bell was looking for someone to write the orchestral parts for her ballet from Tchaikovsky (She received only the melodic lines).

Ms. Bell started out as a concert pianist but when she performed people laughed. She explains it was because wherever she goes she is accompanied by poltergeist activity. It was things flying around the auditorium, she says, that caused all the hilarity.

She is (or was) nowhere near as famous as Rosemary Brown, in Britain, who received in séances music from Beethoven, Mozart, and many other composers, including the conclusion to Schubert's "Unfinished Symphony."

Mrs. Brown, however, produced phonograph rather than poltergeist activity. Mercury recorded her music from Beyond.

AN EARLY AMERICAN POLTERGEIST

Amityville's horrors made all belief in American poltergeists a little more difficult, as I said, even for those determined to believe. It fitted, however, into a long American tradition.

An older and less obviously hyped case involves the Rev. Eliakim Phelps of Stratford, Connecticut, at that time in the nineteenth century when mesmerism, "animal magnetism," the Fox Sister's table-rapping, and other Yankee speculations (which produced a couple of new religions, Mormonism and Christian Science, not to say an atmosphere of religious revival and superstitious wonder) reigned supreme in New England.

Early in March 1850, the Rev. Mr. Phelps seems to have awakened a ghost as a result of joining with a visitor from New York in the new fad of a séance. A few days later, Sunday the tenth, the family returned from morning services to find their home topsy-turvy. It was not the work of a burglar; nothing had been taken, just rearranged chaotically. Was the friend, who was thought to have returned to New York, playing a trick? The Rev.

Thomas William Robertson (1829-1871) was a dramatist and director who introduced many spectacular effects into the staging of Victorian plays. With a magic lantern he created apparitions which thrilled audiences. Tricks were picked up by mediums. When they popularized rapping and spirit trumpets floating around, belief in poltergeists was helped along.

Mr. Phelps stayed home to watch while the rest of the family went to afternoon services. They came back to discover a scene of disorder of which the *paterfamilias* claimed no knowledge. There is a bit of a problem here, but these cases often have, and often gloss over, some minor glitches.

Clothes were laid out on a bed to resemble a corpse laid out for a funeral. In another room clothes and other things had been used to fashion dummies of people praying over open bibles. It was decided that all these picturesque scenes could not have been done, consciously or unconsciously, by the Reverend alone in the time he had been alone in the house.

The next day there were fearful screams, sounds as if the building were being demolished, objects flying through the air, a candlestick jumping off the mantelpiece to beat itself into smithereens on the hearth. The two children, ages sixteen and twelve, especially the younger one (a boy named Harry) were violently attacked by invisible hands. At one point Harry was thrown down a well, at another point trussed up in a tree. The house was in a shambles. As many as seventy-two window panes were smashed.

Back to table-rapping (which precipitated the whole chain of events) for the Reverend. He learns that the ghost is a dead man who is being tortured in hell for having cheated Mrs. Phelps in a business deal. The spirit adds to rapping little notes penned when the Reverend is not watching and even a warm if somewhat damp hand under the table.

Enter on the scene Andrew Jackson Davis. You can read all about this extraordinary character in the essay on him I contributed to in *Encyclopedia USA*. Briefly: he came from a very poor family in upstate New York, was taken under the wing of an older gentleman who convinced him he had occult powers, and soon was writing huge tomes dictated to him by spirit voices! He considered himself an expert on spirits, and at the home of the Rev. Mr. Phelps he announced he was in touch with not only the poor dead clerk but a passel of other folks from Beyond. Whether it was Davis' idea or the Reverend's, now that hundreds of dollars worth of damage had been done to their home, the wife was hysterical and the children beaten and bruised and traumatized for life, it was decided to ship Mrs. Phelps, the daughter Anna, and the son Harry off to Philadelphia.

The ghosts apparently got what they wanted. They did not pursue the Phelpses to Philadelphia, and the restless spirits that Rev. Mr. Phelps had foolishly stirred up by his silly séance returned to their infernal residences.

Colin Wilson calls the poltergeists at the Phelps house "the usual crowd of invisible juvenile delinquents" but still rates the case as "one of the most spectacular cases of poltergeist disturbance on record."

Actually, it does have just about everything. A colorful chapter in the credulousness of still-rural America in the nineteenth century, a time when phrenology and psychology were pretty much on a par and homespun theologies were burgeoning. A motive for the arrival of a ghost. Communicative, sometimes even clever or ribald spirits, who turn very nasty and are never shy about performing dramatically for witnesses. Sweet children as targets. Proof of the existence of hell (always nice for a man of the cloth to have at hand). Terrific confusion and destruction, not just sighs and whimpers and a chill falling over the room as somebody transparent floats through. Spectacular séances. A visiting expert of note. Even a moral: don't fool with séances; you may unleash more than you can handle.

CORNWALL

The duchy of Cornwall, effectively cut off from the rest of the island of Britain until bridges were built in the West Country in the nineteenth century, has always been said to be a hotbed of chill ghosts. Peter Underwood and others have written about its many specters. In Cornwall, you don't have to be on ley lines to feel you are in places of power on the deserted heaths, amid ancient rock circles, along the rugged coasts where a major industry used to be the lighting of false beacons to lure ships to destruction on the rocks (the cargoes were stolen, the crews murdered). Here the moonrakers were said to scoop the reflection of the moon off the calm standing pools, rendering the night dark for shipwrecking, smuggling, and other nefarious deeds.

In the mines of Germany, said Paracelsus, who discovered the element cobalt, was a malicious sprite called *Kobold*. In Cornwall they have a kinder, gentler equivalent in the mines in the person of Blue Cap, or Cutty Soams, who is usually helpful, only occasionally mysterious, and likely to be your friend if you leave tallow and food around for him. In the United States, where lots of Cornish miners immigrated in the nineteenth century, these mine sprites, whom one can hear knocking as they work underground, are called Knockers, or Tommyknockers. You can read about them at work in the Mamie R. Mine in Cripple Creek, Colorado, in Maryjoy Martin's *Twilight Dwellers: Ghosts, Ghouls and Goblins of Colorado* (1985). We have our own, albeit imported, Cornish ghosts.

FLAMMARION ON POLTERGEISTS

Camille Flammarion, as quoted by Colin Wilson:

> These spirits are not necessarily the souls of the dead; for other kinds of spiritual beings may exist, and space may be full of them without our ever knowing anything about it, except under unusual circumstance. Do we not find in different ancient literatures demons, angels, gnomes, goblins, sprites, specters, elementals, etc.? Perhaps these legends are not without some foundation in fact.

What I find missing in so much superstitious speculation is an emphasis on the probable rather than a stress on the fact that anything in nature is possible. That, and a leap to judgment that is similar to the leap of faith. Is belief in the occult (which means only "hidden") like belief in religion (which speaks of the unknowable)? Are both superstition and religion necessary hoaxes to preserve order in life? On the subject of poltergeists and all other spiritual creatures, and their Creator, can we not seek "the true philosophy" of which Schopenhauer writes in his *Dialogue on Religion*?

> We will not abandon the hope that eventually mankind will reach a point of maturity and education so that it can on the one hand produce and on the other hand accept the true philosophy.

Meanwhile we seem to be children who want to be sure of everything, whether hidden from us for a while or forever, and even claim we know it all, pontificating about angels and devils, ghosts and poltergeists, vampires and God Himself. We construct theology and demonology, faith and superstition on the same shaky foundations and ignorantly defend one against the other.

Here I am concerned only with poltergeists that may be the souls of the dead. I claim to have no last word on them. For other kinds of supernatural creatures—except angels, a topic I consider adequately covered by a host of modern books answering to or creating the current angel craze—you will have to go to *The Complete Book of Devils and Demons*. There all the possibilities are discussed, from The Devil as a real person to The Devil as a convenient anthropomorphizing of our abstract idea of evil, from fallen

The nineteenth-century Curé d'Ars was persecuted by poltergeists. On occasion they nearly tore apart buildings in which he was lodged.

angels as foreign gods to fairies as primitive people of prehistory. From the clerics of the Middle Ages who believed that the air was thronged with invisible powers—Alfonse de Spina undertook to give a census of them— to the hardheaded modern Scandinavian who would not think of siting a new house on any spot the trolls do not approve, people have always believed in what Cotton Mather in Puritan New England called "the wonders of the invisible world."

It is the fact of their belief that I am sure about, not anything else. It is the fact of their belief that can tell us something real and useful about the only subject on which we can pretend to any actual knowledge; that is, human behavior. On poltergeists, as on many other things, I must say my interest is in the human face reflected in that mirror, not the mirror itself. Any child can see a human face in a mirror, even though the child could never explain how the mirror works, or reverses the image.

AROUND THE WORLD

From Time-Life's *The Mysterious World*:

EBERBACH VALLEY: The clatter of a spectral army over this German valley, said to signal war's onset or end, was reported just before Germany's 1945 defeat....

PLAINS OF MARATHON: In these fields north of Athens— scene of a bloody battle in which the Athenians repelled the Persians in 490 BC—people supposedly heard the screams of the wounded and the whistle of spears for years afterward....

SAN QUENTIN [FRANCE]: In 1849 a barrage of invisible projectiles pierced kitchen windows without shattering them.... The spirit believed responsible went away after a servant was discharged.

SCHWEIZER-RENKE: A farmer near this South African town said he was stunned to see bread pans, flatirons, a pot, and the meat he was frying move unaided to the oven—the work, it was thought, of a pesky spirit called Old Griet.

And there are many British and other "cases ancient and modern" in Colin Wilson's "study in destructive haunting," *Poltergeist!* (1981). British poltergeists have been reported in royal residences, ancient castles, low-rent housing estates, elegant manor houses, busy inns and pubs, big city residences both grand and humble, and little country cottages.

A British friend visiting me when an oil portrait of a Victorian lady fell off the wall in my library, with a crash, would not for a moment hear of passing traffic shaking the house. Surely it was a sign I ought to get rid of the picture right away! I was so pressed to do so, I sold it at auction and made so much on the deal I was able to replace it with a much better painting. I hope the grim Victorian sitter is happier where she is now.

HOTEL DEL CORONADO

This giant old hostelry in San Diego is haunted by the ghost of a long-departed true elegance, but it is still picturesque and cheerfully touristy. If and when you check in, you might be interested to know that poltergeist activity has been reported in Room 3502. You may or may not wish to request it.

GETTING IN TOUCH

If you do have a destructive or prankish spirit in the house—puck, *puca*, poltergeist or whatever—I suppose there is not much you can do but move, or get used to it. One family so oppressed nicknamed their spirit "Old Jeffrey" and made it a part of the family, as it were. To contact it seems impossible. In the words of Sir Max Beerbohm's famous parody of the peculiar style of Henry James, there are "too many dark, too many buzzing and bewildering and all frankly not negotiable leagues in between."

To mention another humorist, James Thurber, I recall a book of his called *Leave Your Mind Alone*. I think *Leave the Spirit World Alone* might be equally good advice. If it does exist, you may be in touch with it in person quite soon enough.

A LITTLE LIBRARY ON THE POLTERGEIST

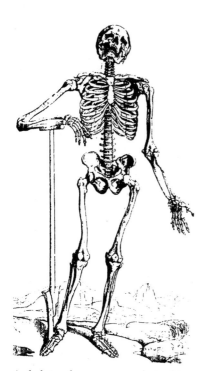

A skeleton leans on a spade in this picture from Andreas Vesalius' ground-breaking book on anatomy, *De Humani Corporis Fabrica* (1543).

Gerald Brittle, *The Demonologist* (1980, reprinted 1991)

Hereward Carrington and Nandor Fodor, *The Story of the Poltergeist down the Centuries* (1953)

David Cohen, *Poltergeists and Hauntings* (1965)

Nandor Fodor, *Haunted People: The Poltergeists Down the Ages* (1951)
    "   ", *On the Trail of the Poltergeist* (1958)

Alan Gault and A. D. Cornell, *Poltergeists* (1979)

Michael Goss, *Poltergeists: An Annotated Bibliography* [c. 1880-1975] (1979)

J. A. Gridley, *Astounding Facts from the Spirit World* (1854)

G. Jahoda, *The Psychology of Superstition* (1970)

Milbourne Christopher, *ESP, Seers, and Psychics* (1970)

A. R. G. Owen, *Can We Explain the Poltergeist?* (1964)

Emily Peach, *Things that Go Bump in the Night* (1991)

Ronald Pearsall, *The Table-Rappers* (1972)

Guy Lyon Playfair, *This House is Haunted: An Investigation of the Enfield* [Middlesex] *Poltergeist* (1980)
Frank Podmore, *Mediums of the Nineteenth Century* (reprinted 1963)
Harry Price, *The Most Haunted House in England* [Borley Rectory] (1940)
"   ", *Poltergeist over England* (1945)
Charles Richet, *Thirty Years of Psychical Research* (1923)
William G. Roll, *The Poltergeist* (1972)
Sacheverell Sitwell, *Poltergeists* (1940)
Andrew Tackaberry, *Famous Ghosts, Phantoms and Poltergeists* (1953)
Herbert Thurston, SJ, *Ghosts and Poltergeists* (1953)
Colin Wilson, *Poltergeist!* (1981)

THE SAUCHIE POLTERGEIST (1960)

Owen's book, mentioned just above, contains a sober description of an alleged poltergeist in Scotland. In America we tend to get publicity-seeking families and investigators with an ax to grind, reporters with a story to sensationalize. In contrast, the Sauchie case, centering around a little girl of eleven, seems to involve people who sought neither notoriety nor cash from the tabloids. They were people who were stunned at what they saw but did not even try to explain it. Most importantly, the witnesses kept good notes and were very reliable members of the community: doctors, clergymen, and a primary schoolteacher.

This is not to say that people must have high standing in the community or a professional status before occult activity involving them can be believed, but it might help. To see a hustling hick trying to peddle his story of UFO abduction to the press, or an ex-cop who retired early so he could dress up in a Hollywood-inspired costume (The Blue Knight) and declare that he is the embodiment (maybe the close associate, I'm not certain) of the Archangel Michael, does not mean nothing else strange ever occurs. But it does make one wonder why it so often seems to happen to people like that. If the president of the United States, or the president of a large corporation, or even a medium-sized college, were to claim to have been abducted by aliens, we might believe it more readily. If Jimmy Carter said he'd seen the ghost of Vince Foster, I'd be interested. If and when Matilda Krim hears rappings, let me know.

In the case of the Sachie poltergeist, rappings were heard (and tape-recorded by witnesses) in the girl's bedroom, and a large piece of furniture acted up. In the classroom, a desk floated up into the air behind the girl, the pointer for the blackboard vibrated and fell off the table, and when the table itself began to revolve the girl burst into tears and took responsibility for the strange things that always happened wherever she went.

The tot could do nothing as sensational as Carrie did in Stephen King's tale, but she did seem to create disturbance that no one could explain. Apparently she produced effects not maliciously but unconsciously.

I wonder whatever happened to her. Did anyone ever prove conclusively that she was responsible, or had some incorporeal entity attached itself to her? In the long run, was anything established which (in the words of Robert Boyle in the seventeenth century) might completely overcome common prejudice against any such phenomena, "all [our] settled indisposition to believe strange things?"

That phrase is quoted by William Roll in his instructive article "Poltergeists" in the *Encyclopedia of Parapsychology* (ed. Benjamin B. Wolman, *et al.*, 1977). Roll definitely is a believer, but the design of research and the methods of investigation he presents are sound. He considers, in addition to the Sauchie case, that of Runcorn (studied by Dingwall and Hall, 1958), Seaford (Pratt and Roll, 1958), Newark (Roll, 1969), Indianapolis (Roll, 1970), and others. He recommends surveys by Barrett (1911), Cox (1961), Zorab (1964, 1973), and others. I believe, however, that the Sauchie case is the more straightforward and presents the problems very simply and paradigmatically.

THE BUSINESS IN COLUMBUS, OHIO

In 1984 a rather unpleasant little girl named Tina Resch claimed to be the center of poltergeist activity. This put the modest household of her unexceptional foster parents on the front page of the Columbus (Ohio) newspaper. There was Tina, fourteen, with the telephone floating near her! "Poltergeist? Or only a Teen-Ager?," asked *Readers Digest* 125 (December 1964), 141-145, and did not stay for an answer. It was noted that the phenomena did not resume. William Roll of the Psychical Research Foundation in North Carolina reported he could find no sign of trickery. Perhaps he did not look hard enough.

Tina got back in the papers in 1995. She pleaded guilty to the brutal murder of her three-year-old daughter and was sentenced to life imprisonment. Kendrick Frazier in "'Columbus Poltergeist' Tina Resch Imprisoned in Daughter's Murder," *Skeptical Inquirer* 19 [March/April 1995], 3, tended to suggest that we ought to have regarded Tina with more suspicion from the very start.

A VARIATION ON "THE DEVIL MADE ME DO IT"

When he was arrested for murdering a two-year-old child, whom he had been baby-sitting, James Fenwick told the Old Bailey (London's central criminal court) that the baby had been attacked by a poltergeist. It's in the Manchester *Guardian* for 25 October 1995, 1, 10.

"THEY'RE HERE!"

So screamed Heather O'Rourke, the tiny star of the movie, *Poltergeist*. She was famous at 10, dead at 12. The public listened.

Poltergeist would not go away. There was a *Poltergeist II: The Other Side* (which even *People's* critic panned for a weak script and bad direction, while *Macleans* politely said it was a sloppy sequel), and *Poltergeist III* (Peter Travers in *People* pronounced it dreadful, though a lot of people enjoyed laughing at its unintentional humor). Everyone associated with all three films is permanently disgraced, though the flacks tried to say that their clients were blamed for taking good jobs in bad movies. Can and should movie moguls resist making bad movies if, with stars and hype and a public that is undemanding, they can make money out of trash? Not for us to decide, I suppose.

Money does get made. Now we have *Poltergeist: The Legacy* on television. "Boo, humbug!" was how Tom Shales greeted it in *The Washington Post.* Yes, it is trashy. In the commercial world, can anyone be blamed for recycling trash? Sean Mitchell's review in *TV Guide* (27 July—2 August 1996), 34-35, was too kind. *TV Guide* is not known for John Simon-pure critics. But to be brief and accurate we here can say: the show was garbage and the people who watch it are gleefully consuming garbage. Dumb shows and stupid audiences in the Good Ol' USA? You bet. "They're *here!*"

MARY DUNBAR AND THE WITCHES AT ISLAND MAGEE

There is an interesting set of poltergeist-like experiences detailed in the pamphlet published in Belfast under the title *A Narrative of the Sufferings of a Young Girl called Mary Dunbar, Who was Strangely Molested by Spirits and Witches at Mr. James Haltridge's House, Parish of Island Magee, near Carrickfergus, in the County of Antrim, and Province of Ulster, in Ireland, and in Some Other Places to which She was Removed during Her Disorder; As Also the Aforesaid Mr. Haltridge's House being haunted by Spirits in the Latter End of 1710 and Beginning of 1711* (1822).

Reverend James Haltridge had been minister at Island Magee for some time when one day his widow was assailed by small stones thrown in her kitchen when there was no one else around. Then her bedclothes were pulled off her at night, and finally there was the appearance of a ghostly lad of ten or twelve who appeared and silently moved around her room or sat quietly beside her at the fire. At this point the lad did not seem threatening.

Months later, the ghost appeared again, this time breaking a glass in the window and thrusting through a book which Mrs. Haltridge had long ago mislaid. Now the lad spoke up. He said The Devil taught him to read— and that he was going to put everyone in the house to the sword. He started to dig a hole in the yard with the sword. It would be, he declared, the grave of a person now living in the house who was soon to die.

A few days later, clothes in Mrs. Haltridge's bedroom were several times moved around and finally arranged on the bed to resemble a corpse laid out. (Oddly, the same sort of thing happened in the next century in a New

England Family's house—but that is another story, and one you have already heard). One night Mrs. Haltridge awakened to say she felt she had been stabbed in the back. They moved her to another room, but the shifting around of bedclothes and other clothes continued. Some were found folded in rooms some distance away. Despite the prayers of the local minister and others, on 22 February 1711, Mrs. Haltridge died mysteriously, the bedclothes having been ripped off her one last time.

After the death of her mother-in-law, the younger Mrs. Haltridge brought into the house as a servant a girl of about eighteen named Mary Dunbar. Now the goings-on in the house, which already had been the subject of much local gossip, were to become public scandal. Mary Dunbar's clothes were mysteriously transported from one place to another, she found the dead Mrs. Haltridge's nightcap tied up in some of them, and she began to complain of mysterious pains (as of knife wounds). She began to have fits. She recovered from her fits to name supposed witches. She said she knew the women who were responsible.

The mayor arrested some of the women Mary Dunbar named. They included Jane Latimer (Carrickfergus), Janet Mean (Broad Island), Margaret Mitchell ("Mrs. Ann," Kilroot), and these from Island Magee: Catherine M'Calmont, Elizabeth Sellar and her sister Janet Liston (Sellar), and Janet Carson. Mary Dunbar was unable to identify a "woman blind in one eye" whom she also accused of tormenting her, but these others Mary Dunbar identified and accused. She was joined in court by a number of witnesses, highly respected locally, who swore they saw her thrown into fits, vomiting pins, buttons, and feathers, etc., and sorely used by witchcraft.

One of the judges (Upton) told the jury that the accused women were good churchgoers and could not be convicted on the basically unsupported allegations of Mary Dunbar. However, his brother on the bench (Macartney) instructed the jury that a guilty verdict was certainly possible. He left the matter to them and the jury declared the accused women guilty. They were sentenced to a year in jail and four appearances in the pillory. One of them, on one occasion in the pillory, was so pelted by the mob that she lost an eye.

Thus ended, with stones flying as it had begun with stones flying, the last convictions for witchcraft ever upheld in Ireland. The long history of Irish witchcraft trials, beginning with that of Dame Alice Kyteler in the early fourteenth century, ended thus 400 years later.

PHYSICAL EVIDENCE

Some people claim that haunting spirits can do more than float about transparently, and walk through solid walls. They claim ghosts can create physical evidence too.

In Spain there was the case of faces that appeared on the tile floor of a house built over a graveyard. In Italy there was the bloody handprint of a woman who was murdered; it appeared again and again on the wall, no matter how often it was scrubbed off. In Holland, where a counterfeiter was executed in the sixteenth century by being filled up with water until she died, there is a house where the taps mysteriously turn on and where water soaks all sorts of things mysteriously. In Scotland individual roses kept appearing on a dining room table, and in Georgia a century ago blood dripped onto the dining room table of the Walsingham family, accompanied by fearful noises in the room above. This did not stop until the family moved out. That often seems to be the best way to deal with trouble.

GHOSTLY LIGHTS

People have long reported will-o'-the-wisps and other phantom lights and some have attributed them to ghosts maliciously trying to lead travelers astray. In the 1880s at María, Texas, ghost lights got a lot of attention but today, more than a century later, mysterious lights are likely to be ascribed to hoaxes, headlights, even UFOs, almost anything but ghosts. The burning of marsh grasses is, I admit, quite a sight to see, and one can imagine the ignorant being very frightened.

AN ANECDOTE OF A POLTERGEIST

From James Pettit Andrews (1737?-1797)'s *Anecdotes Ancient and Modern* (1790):

> Friday, October 4 at eleven set out from Yarum for Skinningrave, the house of one Mr. Appleby, of which Mr. Jackson was giving a very odd account he had from the Rev. Mr. Midgeley of an apparition which haunted the house in a very remarkable manner. As I am very incredulous in these notions of spirits, I was determined to take a journey thither to know the truth, and, if possible, to have all conviction, either by ocular or auricular proof. Accordingly, I arrived there about eight at night, and asking for Mr. Appleby (whom I found a sensible man, with a great gentility of behavior for a tanner), I told him I had taken the liberty, after hearing such and such reports, to come and ask a few questions relating to a spirit that was said to trouble his house; and that if it would not be inconvenient, I should be obliged to him if he would accommodate me with a room all night.
>
> He told me I was extremely welcome, and that he was obliged to any gentlemen that would give themselves the trouble to come; and did not doubt but that he should satisfy them, by the account he would give them, which he declared, as he should answer at the great tribunal, should be true, sincere, and undisguised, and should contain no incident but what had happened and been transacted

in his house (at first to the grief and amazement of himself, his wife, and four servants) by this invisible and unaccountable agent. He said that it was five weeks since it had left them, and that once before they were quit of it for three weeks, and then it returned, with double the noise and confusion they had before.

In the first place he assured me they had never seen anything, but that the noise and havoc which they had in the house was amazing; that they all were so frightened that one night about one o'clock they thought to quit the house and retire to a neighbor; that they could get no sleep by reason of their beds being stripped of the clothes and thrown upon the ground; that the women were thrown into fits by being oppressed with a weight upon their stomachs, equal to an hundredweight. Upon this they moved all their beds into one room, determined to share an equal fate; so that two men lay in one bed, two women in another, and the man and his wife in the third. No sooner were they in bed but the spirit visited them, the door being locked and barred. It first walked along the room, something like a man, but with an uncommon step. Immediately the maids cried out they were next to death, by a monstrous weight upon them; on which Mr. Appleby immediately came to their relief; that upon approaching the beds, something

Poltergeists had plenty to work with in the overfurnished homes of Victorian England.

leaped off, walked round him, which he, being a man of courage, followed and endeavored to take hold of, but in vain. Upon this he retired to his bed, and immediately the maids called out they were losing the clothes off the bed. He told them to pull hard, which they did, but they were immediately taken with a violent force and thrown upon the men. After this it rattled a chain with a great noise round the room; and instantaneously they were alarmed with a noise over their heads of a man threshing, as it were, threshing corn with a flail, and in a minute was answered by another; and this continued for fifteen minutes in a very regular way, stroke for stroke, as if two men were threshing. Then it descended into the room where they were in bed, and acted the same.

Another night it came grunting like a hog, and after imitated the noise of a swine eating its food; sometimes it would, in the middle of the room, make a noise like the pendulum of a clock, only much faster. And he assured me that it continued in their room one morning in June till past five o'clock; and Mrs. Appleby and all of them saw the clothes taken off them and flung with violence upon the maidservants; but nothing could they discover, neither conceive how they were thus strangely conveyed.

Upon these surprising things being done, it was rumored abroad that the house was strongly haunted; and Mr. Moore, the landlord, and Justice Beckwith went to Appleby, and often talking with him and examining the servants and telling them this was a concerted scheme among them for some purpose, they agreed to sit up all night. As they were putting the glass about, something entered the room, accompanied with a noise like squirting water out of a squirt, upon which they, with a change of countenance, asked him what that was. Appleby answered, "It was only a taste of what he every night had a sufficiency of." Mr. Moore advised him to keep a gun laden, and when he heard it in the room to discharge the piece.

The night following, the family being in bed as usual, it came, and making a sudden stand, threw something upon the ground, which seemed to them as if some sort of seed had fallen out of a paper. In the morning Mrs. Appleby, looking about the room, wondering what it could be that had been cast upon the ground, gathered up a considerable quantity of gunpowder in corns, which greatly surprised her. The next night it came in the same manner, but what it let fall made a greater noise, like shot, and in the morning they, to their real astonishment, found a great many shots. This afforded room for strange conjectures; and accordingly she told me she then did not know what to think, whether it was really an apparition or not; for that the scattering of this powder and shot the very two succeeding nights after Mr. Moore advised them to shoot greatly disconcerted them, though again, upon reflection, they had had so many proofs of something more than it was possible for any human creature to perform, that she was again led to believe it must be something not of this world, and that in the throwing down the powder and shot, it might be done in contempt, and was as much as to say, "What, you would shoot me?"

Once when it was in the midst of its career, one of the men, after composing himself for the purpose, addressed it in these words: In the name of God the Father, Son, and Holy Ghost, what art thou, and what dost thou want? If any person here can contribute to thy ease, speak, and nothing shall be omitted that can procure it. During the time he was speaking it was silent, but immediately upon his ceasing it began its usual noise. Then he spoke again the same words, but no answer followed. Mr. Appleby declared that one night when his servants were very merry, dancing and making a considerable noise, this goblin made so much greater disturbance over their heads, as one would have thought that twenty people were dancing there. Upon which he went up then with a light, but nothing could he discover.

When he told me this surprising narration, which he delivered with so much plainness and sincerity, free from embarrassment, I own I was something staggered, for he gave not the least cause to suspect his veracity. And upon my examining all his servants, they, without any hesitation, confirmed what their master had advanced: so that my expectation of hearing the reports, which I had heard, refuted was entirely frustrated, and I no little surprised to hear them so strongly vouched. I desired to lie in the room which this troublesome guest the most frequented; but they told me it occupied the whole house and no room escaped. So I retired to my apartment at eleven and read Milton till about one, then went to bed, not without wishing (yet not presumptuously) that I might have some strange conviction before morning, but met with none; and after a good night's sleep, arose at seven.

"A PUTTERGEIST"

Lance Morrow in an essay in *Time* (30 June 1997) writes of noises like someone walking around at four in the morning in the old farmhouse that Morrow and his wife bought and moved into. It sounded like "a man going about early-morning chores." Morrow concludes:

> An amputee may harbor in his nerves the ghost of the missing leg—his former completeness. Perhaps out of habit our house believes, down in its planks and nails, that the old man still gets up at four and busies himself at coffee and oatmeal. A puttergeist.

SIGH FACTOR

Typical of the no-brain "chronicles of the paranormal" on TV is *The Psi Factor*. Dan Aykroyd as host, reading some badly-carpentered prose, is less funny than usual. Researchers with lots of equipment with bells and whistles say "affirmative" instead of "yes." They dither uselessly. Their acting is atrocious.

A poltergeist episode involved the McAllisters, a couple building a dream house that becomes a nightmare because it starts "to behave as though it had a mind of its own." Glass is smashed, power tools turn aggressive, the floor heats up, the beams fall down, a robot probe is destroyed, special effects are seen, "a big black figure, I dunno, a shadow or something." Right. Time to get out. The house is sold for a fraction of its cost, the family is glad to have been warned of future unhappiness they might have had in the house, and the commentator concludes that a home must be built on "love." Thanks.

Meanwhile you have watched a high-tech investigation of God knows what with some grimly serious, very inept actors getting their licks between commercials.

This is one of those programs that asks the question: Is there intelligent life in outer space? I hope not. This is the kind of show we wouldn't want them to pick up.

Another question: What is there about poltergeist phenomenon that leads to scripts that are dumber than those of ghost or vampire movies? But I repeat myself.

ANOTHER POLTERGEIST IN BRAZIL

Brazil may be the most superstitious country on earth. Guy Playfair has a book, *The Flying Cow* (1975), in which he calls Brazil "the world's most psychic country," which may be a nicer way of putting it. Here's one of Brazil's poltergeist stories.

On 18 July 1972 in Socoraba, the Ribiero family was attacked by invisible forces that flung the furniture around and badly scalded a young girl who was holding a kettle. The Ribiero family moved away and was never heard from again. End of story.

A great deal of literature of poltergeist phenomena runs not very differently from this. Brazil, however, does have strange stories in connection with Brasilia (1960), São Paulo (1972), Carapicuiba (1974), etc. Occasionally *candomblé* priests exorcize poltergeists; they consider them to be sent by black magicians as what one authority has called "psychic hit men."

"Dion Fortune" (a somewhat formidable lady) and others have written extensively on defending oneself from such evil attacks. In nineteenth-century France there were a number of notable cases of psychic wars between black magicians allegedly employing demons. Although Playfair in *The Flying Cow* and in *The Indefinite Boundary: An Investigation of the Relationship between Matter and Spirit* (1976) tries to connect poltergeists and demons produced by the black arts, and discusses stones thrown as *despacho* cursed objects, it is generally agreed that poltergeists are seldom demonic forces. In Brazil, poltergeists and demons are confused in certain native religions of African origin.

JUMBIES

The names of rambunctious spirits are legion; in the West Indies they are called jumbies. See, for example, "Stone-Throwing in the West Indies," *Light* 26 (13 January 1906), 30. It quotes a report in The Port-of-Spain,

Trinidad, *Mirror* for 21 November 1905. People still believe in jumbies there, nearly a century later.

G. W. LAMBERT, CB

It is a pleasure to remember G. W. Lambert, a distinguished and lifelong student of the occult. I mentioned him earlier, in passing. Now I note him a little more. He was president of the Society for Psychical Research (1955) and kindly vetted my introduction to the reprint edition of its papers in two volumes of *Phantasms of the Living*. He also introduced me to a number of leading British occultists of the time (the sixties). His own principal efforts were directed toward the exposure of fraudulent mediums, but he published extensively on poltergeists as well and conducted lively correspondence in the pages of the *Journal of the Society for Psychical Research*.

Lambert, an important civil servant in his professional life, became fascinated with the occult when as a boy he heard F. W. H. Myers speak at his Public School. Lambert explained the conjuring tricks of mediums and sought physical causes for poltergeist effects in earth tremors and coastal weather. He was critical of Fodor and others whose investigations he did not consider sufficiently rigorous. He answered various critics and conceded to Canon Pearce-Higgins that the physical theory would not cover every case (as when objects were not simply displaced but rearranged). Lambert's plotting of reported cases on a map of the British Isles and his discovery that poltergeist activity there seems to have a season (October through March) are interesting points. The subject deserves more men of his intellectual caliber and honesty.

NANDOR FODOR

Another interesting authority on poltergeist phenomena is the psychologist, Dr. Fodor. His interest was sparked by the theories of Freud and the poltergeist theories (and powers) of Jung. Dr. Fodor wrote importantly on cases in the UK (Thornton Heath and Aldborough and Chelsea) and Hungary (Kisoros, etc.), Italy (Prigano), and of course the famous Cock Lane (London) and Gef the Talking Mongoose (Isle of Man). He was the author of *On the Trail of the Poltergeist* (1958), *The Haunted Mind* (1959), *Mind over Space* (1962), *Between Two Worlds* (1964), and other works, including a collaboration with Hereward Carrington on *The Story of the Poltergeist down the Centuries* (1953).

Dr. Fodor's theories are connected with spiritualism and mediumship as well as with psychiatry and adolescent sexual energies. A bibliography by Leslie Shepard, who is a noted folklorist but also eminent in occult circles, appears with Dr. Fodor's contribution on poltergeists to the 1966 edition of the *Encyclopedia of Psychic Science*.

WILLIAM G. ROLL

Beginning with investigations of extrasensory perception (ESP) and psychokinesis (movement of objects by the power of the mind) while at Oxford, Roll moved on to questions of survival after death and poltergeist phenomena. He conducted many investigations and wrote *The Poltergeist* (1972) and contributed to various scientific or occult journals. He likewise contributed as an authority on poltergeists to Richard Cavendish's *Encyclopedia of the Unexplained* (1974), to *Research in Parapsychology* (1973-1976) and to Benjamin B. Wolman's *Handbook of Parapsychology* (1977). He also worked in collaboration with Donald S. Burdick, William Eisler, Joseph Gaither Pratt, John P. Stump, and others. Dr. J. B. Rhine of Duke University wrote the preface to Roll's *The Poltergeist*, and poltergeist activity is closely connected somehow to American scientific interest in ESP and psychokinesis. As science seeks a Unified Theory, so parapsychology and the paranormal in general need some theory that will pull it all together. Dr. Roll has contributed some of the pieces to the puzzle.

HARRY PRICE

Just as reports of poltergeist activity contain a significant admixture of nonsense and fraud, so do the writings of Harry Price. His many contributions to periodicals both occult and otherwise, hard to trace, were all carefully collected in scrapbook form and are preserved in the University of London library. There serious researchers can easily find them. His self-aggrandizement is evident in partly autobiographical works such as *Leaves from a Psychist's Case-Book* (1933), *Confessions of a Ghost Hunter* (1936), *Search for Truth* (1942), *Poltergeist over England* (1945), and (with R. S. Lambert) *The Haunting of Cashen's Gap* (1936). As we have seen above, he appears to have been taken in by the medium Eleanore Zugun (who suffered almost 1000 instances of poltergeist attack, it was claimed) and he perhaps falsified some of the evidence of the famous Borley Rectory phenomena. Price did much to publicize and popularize poltergeists, and for that alone his place in the history of poltergeists is secure.

CONNECTION WITH GHOSTS AND VAMPIRES

Poltergeists have sometimes been associated with vampires, though most people do not know that. In Anthony Masters' *The Natural History of the Vampire* (1972):

> Vampires could appear in the character of a poltergeist and cause poltergeist disturbances. There was a reported incident involving this on the island of Mycore in 1700 when a poltergeist vampire

was supposed to have entered houses after being buried for two days. Furniture was upset, lamps were put out, and the local peasantry panicked.

In my view, the principal connection between vampires, ghosts, and poltergeists lies in ourselves. This is a matter of our psychology and physiology, the powers of our minds to see or invent illusions and, quite possibly, to affect the world around us on occasion and in ways which to us at this stage of human knowledge remain occult in the strict sense, hidden. Not supernatural, just so far unexplained, out of the ordinary, uncanny, beyond our ken.

I have seen the power of voodoo to harm or kill by suggestion. I have seen so-called miraculous and instant cures, attributable (I believe) also to the powers of suggestion. I am convinced that human beings and not heavenly forces can and have produced the stigmata (wounds resembling those of Christ's Passion). I do not believe that miracles can contradict the world of nature, but that natural world seems to me so full of wonders and mysteries that I cannot for myself rule out incredible effects achievable in subjective reality and perhaps even outside ourselves.

Your own mind is a miracle. Why should it not have so-called miraculous powers?

THE POLTERGEIST MAY NOT BE A SPIRIT AT ALL

Of all the theories put forward by so-called experts from demonologists to psychologists, perhaps the most intriguing explanation of the entities or events we call poltergeists is that offered by Nandor Fodor. He wrote in *The Poltergeist down the Centuries* that one poltergeist he had studied might be "a fragment of a living personality that has broken free in some mysterious way of some of the three-dimensional limitations of the mind of the main personality." Another way of putting it is that poltergeist activity may arise consciously or unconsciously from the angers and resentments and sexual frustrations of people, usually female adolescents. It is possible that they are loosed with conscious malice or quite uncontrolled by the person from which the forces emanate. In this way poltergeists might be related to the psychic warfare reported between some magicians, the kind of bad vibrations (you might say) that "Dion Fortune" and many others say we must find ways of turning aside, to protect ourselves.

This still leaves unexplained any activities, if any there be, that defy the ordinary laws of nature, as when telekinesis moves objects by the sheer power of the mind, makes heavy objects rise or fly, produces showers of stones apparently out of nowhere, or creates strange rappings and other annoyances. The unwillingness or inability of the person causing the poltergeist activity to admit responsibility may account for the occasional cases of so-called multiple personality in those around whom poltergeist activity is reported. Whatever part of the personality is to be blamed, how such energies actually operate remains unexplained. Could it be that certain persons can by willpower (or unwillingly) create a sort of electrical field in which solid objects react strangely? Could it be that poltergeists are not spirits of the dead at all (and not demons) but really emanations of mysterious forces produced by the living?

If that were true, poltergeists do not belong here in our discussions of the spirits of the dead, being products of the living. It has also been suggested that ghosts are not spirits of the dead either but a kind of *recording* made by the living and, as it were, imprinted on the ether, remaining (sometimes for long periods) after the death of those responsible. Poltergeists produced by the living and ghosts that are only reminiscences of the once-living, both created not by spirits but by living human beings, one in the present, one in the past! What fascinating ideas! What mysteries!

POLTERGEIST ON THE BAYOU

Because of the prominence of New Orleans and Cajun Country in general in the history of American superstition, I searched high and low for a really good poltergeist story. Perhaps one of the many supposedly haunted houses of the *Vieux Carré* had an interesting poltergeist. Perhaps one of the brooding if tarted up mansions of the Garden district has a mischievous spirit. Nothing useful. So I have asked L. A. de Montluzin, Jr., to write especially for this book a tale of a *Poltergeist on the Bayou*. Here it is published for the first time (though I feel confident so exciting a story will find its way into print elsewhere, later). Something like this might well have happened in Old Louisiana.

Until the Germans came in the early 1800s, to a bog on the Mississippi River thirty miles upstream for New Orleans which they'd been told was productive farmland, there had never been any talk of mischief-ghosts.

POLTERGEIST ON THE BAYOU
by L.A. de Montluzin, Jr.

Des Allemands the Creole real-estate sharpies who sold them the property had called it—"the Land of the Germans." And with their money gone and their energies spent fighting the river currents as they worked their way upstream, that's where the disappointed Allemands decided to stay put.

Although there is really no winter season in southern Louisiana, the air was becoming chilly, so they cut and sawed the huge cypress trees, and built their trim, weatherproof cabins right up on the natural levee beside the river.

Since the land was no good for planting the crops they were used to, they industriously set about fishing and trapping. Then April brought the swirling flood waters from a snow melt in the north, washing away everything they had constructed and saved. The families fled inland before the flood, their tools and clothing and animals piled on their flatboats, making their way down what is now Bayou des Allemands through the swamps, and southward to a broad high and dry area northwest of Barataria Bay.

The native Cajuns had arrived only a generation ago themselves, from Canada, and already contending with Indians and runaway Negroes in the swamps, they were not particularly happy to see them. But the Germans were not now to be intimidated or dislodged, and they set up a new community, today's Des Allemands, learning from the Indians how to plant and trap effectively in this swampy land.

Unlike the Cajuns, they brought with them a strong Protestant work ethic, and the community prospered. But since there were more than twice as many men as women, it wasn't long before the Allemands were paddling their newly-adopted *pirogues* down the bayou to Barataria for the weekly *fais-do-do* dances with the unattached and much freer Cajun girls on Sunday evenings.

Somehow, the language and cultural differences melted to the tunes of the accordion, fiddle, and washboard, accompanied by the beat from a rope on a stick anchored into a rusted-out washtub. Many a fistfight erupted between the Cajun boys and the interlopers; but the Cajun fathers, considering the prosperous Allemands good prospects for their daughters, enforced the peace.

It was not a full year after the beginning of this mingling that Marie Elène Gautreau, the teenage daughter born late to blind René the netmaker and his now–deceased wife Marie Anne, found herself with child as the direct result of liaisons with Wilhelm Krummel, an Allemand almost twenty years her senior.

The Gautreau clan did not object to a marriage; indeed, they welcomed it. But the prospect of uprooting herself from her community of French-speaking friends and family upset young Marie Elène greatly, and so it was decided that Wilhelm would build a new home for himself, Marie, and René just north of the Barataria settlement—still within easy paddling distance of his own kinfolks, but near enough to the Gautreaus, and to the Catholic church, where it was agreed the baby would be baptized.

Everyone in both communities agreed that Marie Antoinette

Krummel, despite the ungainly amalgamation of her dual-heritage name, was one of the most beautiful babies ever born in the swampland. Her flashing eyes stayed bright blue even after infancy, and her striking features and outgoing personality seemed to combine the very best of German strength and French *savoir-faire*.

Several of Wilhelm's friends began visiting the happy home for days at a time, even going with the family to the Catholic church services, which were much more colorful and musical than their traditional, somber Lutheran meetings. Afterward, of course, there were community fish fries, crab and crawfish boils, gumbo and *étouffée*—and sometimes barbecues of *cochon au lait* (suckling pig) or *andouille* sausage. Now sausage was something the Allemands understood, and the andouille and other sausages coming from Marie Elène's kitchen became a prize commodity for miles around, and a favorite in both communities.

In the *bourrée* card games, and the sharing of a powerful liquor distilled at home from sugar cane and corn mash (left over from the grinding of grits), *Wilhelm* became just plain *Willy*. Since there were so many Maries in the community, Marie Elène was referred to as simply Elène, and the baby was called Nettie.

It wasn't very long after Nettie's birth that the poltergeist began to make his presence felt. At the baptism, the poor *père* couldn't seem to get the water out of the baptismal font with the little container customarily used to pour it over the baby's forehead. Twice he spilled the water onto his starched surplice and best cassock, causing him to simply plunge his hand into the font and hurriedly wipe it across Marie Antoinette's brow as he mumbled the sacred words.

At the celebration afterward, it was noted that several people tripped over unseen objects as they danced, and the fiddle-player's strings kept snapping. Doors slammed in people's faces, and an overladen table collapsed. But perhaps this could all be explained by an exuberance of happiness combined with strong drink and merriment, and it was not until sometime later that these events were remarked on at all.

But these incidents continued as little Nettie grew older. Her playmates would often comment of strange happenings surrounding the child. Her mother died in the Yellow Fever epidemic of 1846, when Nettie was only six years old, and at the funeral service in church, the lid on the dimple cypress casket kept popping off. Elène, who had died sitting upright in the middle of the night, had to be strapped into the humble coffin, and her body bolted upright, frightening the combined mourning community half to death. But Nettie only laughed out loud at the startling sight.

No one was ever seriously hurt, you understand. And Nettie was never harmed by the pranks of the mischief-ghost. But her playmates began to understand that this was a protective force for the girl. Another young girl threw a rock at her in a dispute, but the rock veered off and hit her own mother sharply in the forehead. A mischievous boy chased her out into the swamp, where she perched precariously on an old log as he pursued her; but he tripped and fell into the water, narrowly missing a hungry alligator, which had most of his overalls for lunch.

"Don't mess with Nettie," was the word among the children in the community. "She's got a spirit guarding her!"

Of course, the pious in the Cajun community assumed that this was all the work of Nettie's Guardian Angel, and the priest confirmed this. But in Des Allemands, the old people knew better; they had seen the work of poltergeists many times in the old country, but they decided to keep these concerns from their Cajun neighbors.

With no wife to prevent it, Willy's spacious home became the gathering place for the men of both communities. Almost every night the liquor flowed, the sausages fried, the gumbo bubbled, as the music from old blind René's accordion sang out over the swampland. Nettie was by now a teenager, and she had sweet eyes for Hercule, a strapping youth of seventeen whose body was considerably stronger than his mind, but who had a good heart, though an argumentative disposition at times.

As a young man with his own traps and *pirogue*, and a good bit of spending money of his own, Hercule was welcomed into the card games, and he even developed a taste for the strong home brew that was served so freely there. He was a generous winner but a sore and somber loser, and he got into frequent exchanges of words with some of the older men, especially the Allemands.

Nettie would take him aside and calm him down, keeping him out of further trouble, and often insisted that he return to his own home until the next day. One night she paddled him home in her own *pirogue*, creeping up the outside stairs into the attic with him, and, for the first time, she spent the night with him there.

The mischief-ghost continued to bedevil anyone who crossed Nettie. There were broken legs from unexplainable falls, slips, and mishaps. There was a bump on the head from a falling tree branch, the spilling of scalding soup in the lap of a nosy and gossiping neighbor. But the poltergeist never bothered Hercule.

Then came an especially hot Saturday in July. It had been too uncomfortable to trap or even fish after midday, and the men had begun their drinking and celebrating early. Hercule and Nettie had spent the afternoon swimming without clothing in a secret little cove that they had discovered, and the inevitable had of course occurred. But Hercule had brought along a bottle of liquor, and he was already tipsy when they got back to Nettie's house shortly after sundown.

Willy had noted his daughter's growing infatuation with the boy, but had decided, after conferring with René, that he would let nature take its course. Hercule could do a good day's work, and he could certainly assure Nettie of splendid children and a secure living.

Hercule's father, Benoît, was another matter. Even more argumentative and difficult than his son, he had never particularly liked the industrious and prosperous Allemands, especially since he was pretty much a layabout himself. He was jealous of the fruits of their labor, although happy to partake of the free food and liquor that Willy provided.

A number of years before, Benoît had lost a girlfriend to marriage with one of Willy's compatriots, who was even winning in the card game and taunting him! And now Willy's wily daughter was getting serious with Benoît's only son, whom he relied on to do the heavy work around the house, and in the tasks of trapping and skinning. This was outrageous!

Already quite drunk when the two teenagers came in, he jumped up from the card table and began berating his son, his host, and Nettie. She was nothing more than a whore, he shouted directly at her. The confident young girl, sure of her love for Hercule and secure in her own home, screamed right back, advancing right in front of him. When he shoved her back, she reached onto the stove and grabbed the coffee pot, showering him with the boiling liquid.

Stunned but not deterred, Benoît drew his hunting knife and advanced on Nettie. Hercule tried to intervene between them, but because of his own condition, was only partially successful. The knife went up and came striking down as the three of them fell into a heap on the unfinished wooden floor.

Old René had stopped playing his accordion, and all the men had rushed over to intervene in the fighting. As Hercule slowly rose from the floor, Nettie and Benoît remained down, a pool of blood between them. The men turned them over, but saw immediately that Nettie had simply passed out from fright, and been knocked out by the weight of Hercule's body upon hers.

Benoît was dead, the knife sticking out of his chest.

Of course, the sheriff had to be sent for, and the family, reluctant to move Benoît's body, spent the night with their Allemands clan as Hercule repaired home to comfort his mother. The sheriff paddled over the next morning from Grand Isle on the Gulf. He quickly decided that no charges were to be filed.

After all, everyone in the community knew that this was simply the work of Nettie's mischief-ghost!

POLTERGEIST: THE MOVIES

Haunted houses are usually crumbling old piles, but the family that has to suffer all the inconveniences of the poltergeist in these movies begins by taking up residence in a nice new middle-class development. Of course there is a young girl, because poltergeists are attracted, it is said, to the energies of such youngsters. "People in the TV" abduct her. All hell breaks loose. The development has been constructed on the site of an old cemetery, from which the bodies were not removed. This creates a sort of cross between *Night of the Living Dead* and *The Exorcist*, with great violence erupting in an everyday landscape, as with Hitchcock's *The Birds*.

With Steven Spielberg's magic touch added to the direction by Tobe Hooper (*Texas Chainsaw Massacre*), *Poltergeist* (1982) was a massive success. The sequels, as so often happens, were not up to the original, but you already know that.

Poltergeist II: The Other Side (1986) brought back JoBeth Williams and Craig T. Nelson and resurrected Julian Beck (of The Open Theater). It is four years later and the family has moved in with in-laws but the bad guys are still after them. This time Spielberg was not personally involved, and it shows.

Poltergeist III (1988) finds Carol Anne grown up (some), living with relatives in Chicago but still pursued by the evil preacher Kane who gave her so much trouble in *Poltergeist II*. She'll be OK, but you always knew that, and that is one of the reasons the story really lacks interest despite all the shenanigans.

Millions saw these films on television, too. Their existence did much to prevent others from turning out poltergeist movies. Gresham's Law (from economics) applies: the bad drives out the good. We are ready for a first-class poltergeist film.

POLTERGEIST IN BELGRADE

In 1923 at 61 Bosanka Street a poltergeist was reported who may, they feared, have also been a vampire. Religious services were held to exorcize it and plenty of holy water was spilled.

POLTERGEIST IN A CHINA SHOP

In 1967 there were more than 200 incidents of destruction in a warehouse full of ceramic and glass souvenirs. A young man, aged 19, was suspected, but he was carefully watched and though he was identified by some as being the cause of the poltergeist activity he was not personally seen to take any part in it. He was dismissed. The destruction ceased. An adolescent male in such a situation is unusual (if anything about poltergeist activity is usual) as it is the presence of a young female that is normally blamed for flying objects and her removal from the scene that ends the activity.

A POLTERGEIST PLAY

Phelin McDermott and a couple of other British actors brought McDermott's play *78 Hill Lane* to the Off-Off Broadway venue of Performance Space 122 in the East Village in 1998. In the autobiographical drama, McDermott tells of a poltergeist experience in his childhood and its effect on his later life. The only thing remarkable about it was the subject matter.

A NEW HAMPSHIRE POLTERGEIST

It happened at the residence of George Walton in Great Island (New Hampshire) in 1672 and, as "R. C., Esq.," Richard Chamberlain wrote about it in a curious book published in London in 1698, *Lithobolia; or, The Stone-Throwing Devil.*

The poltergeist threw rocks and household objects. They rained down the chimney, flew around the house, hit people as they worked outside. "Stones (some great ones)," wrote Chamberlain, "came thick and three-fold among us," and though he had been a skeptic Chamberlain concluded that he and others by this poltergeist activity were confirmed "in the opinion that there are such things as witches and the effects of witchcraft." Soon that opinion was to be even more widespread, helped along by the writing of Increase Mather and his son Cotton Mather, self-appointed experts on "The Invisible World." Soon persecutions and executions for witchcraft were to blacken the history of New England.

WORTHY OF SERIOUS STUDY

The poltergeist phenomena are especially interesting because of the psychological implications, but not enough work has been done. In these books I seldom recommend articles in periodicals, but you ought to have a look at Joyce Bynum's brief but useful article in the journal of general semantics, *ETC* (Summer 1993, 221-231), aptly entitled "Poltergeists—A Phenomenon Worthy of Serious Study." It is indeed.

6

Ghost Stories

THE GHOST STORY

The ghost story is an art form which has attracted over the centuries some of the world's best writers. Here we cannot print or even excerpt Henry James's *The Turn of the Screw* or even a short story by Sir Pelham Wodehouse (P. G. Wodehouse) about a golfing ghost, but we can offer a few examples.

THE REV. MONTAGUE SUMMERS ON THE GHOST STORY

Summers may or may not have been a properly ordained Roman Catholic priest; opinions differ. He certainly was fascinated by evil and wrote about vampires, demons, and other supernatural things. In addition, he was a lover of literature and edited old books, and staged old plays. In his book *The Vampire* (1928), he says this about a ghost story he has related:

> It is brief and succinct, although there are many details, but every touch tells. No ghost story should be of any [great] length. The horror and the awe evaporate with prolixity. The ghost [in the story he tells] is malevolent and odious. In fiction a helpful apparition is a notable weakness, and the whole narrative becomes flabby.... The authentic note of horror is struck on the eerie suggestion which....is of intent left ill-defined. Nothing could be more crude than an explanation....

It is to be noted that with the rise of the Gothic novel (which Summers wrote about brilliantly in *The Gothic Quest*), authors stretched the tales out to inordinate length and, worse, at the end many of the writers undertook to explain away all the mysteries and to say that nothing supernatural had in fact occurred. With the periodicals that supplanted the triple-decker novels of earlier times in the favor of the ordinary reader, the short story gave the ghost story a new lease on life.

LITERARY ADVICE

Here are three opinions from the treasure trove of D. J. Enright's *The Oxford Book of the Supernatural* (1995).

From the introduction to V. H. Collins' *Ghosts and Marvels* (1924):

> For the ghost story, a slight haze of distance is desirable.... For some degree of actuality is the charm of the best ghost stories, not a very insistent actuality, but one strong enough to allow the reader to identify with the patient.

From Montague Rhodes James in the London *Evening News* (17 April 1931):

> If there is a theme that ought to be kept out of the ghost story, it is that of the charnel house. That and sex.

From Edith Wharton in *All Souls* (1937):

> I read the other day in a book by a fashionable essayist that ghosts went out when the electric light came in. What nonsense!.... As between turreted castles patrolled by headless victims with clanking chains, and the comfortable suburban house with a refrigerator and central heating, where you feel, as soon as you are in it, *That there's something wrong*, give me the latter for sending a chill down the spine!

And from Patricia Craig's review of Michael Cox's *The Oxford Book of Twentieth-Century Ghost Stories* (*Times Literary Supplement*, 6 December 1996, 25):

> The Victorian ghost story, by tending towards excess, in atmosphere and execution, risks toppling over into farce or getting entangled in its own grisly trappings. Once we reach the present century, however, the idea is to start off as matter-of-factly as possible, and then gradually increase the sense of something awry, before letting rip with a particular instance of spine-chilling. The story's impact depends partly on an incongruity between ordinary, natural life, as depicted by the author, and a preternatural occurrence.

A GHOST STORY ADAPTED FROM LUCIAN'S *PHILOPSUEDES*

Because it had the reputation for being haunted, Eubatides' house in Corinth had been empty for a long time. People who attempted to move into it were struck by a ghostly hand and forced to flee. In time the house was abandoned, the roof fell in, and nobody brave enough to enter it could be found.

Now (says Arignotus the Pythagorean) when I heard about this state of affairs, I collected some of my books—I have numerous Egyptian books on the occult—and around midnight I ventured into the house, despite the efforts of my host in the city to keep me out of it, because as soon as he heard what I was going to do he pleaded with me and even clutched at my garments to keep me from doing something he thought absolutely fatal.

Nevertheless, borrowing a horn lantern, I went in, all alone. I put down the lantern in the middle of the principal room, sat on the floor, and calmly began to read my books. It was not long before the ghost made his appearance.

Apparently he assumed that I was an uneducated man and just as easy to terrify as the others had been before me. He was wrong.

You have to understand that this ghost was black as night. He had a sleazy, desiccated look, and his stringy hair hung down limply. Coming close to me, he assailed me from every side, hoping to drive me out of there. Then he began shape shifting: first he turned into a dog, then a fiercer bull, then the fiercest lion. But while he was going through all these metamorphoses I was not idle. Rather, reading my formulas in Egyptian, I let him have the most terrible magical formulas, the most potent magical spells that I had.

By the force of these incantations I pushed the ghost into the furthermost, darkest corner of the room, and there he vanished. Marking the spot where he was last seen, I calmly went off to sleep until morning.

At dawn, everyone who knew of my adventure was waiting anxiously outside the house. They did not dare to come in but believed that if they did, they would find me stone cold, a corpse, because nobody else who had dared to enter the house ever had come out alive. To their immense surprise, out I walked hale and hearty.

I went and found Eubatides and told him that he could have his house back. I would help him get rid of the horrors. Bringing him along with me, and followed by a crowd desirous of seeing the outcome of the adventure, I led Eubatides to the exact spot where the ghost had vanished and convinced him to have his servants take pick and shovel and dig. When they did so, they discovered the remains of a body thrown into the grave a very long time ago, a heap of bones. We took these up and gave them a proper burial ceremony. Since then, that house has never been bothered by ghosts again.

For more classical phantoms, see Lacy Collinson-Morley's *Greek and Roman Ghosts Stories* (1968).

ÆSOP'S FABLE OF THE OLD MAN AND DEATH

Once upon a time there was an old man who had struggled along for a long time carrying a heavy burden. He was so weary that he sat himself down and he said, "I wish that Death would come to me and end this miserable life of mine."

Lo and behold! That very minute who should appear but Death himself. "What can I do for you, old man?" asked Death.

"Well," said the old man, looking at Death, "if you can just help me get this burden up on my back again I think I can carry it for quite a while longer."

MORAL: It is one thing to call for Death but quite another when he appears.

AN OLD, VERY ODD, GHOST STORY

In Iamblichus (Second Century BC) there is a weird story about King Garmos, who falls in love with the beautiful Sidonis. Unfortunately, Sidonis is already in love with Rhodanes. The king has Rhodanes crucified and locks up Sidonis in chains (albeit golden chains) but both of them escape by *pretending to be ghosts*. In the long run, after many adventures, Rhodanes and Sidonis live happily ever after.

The living and the dead. From a manuscript (called Nero A. X because Sir John Cotton had busts of Roman emperors to mark his various bookcases).

THE PROMISE

Thanks to my friend and colleague at The City University of New York, Wayne H. Finke (Baruch CUNY), I can offer you a portion of a story which he has translated for us from the Spanish of Gustavo Adolph Bécquer (1836-1870), a leading post-Romantic poet and fiction writer in a style somewhat like that of Poe. In retelling old *leyendas*, Bécquer is able to create, Finke says, "a strange, unreal world in which characters appear not so much to live as to float; they appear and disappear in a crepuscular atmosphere comparable to that in the paintings and prints of the symbolist artist Odilon Redon."

In this story, the Count of Gómara has to leave his lover, Margarita, to go fight for Don Fernando III, the king who wants to drive the Moors out of Seville. He promises to return, and places on her hand a ring as token of his pledge.

In battle, a mysterious hand turns his horse from running onto the Moorish lances, and saves his life. It deflects an arrow shot at him, saving him again. "It follows me everywhere: in the tent, in battle, by day, by night. Even now—look at it—it rests on my shoulder."

The count eventually hears a minstrel singing *The Ballad of the Dead Hand*:

The girl had a lover
who said he was a squire.
The squire announced
He was going off to war.
"You depart and may not return."
The count with his army
rode out from his castle.
She, who recognized him,
With great sorrow moaned.
"Woe is me, for the count departs
Carrying off my honor!"
As the sorrowing girl wept,
They say the wind repeated,
"Woe to her who trusts in
The promises of a man."
Her brother, who was present,
Heard these words.
"You have dishonored us," says he.
"He swore he would return."
"He will not find you, if he returns,
Where he was wont to meet you."
As the poor unfortunate girl died,
They say the wind repeated,
"Woe to her who trusts in
The promises of a man."
Dead they carried her to the grove
And in the shadow buried her.
But, for all the earth they threw on top,
Her hand could not be covered,

That hand on which she wore
The ring given by the count.
At night, over her sepulcher,
They say the wind repeated,
*"Woe to her who trusts in
The promises of a man."*

The count is then told that "this song is repeated by one and all villagers from the domains of Gómara" and that "the most holy and high judgment of God has permitted that the hand, on which her beloved placed a ring in making her a sacred promise, always remains outside her grave since her burial."

"Perhaps you know the man," the minstrel says to the count, "whose duty it is to keep his promise."

Bécquer concludes the tale thus:

In a poor hamlet beside the road to Gómara I recently saw the very spot where they say the strange ceremony of the count's marriage took place.

After the count, kneeling by the simple grave, had taken Margarita's hand in his, a priest authorized by the pope himself blessed this lugubrious union, and then it is said the wonder ceased and the dead hand sank beneath the earth forever.

At the foot of several ancient, thick trees there is a patch of meadow which, when Spring arrives, is spontaneously covered with marguerites [daisies].

The townsfolk say that Margarita is buried at that spot.

A MEDIEVAL LEGEND FROM RAVENNA

In slightly overheated prose, a lesbian who preferred the more masculine pen name of "Vernon Lee" wrote of *Ravenna and Her Ghosts*. In the course of her travelogue, she gives us a legend retold by Boccaccio, illustrated by Botticelli, versified by Dryden, and part of the European heritage. She claims she is translating from a manuscript "in the barbarous Romagnol dialect of the fifteenth century" obtained "in a manner I am not at liberty to divulge."

About that time (when Messer Guido da Pollenta was lord of Ravenna) men spoke not a little of what happened to Messer Nastasio de Honestis, son of Messer Brunoro, in the forest of Classis. Now the forest of Classis is exceeding vast, extending along the sea-shore between Ravenna and Cervia for the space of some fifteen miles, and has its beginning near the church of Saint Apollinaris, which is in the marsh; and you reach it directly from the gate of the same name, but also, crossing the river Ronco where it is easier to ford, by the gate called Sisa, beyond the houses of the Rasponis. And this forest aforesaid is made of many kinds of noble and useful trees, to wit, oaks, both free standing and in bushes, ilexes, elms, poplars, bays, and many plants of smaller growth but great dignity and pleasantness, as hawthorns, barberries, blackthorn, blackberry, brier-rose, and the thorn called marrucca, which bears pods resembling small hats or cymbals, and is excellent for hedging. But principally does this noble forest consist of pine-trees, exceeding lofty and perpetually green; whence indeed the arms of this ancient city, formerly the seat of the Emperors of Rome, are none other than a green pine-tree.

And the forest aforesaid is well stocked with animals, both such as run and creep, and many birds. The animals are foxes, badgers, hares, rabbits, ferrets, squirrels, and wild boars, the which issue forth and eat the young crops and grub the fields with incredible damage to all concerned. Of the birds it would be too long to speak, both of those which are snared, shot with cross-bows, or hunted with the falcon; and they feed of fish in the ponds and streams of the forest, and grasses and berries, and the pods of the white vine [clematis] which covers the grass on all sides.

And the manner of Messer Nastasio being in the forest was thus, he being at the time a youth of twenty years or thereabouts, of illustrious birth, and comely person and learning and prowess, and modest and discreet bearing. It so happened that he was enamoured of the daughter of Messer Hostasio de Traversariis. The damsel was lovely but exceeding coy and shrewish, and would not consent to marry him. This despite the desire of her parents, who in everything, as happens with only daughters of old men (for Messer Hostasio was well stricken in years), sought only to please her. Whereupon Messer Nastasio, fearing lest the damsel might despise his fortunes, wasted his substance in presents and feastings and housings, but all to no avail.

When it happened that having spent nearly all he possessed and ashamed to show his poverty and his unlucky love before the eyes of his townsmen, he betook him to the forest of Classis, it being autumn, on the pretext of snaring birds, but intending to take privily the road to Rimini and thence to Rome, and there seek his fortune. And Nastasio took with him fowling-nets, and bird-lime, and tame owls, and two horses (one of which was ridden by his servant), and food for some days; and they alighted in the midst of the forest, and slept in one of the fowling-huts of cut branches set up by the citizens of Ravenna for their pleasure.

And it happened that on the afternoon of the second day (and it chanced to be Friday) of his stay in the forest, Messer Nastasio, being exceeding sad in his heart, went forth towards the sea to muse upon the unkindness of his beloved and the hardness of his fortune. Now you should know that near the sea, where you can clearly hear its roar even on windless days, there is in that forest a clear place, made as by the hand of man, set round with tall pines even like a garden, but in the shape of a horse-course, free from bushes and pools, and covered with the finest greensward. Here, Nastasio sat him on the trunk of a pine. The hour was sunset, and the weather being uncommon clear he heard a rushing sound in the distance, as of the sea; and there blew a death-cold wind; and then came sounds of crashing branches, and neighing of horses, and yelping of hounds, and halloes and horns. And Nastasio wondered greatly, for that was not the hour for hunting; and he hid behind a great pine trunk, fearing to be recognized. And the sounds came nearer, even of horns and hounds, and the shouts of huntsmen; and the bushes rustled and crashed, and the hunt rushed into the clearing, horsemen and foot, with many hounds. And behold, what they pursued was not a wild boar, but something white that ran erect, and it seemed to Messer Nastasio, as if it greatly resembled a naked woman; and it screamed piteously.

Now when the hunt had swept past, Messer Nastasio rubbed his eyes and wondered greatly. But even as he wondered, and stood in the middle of the clearing, behold, part of the hunt swept back, and the thing which they pursued ran in a circle on the greensward, shrieking piteously. And behold, it was a young damsel, naked, her hair loose and full of brambles, with only a tattered cloth around her middle. And as she came near to where Messer Nastasio was standing (but no one of the hunt seemed to heed him) the hounds were upon her, barking furiously, and a hunter on a black horse, black even as night. And a cold wind blew and caused Nastasio's hair to stand on end; and he tried to cry out, and to rush forward, but his voice died in his throat and his limbs were heavy and covered with sweat, and refused to move.

Then the hounds fastened on the damsel threw her down, and he on the black horse turned swiftly, and transfixed her, shrieking dismally with a boar-spear. And those of the hunt galloped up, and wound their horns; and he on the black horse, which was a stately youth habited in a coat of black and gold, and black boots and black feathers on his hat, threw his reins to a groom, and alighted and approached the damsel where she lay, while the huntsmen were holding back the hounds and winding their horns. Then he drew a knife, such as are used by huntsmen, and driving its blade into the damsel's side, cut out her heart, and threw it, all smoking, into the midst of the hounds. And a cold wind rustled through the bushes, and all had disappeared, horses, and huntsmen, and hounds. And the grass was untrodden as if no man's foot or horse's hoof had passed there for months.

And Messer Nastasio shuddered, and his limbs loosened, and he knew that the hunter on the black horse was Messer Guido degli Anastagi, and the damsel Monna Filomena, daughter of the Lord of Gambellara. Messer Guido had loved the damsel greatly, and been flouted by her, and leaving his home in despair, had been killed on the way by robbers, and Monna

Filomena had died shortly after. The tale was still fresh in men's memories, for it had happened in the city of Ravenna barely five years before. And those whom Nastasio had seen, both the hunter and the lady, and the huntsmen and horses and hounds, were the spirits of the dead.

When he had recovered his courage, Messer Nastasio sighed and said unto himself: "How like is my fate to that of Messer Guido! Yet would I never, even when a spectre, without weight or substance, made of wind and delusion, and arisen from hell, act with such cruelty towards her I love." And then he thought: "Would that the daughter of Messer Pavolo de Traversariis might hear of this! For surely it would cause her to relent!" But he knew that his words would be in vain, and that none of the citizens of Ravenna, and least of all the damsel of the Traversari, would believe them, but rather esteem him a madman.

Now it came about that when Friday came round once more, Nastasio, by some chance, was again walking in the forest-clearing by the great pines, and he had forgotten; when the sea began to roar, and a cold wind blew; and there came through the forest the sound of horses and hounds, causing Messer Nastasio's hair to stand up and his limbs to grow weak as water. And he on the black horse again pursued the naked damsel, and struck her with his boar-spear, and cut out her heart and threw it to the hounds; the which hunter and damsel were the ghosts of Messer Guido, and of Madonna Filomena, daughter of the Lord of Gambellara, arisen out of Hell. And in this fashion did it happen for three Fridays following, the sea beginning to moan, the cold wind to blow and the spirits to hunt the deceased damsel at twilight in the clearing among the pine-trees.

Now when Messer Nastasio noticed this, he thanked Cupid, which is the Lord of all lovers, and devised in his mind a cunning plan. And he mounted his horse and returned to Ravenna, and gave out to his friends that he had found a treasure in Rome; and that he was minded to forget the damsel of the Traversari and seek another wife. But in reality he went to certain money-lenders, and gave himself into bondage, even to be sold as a slave to the Dalmatian pirates if he could not repay his loan. And he published that he desired to take to him a wife, and for that reason would feast all his friends and the chief citizens of Ravenna, and regale them with a pageant in the pine forest, where certain foreign slaves of his would show wonderful feats for their delight. And he sent forth invitations, and among them to Messer Pavolo de Traversariis and his wife and daughter. And he bid them for a Friday, which was also the eve of the Feast of the Dead.

Meanwhile he took to the pine forest carpenters and masons, and such as paint and gild cunningly, and waggons of timber, and cut stone for foundations, and furniture of all kinds; and the waggons were drawn by four and twenty yoke of oxen, grey oxen of the Romagnol breed. And he caused the artisans to work day and night, making great fires of dry myrtle and pine branches, which lit up the forest all around. And he caused them to make foundations, and build a pavilion of timber in the clearing which is the shape of a horse-course, surrounded by pines. The pavilion was oblong, raised by ten steps above the grass, open all round and reposing on arches and pillars; and there was a projecting *abacus* under the arches over the capitals, after the Roman fashion; and the pillars were painted red, and the capitals red also picked out with gold and blue, and a shield with the arms of the Honestis on each. The roof was raftered, each rafter painted with white lilies on a red ground, and heads of youths and damsels; and the roof outside was made of wooden tiles, shaped like shells and gilded. And on the top of the roof was a weather-vane; and the vane was a figure of Cupid, god of love, cunningly carved of wood and painted like life, and he flies, poised in air, and shoots his darts on mortals. He was winged and blindfolded, to show that love is inconstant and no respecter of persons; and when the wind blew, he turned about, and the end of his scarf, which was beaten metal, swung in the wind.

Now when the pavilion was ready, within six days of its beginning, carpets were spread on the floor, and seats placed, and garlands of bay and myrtle slung from pillar to pillar between the arches. And tables were set, and sideboards covered with gold and silver dishes and trenchers; and a raised place, covered with arras, was made for the players of fifes and drums and lutes; and tents were set behind for the servants, and fires prepared for cooking meat. White oxen and sheep were brought from Ravenna in wains, and casks of wine, and fruit and white bread, and many cooks, and serving-men, and musicians, all habited gallantly in the colours of the Honestis, which are vermilion and white, parti-coloured, with black stripes; and they wore doublets laced with gold, and on their breast the arms of the house of Honestis, which are a dove holding a leaf.

Now on Friday the eve of the Feast of the Dead, all was ready, and the chief citizens of Ravenna set out for the forest of Classis, with their wives and children and servants, some on horseback, and others in wains drawn by oxen, for the tracks in that forest are deep. And when they arrived, Messer Nastasio welcomed them and thanked them all, and conducted them to their places in the pavilion. Then all wondered greatly at its beauty and magnificence, and chiefly Messer Pavolo de Traversariis; and he sighed, and thought within himself, "Would that my daughter were less shrewish, that I might have so noble a son-in-law to prop up my old age!" They were seated at the tables, each according to their dignity, and they ate and drank and praised the excellence of the cheer; and flowers were scattered on the tables, and young maidens sang songs in praise of love, most sweetly.

Now when they had eaten their fill, and tables been removed, and the sun was setting between the pine-trees, Messer Nastasio caused them all to be seated facing the clearing, and a herald came forward, in the livery of the Honestis, sounding his trumpet and declaring in a loud voice that they should now witness a pageant, the which was called the Mystery of Love and Death. Then the musicians struck up, and began a concert of fifes and lutes, exceeding sweet and mournful. And at that moment the sea began to moan, and a cold wind to blow; a sound of horsemen and hounds and horns and crashing branches came through the wood; and the damsel, the daughter of the Lord of Gambellara, rushed naked, her hair streaming and her feet torn, across the grass, pursued by the hounds, and by the ghost of Messer Guido on the black horse, the nostrils of which were filled with fire.

Now when the ghost of Messer Guido struck that damsel with the boar-spear, and cut out her heart, and threw it, while the others wound their horns, to the hounds, and all vanished, Messer Nastasio de Honestis, seizing the herald's trumpet, blew in it, and cried in a loud voice, "The Pageant of Death and Love! The Pageant of Death and Love! Such is the fate of cruel damsels!" and the gilt Cupid on the roof swung round creaking dreadfully, and the daughter of Messer Pavolo uttered a great shriek and fell on the ground in a swoon.

Here the Romagnol manuscript comes to a sudden end, the outer sheet being torn through the middle. But we know from the Decameron that the damsel of the Traversari was so impressed by the spectre-hunt she had witnessed that she forthwith relented towards Nastaio degli Honesti and married him, and that they lived happily ever after. Whether or not that part of the pine forest of Classis still witnesses this ghostly hunt, we have no means of knowing.

BILOCATION

You can't be in two places at the same time, people say. Others disagree. Maybe you could be dying in India and appearing in England at the same time to let your relatives know. Many instances of that were offered to The Society for Psychical Research in the nineteenth century particularly. Maybe you could be dead and in the grave, or in Heaven, and walk around on earth as a ghost. You might even be able to bilocate, as the term goes, while still alive.

Hagiographies report a number of instances of saints and the blessed in two places at the same time. St. Francis Xavier, St. Anthony of Padua, Blessed Angelo of Acri and Blessed Martin of Porres were all said to have performed this trick. St. Joseph of Cupertino—he got into one of my earlier books by giving a pope an exhibition not just of levitation but of flying—and St. Alfonse Liguori were both said to have appeared in ghostly form, while still alive themselves, to assist at the bedsides of dying persons.

The werewolf was said sometimes to go forth as a spirit and take lupine form while the human body lay in a kind of trance at home, an out-of-body experience.

If the living can send the spirit on out of body experiences, perhaps after death the spirit can be free of the body. This is a theory of great interest to those who believe in ghosts.

Montague Summers brings up the subject in connection with one of the stories *(The Ghost Detective)* he includes in his anthology of Victorian ghost stories and he quotes the jargon of the Rev. F. P. Siegfried, who wrote:

> Should God choose to deprive a body of its extensional relation to this place and thus, so to speak, delocalize the material substance, the latter would be quasi spiritualized and would thus, besides its natural circumscriptive location, be capable of receiving definitive and consequently multiple location; for in this case the obstacle to bilocation, viz., actual local extension, would have been removed. Replication does not involve multiplication of the body's substance, but only the multiplication of its local relations to other bodies. The existence of its substance in one place is contradicted only by non-existence in that same place, but says nothing *per se* about existence or non-existence elsewhere.

THE DREAM
by Joseph Sheridan Le Fanu

Le Fanu, despite his surname, was born in Dublin and, as his middle name suggests, he was related to the dramatist Richard Brinsley Sheridan. Trained as a lawyer, he never practiced but rather from an early age contributed to the *Dublin University Magazine*, of which, near the end of his busy literary life, he became proprietor and editor. He wrote ballads and many other kinds of literature but he reigns as a master of the fiction of mystery and terror: *The House by the Churchyard* (1863) and *Uncle Silas* (1864), other novels whose basic ideas often appeared in short stories, and the collection of short stories published under the title of *In a Glass Darkly* (1872). Here is one of his short stories, a ghost tale that was to be much imitated in the rest of his century and the next. It is called *The Dream*. It is strange here, for it is the story of what you might call a ghost before he died. Read on.

DREAMS! What age, or what country of the world, has not felt and acknowledged the mystery of their origin and end? I have thought not a little upon the subject, seeing it is one which has been often forced upon my attentions, and sometimes strangely enough; and yet I have never arrived at anything which at all appeared a satisfactory conclusion. It does appear that a mental phenomenon so extraordinary cannot be wholly without its use. We know, indeed, that in the olden times it has been made the organ of communication between the Deity and His creatures; and when a dream produces upon a mind, to all appearance hopelessly reprobate and depraved, an effect so powerful and so lasting as to break down the inveterate habits, and to reform the life of an aban-doned sinner, we see in the result, in the reformation of morals which appeared incorrigible, in the reclamation of a human soul which seemed to be irretrievably lost, something more than could be produced by a mere chimera of the slumbering fancy, something more than could arise from the capricious images of a terrified imagination. And while Reason rejects as absurd the superstition which will read a prophecy in every dream, she may, without vio-lence to herself, recognize, even in the wildest and most incon-gruous of the wanderings of a slumbering intellect, the evidences and the fragments of a language which may be spoken, which *has* been spoken, to terrify, to warn and to command. We have rea-son to believe, too, by the promptness of action which in the age of the prophets followed all intimations of this kind, and by the strength of conviction and strange permanence of the effects result-ing from certain dreams in latter times—which effects we ourselves may have witnessed—that when this medium of communications has been employed by the Deity, the evidences of His presence have been unequivocal. My thoughts were directed to this subject in a manner to leave a lasting impression upon my mind, by the events which I shall now relate, the statement of which, however extra-ordinary, is nevertheless accurate.

About the year 17—, having been appointed to the living of C——h, I rented a small house in the town which bears the same name: one morning in the month of November, I was awakened before my usual time by my servant, who bustled into my bedroom for the purpose of announcing a sick call. As the Catholic Church holds her last rites to be totally indispensable to the safety of the departing sinner, no conscientious clergyman can afford a moment's unnecessary delay, and in little more than five minutes I stood ready, cloaked and booted for the road, in the small front parlour in which the messenger, who was to act as guide, awaited my coming. I found a poor little girl crying piteously near the door, and after some slight difficulty I ascertained that her father was either dead or just dying.

"And what may be your father's name, my poor child?" said I. She held down her head as if ashamed. I repeated the question, and the wretched little creature burst into floods of tears still more bitter than she had shed before. At length, almost angered by conduct which appeared to me so unreasonable, I began to lose patience, and I said rather harshly:

"If you will not tell me the name of the person to whom you would lead me, your silence can arise from no good motive, and I might be justified in refusing to go with you at all."

"Oh, don't say that—don't say that!" cried she. "Oh, sir, it was that I was afeard of when I would not tell you—I was afeard, when you heard his name, you would not come with me; but it is no use hidin' it now—it's Pat Connell, the carpenter, your honour."

She looked in my face with the most earnest anxiety, as if her very existence depended upon what she should read there. I relieved the child at once. The name, indeed, was most unpleasantly familiar to me; but, however fruitless my visits and advice might have been at another time, the present was too fearful an occasion to suffer my doubts of their utility, or my reluctance to re-attempting what appeared a hopeless task, to weigh even against the lightest chance that a consciousness of his imminent danger might produce in him a more docile and tractable disposition. Accordingly I told the child to lead the way, and followed her in silence. She hurried rapidly through the long narrow street which forms the great thoroughfare of the town. The darkness of the hour, rendered still deeper by the close approach of the old-fashioned houses, which lowered in tall obscurity on either side of the way; the damp, dreary chill which renders the advance of morning peculiarly cheerless, combined with the object of my walk— to visit the death-bed of a presumptuous sinner, to endeavour, almost against my own conviction, to infuse a hope into the heart of a dying reprobate—a drunkard but too probably perishing under the consequences of some mad fit of intoxication; all these circumstances served to enhance the gloom and solemnity of my feelings, as I silently followed my little guide, who with quick steps traversed the uneven pavement of the main street. After a walk of about five minutes, she turned off into a narrow lane of that obscure and comfortless class which is to be found in almost all small old-fashioned towns, chill, without ventilation, reeking with all manner of offensive effluvia, and lined by dingy, smoky, sickly and pent-up buildings, frequently not only in a wretched but in a dangerous condition.

"Your father has changed his abode since I last visited him, and, I am afraid, much for the worse," said I.

"Indeed he has, sir; but we must not complain," replied she. "We have to thank God that we have lodging and food, though it's poor enough, it is, your honour."

Poor child! thought I. How many an older head might learn wisdom from thee—how many a luxurious philosopher, who is skilled to preach but not to suffer, might not thy patient words put to the blush! The manner and language of my companion were alike above her years and station; and, indeed, in all cases in which the cares and sorrows of life have anticipated their usual date, and have fallen, as they sometimes do, with melancholy prematurity to the lot of childhood, I have observed the result to have proved uniformly the same. A young mind, to which joy and indulgence have been strangers, and to which suffering and self-denial have been familiarized from the first, acquires a solidity and an elevation which no other discipline could have bestowed, and which, in the present case, communicated a striking but mournful peculiarity to the manners, even to the voice, of the child. We paused before a narrow, crazy door, which she opened by means of a latch, and we forthwith began to ascend the steep and broken stairs which led to the sick man's room.

As we mounted the flight after flight towards the garret-floor, I heard more and more distinctly the hurried talking of many voices. I could also distinguish the low sobbing of a female. On arriving upon the uppermost lobby, these sounds became fully audible.

"This way, your honour," said my little conductress; at the same time, pushing open a door of patched and half-rotten plank, she admitted me into the squalid chamber of death and misery. But one candle, held in the fingers of a scared and haggard-looking child, was burning in the room, and that so dim that all was twilight or darkness except within its immediate influence. The general obscurity, however, served to throw into prominent and startling relief the deathbed and its occupant. The light fell with horrible clearness upon the blue and swollen features of the drunkard. I did not think it possible that a human countenance could look so terrific. The lips were black and drawn apart; the teeth were firmly set; the eyes a little unclosed, and nothing but the whites appearing. Every feature was fixed and livid, and the whole face wore a ghastly and rigid expression of despairing terror such as I never saw equaled.

His hands were crossed upon his breast, and firmly clenched; while, as if to add to the corpse-like effect of the whole, some white cloths, dipped in water, were wound about the forehead and temples.

As soon as I could remove my eyes from this horrible spectacle, I observed my friend Dr. D———, one of the most humane of a humane profession, standing by the bedside. He had been attempting, but unsuccessfully, to bleed the patient, and had now applied his finger to the pulse.

"Is there any hope?" I inquired in a whisper.

A shake of the head was the reply. There was a pause, while he continued to hold the wrist; but he waited in vain for the throb of life—it was not there: and when he let go the hand it fell stiffly back into its former position upon the other.

"The man is dead," said the physician, as he turned from the bed where the terrible figure lay.

Dead! thought I, scarcely venturing to look upon the tremendous and revolting spectacle. Dead! without an hour for repentance, even a moment for reflection. Dead! without the rites which even the best should have. Was there a hope for him? The glaring eyeball, the grinning mouth, the distorted brow—that unutterable look in which a painter would have sought to embody the fixed despair of the nethermost hell—these were my answer.

The poor wife sat at a little distance, crying as if her heart would break—the younger children clustered round the bed, looking with wondering curiosity upon the form of death, never seen before.

When the first tumult of uncontrollable sorrow had passed away, availing myself of the solemnity and impressiveness of the scene, I desired the heart-stricken family to accompany me in prayer, and all knelt down while I solemnly and fervently repeated some of those prayers which appeared most applicable to the occasion. I employed myself thus in a manner which I trusted was not unprofitable, at least to the living, for about ten minutes; and having accomplished my task, I was the first to arise.

I looked upon the poor, sobbing, helpless creatures who knelt so humbly around me, and my heart bled for them. With a natural transition I turned my eyes from them to the bed in which the body lay; and, great God! What was the revulsion, the horror which I experienced on seeing the corpse-like, terrific thing seated half upright before me. The white cloths which had been wound about the head had now partly slipped from their position, and were hanging in grotesque festoons about the face and shoulders, while the distorted eyes leered from amid them—

"A sight to dream of, not to tell."
[Samuel Taylor Coleridge, *Christabel*, l. 253]

I stood actually riveted to the spot. The figure nodded its head and lifted its arm, I thought, with a menacing gesture. A thousand confused and horrible thoughts at once rushed upon my mind. I had often read that the body of a presumptuous sinner, who, during life, had been the willing creature of every satanic impulse, had been known, after the human tenant had deserted it, to become the horrible sport of demoniac possession.

I was roused by the piercing scream of the mother, who now, for the first time, perceived the change which had taken place. She rushed towards the bed, but, stunned by the shock and overcome by the conflict of violent emotions, before she reached it she fell prostrate upon the floor.

I am perfectly convinced that had I not been startled from the torpidity of horror in which I was bound by some powerful and arousing stimulant, I should have gazed upon this unearthly apparition until I had fairly lost my senses. As it was, however, the spell was broken—superstition gave way to reason: the man whom all believed to have been actually dead was living!

Dr. D——— was instantly standing by the bedside, and upon examination he found that a sudden and copious flow of blood had taken place from the wound which the lancet had left; and this, no doubt, had effected his sudden and almost supernatural restoration to an existence from which all thought he had been forever removed. The man was still speechless, but he seemed to understand the physician when he forbade his repeating the painful and fruitless attempts which he made to articulate, and he at once resigned himself quietly into his hands.

I left the patient with leeches upon his temples, and bleeding freely, apparently with little of the drowsiness which accompanies apoplexy. Indeed, Dr. D——— told me that he had never before witnessed a seizure which seemed to combine the symptoms of so many kinds, and yet which belonged to none of the recognized classes; it certainly was not apoplexy, catalexy, nor *delirium tremens*, and yet it seemed, in some degree, to partake of the properties of all. It was strange, but stranger things are coming.

During two or three days Dr. D——— would not allow his patient to converse in a manner which could excite or exhaust him, with anyone; he suffered him merely as briefly as possible to express his immediate wants. And it was not until the fourth day after my early visit, the particulars of which I have just detailed, that it was thought expedient that I should see him, and then only because it appeared that his extreme importunity and impatience to meet me were likely to retard his recovery more than the mere exhaustion attendant upon a short conversation could possibly do. Perhaps, too, my friend entertained some hope that if by holy confession his patient's bosom were eased of the perilous stuff which no doubt oppressed it, his recovery would by more assured and rapid. It was then, as I have said, upon the fourth day after my first professional call that I found myself once more in the dreary chamber of want and sickness.

The man was in bed, and appeared low and restless. On my entering the room he raised himself in the bed, and muttered, twice or thrice:

"Thank God! thank God!"

I signed to those of his family who stood by to leave the room, and took a chair beside the bed. So soon as we were alone, he said, rather doggedly:

"There's no use in telling me of the sinfulness of bad ways— I know it all. I know where they lead to—I have seen everything about it with my own eyesight, as plain as I see you." He rolled himself in the bed, as if to hide his face in the clothes; and then suddenly raising himself, he exclaimed with startling vehemence, "Look, sir! there is no use in mincing the matter: I'm blasted with the fires of hell; I have been in hell. What do you think of that? In hell—I'm lost forever—I have not a chance. I am damned already—damned—damned!"

The end of this sentence he actually shouted. His vehemence was perfectly terrific; he threw himself back, and laughed, and sobbed hysterically. I poured some water into a tea-cup, and gave it to him. After he had swallowed it, I told him if he had anything to communicate to do so as briefly as he could, and in a manner as little agitating to himself as possible; threatening at the same time, though I had no intention of doing so, to leave him at once in case he again gave way to such passionate excitement.

"It's only foolishness," he continued, "for me to try to thank you for coming to such a villain as myself at all. It's no use for me to wish good to you, or to bless you; for such as me has no blessings to give."

I told him that I had but done my duty, and urged him to proceed to the matter which weighed upon his mind. He then spoke nearly as follows:

"I came in drunk of Friday night last, and got to my bed here; I don't remember how. Sometime in the night it seemed to me I

wakened, and feeling uneasy in myself, I got up out of the bed. I
wanted the fresh air; but I would not make a noise to open the window, for fear I'd waken the crathurs. It was very dark and troublesome to find the door; but at last I did get it, and I groped my
way out, and went down as easy as I could. I felt quite sober, and
I counted the steps one after another, as I was going down, that I
might not stumble at the bottom.

"When I came to the first landing-place—God be about us
always!—the floor of it sunk under me, and I went down—down—
down, till the senses almost left me. I do not know how long I was
falling, but it seemed to me a great while. When I came rightly to
myself at last, I was sitting near the top of a great table; and I could
not see the end of it, if it had any, it was so far off. And there was
men beyond reckoning sitting down all along by it, at each side,
as far as I could see at all. I did not know at first was it in the open
air; but there was a close smothering feel in it that was not natural. And there was a kind of light that my eyesight never saw
before, red and unsteady; and I did not see for a long time where
it was coming from, until I looked straight up, and then I seen that
it came from great balls of blood-coloured fire that were rolling
high overhead with a sort of rushing, trembling sound, and I perceived that they shone on the ribs of a great roof of rock that was
arched overhead instead of the sky. When I seen this, scarce knowing what I did, I got up, and I said, 'I have no right to be here; I
must go.' And the man that was sitting at my left hand only smiled,
and said, 'Sit down again; you can *never* leave this place.' And his
voice was weaker than any child's voice I ever heard; and when he
was done speaking he smiled again.

"Then I spoke out very loud and bold, and I said, 'In the name
of God, let me out of this bad place.' And there was a great man
that I did not see before, sitting at the end of the table that I was
near; and he was taller than twelve men, and his face was very proud
and terrible to look at. And he stood up and stretched out his hand
before him; and when he stood up, all that was there, great and
small, bowed down with a sighing sound; and a dread came on my
heart, and he looked at me, and I could not speak. I felt I was his
own, to do what he liked with, for I knew at once who he was; and
he said, 'If you promise to return, you may depart for a season;'
and the voice he spoke with was terrible and mournful, and the
echoes of it went rolling and swelling down the endless cave, and
mixing with the trembling of the fire overhead; so that when he
sat down there was a sound after him, all through the place, like
the roaring of a furnace. And I said, with all the strength I had, 'I

promise to come back—in God's name let me go!'

"And with that I lost the sight and hearing of all that was there, and when my senses came to me again I was sitting in the bed with the blood all over me, and you and the rest praying around the room."

Here he paused, and wiped away the chill drops which hung upon his forehead.

I remained silent for some moments. The vision which he had just described struck my imagination not a little, for this was long before Vathek [William Beckford's oriental tale] and the "Hall of Eblis" [a story about the devil] had delighted the world; and the description which he gave had, as I received it, all the attractions of novelty beside the impressiveness which always belongs to the narration of an *eye-witness*, whether in the body or in the spirit, of the scenes which he describes. There was something, too, in the stern horror with which the man related these things, and in the incongruity of his description with the vulgarly received notions of the great place of punishment, and of its presiding spirit, which struck my mind with awe, almost with fear. At length he said, with an expression of horrible, imploring earnestness which I shall never forget:

"Well, sir, is there any hope; is there any chance at all? or is my soul pledged and promised away for ever? is it gone out of my power? must I go back to the place?"

In answering him, I had no easy task to perform; for however clear might be my internal conviction of the groundlessness of his fears, and however strong my skepticism respecting the reality of what he had described, I nevertheless felt that his impression to the contrary, and his humility and terror resulting from it, might be made available as no mean engines in the work of his conversion from profligacy, and of his restoration to decent habits and to religious feeling.

I therefore told him that he was to regard his dream rather in the light of a warning than in that of a prophecy; that our salvation depended not upon the word or deed of a moment, but upon the habits of a life; that, in fine, if he at once discarded his idle companions and evil habits, and firmly adhered to a sober, industrious and religious course of life, the powers of darkness might claim his soul in vain, for that there were higher and firmer pledges than human tongue could utter, which promised salvation to him who should repent and lead a new life.

I left him much comforted, and with a promise to return upon the next day. I did so, and found him much more cheerful, and without any remains of the dogged sullenness which I suppose had arisen from his despair. His promises of amendment were given in that tone of deliberate earnestness which belongs to deep and solemn determination; and it was with no small delight that I observed, after repeated visits, that his good resolutions, so far from failing, did but gather strength by time, and when I saw that man shake off the idle and debauched companions whose society had for years formed alike his amusement and his ruin, and revive his long-discarded habits of industry and sobriety, I said within myself, There is something more in all this than the operation of an idle dream.

One day, some time after his perfect restoration to health, I was surprised, on ascending the stairs for the purpose of visiting this man, to find him busily employed in nailing down some planks upon the landing-place, through which, at the commencement of his mysterious vision, it seemed to him that he had sunk. I perceived at once that he was strengthening the floor with a view to securing himself against such a catastrophe, and could scarcely forbear a smile as I bid "God bless his work."

He perceived my thoughts, I suppose, for he immediately said:

"I can never pass over that floor without trembling. I'd leave this house if I could, but I can't find another lodging in the town so cheap, and I'll not take a better till I've paid off all my debts, please God; but I could not be easy in my mind till I made it as safe as I could. You'll hardly believe me, your honour, that while I'm working, maybe a mile away, my heart is in a flutter the whole way back with the bare thoughts of the two little steps I have to walk upon this bit of a floor. So it's no wonder, sir, I'd thry to make it sound and firm with any idle timber I have."

I applauded his resolution to pay off his debts, and the steadiness with which he pursued his plans of conscientious economy, and passed on.

Many months elapsed, and still there appeared no alteration in his resolutions of amendment. He was a good workman, and with his better habits he recovered his former extensive and profitable employment. Everything seemed to promise comfort and respectability. I have little more to add, and that shall be told quickly. I had one evening met Pat Connell, as he returned from his work, and as usual, after a mutual, and on his side respectful salutation, I spoke a few words of encouragement and approval. I left him industrious, active, healthy—when next I saw him, not three days after, he was a corpse.

The circumstances which marked the event of his death were somewhat strange—I might say fearful. The unfortunate man had accidentally met an old friend just returned, after a long absence; and in a moment of excitement, forgetting everything in the warmth of his joy, he yielded to his urgent invitation to accompany him into a public-house, which lay close by the spot where the encounter had taken place. Connell, however, previously to entering the room, had announced his determination to take nothing more than the strictest temperance would warrant.

But oh! who can describe the inveterate tenacity with which a drunkard's habits cling to him through life? He may repent, he may reform, he may look with actual abhorrence upon his past profligacy; but amid all this reformation and compunction, who can tell the moment in which the base and ruinous propensity may not recur, triumphing over resolution, remorse, shame, everything, and prostrating its victim once more in all that is destructive and revolting in that fatal vice?

The wretched man left the place in a state of utter intoxication. He was brought home nearly insensible, and placed in his bed. The younger part of the family retired to rest much after their usual hour; but the poor wife remained up sitting by the fire, too much grieved and shocked at the occurrence of what she had so little expected, to settle to rest. Fatigue, however, at length overcame her, and she sank gradually into an uneasy slumber. She could not tell how long she had remained in this state; but when she awakened, and immediatcly on opening her eyes, she perceived by the faint red light of the smouldering turf embers two persons, one of whom she recognized as her husband, noiselessly gliding out of the room.

"Pat, darling, where are you going?" said she.

There was no answer—the door closed after them; but in a moment she was startled and terrified by a loud and heavy crash, as if some ponderous body had been hurled down the stair.

Much alarmed, she started up, and going to the head of the staircase she called repeatedly upon her husband, but in vain.

She returned to the room, and with the assistance of her daughter whom I had occasion to mention before, she succeeded in finding and lighting a candle, with which she hurried again to the head of the staircase.

At the bottom lay what seemed to be a bundle of clothes, heaped together, motionless, lifeless—it was her husband. In going down the stairs, for what purpose can never now be known, he had fallen helplessly and violently to the bottom, and, coming head foremost, the spine of the neck had been dislocated by the shock, and instant death must have ensued.

The body lay upon that landing-place to which his dream had referred.

It is scarcely worth endeavouring to clear up a single point in a narrative where all is mystery; yet I could not help suspecting that the second figure which had been seen in the room by Connell's wife on the night of his death might have been no other than his own shadow.

I suggested this solution of the difficulty; but she told me that the unknown person had been considerably in advance of her husband, and on reaching the door had turned back as if to communicate something to his companion.

It was, then, a mystery.

Was the dream verified?—whither had the disembodied spirit sped? Who can say? We know not. But I left the house of death that day in a state of horror which I could not describe. It seemed to me that I was scarce awake. I heard and saw everything as if under the spell of a nightmare. The coincidence was terrible.

THE TALE OF COUNT BERTHOLD

The man who wrote of the occult under the *nom de plume* of "Paul Christian" was a librarian at The Arsenal in Paris. There he found many rare documents for his nineteenth-century *History and Practice of Magic* (translated 1963). In that book he tells a story about Count Berthold's marvelous adventures. I shall retell it for you.

One stormy night a weary traveler arrived at the nobleman's castle. It was perched on a mountain crag near Nôtre Dame des Eremites, to which the traveler was going, barefoot, in search of a miracle for his son. The nobleman gave the traveler "God's portion," food reserved for hospitality for the poor, and paid no more attention to him. He continued to carouse with his friends. The traveler was shocked to hear the count and his friends blaspheme.

"If The Devil himself crossed my path," boasted the count, "I should no more fall back before him than I would before The Deity." And the count drank to Satan: "I offer him a thousand thanks if he will be so kind to escort me tonight." Then he rode out into the storm.

On the mountain road he was afraid. Brave on the battlefield, where he could see the enemy, the count had a superstitious dread of the unseen, the *Bergmainnlein* [mountain spirits]. Suddenly those supernatural powers did make themselves visible: two monstrous hands, bathed in a ghastly green light, appeared at the head of his horse. He forced his steed ahead and the hands vanished, only to be replaced by two ghostly knights in black armor who rode up from behind.

The black knights drew the count on higher and higher over the crags until they reached eternal snows and there, from the depths of an enormous trench, a voice cried: "Give us the blasphemer!"

Just as he was about to plunge with his horse into the abyss, the count cried, "My God! I am lost!"

It was perhaps the first time in all his life that the count had called upon God, but at this the black knights withdrew and in the distance was suddenly revealed to the count the statue of The Blessed Virgin which stood on top of the church at Nôtre Dame des Eremites. Using that mysteriously illuminated statue as his guide, the count made his way back over treacherous mountain crags, all the while resolving to dedicate his life to the The Virgin.

So he did, for when he reached the monastery attached to the church—a monastery where the monks told him that during the night the church bell had rung miraculously with no one touching it—he stayed there and spent the rest of his life faithful to his vow of leaving the world and serving The Virgin.

Such pious medieval tales as this contrived to recall beliefs in the old pagan superstitions and to make the average person more religious, and more superstitious about ghosts and other supernatural manifestations.

AN ELIZABETHAN GHOST STORY

Wicked Will Darrel lived at Littlecote, a Tudor mansion west of Hungerford in Berkshire. He committed incest with his sister and as a result of this vile affair a baby was conceived. When the time came for the woman to deliver, Wicked Will sent servants to bring to him Mother Barnes, a midwife who lived at Great Shefford, nearby. They blindfolded her and brought her secretly to a bedchamber in Wicked Will's mansion.

Mother Barnes delivered the baby and wrapped the boy in her apron to take him to his father. She found Wicked Will standing by the fireplace in a downstairs room. He snatched the child from her, threw him into the fire, and held him there with his boot until the unfortunate newborn was burned to death.

The horrified midwife was kept under guard in the house until, blindfolded, she could be taken back by the servants to her own home. But she was a shrewd woman. Unobserved, she cut a piece of the bed hangings to prove she had been in the bedroom and she silently counted the steps down to the room where Wicked Will destroyed his unwanted son.

With her evidence Wicked Will was brought to trial before Sir John Popham (1531?-1607) but by that time the midwife herself was dead. Wicked Will went free. Soon after he died, injured in a riding accident. The locals spread the story that Wicked Will's horse had been startled by the appearance of the ghost of the baby in the road.

People still point to the place called Will's Stile (or sometimes Darrel's Stile) where Wicked Will saw the ghost that cost him his life.

Now, they say, the ghost of both the baby and the mother are to be seen on occasion in that bedroom at Littlecote. Moreover, the ghost of Mother Barnes, with the baby in her apron, is said to appear now and then on that stairway in the house. The house, by the way, on the death of Wicked Will was acquired in 1589 by none other than Sir John, the judge who let Wicked Will go free because Mother Barnes was not alive to testify at the trial.

THE STATUE

This is my retelling of a traditional Swedish folktale, and it is a curious one. Stories of ghosts are common in folktales, but this one starts with a man insulting ghosts and takes a few surprising turns. Because it is not your

Canterburies
DREAME:
IN WHICH
The Apparition of Cardinall *Wolfey* did present himfelfe unto him on the fourteenth of May laſt paſt:

It being
The third night after my Lord of STRAFFORD had taken his fare-well to the WORLD.

Printed in the yeare 1641.

ordinary ghost story, I place it here rather than later under folklore. I believe you will enjoy it.

Once upon a time two men were walking through a churchyard, and one of them raised his cap reverently and said, "God bless all who rest here!"

"They have made their own beds and they must lie in them," said the other fellow. "They're getting whatever they deserve."

The revenge of the ghosts was swift. In an instant, the fellow was turned to stone.

No one could help him until a new pastor came to the church and moved the statue into his study. There he prayed over it every day and every night, and every time he came to "May God banish all evil from this house!" he heard a laugh. Did it come from the statue?

No, that was foolish. Or was it? No one was listening, so at last the pastor got up the courage to address the statue.

"Was that you laughing?"

Miracle of miracles, the statue spoke, "Yes, it was."

"And why do you laugh?"

You'll recall that the fellow who was turned into this statue was always pretty frank in his speech, so he up and told the pastor exactly what was so amusing. It was that the pastor, though so kind as to worry about the fate of the statue, was cruel to his wife, criticizing her all the time. And that brought little devils into the house every time he did that. Of course when he prayed that all evil be banished from the house they all had to troop out again. All this coming and going, especially as there was one little devil that limped a bit and always was tardy coming in and going out, trying to scurry after the others, was very funny, if you could see it. And the statue could!

So the pastor took the matter to heart and began to treat his wife better. The little devils ceased to visit, and the statue, having done a good deed, thus atoned for his insensitivity about the dead and came to life for a moment. Then he died a natural death. The parson had him buried in that same graveyard. There he rested peacefully ever after, in the fellowship of the very ghosts with whom he had once been so unsympathetic. The parson, having learned his lesson, lived the rest of his life happily with his wife.

THE HAND

Guy de Maupassant wrote a short story by this title in which a French magistrate in Corsica tells of Sir John Rowell, an Englishman, who showed him a gruesome souvenir; a severed human hand.

> It was a hand, a man's hand. Not a clean white hand of a skeleton but a blackened, desiccated hand, with yellow nails, bare muscles,

betraying old traces of blood, black blood, crusted around the bones, which had been cut off clean as with an ax about the middle of the forearm. Around the wrist of this filthy object was riveted a strong chain, which was attached to a ring strong enough to hold an elephant.

"What is that?" I asked.

"That is my worst enemy," the Englishman calmly replied.

The Englishman said he had cut off the hand of an American years before. Now he was afraid. "That hand is constantly trying to escape," the Englishman said. "The chain is necessary."

Later the Englishman was found dead, bearing all the marks of strangulation by a powerful hand. There had been a terrific struggle, and in it the Englishman had bitten off one of the fingers of the dead hand. It was clamped in his teeth, and on his dead face was an expression of the utmost terror.

Still later the hand, missing one finger, was found on the grave of the Englishman.

> The ladies [to whom the magistrate told the tale] were horrified, pale and trembling.
>
> "But the mystery is not solved. There is no explanation. We shall never be able to sleep if you do not tell us your own opinion of the matter."
>
> The magistrate gave a rather grim smile.
>
> "Well, ladies, I fear I shall deprive you of nightmares. It's my theory that the owner of that hand was not dead at all and that he came looking for his lost hand with the one that was left to him. But explaining how he did it is beyond me. It was a sort of revenge."
>
> Another lady protested: "No, that can't be the real explanation."
>
> Still smiling, the tale teller answered: "I warned you that it wouldn't satisfy you."

As the magistrate had remarked even before he began the tale, to some people it "really appeared to have an element of the supernatural in it" but, as he assured them, he himself had not "for one instant attributed anything of the supernatural to this incident" and always believed "in normal cases solely."

DISEASE AND GHOSTS

People have long believed that Plague is one of the Four Horsemen of the Apocalypse, and primitive people ascribe diseases to malevolent spirits. Stories of ghosts transmitting diseases, however, are rare. Here is an Irish tale of disease and ghosts.

Brian O'Hanaray inherited from his father of the same name (a captain in the Irish Guards) a wild streak and through his mother (daughter of an Irish lord, the Marquis of Montalan) a great fortune and a title. On his mother's side as well there was wildness: his grandfather, Marquis of Montalan, was extravagant and eccentric.

Soon after he came into his fortune (1788), the new marquis bought additional property to extend his holdings and on it was a ruined Cistercian Abbey. Despite an old curse engraved on a slab of flint warning everyone off, a warning that superstitious locals had honored for six centuries, the marquis took the marble from a private chapel for the new house of Portaranmore he was building and he rifled the tomb of a long-dead abbot, which was filled with gold and silver and jeweled ecclesiastical pieces. As the theatrical prose of James Reynolds in *Ghosts in Irish Houses* (1947) put it:

> Standing, swaying, in a wide, pointed niche was the panoplied skeleton of a man. On his head was a tall, spiked miter. A shredding purple and vermilion cope, heavily bossed in gold, hung crazily from the shoulder bones. A trefoiled crozier, richly jeweled, leaned out at an angle from the crook of a bony arm. Piled helter-skelter about the feet of this cadaver was every kind of altar gear—gold chalices and silver and gold reliquaries, covered with magnificent jewels which smoldered or flashed in the wavering light. The Abbot Fenir trampled for the last time on his riches.

The marquis was so terrified as the corpse fell toward him and the stench of decay rose up, the cerements disintegrating in the air, he vowed to give all the treasure to the nuns at Lisdoonvarna. And they did good work with the money that came from such as they sold, although people were worried about silver chalices that had never tarnished and never would! But it is said the abbot's ghost was still going to exact revenge.

The very night that a great party of house warming blazed at Portaranmore, the marquis was confronted on the stairs by the abbot's ghost. Staggering away, he reached out to steady himself and was touched on the left hand with a piece of the stinking cerements.

Thereafter his hand developed "a gray spot, which burned fiercely... the size of a guinea." He fled Portaranmore and for years wandered all over The Continent, hiding his bandages. Then he returned to live in the dower house of Portaranmore, at Knockaleedy Rasp, a small and melancholy house cut into the rocks, "in the teeth of the wind, and the eye of the setting sun." He had the great staircase of Portaranmore torn out and the remains of the private chapel razed, but for twenty years he never went near the great house.

When he died at Knockaleedy, his hand was found to be "red, bloated, splotched in white" and it is said that his servant saw "a thin trail of gray smoke lift from it."

Was this horrible condition created by the guilty mind of the reckless marquis, or was it the curse of the abbot's ghost?

More startling curses are recounted in *The Complete Book of Spells, Curses, and Magical Recipes*, the book which precedes this one in this series. But I still am not certain how some of them could function purely on the basis of the victim's self-destructive superstitions. The relationships between spiritual health and physical health are more complex than the stigmata and hysterical paralysis. They have never been explained fully to my personal satisfaction by science, Christian Science, or Scientology.

THE TALE OF THE DREAM FROM *THE THOUSAND AND ONE NIGHTS*

This is a story rather related to ghosts, figures that come to us in our dreams. You may say this is not a ghost story, but it is certainly a good story.

Once there was a merchant in Baghdad who had lost all his money and had a difficult time just staying alive. But one night, after he had lain down to sleep with a heavy heart as usual, a man appeared to him in a dream and said, "Your fortune awaits you in Cairo. Go there to seek it."

So desperate was the merchant that when he woke up, remembering the figure who had appeared to him in his dream and the message of hope, he set off for Cairo. He reached that city after a long and tiring journey and, having no money to stay at an inn, he curled up in the courtyard of a mosque. There, completely exhausted, he went to sleep.

Now, as the will of Allah would have it, some evil men had entered the mosque and, breaking down a wall that separated it from a private house, went into the house to burgle it. But the terrific noise alerted the occupants of the house and they raised the alarm, which brought the police.

The would-be burglars ran off, but the sleeping merchant was found in the courtyard of the mosque and was severely beaten by the police and then dragged off to jail.

Days later he was taken from his cell and brought before the chief of police, who asked him who he was and what he was doing there. The merchant explained that a figure had appeared to him in a dream and had told him he would find his fortune in Cairo. All he had found, however, was beating and imprisonment, and he had committed no crime.

"You were foolish to come all the way to Cairo on the strength of a promise in a dream," said the policeman. "I myself have had a man come to me in a dream on three different occasions, describing a house in Baghdad and telling where in the garden is buried a great treasure." And he told the merchant all the details of the dream and the house.

"Still I have not been foolish enough to go all the way to Baghdad. No, not for three dreams," said the policeman.

"Here is enough money for you to go back home. Do so, and forget your dream," he said to the merchant.

The merchant humbly accepted the money and rushed home, for the house and the garden in the policeman's dream were his own house and garden. He dug up the treasure in the garden, the promise of his dream was fulfilled, and he was rich again for the rest of his life.

THE HAUNTED HOUSE
From the Mss. Of the Late Diedrich Knickerbocker
[Washington Irving, *Bracebridge Hall*]

Formerly almost every place had a house of this kind. If a house was seated on some melancholy place, or built in some old romantic manner, or if any particular accident had happened in it, such as murder, sudden death, or the like, to be sure that house had a Mark set on it, and was afterwards esteemed the habitation of a ghost.

Bourne's Antiquities

In the neighbourhood of the ancient city of the Manhattoes there stood, not very many years since, an old mansion, which, when I was a boy, went by the name of the Haunted House. It was one of the very few remains of the architecture of the early Dutch settlers, and must have been a house of some consequence at the time when it was built. It consisted of a centre and two wings, the gable ends of which were shaped like stairs. It was built partly of wood, and partly of small Dutch bricks, such as the worthy colonists brought with them from Holland, before they discovered that bricks could be manufactured elsewhere. The house stood remote from the road, in the centre of a large field, with an avenue of old locust [acacia] trees leading up to it, several of which had been shivered by lightning, and two or three blown down. A few apple trees grew straggling about the field; there were traces also of what had been a kitchen-garden; but the fences were broken down, the vegetables had disappeared, or had grown wild and turned to little better than weeds, with here and there a ragged rose-bush, or a tall sunflower shooting up from among brambles, and hanging its head sorrowfully, as if contemplating the surrounding desolation. Part of the roof of the old house had fallen in, the windows were shattered, the pannels of the doors broken, and mended with rough boards, and there were two rusty weathercocks at the ends of the house which made a great jingling and whistling as they whirled about, but always pointed wrong. The appearance of the whole place was forlorn and desolate at the best of times; but, in unruly weather, the howling of the wind about the crazy old mansion, the screeching of the weathercocks, the slamming and banging of a few loose window-shutters, had altogether so wild and dreary an effect, that the neighbourhood stood perfectly in awe of the place, and pronounced it the rendezvous of hobgoblins. I recollect the old building well; for I remember how many times, when an idle, unlucky urchin, I have prowled round its precincts, with some of my graceless companions, on holiday afternoons, when out on a freebooting cruise among the orchards. There was a tree standing near the house that bore the most beautiful and tempting fruit; but then it was on enchanted ground, for the place was so charmed by frightful stories that we dreaded to approach it. Sometimes we would venture in a body, and get near the Hesperian tree, keeping an eye upon the old mansion, and darting fearful glances into its shattered windows; when, just as we were about to seize upon our prize, an exclamation from one of the gang, or an accidental noise, would throw us all into a panic, and we would scamper headlong from the place, nor stop until we had got quite into the road. Then there were sure to be a host of fearful anecdotes told of strange cries and groans, or of some hideous face suddenly seen staring out of one of the windows. By degrees we ceased to venture into these lonely grounds, but would stand at a distance and throw stones at the building; and there was something fearfully pleasing in the sound as they rattled along the roof, or sometimes struck some jingling fragments of glass out of the windows.

The origin of this house was lost in the obscurity that covers the early period of the province, while under the government of their high mightiness the states-general. Some reported it to have been a country residence of Wilhelmus Kieft, commonly called the Testy, one of the Dutch governors of New Amsterdam; others said that it had been built by a naval commander who served under Van Tromp, and who, on being disappointed of preferment, retired from the service in disgust, became a philosopher through sheer spite, and brought over all his wealth to the province, that he might live according to his humour, and despise the world. The reason of its having fallen to decay was likewise a matter of dispute; some said that it was in chancery, and had already cost more than its worth in legal expenses; but the most current, and, of course, the most probable account, was that it was haunted, and that nobody could live quietly in it. There can, in fact, be very little doubt that this last was the case, there were so many corroborating stories to prove it,—not an old woman in the neighborhood but could furnish at least a score. There was a gray-headed curmudgeon of a Negro that lived hard by, who had a whole budget of them to tell, many of which had happened to himself. I recollect many a time stopping with my schoolmates, and getting him to relate some. The old crone lived in a hovel, in the midst of a small patch of potatoes, and Indian corn, which his master had given him on setting him free. He would come to us, with his hoe in hand, and as we sat perched, like a row of swallows, on the rail of the fence, in the mellow twilight of a summer evening, he would tell us such fearful stories, accompanied by such awful rollings of his white eyes, that we were almost afraid of our own footsteps as we returned home afterwards in the dark.

Poor old Pompey! many years are past since he died, and went to keep company with the ghosts he was so fond of talking about. He was buried in a corner of his own little potato patch; the plough soon passed over his grave, and levelled it with the rest of the field, and nobody thought any more of the gray-headed Negro. By singular chance I was strolling in that neighbourhood several years afterwards, when I had grown up to be a young man, and I found a knot of gossips speculating on a skull which had just been turned up by a ploughshare. They of course determined it to be the remains of some one that has been murdered, and they had raked up with it some of the traditionary tales of the haunted house. I knew it at once to be the relic of poor Pompey, but I held my tongue; for I am too considerate of other people's enjoyment ever to mar a story of a ghost or a murder. I took care, however, to see the bones of my old friend once more buried in a place where they were not likely to be disturbed...

THE ADVENTURE OF THE
GERMAN STUDENT

Washington Irving (1783-1859) is most famous for *Rip Van Winkle* and *The Legend of Sleepy Hollow*, but here, after his story of the kind of "haunted" house so many children have known, is Irving's Gothic tale in the European fashion he made popular in America. It is from his well-received *Tales of a Traveller* (1824).

> On a stormy night, in the tempestuous times of the French revolution, a young German was returning to his lodgings, at a late hour, across the old part of Paris. The lightning gleamed, and the loud claps of thunder rattled through the lofty narrow streets—but I should first tell you something about this young German.

Gottfried Wolfgang was a young man of good family. He had studied for some time at Göttingen, but being of a visionary and enthusiastic character, he had wandered into those wild and speculative doctrines which have so often bewildered German students. His secluded life, his intense application, and the singular nature of his studies, had an effect on both mind and body. His health was impaired; his imagination diseased. He had been indulging in fanciful speculations on spiritual essences, until, like Swedenborg, he had an ideal world of his own around him. He took up a notion, I do not know from what cause, that there was an evil influence.... [which] produced the most gloomy effects. He became haggard and desponding. His friends discovered the mental malady preying upon him, and determined that the best cure was a change of scene; he was sent, therefore, to finish his studies amid the splendors and gayeties of Paris.

Wolfgang arrived at Paris at the breaking out of the revolution. The popular delirium at first caught his enthusiastic mind, and he was captivated by the political and philosophical theories of the day: but the scenes of blood which followed shocked his sensitive nature, disgusted him with society and the world, and made him more than ever a recluse. He shut himself up in a solitary apartment in the *Pays Latin*, the quarter of the students. There, in a gloomy street not far from the monastic walls of the Sorbonne, he pursued his favorite speculations. Sometimes he spent hours together in the great libraries of Paris, those catacombs of departed authors, rummaging among their hoards of dusty and obsolete works in quest of food for his unhealthy appetite. He was, in a manner, a literary ghoul, feeding in the charnel-house of decayed literature.

Wolfgang, though solitary and recluse, was of an ardent temperament, but for a time it operated merely upon his imagination. He was too shy and ignorant of the world to make any advances to the fair, but he was a passionate admirer of female beauty, and in his lonely chamber would often lose himself in reveries on forms and faces which he had seen, and his fancy would deck out images of loveliness far surpassing the reality.

While his mind was in this excited and sublimated state, a dream produced an extraordinary effect upon him. It was of a female face of transcendent beauty. So strong was the impression made, that he dreamt of it again and again. It haunted his thoughts by day, his slumbers by night; in fine, he became passionately enamoured of this shadow of a dream. This lasted so long that it became one of those fixed ideas which haunt the minds of melancholy men, and are at times mistaken for madness.

Such was Gottfried Wolfgang, and such his situation at the time I mentioned. He was returning home late one stormy night, through some of the old and gloomy streets of the Marais, the ancient part of Paris. The loud claps of thunder rattled among the high houses of the narrow streets. He came to the Place de Grève, the square where public executions are performed. The lightning quivered about the pinnacles of the ancient Hôtel de Ville, and shed flickering gleams over the open space in front. As Wolfgang was crossing the square, he shrank back with horror at finding himself close by the guillotine. It was the height of the reign of terror, when this dreadful instrument of death stood ever ready, and its scaffold was continually running with the blood of the virtuous and the brave. It had that very day been actively employed in the work of carnage, and there it stood in grim array, amidst a silent and sleeping city, waiting for fresh victims.

Wolfgang's heart sickened within him, and he was turning shuddering from the horrible engine, when he beheld a shadowy form, cowering as it were at the foot of the steps which led up to the scaffold. A succession of vivid flashes of lightning revealed it more distinctly. It was a female figure, dressed in black. She was seated on one of the lower steps of the scaffold, leaning forward, her face hid in her lap; and her long dishevelled tresses hanging to the ground, streaming with the rain which fell in torrents. Wolfgang paused. There was something awful in this solitary monument of woe. The female had the appearance of being above the common order. He knew the times to be full of vicissitude, and that many a fair head, which had once been pillowed on down, now wandered houseless. Perhaps this was some poor mourner whom the dreadful axe had rendered desolate, and who sat here heartbroken on the strand of existence, from which all that was dear to her had been launched into eternity.

He approached, and addressed her in the accents of sympathy. She raised her head and gazed wildly at him. What was his astonishment at beholding, by the bright glare of the lightning, the very face which had haunted him in his dreams. It was pale and disconsolate, but ravishingly beautiful.

Trembling with violent and conflicting emotions, Wolfgang again accosted her. He spoke something of her being exposed at such an hour of the night, and to the fury of such a storm, and offered to conduct her to her friends. She pointed to the guillotine with a gesture of dreadful signification.

"I have no friend on earth!" said she.

"But you have a home," said Wolfgang.

"Yes—in the grave!"

The heart of the student melted at the words.

"If a stranger dare make an offer," said he, "without danger of being misunderstood, I would offer my humble dwelling as a shelter; myself as a devoted friend. I am friendless myself in Paris, and a stranger in the land; but if my life would be of service, it is at your disposal, and should be sacrificed before harm or indignity should come to you."

There was an honest earnestness in the young man's manner that had its effect. His foreign accent, too, was in his favor; it showed him not to be a hackneyed inhabitant of Paris. Indeed, there is an eloquence in true enthusiasm that is not to be doubted. The homeless stranger confided herself implicitly to the protection of the student.

He supported her faltering steps across the Pont Neuf, and by the place where the statue of Henry the Fourth had been overthrown by the populace. The storm had abated, and the thunder rumbled at a distance. All Paris was quiet; that great volcano of human passion slumbered for a while, to gather fresh strength for the next day's eruption. The student conducted his charge through the ancient streets of the *Pays Latin*, and by the dusky walls of the Sorbonne, to the great dingy hotel which he inhabited. The old portress who admitted them stared with surprise at the unusual sight of the melancholy Wolfgang with a female companion.

On entering his apartment, the student, for the first time, blushed at the scantiness and indifference of his dwelling. He had but one chamber—an old-fashioned saloon—heavily carved, and fantastically furnished with the remains of former magnificence, for it was one of those hotels in the quarter of the Luxembourg palace, which had once belonged to nobility. It was lumbered with books and papers, and all the usual apparatus of a student, and his bed stood in a recess at one end.

When lights were brought, and Wolfgang had a better opportunity of contemplating the stranger, he was more than ever intoxicated by her beauty. Her face was pale, but of a dazzling fairness, set off by a profusion of raven hair that hung clustering about it. Her eyes were large and brilliant, with a singular expression approaching almost to wildness. As far as her black dress permitted her shape to be seen, it was of perfect symmetry. Her whole appearance was highly striking, though she was dressed in the simplest style. The only thing approaching to an ornament which she wore, was a broad black band round her neck, clasped by diamonds.

The perplexity now commenced with the student how to dispose of the helpless being thus thrown upon his protection. He thought of abandoning his chamber to her, and seeking shelter for himself elsewhere. Still, he was so fascinated by her charms, there seemed to be such a spell upon his thoughts and senses, that he could not tear himself from her presence. Her manner, too, was singular and unaccountable. She spoke no more of the guillotine. Her grief had abated. The attention of the student had first won her confidence, and then, apparently, her heart. She was evidently an enthusiast like himself, and enthusiasts soon understand each other.

In the infatuation of the moment, Wolfgang avowed his passion for her. He told her the story of his mysterious dream, and how she had possessed his heart before he had even seen her. She was strangely affected by his recital, and acknowledged to have felt an impulse towards him equally unaccountable. It was the time for wild theory and wild actions. Old prejudices and superstitions were done away; everything was under the sway of the "Goddess of Reason." Among other rubbish of the old times, the forms and ceremonies of marriage began to be considered superfluous bonds for honorable minds. Social compacts were the vogue. Wolfgang was too much of a theorist not to be tainted by the liberal doctrines of the day.

"Why should we separate?" said he: "our hearts are united; in the eye of reason and honor we are as one. What need is there of sordid forms to bind high souls together?"

The stranger listened with emotion: she had evidently received illumination at the same school.

"You have no home nor family," continued he: "let me be everything to you, or rather let us be everything to one another. If form is necessary, form shall be observed—there is my hand. I pledge myself to you forever."

"Forever?" said the stranger, solemnly.

"Forever!" replied Wolfgang.

The stranger clasped the hand extended to her: "Then I am yours," murmured she, and sank upon his bosom.

The next morning the student left his bride sleeping, and sallied forth at an early hour to seek more spacious apartments suitable to the change in his situation. When he returned, he found the stranger lying with her head hanging over the bed, and one arm thrown over it. He spoke to her, but received no reply. He advanced to awaken her from her uneasy posture. On taking her hand, it was cold—there was no pulsation—her face was pallid and ghastly. In a word, she was a corpse.

Horrified and frantic, he alarmed the house. A scene of confusion ensued. The police was summoned. As the officer of police entered the room, he started back on beholding the corpse.

"Great heaven!" cried he, "how did this woman come here?"

"Do you know anything about her?" said Wolfgang eagerly.

"Do I?" exclaimed the officer: "she was guillotined yesterday."

He stepped forward; undid the black collar round the neck of the corpse, and the head rolled on the floor!

The student burst into a frenzy. "The fiend! The fiend has gained possession of me!" shrieked he: "I am lost forever."

They tried to soothe him, but in vain. He was possessed with the frightful belief that an evil spirit had reanimated the dead body to ensnare him. He went distracted, and died in a madhouse.

Here the old gentleman with the haunted head finished his narrative.

"And is this really a fact?" said the inquisitive gentleman.

"A fact not to be doubted," replied the other. "I had it from the best authority. The student told it to me himself. I saw him in a madhouse in Paris."

THE DEAD MAN WHO WAS KILLED AGAIN

Ambrose Bierce's story about the *Occurrence at Owl Creek Bridge* is deservedly famous, but you are unlikely to know of his strange tale called *One Summer Night*. In it a man in his coffin is killed again. You might say it is the story that proceeds that of a vengeful ghost, the details of which are left to the reader to supply.

The story tells of three graverobbers, two medical students and the caretaker of the cemetery, a man named Jess. They dig up the grave of Henry Armstrong, and as they remove the coffin lid, they see Henry sit up in the coffin. The two medical students run off, terrified.

The next day the medical students see Jess' wagon at the medical school and inside the building, stretched out on a slab, is the corpse of Henry Armstrong, "the head defiled with blood and clay from a blow with a spade." Jess is standing by.

"I'm waiting for my pay," says Jess.

FJELKINGE'S GHOST

During the early half of the Seventeenth Century many of the best estates in Skåne [in Southern Sweden] belonged to the family of Barkenow, or more correctly, to the principal representative of the family, Madame Margaretta Barkenow, daughter of the renowned general and governor-general, Count Rutger von Ascheberg, and wife of colonel Kjell Kristofer Barkenow.

A widow at twenty-nine, she took upon herself the management of her many estates, in the conduct of which she ever manifested an indomitable, indefatigable energy, and a never-ceasing care for her numerous dependents.

On a journey over her estates, Madame Margaretta came, one evening, to Fjelkinge's inn, and

The very fashion plate of ghosts in the traditional sheet (actually a shroud).

insisted on sleeping in a room which was called the "ghost's room." A traveler had, a few years before, slept in this room, and, as it was supposed, had been murdered, at least the man and his effects had disappeared, leaving no trace of what had become of them. After this his ghost appeared in the room nightly, and those who were acquainted with the circumstance, traveled to the next post, in the dark, rather than choose such quarters for the night. Margaretta was, however, not among this number. She possessed greater courage, and without fear chose the chamber for her sleeping room.

After her evening prayers she retired to bed to sleep, leaving the lamp burning. At twelve o'clock she was awakened by the lifting up of two boards in the floor, and from the opening a bloody form appeared, with a cloven head hanging upon its shoulders.

"Noble lady," whispered the apparition, "I beg you prepare, for a murdered man, a resting place in consecrated ground, and speed the murderer to his just punishment."

Pure in heart, therefore not alarmed, Lady Margaretta beckoned the apparition to come nearer, which it did, informing her that it had entreated others, who after the murder had slept in the room, but that none had the courage to comply. Then Lady Margaretta took from her finger a gold ring, laid it in the gaping wound, and bound the apparition's head up with her pocket handkerchief. With a glance of unspeakable thankfulness the ghost revealed the name of the murderer and disappeared noiselessly beneath the floor.

The following morning Lady Margaretta instructed the bailiff of the estate to assemble the people at the post house, where she informed them what had happened during the night, and commanded that the planks of the floor be taken up. Here, under the ground, was discovered a half decomposed corpse, with the countess' ring in the hole in its skull, and her handkerchief bound around its head.

At sight of this, one of those present grew pale and fainted to the ground. Upon being revived he confessed that he had murdered the traveler and robbed him of his goods. He was condemned to death for his crime, and the murdered man received burial in the parish churchyard.

The ring, which is peculiarly formed and set with a large grayish chased stone, remains even now in the keeping of the Barkenow family, and is believed to possess miraculous powers in sickness, against evil spirits and other misfortunes. When one of the family dies it is said that a red, blood-like spot appears upon the stone.

THE JEALOUS HUSBAND

Russian folklore is rich in tales of ghosts and poltergeists, vampires and kitchen spirits, and more. Here is a legend that the theosophist Helena Blavatsky used to like to tell.

Everyone knows that when January marries May there will be trouble: Chaucer and many after him in English literature recount the hijinks that follow when an old man takes a much younger bride. There is the story of an old Russian governor who married an unwilling and very much younger person. The marriage was a disaster but, fortunately for her, the husband soon died. Before he did, however, he warned his wife that if she had anything to do with a man after he shuffled off this mortal coil he would come back and punish her.

She was still young, her sex life had been extremely unsatisfying, and of course she took up with a man of her own age whom she had wanted to marry in the first place but had not. And of course the ghost of the dead governor rose in anger. Every night his spectral coach rattled out of the cemetery and up to his old residence. There he assaulted his wife, beating her severely. Anyone who tried to stand in the way was simply swept aside by a strong, invisible force.

They had to dig up the dead governor and burn his corpse before the assaults stopped.

THE MOST AMUSING GHOST STORY EVER TOLD

You'll have to read it to see what I mean. In it "Saki" (H. H. Munro) wrote one of the most unforgettable short stories in English. Stuart L. Astor and I had to include it in our *British Short Stories: Classics and Criticism* (1968). It is called *The Open Window*. In it, we wrote, "his life-long delight in practical jokes and irresponsible admiration—indeed, identification with—inventive and ungovernable children are demonstrated in their purest form." It's a masterfully short short story. Here it is:

"My aunt will be down presently, Mr Nuttel," said a very self-possessed young lady of fifteen; "in the meantime you must try and put up with me."

Framton Nuttel endeavoured to say the correct something which should duly flatter the niece of the moment without unduly discounting the aunt that was to come. Privately he doubted more than ever whether these formal visits on a succession of total strangers would do much towards helping the nerve cure which he was supposed to be undergoing.

"I know how it will be," sister had said when he was preparing to migrate to this rural retreat; "you will busy yourself down there and not speak to a living soul, and your nerves will be worse than ever from moping. I shall just give you letters of introduction to all the people I know there. Some of them, as far as I can remember, were quite nice."

Framton wondered whether Mrs Sappleton, the lady to whom he was presenting one of the letters of introduction, came into the nice division.

"Do you know many of the people round here?," asked the niece, when she judged that they had had sufficient silent communion.

"Hardly a soul," said Framton. "My sister was staying here, at the rectory, you know, some four years ago, and she gave me letters of introduction to some of the people here."

He made the last statement in a tone of distinct regret.

"Then you know practically nothing about my aunt?" pursued the self-possessed young lady.

"Only her name and address," admitted the caller. He was wondering whether Mrs Sappleton was in the married or widowed state. An indefinable something about the room seemed to suggest masculine habitation.

"Her great tragedy happened just three years ago," said the child, "that would be since your sister's time."

"Her tragedy?" asked Framton; somehow in this restful country spot tragedies seemed out of place.

"You may wonder why we keep that window wide open on an October afternoon," said the niece, indicating a large French window that opened on to a lawn.

"It is quite warm for the time of year," said Framton; "but has that window got anything to do with the tragedy?"

"Out that window, three years ago to a day, her husband and her two young brothers went off for their day's shooting. They never came back. In crossing the moor to their favourite snipe-shooting grounds they were all three engulfed in a treacherous piece of bog. It had been that dreadful wet summer, you know, and places that were safe in other years gave way suddenly without warning. Their bodies were never recovered. That was the dreadful part of it." Here the child's voice lost its self-possessed note and became falteringly human. "Poor aunt always thinks that they will come back some day, they and the little brown spaniel that was lost with them, and walk in at that window just as they used to do. That is why the window is kept open every evening until it is quite dark. Poor dear aunt, she had often told me how they went out, her husband with his white waterproof coat over his arm, and Ronnie, her youngest brother, singing 'Bertie, why do you bound?' as he always did to tease her, because she said it got on her nerves. So you know, sometimes on still, quiet evenings like this, I almost get a creepy feeling that they will all walk in through that window—"

She broke off with a little shudder. It was a relief to Framton when the aunt bustled into the room with a whirl of apologies for being late in making her appearance.

"I hope Vera has been amusing you?" she said.

"She has been very interesting," said Framton.

"I hope you don't mind the open window," said Mrs Sappleton briskly; "my husband and brothers will be home directly from shooting and they always come in this way. They've been out for snipe in the marshes to-day, so they'll make a fine mess over my poor carpets. So like you men-folks, isn't it?"

She rattled on cheerfully about the shooting and the scarcity of birds, and the prospects for duck in the winter. To Framton it was all purely horrible. He made desperate but only partially successful effort to turn the talk on to a less ghastly topic; he was conscious that his hostess was giving him only a fragment of her attention, and her eyes were constantly straying past him to the open window and the lawn beyond. It was certainly an unfortunate coincidence that he should have paid his visit on this tragic anniversary.

"The doctors agree in ordering me a complete rest, an absence of mental excitement, and avoidance of anything in the nature of violent physical exercise," announced Framton, who laboured under the tolerably wide-spread delusion that total strangers and chance acquaintances are hungry for the least detail of one's ailments and infirmities, their cause and cure. "On the matter of diet they are not so much in agreement," he continued.

"No?" said Mrs Sappleton, in a voice which only replaced a yawn at the last moment. Then she suddenly brightened into alert attention—but not to what Framton was saying.

"Here they are at last!" she cried. "Just in time for tea, and don't they look as if they were muddy up to the eyes!"

Framton shivered slightly and turned toward the niece with a look intended to convey sympathetic comprehension. The child was staring out through the open window with dazed horror in her eyes. In a chill shock of nameless fear Framton swung round in his seat and looked in the same direction.

In the deepening twilight three figures were walking across the lawn towards the window; they all carried guns under their arms, and one of them was additionally burdened with a white coat hung over his shoulders. A tired brown spaniel kept close at their heels. Noiselessly they neared the house, and then a hoarse young voice chanted out of the dusk: "I said, Bertie, why do you bound?"

Framton grabbed wildly at his stick and hat; the hall-door, the gravel-drive, and the front gate were dimly-noted stages in his headlong retreat. A cyclist coming along the road had to run into the hedge to avoid imminent collision.

"Here we are, my dear," said the bearer of the white mackintosh, coming in through the window; "fairly muddy, but most of it's dry. Who was that who bolted out as we came in?"

"A most extraordinary man, a Mr Nuttel," said Mrs Sappleton; "could only talk about his illness, and dashed off without a word of good-bye or apology when you arrived. One would think he had seen a ghost."

"I expect it was the spaniel," said the niece calmly; "he told me he had a horror of dogs. He was once hunted into a cemetery somewhere on the banks of the Ganges by a pack of pariah dogs, and had to spend the night in a newly dug grave with the creatures snarling and snapping and grinning and foaming just above him. Enough to make anyone lose their nerve."

Romance at short notice was her specialty.

"Saki" (his pen name was taken from the cupbearer to the gods) always shows wit in naming his characters. Here the little girl who lies so well is named Vera, which means "Truth."

The best anthologies of British occult stories were edited by Lord Halifax and Lady Cynthia Asquith and the Rev. Montague Summers, if after this playful twist on regular ghosts stories you want the genuine article. Someone should reprint the anonymous anthologies of *The Best Ghost Stories* (1919) and *A Century of Thrillers* (1934, with a second series 1935) and *A Century of Ghost Stories* (1936).

THE YELLOW WALLPAPER

You can think of the following story as one concerning ghosts or insanity. The way feminists see it today, whatever else it may be it is a minor but absolutely politically correct masterpiece documenting the oppression of women. American stories have rather infrequently made women into the

A crude illustration of 1709 accompanied the startling tale of Christopher Slaughterwood of Guildford, who came back from the dead with the executioner's rope still around his neck to demand vengeance on those who (falsely?) sent him to the gallows.

melodramatically crazy narrators or the kind we find among men in the tales of Poe. Women have given us neurotic or even crazy narrators, too. Think of Eudora Welty's *Why I Live at the P.O.* The following story, written in 1890, printed in 1899, has a narrator you will not soon forget. A great deal of power comes from the fact that the story is in part autobiographical.

The author of *The Yellow Wallpaper* was Charlotte Perkins Gilman (1860-1935), poet, fiction writer, feminist activist. She knew all about depression arising from the oppression of women, limited careers for women in a male-dominated society, and marriage as a sort of prison. She herself might well have gone mad had she not firmly pushed out of the way anyone who stood in her path. She discarded her husband, turned to women's causes, and wrote and spoke out in all senses of the phrase "with a vengeance." *The Yellow Wallpaper* is probably her most artistic, most enduring work, though it must be said that just now it is hugely overpraised because of the popularity of its feminist sentiments. Mrs. Gilman is no Edith Wharton, no Toni Morrison.

I choose to give her story space in my limited anthology because I believe you will find it more accessible than ghost stories by even better and more famous American women writers. It also helps me to put in your mind the problem of mental imbalance. Ignored or not, that is always an undercurrent in the discussion of the occult. Are those who report hauntings insane? Are they hallucinating? Is it, on the other hand, possible that many actual events that science should have investigated go unreported because people who have had experiences fear they will be called unhinged if they talk about them?

I once said about magic that those who talk don't know and those who know don't talk. Something of the like might be said about experiences such as the terrifying one that is reported in *The Yellow Wallpaper*. Mrs. Gilman *puts you through it* with unusual power.

Here we have a woman's breakdown followed by a rest cure that forbids her to write and drives her insane. This story has achieved the status of a Women's Liberation classic. A critical edition and casebook about it have been published (Julie Bates Dock, Penn State University Press). The critics have written a good deal—perhaps I ought to say, "a lot"—about it. America's greatest literary critic, Edmund Wilson, were he around today might have repeated his canard that women's literature is nothing but complaining. You read the story and see what you think.

It is very seldom that mere ordinary people like John and myself secure ancestral halls for the summer.

A colonial mansion, a hereditary estate, I would say a haunted house, and reach the height of romantic felicity— but that would be asking too much of fate!

Still I will proudly declare that there is something queer about it.

Else, why should it be let so cheaply? And why have stood so long untenanted?

John laughs at me, of course, but one expects that in marriage.

John is practical in the extreme. He has no patience with faith, an intense horror of superstition, and he scoffs openly at any talk of things not to be felt and seen and put down in figures.

John is a physician, and *perhaps*—(I would not say it to a living soul, of course, but this is dead paper and a great relief to my mind)—*perhaps* that is one reason I do not get well faster.

You see he does not believe I am sick!

And what can one do?

If a physician of high standing, and one's own husband, assures friends and relatives that there is really nothing the matter with one but temporary nervous depression—a slight hysterical tendency—what is one to do?

My brother is also a physician, and also of high standing, and he says the same thing.

So I take phosphates or phosphites—whichever it is, and tonics, and journeys, and air, and exercise, and am absolutely forbidden to "work" until I am well again.

Personally, I disagree with their ideas.

Personally, I believe that congenial work, with excitement and change, would do me good.

But what is one to do?

I did write for a while in spite of them; but it *does* exhaust me a good deal— having to be so sly about it, or else meet with heavy opposition.

I sometimes fancy that in my condition if I had less opposition and more society and stimulus—but John says the very worst thing I can do is to think about my condition, and I confess it always makes me feel bad.

So I will let it alone and talk about the house.

The most beautiful place! It is quite alone, standing well back from the road, quite three miles from the village. It makes me think of English places that you read about, for there are hedges and walls and gates that lock, and lots of separate little houses for the gardeners and people.

There is a *delicious* garden! I never saw such a garden—large and shady, full of box-bordered paths, and lines with long grape-covered arbors with seats under them.

There were green houses, too, but they are all broken now.

There was some legal trouble, I believe, something about the heirs and coheirs; anyhow, the place has been empty for years.

That spoils my ghostliness, I am afraid, but I don't care—there is something strange about the house—I can feel it.

I even said so to John one moonlight evening, but he said what I felt was a *draught,* and shut the window.

I get unreasonably angry with John sometimes. I'm sure I never used to be so sensitive. I think it is due to this nervous condition.

But John says if I feel so, I shall neglect proper self-control; so I take pains to control myself—before him, at least, and that makes me very tired.

I don't like our room a bit. I wanted one downstairs that opened on the piazza and had roses all over the window, and such pretty old-fashioned chintz hangings! But John would not hear of it.

He said there was only one window and not room for two beds, and no near room for him if he took another.

He is very careful and loving, and hardly lets me stir without special direction.

I have a schedule prescription for each hour in the day; he takes all care from me, and so I feel basely ungrateful not to value it more.

He said we came here solely on my account, that I was to have perfect rest and all the air I could get. "Your exercise depends on your strength, my dear," said he, "and your food somewhat on your appetite; but air you can absorb all the time." So we took the nursery at the top of the house.

It is a big, airy room, the whole floor nearly, with windows that look all ways, and air and sunshine galore. It was nursery first and then playroom and gymnasium, I should judge; for the windows are barred for little children, and there are rings and things in the walls.

The paint and paper look as if a boys' school had used it. It is stripped off—the paper—in great patches all around the head of my bed, about as far as I can reach, and in a great place on the other side of the room low down. I never saw a worse paper in my life.

One of those sprawling flamboyant patterns committing every artistic sin.

It is dull enough to confuse the eye in following, pronounced enough to constantly irritate and provoke study, and when you follow the lame uncertain curves for a little distance they suddenly commit suicide—plunge off at outrageous angles, destroy themselves in unheard of contradictions.

The color is repellent, almost revolting; a smouldering unclean yellow, strangely faded by the slow-turning sunlight.

It is a dull yet lurid orange in some places, a sickly sulphur tint in others.

No wonder the children hated it! I should hate it myself if I had to live in this room long.

There comes John, and I must put this away,—he hates to have me write a word.

We have been here two weeks, and I haven't felt like writing before, since that first day.

I am sitting by the window now, up in this atrocious nursery, and there is nothing to hinder my writing as much as I please, save my lack of strength.

John is away all day, and even some nights when his cases are serious.

I am glad my case is not serious!

But these nervous troubles are dreadfully depressing.

John does not know how much I really suffer. He knows there is no *reason* to suffer, and that satisfies him.

Of course it is only nervousness. It does weigh on me so not to do my duty in any way!

I meant to be such a help to John, such a real rest and comfort, and here I am a comparative burden already!

Nobody would believe what an effort it is to do what little I am able,—to dress and entertain, and order things.

It is fortunate Mary is so good with the baby. Such a dear baby!

And yet I *cannot* be with him, it makes me so nervous.

I suppose John never was nervous in his life. He laughs at me so about this wallpaper!

At first he meant to repaper the room, but afterwards he said that I was letting it get the better of me, and that nothing was worse for a nervous patient than to give way to such fancies.

He said that after the wallpaper was changed it would be the heavy bedstead, and then the barred windows, and then the gate at the head of the stairs, and so on.

"You know the place is doing you good," he said, "and really, dear, I don't care to renovate the house just for a three months' rental."

"Then do let us go downstairs," I said, "there are such pretty rooms there."

Then he took me in his arms and called me a blessed little goose, and said he would go down to the cellar, if I wished, and have it whitewashed into the bargain.

But he is right enough about the beds and windows and things.

It is an airy and comfortable room as any one need wish, and, of course, I would not be so silly as to make him uncomfortable just for a whim.

I'm really getting quite fond of the big room, all but that horrid paper.

Out of one window I can see the garden, those mysterious deep-shaded arbors, the riotous old-fashioned flowers, and bushes and gnarly trees.

Out of another I get a lovely view of the bay and a little private wharf belonging to the estate. There is a beautiful shaded lane that runs down there from the house. I always fancy I see people walking in these numerous paths and arbors, but John has cautioned me not to give way to fancy in the least. He says that with my imaginative power and habit of story-making, a nervous weakness like mine is sure to lead to all manner of excited fancies, and that I ought to use my will and good sense to check the tendency. So I try.

I think sometimes that if I were only well enough to write a little it would relieve the press of ideas and rest me.

But I find I get pretty tired when I try.

It is so discouraging not to have any advice and companionship about my work. When I get really well, John says we will ask Cousin Henry and Julia down for a long visit; but he says he would as soon put fireworks in my pillow-case as to let me have those stimulating people about now.

I wish I could get well faster.

But I must not think about that. This paper looks to me as if it *knew* what a vicious influence it had!

There is a recurrent spot where the pattern lolls like a broken neck and two bulbous eyes stare at you upside down.

I get positively angry with the impertinence of it and the everlastingness. Up and down and sideways they crawl, and those absurd, unblinking eyes go all up and down the line, one a little higher than the other.

I never saw so much expression in an inanimate thing before, and we all know how much expression they have! I used to lie awake as a child and get more entertainment and terror out of blank walls and plain furniture than most children could find in a toy-store.

I remember what a kindly wink the knobs of our big, old bureau used to have, and there was one chair that always seemed like a strong friend.

I used to feel that if any of the other things looked too fierce I could always hop into that chair and be safe.

The furniture in this room is no worse than inharmonious, however, for we had to bring it all from downstairs. I suppose when this was used as a playroom they had to take the nursery things out, and no wonder! I never saw such ravages as the children have made here.

The wall-paper, as I said before, is torn off in spots, and it sticketh closer than a brother—they must have had perseverance as well as hatred.

Then the floor is scratched and gouged and splintered, the plaster itself is dug out here and there, and this great heavy bed which is all we found in the room, looks as if it had been through the wars.

But I don't mind it a bit—only the paper.

There comes John's sister. Such a dear girl as she is, and so careful of me! I must not let her find me writing.

She is a perfect and enthusiastic housekeeper, and hopes for no better profession. I verily believe she thinks it is the writing which makes me sick!

But I can write when she is out, and see her a long way off from these windows.

There is one that commands the road, a lovely shaded winding road, and one that just looks off over the country. A lovely country, too, full of great elms and velvet meadows.

This wall-paper has a kind of sub-pattern in a different shade, a particularly irritating one, for you can only see it in certain lights, and not clearly then.

But in the places where it isn't faded and where the sun is just so—I can see a strange, provoking, formless sort of figure, that seems to skulk about behind that silly and conspicuous front design.

There's sister on the stairs!

Well, the Fourth of July is over! The people are all gone and I am tired out. John thought it might do me good to see a little company, so we just had mother and Nellie and the children down for a week.

Of course, I didn't do a thing. Jennie sees to everything now.

But it tired me all the same.

John says if I don't pick up faster he shall send me to Weir Mitchell in the fall.

But I don't want to go there at all. I had a friend who was in his hands once, and she says he is just like John and my brother, only more so!

Besides, it is such an undertaking to go so far.

I don't feel as if it was worth while to turn my hand over for anything, and I'm getting dreadfully fretful and querulous.

I cry at nothing, and cry most of the time.

Of course I don't when John is here, or anybody else, but when I am alone.

And I am alone a good deal just now. John is kept in town very often by serious cases, and Jennie is good and lets me alone when I want her to.

So I walk a little in the garden or down that lovely lane, sit on the porch under the roses, and lie down up here a good deal.

I'm getting really fond of the room in spite of the wall-paper. Perhaps *because* of the wall-paper.

It dwells in my mind so!

I lie here on this great immovable bed—it is nailed down, I believe—and follow that pattern about by the hour. It is as good as gymnastics, I assure you. I start, we'll say, at the bottom, down in the corner over there where it has not been touched, and I determine for the thousandth time that I *will* follow that pointless pattern to some sort of a conclusion.

I know a little of the principle of design, and I know this thing was not arranged on any laws of radiation, or alternation, or repetition, or symmetry, or anything else that I ever heard of.

It is repeated, of course, by the breadths, but not otherwise.

Looked at in one way each breadth stands alone, the bloated curves and flourishes-a kind of "debased Romanesque" with *delirium tremens*—go waddling up and down in isolated columns of fatuity.

But, on the other hand, they connect diagonally, and the sprawling outlines run off in great slanting waves of optic horror, like a lot of wallowing seaweeds in full chase.

The whole thing goes horizontal breadth for a frieze, and that adds wonderfully to the confusion.

There is one end of the room where it is almost intact, and there, when the crosslights fade and the low sun shines directly upon it, I can almost fancy radiation after all,—the interminable grotesques seem to form around a common centre, and rush off in headlong plunges of equal distraction.

It makes me tired to follow it. I will take a nap I guess.

I don't know why I should write this.

I don't want to.

I don't feel able.

And I know John would think it absurd. But I *must* say what I feel and think in some way—it is such a relief!

But the effort is getting to be greater than the relief.

Half the time now I am awfully lazy, and lie down ever so much.

John says I mustn't lose my strength, and has me take cod liver oil and lots of tonics and things, to say nothing of ale and wine and rare meat.

Dear John! He loves me very dearly, and hates to have me sick. I tried to have a real earnest reasonable talk with him the other day, and tell him how I wish he would let me go and make a visit to Cousin Henry and Julia.

But he said I wasn't able to go, nor able to stand it after I got there; and I did not make out a very good case for myself, for I was crying before I had finished.

It is getting to be a great effort for me to think straight. Just this nervous weakness I suppose.

And dear John gathered me up in his arms, and just carried me upstairs and laid me on the bed, and stayed by me and read to me till it tired my head.

He said I was his darling and his comfort and all he had, and that I must take care of myself for his sake, and keep well.

He says no one but myself can help me out of it, that I must use my will and self-control and not let any silly fancies run away with me.

There's one comfort, the baby is well and happy, and does not have to occupy this nursery with the horrid wall-paper.

If we had not used it, that blessed child would have! What a fortunate escape! Why, I wouldn't have a child of mine, an impressionable little thing, live in such a room for worlds.

I never thought of it before, but it is lucky that John kept me here after all, I can stand it so much easier than a baby, you see.

Of course I never mention it to them any more—I am too wise,—but I keep watch of it all the same.

There are things in that paper that nobody knows but me, or ever will.

Behind that outside pattern the dim shapes get clearer every day.

It is always the same shape, only very numerous.

And it is like a woman stooping down and creeping about behind that pattern. I don't like it a bit. I wonder—I begin to think—I wish John would take me away from here!

It is so hard to talk with John about my case, because he is so wise, and because he loves me so.

But I tried it last night.

It was moonlight. The moon shines in around just as the sun does.

I hate to see it sometimes, it creeps so slowly, and always comes in by one window or another.

John was asleep and I hated to waken him, so I kept still and watched the moonlight on that undulating wall-paper till I felt creepy.

The faint figure behind seemed to shake the pattern, just as if she wanted to get out.

I got up softly and went to feel and see if the paper *did* move, and when I came back John was awake.

"What is it, little girl?" he said. "Don't go walking about like that—you'll get cold."

I thought it was a good time to talk, so I told him that I really was not gaining here, and that I wished he would take me away.

"Why darling!" said he, "our lease will be up in three weeks, and I can't see how to leave before."

"The repairs are not done at home, and I cannot possibly leave town just now. Of course if you were in any danger, I could and would, but you really are better, dear, whether you can see it or not. I am a doctor, dear, and I know. You are gaining flesh and color, your appetite is better, I feel really much easier about you."

"I don't weigh a bit more," said I, "nor as much; and my appetite may be better in the evening when you are here, but it is worse in the morning when you are away!"

"Bless her little heart!" said he with a big hug, "she shall be as sick as she pleases! But now let's improve the shining hours by going to sleep, and talk about it in the morning!"

"And you won't go away?" I asked gloomily.

"Why, how can I, dear? It is only three weeks more and then we will take a nice little trip of a few days while Jennie is getting the house ready. Really dear you are better!"

"Better in body perhaps—" I began, and stopped short, for he sat up straight and looked at me with such a stern, reproachful look that I could not say another word.

"My darling," said he, "I beg of you, for my sake and for our child's sake, as well as for your own, that you will never for one instant let that idea enter your mind! There is nothing so dangerous, so fascinating, to a temperament like yours. It is a false and foolish fancy. Can you not trust me as a physician when I tell you so?"

So of course I said no more on that score, and we went to sleep before long. He thought I was asleep first, but I wasn't, and lay there for hours trying to decide whether that front pattern and the back pattern really did move together or separately.

On a pattern like this, by daylight, there is a lack of sequence, a defiance of law, that is a constant irritant to a normal mind.

The color is hideous enough, and unreliable enough, and infuriating enough, but the pattern is torturing.

You think you have mastered it, but just as you get well underway in following, it turns a back-somersault and there you are. It slaps you in the face, knocks you down, and tramples upon you. It is like a bad dream.

The outside pattern is a florid, arabesque, reminding one of a fungus. If you can imagine a toadstool in joints, an interminable string of toadstools, budding and sprouting in endless convolutions—why, that is something like it.

That is, sometimes!

There is one marked peculiarity about this paper, a thing nobody seems to notice but myself, and that is that it changes as the light changes.

When the sun shoots in through the east window—I always watch for that first long, straight ray—it changes so quickly that I never can quite believe it.

That is why I watch it always.

By moonlight—the moon shines in all night when there is a moon—I wouldn't know it was the same paper.

At night in any kind of light, in twilight, candle light, lamplight, and worst of all by moonlight, it becomes bars! The outside pattern I mean, and the woman behind it is as plain as can be.

I didn't realize for a long time what the thing was that showed behind, that dim sub-pattern, but now I am quite sure it is a woman.

By daylight she is subdued, quiet. I fancy it is the pattern that keeps her so still. It is so puzzling. It keeps me quiet by the hour.

I lie down ever so much now. John says it is good for me, and to sleep all I can.

Indeed he started the habit by making me lie down for an hour after each meal

It is a very bad habit I am convinced, for you see I don't sleep. And that cultivates deceit, for I don't tell them I'm awake—O no!

The fact is I am getting a little afraid of John.

He seems very queer sometimes, and even Jennie has an inexplicable look.

It strikes me occasionally, just as a scientific hypothesis,—that perhaps it is the paper!

I have watched John when he did not know I was looking, and came into the room suddenly on the most innocent excuses, and I've caught him several times *looking at the paper*! And Jennie too. I caught Jennie with her hand on it once.

She didn't know I was in the room, and when I asked her in a quiet, a very quiet voice, with the most restrained manner possible, what she was doing with the paper—she turned around as if she had been caught stealing, and looked quite angry—asked me why I should frighten her so!

Then she said that the paper stained everything it touched, that she had found yellow smooches on all my clothes and John's, and she wished we would be more careful!

Did not that sound innocent? But I know she was studying that pattern, and I am determined that nobody shall find it out but myself!

Life is very much more exciting now than it used to be. You see I have something more to expect, to look forward to, to watch. I really do eat better, and am more quiet than I was.

John is so pleased to see me improve! He laughed a little the other day, and said I seemed to be flourishing in spite of my wallpaper.

I turned it off with a laugh. I had no intention of telling him it was *because* of the wall-paper—he would make fun of me. He might even want to take me away.

I don't want to leave now until I have found it out. There is a week more, and I think that will be enough.

I'm feeling ever so much better! I don't sleep much at night, for it is so interesting to watch developments; but I sleep a good deal in the daytime.

In the daytime it is tiresome and perplexing.

There are always new shoots on the fungus, and new shades of yellow all over it. I cannot keep count of them, though I have tried conscientiously.

It is the strangest yellow, that wall-paper! It makes me think

of all the yellow things I ever saw—not beautiful ones like but-
tercups, but old foul, bad yellow things.

But there is something else about that paper—the smell! I
noticed it the moment we came into the room, but with so much
air and sun it was not bad. Now we have had a week of fog and
rain, and whether the windows are open or not, the smell is here.

It creeps all over the house.

I find it hovering in the dining-room, skulking in the parlor,
hiding in the hall, lying in wait for me on the stairs.

It gets into my hair.

Even when I go to ride, if I turn my head suddenly and surprise it—there is that smell!

Such a peculiar odor, too! I have spent hours in trying to ana-
lyze it, to find what it smelled like.

It is not bad at first, and very gentle, but quite the subtlest,
most enduring odor I ever met.

In this damp weather it is awful, I wake up in the night and
find it hanging over me.

It used to disturb me at first. I thought seriously of burning
the house—to reach the smell.

But now I am used to it. The only thing I can think of that it
is like is the *color* of the paper! A yellow smell.

There is a very funny mark on this wall, low down, near the
mopboard. A streak that runs round the room. It goes behind every
piece of furniture, except the bed, a long, straight, even *smooch*, as
if it had been rubbed over and over.

I wonder how it was done and who did it, and what they did
it for. Round and round and round—round and round and round—
it makes me dizzy!

I really have discovered something at last.

Through watching so much at night, when it changes so, I have
finally found out.

The front pattern *does* move—and no wonder! The woman
behind shakes it!

Sometimes I think there are a great many women behind, and
sometimes only one, and she crawls around fast, and her crawling
shakes it all over.

Then in the very bright spots she keeps still, and in the very
shady spots she just takes hold of the bars and shakes them hard.

And she is all the time trying to climb through. But nobody
could climb through that pattern—it strangles so; I think that is
why it has so many heads.

They get through, and then the pattern strangles them off and
turns them upside down, and makes their eyes white!

If those heads were covered or taken off it would not be half so bad.

I think that woman gets out in the daytime!

And I'll tell you why—privately—I've seen her!

I can see her out of every one of my windows!

It is the same woman, I know, for she is always creeping, and most women do not creep by daylight.

I see her on that long road under the trees, creeping along, and when a carriage comes she hides under the blackberry vines.

I don't blame her a bit. It must be very humiliating to be caught creeping by daylight!

I always lock the door when I creep by daylight. I can't do it at night, for I know John would suspect something at once.

And John is so queer now, that I don't want to irritate him, I wish he would take another room! Besides, I don't want anybody to get that woman out at night but myself.

I often wonder if I could see her out of all the windows at once.

But, turn as fast as I can, I can only see out of one at one time.

And though I always see her, she *may* be able to creep faster than I can turn!

I have watched her sometimes away out in the open country, creeping as fast as a cloud shadow in a high wind.

If only that top pattern could be gotten off from the under one! I mean to try it, little by little.

I have found out another funny thing, but I shan't tell it this time! It does not do to trust people too much.

There are only two more days to get this paper off, and I believe John is beginning to notice. I don't like the look in his eyes.

And I heard him ask Jennie a lot of professional questions about me. She had a very good report to give.

She said I slept a good deal in the daytime.

John knows I don't sleep very well at night, for all I'm so quiet!

He asked me all sorts of questions, too, and pretended to be very loving and kind.

As if I couldn't see through him!

Still, I don't wonder he acts so, sleeping under this paper for three months.

It only interests me, but I feel sure John and Jennie are secretly affected by it.

Hurrah! This is the last day, but it is enough. John to stay in town overnight, and won't be out until this evening.

Jennie wanted to sleep with me—the sly thing! But I told her I should undoubtedly rest better for a night all alone.

That was clever, for really I wasn't alone a bit! As soon as it was moonlight and that poor thing began to crawl and shake the pattern, I got up and ran to help her.

I pulled and she shook, I shook and she pulled, and before morning we had peeled off yards of that paper.

A strip about as high as my head and half around the room.

And then when the sun came and that awful pattern began to laugh at me, I declared I would finish it to-day!

We go away to-morrow, and they are moving all my furniture down again to leave things as they were before.

Jennie looked at the wall in amazement, but I told her merrily that I did it out of pure spite at the vicious thing.

She laughed and said she wouldn't mind doing it herself, but I must not get tired.

How she betrayed herself that time!

But I am here, and no person touches this paper but me,—not *alive*!

She tried to get me out of the room—it was too patent! But I said it was so quiet and empty and clean now that I believed I would lie down again and sleep all I could; and not to wake me even for dinner—I would call when I woke.

So now she is gone, and the servants are gone, and the things are gone, and there is nothing left but that great bedstead nailed down, with the canvas mattress we found on it.

We shall sleep downstairs to-night, and take the boat home to-morrow.

I quite enjoy the room, now it is bare again.

How those children did tear about here!

This bedstead is fairly gnawed!

But I must get to work.

I have locked the door and thrown the key down into the front path.

I don't want to go out, and I don't want to have anybody come in, till John comes.

I want to astonish him.

I've got a rope up here that even Jennie did not find. If that woman does get out, and tried to get away, I can tie her!

But I forgot I could not reach far without anything to stand on!

This bed will *not* move!

I tried to lift and push it until I was lame, and then I got so angry I bit off a little piece at one corner—but it hurt my teeth.

Then I peeled off all the paper I could reach standing on the floor. It sticks horribly and the pattern just enjoys it! All those strangled heads and bulbous eyes and waddling fungus growths just shriek with derision!

I am getting angry enough to do something desperate. To jump out of the window would be admirable exercise, but the bars are too strong even to try.

Besides I wouldn't do it. Of course not. I know well enough that a step like that is improper and might be misconstrued.

I don't like to *look* out of the windows even—there are so many of those creeping women, and they creep so fast.

I wonder if they all come out of that wall-paper as I did?

But I am securely fastened now by my well-hidden rope—you don't get *me* out in the road there!

I suppose I shall have to get back behind the pattern when it comes night, and that is hard!

It is so pleasant to be out in this great room and creep around as I please!

I don't want to go outside. I won't. Even if Jennie asks me to.

For outside you have to creep on the ground, and everything is green instead of yellow.

But here I can creep smoothly on the floor, and my shoulder just fits in that long smooch around the wall, so I cannot lose my way.

Why there's John at the door!

It is no use, young man, you can't open it!

How he does call and pound!

Now he's crying for an axe.

It would be a shame to break down that beautiful door!

"John dear!" said I in the gentlest voice, "the key is down by the front steps, under a plaintain leaf!"

That silenced him for a few moments.

Then he said—very quietly indeed, "Open the door, my darling!"

"I can't" said I. "The key is down by the front door under a plaintain leaf!"

And then I said it again, several times, very gently and slowly, and said it so often that he had to go and see, and he got it of course, and came in. He stopped short by the door.

"What is the matter?" he cried. "For God's sake, what are you doing!"

I kept on creeping just the same, but I looked at him over my shoulder.

"I've got out at last," said I, "in spite of you and Jennie. And I've pulled off most of the paper, so you can't put me back!"

Now why should that man have fainted? But he did, and right across my path by the wall, so that I had to creep over him every time!

THE BEST GHOST AND VAMPIRE TALES

There follows a list that was warmly received by readers of *The Complete Book of Vampires* and so I reprint it here for any who missed it.

Robert Aikman, *Ringing the Changes*
Woody Allen, *Count Dracula*
Michael Arlen, *The Ghoul of Golder's Green*
M. R. S. Andrews, *Dundonald's Destroyer*
Enid Bagnold, *The Amorous Ghost*
J. Kendrick Bangs, *The Water Ghost of Harrowby Hall*
Sabine Baring-Gould, *A Dead Finger*
E. F. Benson, *Mrs. Amworth*
Ambrose Bierce, *Cold Greeting*
Algernon Blackwood, *The Empty House*
Elizabeth Bowen, *The Cheery Soul*
Elizabeth Bowen, *Green Holly*
"M. Bowen," *Avenging of Ann Leete*
Ray Bradbury, *The Man Upstairs*
Mary Elizabeth Braddon, *Good Lady Ducayne*
Charlotte Brontë, *Napoleon and the Spectre*
William Cullen Bryant, *Indian Spring*
Donn Byrne, *Mrs. Dutton Intervenes*
Sir A. Caldecott, *Authorship Disputed*
G. K. Chesterton, *Vampire of the Village*
Irving S. Cobb, *The Second Coming of a First Husband*
Wilkie Collins, *The Ghost's Touch*
A. E. Coppard, *Adam and Eve and Pinch Me*
F. Marion Crawford, *For the Blood is the Life*
"Clemence Dane," *Spinster's Rest*
M. P. Dare, *Unholy Relics*
Walter de la Mare, *Seaton's Aunt*
August W. Derleth, *Just a Song at Twilight*
Charles Dickens, *The Signal-Man*
C. C. Dobie, *Elder Brother*
Sir Arthur Conan Doyle, *Lot No. 249*
Edward, Lord Dunsany, *The Haunting of Halahanstown*
Lawrence Durrell, *Carnival*
Mary E. Wilkins Freeman, *The Gentle Ghost*
R. A. Freeman, *The Apparition of Burling Court*

Jane Gardam, *The Meeting House*
Elizabeth Gaskell, *The Old Nurse's Story*
Théophile Gautier, *La Morte amoreuse*
J. Gloag, *Lady without Appetite*
"Maxim Gorki," *The Story of a Novel*
C. I. M. Graves, *The Cost of Wings*
Sir H. Rider Haggard, *Only a Dream*
Knut Hamsun, *An Apparition*
Thomas Hardy, *Withered Arm*
Bret Harte, *A Child's Ghost Story*
L. P. Hartley, *Travelling Grave*
Nathaniel Hawthorne, *The Gray Champion*
Lafcadio Hearn, *Shriyö*
James Hogg, *The Mysterious Bridge*
Elizabeth Jane Howard, *Three Miles Up*
Robert E. Howard, *The Horror from the Mound*
William Dean Howells, *His Apparition*
Robert Thurston Hopkins, *The Vampire of Woolpit Grange*
Noel Hynd, *A Vampire*
W. E. Ingersoll, *The Centenarian*
Washington Irving, *The Adventure of the German Student*
C. Jacobi, *Revelations in Black*
Henry James, *The Turn of the Screw*
Montague Rhodes James, *The Thin Ghost*
W. W. Jacobs, *The Monkey's Paw*
Rudyard Kipling, *They*
Heinrich V. Kleist, *The Beggar Woman of Locarno*
Owen Lattimore, *Ghosts of Wulakai*
Stephen Leacock, *Buggam Grange*
"Vernon Lee," *Oke of Okehurst*
Joseph Sheridan LeFanu, *The Ghost and the Bone-Setter*
Penelope Lively, *Revenant as Typewriter*
F. B. Long, *It Will Come to You*
H. P. Lovecraft and August W. Derleth, *The Survivor*
Alison Lurie, *The Highboy*
Edward, Lord Lytton, *The Haunted and the Haunters*
Arthur Machen, *Munitions of War*
John Mansfield, *Ghosts*
Don Marquis, *Too American*
Richard Matheson, *The Funeral*
Guy de Maupassant, *La Horla*
André Maurois, *The House*
R. H. Middleton, *On the Brighton Road*

Lálmán Mikszáth, *Fiddlers Three*
P. Morand, *Chinese Phantoms*
William Morris, *The Lovers*
Arthur Morrison, *Chamber of Light*
Jan Neruda, *The Vampire*
Charles Nodier, *Inés de las Sierras*
F. J. O'Brien, *What Was It?*
Margaret Wilson Oliphant, *The Open Door*
R. C. O'Neill, *The Lady and the Ghost*
Oliver Onions, *The Beckoning Fair One*
Thomas Nelson Page, *No Haid Pawn*
Barry Pain, *Not on the Passenger List*
Elia Wilkinson Peattie, *From the Loom of the Dead*
E. Peirce, *The Doom of the House of Duryea*
Eden Phillpotts, *Grimm's Ghost*
Luigi Pirandello, *The Haunted House*
Edgar Allan Poe, *Berenice*
T. F. Powys, *I Came as a Bride*
Sir Arthur Quiller-Couch, *The Haunted Yacht*
Simon Raven, *Chriseis*
Victor Roman, *Four Wooden Stakes*
A. L. Rowse, *All Souls' Night*
Alan Ryan, *Baby's Blood*
"Saki," *Laura*
Sir Walter Scott, *The Tapestried Chamber*
William Gilmore Simms, *Carl Werner*
Lady Eleanor Furneaux Smith, *Satan's Circus*
Evelyn E. Smith, *Softly, While You're Sleeping*
Stanislaus Eric Stenbock, *The True Story of a Vampire*
Robert Louis Stevenson, *Thrawn Janet*
Frank R. Stockton, *The Transferred Ghost*
Bram Stoker, *The Judge's House*
Harriet Beecher Stowe, *Tom Toothacher's Ghost Story*
Sir Rabindranath Tagore, *The Hungry Stones*
James Thurber, *The Night the Ghost Got In*
Johann Ludwig Tieck, *Wake Not the Dead*
Ivan Turgenev, *Apparitions*
"Mark Twain," *Ghost Story*
A. E. Van Vogt, *Asylum*
H. Russell Wakefield, *The Seventeenth Hole at Duncaster*
Sir Hugh Walpole, *Mrs. Lunt*
H. G. Wells, *The Inexperienced Ghost*
Eudora Welty, *The Purple Hat*

Edith Wharton, *Afterward*
Oscar Wilde, *The Canterville Ghost*
Virginia Woolf, *The Haunted House*
Alexander Woolcott, *Full Fathom Five*
P. C. Wren, *Fear*
"S, Ex-Private," *Smee*
Israel Zangwill, *The Double-Barrelled Ghost*
Arnold Zweig, *An Apparition*

and

Anon, *Ghost Stories. Collected with a Particular View to Counteract the Vulgar Belief in Ghosts and Apparitions* (1823, reprinted 1865)
H. Addington Bruce, *Historic Ghosts and Ghost Hunters* (1908)
John Canning, *Fifty Great Ghost Stories* (1966)
Michael Cox, *The Oxford Book of Twentieth-Century Ghost Stories* (1996)
Cristopher Frayling, *The Vampire: A Bedside Companion* (1978)
Joseph L. French, *Great Ghost Stories* (1918)
Peter Haining, *Great Tales of Terror From Europe and America* (1973)
"   ," *Vampire: Chilling Tales of the Undead* (1985)
Sharon Jarvis, *True Tales of the Uninvited* (1989)
Alexander Lang, *Great Ghost Stories of the World* (1939)
Geoffrey Palmer and Noël Lloyd, *Ghost Stories Round the World* (1965)
Leslie Shepard, *The Dracula Book of Great Vampire Stories* (1977)
Richard "Red" Skelton, *A Red Skeleton in Your Closet* (1965)
Andrew Tackaberry, *Famous Ghosts, Phantoms, and Poltergeists for the Millions* (1966)
Devendra P. Varma, *Voices from the Vaults* (1987)
Ornella Volta and Valeria Riva, *The Vampire: An Anthology* (1963)

FILL IN THE BLANKS

Charles W. Morton for years entertained readers in *The Atlantic* and other periodicals with his wit and wisdom. In *A Slight Sense of Outrage* (1955) he reprinted his *All-Purpose Ghost Story*. All you have to do is fill in the blanks (in the full version he comments amusingly on how to do that). For the full article you will have to seek out the book, but this is all you need to create your own clichéd ghost story:
"I don't believe in ghosts—yet how else to account for what happened to me that night in ____"....
"It was late in the afternoon when I finally reached ____" he continues. "I had been ___ing hard all day and I was looking forward to a ____, a good____, and the possibility of ____ next morning"....
"There was nothing about the outward appearance of No.___ that was in the least unusual, but as I mounted the steps and rang the bell I had a

sudden feeling of ____. I noticed, too, that a ____ across the street seemed to be eyeing me rather closely, but I must confess that I thought nothing of it at the time"....

"I realized when Blank answered the door himself that his servants must have left and that we were alone in the house"....

"The warmth of my welcome was like old times, but I was hardly prepared for Blank's appearance. He was much ____er than when I had last seen him; his ____, which I remembered as downright ____, was now quite ____. His ____s, too, were no longer as I had known them. All in all, he seemed like a man who had ____ed, if I may be permitted the word"....

"I could not help noticing, as we exchanged greetings, Blank's ____; it was very old, as I could tell at a glance, and of curious workmanship"....

"The room to which blank showed me seemed cheery enough," the story goes on, "but I was struck by the huge ____ which occupied almost one entire wall. Once or twice, as I turned suddenly and looked at it, I could have sworn that it was ____ing, but this, of course, was absurd. ____s simply do not ____, I told myself"....

At this point there can be a dinner, with as much foody folderol as is desired but soon both men go off to their beds. The story picks up speed:

"So far as I could tell, my room was just as I had left it, but the ____ seemed even larger that before. Its bulk dwarfed everything else, and I was uncomfortably aware of it as I dropped off to sleep.

"I have no way of judging how long I slept, but suddenly I was wide awake. The room was pitch black; all was still. Then I heard, faintly and as at a great distance, the sound of ____ing. It was as if a very____ ____, or a ____, were being ____ed, far away. I cannot describe the feeling of ____, of ____, of sheer ____, that swept over me. The ____ing grew louder. It seemed to be coming from the general direction of the vast ____ that I have mentioned. My ____ was ____. I tried to ____, but to no avail. Suddenly I realized that I could see taking form in the darkness the unmistakable outlines of a ____ (italics)!

"At that point I must have ____ ____ altogether, for the next thing I knew it was ____ ____, and Blank was ____ing ____ ____ ____ jug of hot water.

"I ____ ____ ____ ____, Blank ____ ____ ____ ____, and the house was sold. Shortly afterwards, I came upon this story in the evening paper:

"Workmen ____ing an old house at No. ___ ___ Street discovered today in the wall of a bedroom the mummified remains of a ____. Police are investigating."

7

Ghosts and Poltergeists in Literature and Folklore

THE POPULAR IMAGINATION

This chapter hopes to give the reader some idea about the nature and extent of ghost and poltergeist figures in the popular imagination. Here is more from literature and folklore and even from the worlds of film, television, music, and other arts. *The Complete Book of Werewolves*, which will follow this book and conclude the series, will attempt to list and describe all the books and films devoted to werewolves and cases of transformation, but there are too many instances of the ghost and poltergeist in such media for me to attempt completeness here in a book already longer than others in this series.

THE FIRST THING AT THE LAST

The first thing that must be done at the time of someone's death for the benefit of the dead, varies from culture to culture. Here is a predicament that a Jew gets into in Nathan Englander's clever short story *The Twenty-Seventh Man* (1998):

> The morning that Mendel Muskatev awoke to find his desk was gone, his room was gone, and the sun was gone, he assumed he had died. This worried him, so he said the prayer for the dead, keeping himself in mind. Then he wondered if one was allowed to do such a thing, and worried instead that the first thing he had done upon being dead was sin.

PHANTOM SHIPS

The most famous of these is the Flying Dutchman. All its crew dead, it is said to sail the seven seas with full sails even when the sea is becalmed.

The phantom ship delivers mail addressed to people long dead. It has been, as we note elsewhere, the subject of fiction and opera.

But also in fiction we find ghost ships in stories by M. H. Barker, F. S. Bassett, C. L. Carmer, A. O. DeBlacam, Captain Frederick Marryat, and many others. Notable in American literature are Washington Irving's *The*

HAMLET.
Horatio: "Stay, illusion! If thou hast any sound or use of voice Speak to me."

Storm Ship, Edgar Allen Poe's *Ms. Found in a Bottle*, Bret Harte's *The Legend of Devil's Point*, Frank Norris' *The Ship that Saw a Ghost*, and some recent tales of the uncanny and the unexplained in connection with real vessels lost at sea. Long before flying saucers we had ghost ships.

In Scandinavian folklore, there is the tradition of a Man on Board. This ghost performs tasks such as shifting cargo, stoking coal, rowing, etc. He flees the ship just before it sinks.

Such phenomena as St. Elmo's Fire (with its apparently ghostly lights) and other things seen at sea by traditionally superstitious sailors have contributed mightily to tales of ghosts on the ocean waves.

If you have ever stood alone by moonlight on the deck of a quiet ship you know the feeling of some Presence that goes far toward explaining the superstitions of sailors. No wonder ghosts at sea are the most captivating.

A FRIENDLY GHOST

No, not Casper in the cartoons, though that figure (sinking in popularity but still in the Top Ten with the Under Tens) has done something to keep children from being too frightened of specters.

I mean Jack, the friendly ghost in *The Old Wives' Tale* (1595), by George Peele (*c.*1558-1598). This is a comedy with folklore material. The ghost helps to destroy the enchantment by which a nasty magician, Sacrapant, holds the heroine, the beautiful Delia. Milton's more famous masque of *Comus* repeats some of Peele's romantic story. I mention this old play by one of the University Wits of Shakespeare's time to make the point that not all ghosts in literature are unpleasant. The Grateful Dead can be of great use to the living.

FROM GEOFFREY CHAUCER

"Now, sire," quod she, "but a word er I go.
My child is dead withinne thise wykes two,
Soone after that ye wente out of this toune."
    "His death saugh I by revelacioun,"
Seide this frere, "at hoom in our dortout.
I dar we; seyn that, er that half an hour
After his death, I saugh hym born to blisse
In myn avision, so God me wisse!
So dide oure sexteyn and oure fermerer,
That han been trewe freres fifty yeer...."

SOPHONISBA

This is the title of a play by John Marston which either predated Shakespeare's *Macbeth* by a little and gave The Bard some ideas about super-

natural sensations to include or, alternatively, had to compete with the popularity of such crowd-grabbing material as *Macbeth* offered when both plays
were presented in 1606.

Marston's witch, called Erictho, is—name and all—right out of the sixth

The Ars Moriendi (Art of Dying, c. 1471) shows angels and devils contending for
the soul of the dying man.

book of the *Pharsalia* by the Latin writer Lucian. Erictho lives in a sort of desecrated temple which boys have covered with obscene graffiti. And the neighborhood is terrible!

> Down in a pit, o'er-grown with brakes and briars,
> Close by the ruin of a shaken abbey,
> Torn, with an earthquake, down unto the ground,
> Mongst graves and grott[oe]s, near an old charnel-house.
> She makes fierce spoil, and swells with wicked triumph
> To bury her lean knuckles in his eyes.

No wonder ghosts come back for vengeance after helpless corpses receive rude treatment like that! And you thought dramatic entertainment got gory and gruesome only when the likes of *Halloween* and *Tales from the Crypt* came along! It's the tradition, not the times. This stuff "will play in Peoria." It played at Shakespeare's Globe and Blackfriars, too.

SHAKESPEARE'S GHOSTS ONSTAGE

The ghost in *Hamlet* is the most famous one of all. Tradition says Shakespeare himself played the part of The Ghost. *Macbeth* has ghosts and also a ghostly dagger in the air, and *Richard III* had almost a dozen ghosts in one scene as, the night

John Dickenson in 1598 published *Greene in Conceipt*, a "Tragique Historie of faire Valeria of London," supposed to have been penned by Robert Greene. Greene was one of the "University Wits" of Shakespeare's early days in the theater. Greene is shown here risen from his grave (wearing his shroud). "Ghost-written" indeed!

before his death, the king's past rises up to confront him. The Elizabethans firmly believed in ghosts and in demons.

RICHARD BARNFIELD (1574-1627) ON "MAN'S LIFE"

> Man's life is well comparèd to a feast,
> Furnished with choice of all variety;
> To it comes Time; and as a bidden guest
> He sets him down, in pomp and majesty;
> The three-fold Age of man the waiters be.
> Then with an earthen voider (made of clay)
> Comes death and takes the table clean away.

CARDENIO; OR, THE SECOND MAIDEN'S TRAGEDY

This is a strange, anonymous play of Shakespeare's time that some critics (principally the autograph expert, Charles Hamilton) say Shakespeare wrote or had some hand in writing. The ghost in it is that of the wife of Govanius. She kills herself when she thinks her husband, whom The Tyrant has deposed, is dead. He isn't. He just fainted when she asked him to kill her rather than let her fall into the hands of The Tyrant. Things get very melodramatic.

The Tyrant, necrophiliac as well as general nogoodnik, breaks open the lady's tomb and hires a makeup expert to pretty up the corpse for him. He may not be able to have the live lady, but he has serious designs on the dead one. What the mad Tyrant doesn't realize is that the makeup man is our old friend Govanius in disguise. So Govanius puts poison in the lipstick on the corpse and *bingo*, when The Tyrant kisses the corpse it is all over for him.

THE GHOST URGES REVENGE

Jasper Heywood translated into English ten plays of the Roman dramatist Seneca, and suddenly the Elizabethan stage was full of Senecan gore and horrible revenge, from the first Elizabethan blank-verse tragedy (Norton and Sackville's *Gorboduc*) onwards. One of the masters of the Senecan mode was John Marston (1576-1634). He had a brief career writing for the stage, giving it up after less than half a dozen years to take holy orders, but his two plays, *Antonio and Mellida* and *Antonio's Revenge*, both published in quarto in 1602, show power. Incidentally, he seems to have given Shakespeare some good ideas for rewriting a play by Thomas Kyd about a gloomy Dane called Hamlet.

In Shakespeare's *Hamlet*, too famous to take up space here, is perhaps the most famous theatrical ghost of all, as I said earlier. Here are two scenes by Marston, which Shakespeare must have loved. In the first, Antonio speaks with the ghost of his father. In the second, the ghost speaks with his widow. Work with the Elizabethan spelling. Note that the original audiences were expected to be able to understand the Latin tags.

> *Enter two pages, the one with two tapers, the other with a chafing dish: a perfume in it.* Antonio, *in his night gowne, and a night cap, unbrac't, following after.*

> ANTONIO. The black iades of swart night trot foggy rings
> Bout heavens browe. Tis now starke dead night.
> Is this Saint *Markes* Church?

> 1 PAGE. It is, my Lord.

ANTONIO. Where stands my father's hearse?

2 PAGE. Those streamers beare his armes. I, that is it.

ANTONIO. Set tapers to the toumbe, a lampe the Church:
Give me the fire. Now depart and sleepe.   [*Exeunt* PAGES
I purifie the ayre with odorous fume.
Graves, valts, and toumbes, groane not to beare my weight.
Colde flesh, bleake trunkes, wrapt in your half-rot shrowdes,
I presse you softly, with a tender foote.
Most honour'd sepulchre, vouchsafe a wretch
Leave to weepe over thee. Toumb, Ile not be long
Ere I creepe in thee, and with bloodlesse lips
Kisse my cold fathers cheeke. I pree thee, grave,
Provide soft mould to wrap my carcasse in.
Thou royal spirit of *Andrugio*, where ere thou hoverst
(Ayrie intellectt) I heave up tapers to thee (viewe thy son)
In celebration of dewe obsequies.
Once every night, Ile dewe thy funerall hearse
With my religious teares.
O blessed father of a cursèd son,
Thou diedst most happie, since thou livedst not
To see thy sonne most wretched, and thy wife
Pursu'd by him that seekes my guiltlesse blood.
O, in what orbe thy mightie spirit soares.
Stoop and beat downe this rising fog of shame,
That strives to blur thy blood, and girt defame
About my innocent and spotlesse browes.
Non est mori miserum, sed misere mori.

ANDRUGIO. Thy pangs of anguish rip my cerecloth up:
And loe the ghoast of ould *Andrugio*
Forsakes his coffin. *Antonio*, revenge.
I was impoyson'd by *Piero's* hand:
Revenge my bloode; take spirit gentle boy:
Revenge my bloode. Thy *Mellida*, is chaste:
Onely to frustrate thy pursuite in love,
Is blaz'd unchaste. Thy mother yeelds consent
To be his wife, & give his bloode a sonne,
That made her husbandlesse, and doth complot
To make her sonlesse: but before I touch
The banks of rest, my ghoast shall visite her.
Thou vigor of my youth, iuyce of my love,
Seize on revenge, graspe the sterne bended front
Of frowning vengeance, with unpaized clutch.

Alarum *Nemesis*, rouze up thy bloode,
Isuent some stratageme of vengeance:
Which but to thinke on, may like lightning glide,
With horror through thy breast; remember this.
Scelera non vlcisceris, nisi vincis. [*Exit* ANDRUGIO'S GHOST.

MARIA. God night *Nutriche*. Pages, leave the roome.
The life of night growes short, tis almost dead.
         [*Exeunt* PAGES *and* NUTRICHE.
O thou cold widdowe bed, sometime thrice blest,
By the warme pressure of my sleeping Lord:
Open thy leaves, and whilst on thee I treade,
Groane out. Alas, my dear *Andrugio's* deade.
    [MARIA *draweth the courtaine: and the ghost of*
     ANDRUGIO *is displayed, sitting on the bed.*
Amazing terror, what portent is this?

ANDRUGIO. Disloyal to our Hymniall rites,
What raging heat rains in thy strumpet blood?
Hast thou so soone forgot *Andrugio*?
Are our love-bands so quickly cancellèd?
Where lives thy plighted faight unto this breast?
O weake *Marya*! Go to, calme thy feares.
I pardon thee, poore soule. O shed no teares,
Thy sex is weake. That black incarnate fiende
May trippe thy faith, that hath orethrowne my life:
I was impoyson'd by *Piero's* hand.
With my sonne, to bend up straind revenge.
Maintaine a seeming favour to his suite,
Till time may forme our vengeance absolute.
  [*Enter* ANTONIO, *his armes bloody: a torch and a poniard* [dagger]

ANTONIO. See, unamaz'd, I will beholde thy face,
Outstare the terror of thy grimme aspect,
Daring the horred'st object of the night.
Looke how I smoake in blood, reeking the steame
Of foming vengeance. O my soule's inthroan'd
In the trumphant chariot of revenge.
My thinks I am all ayre, and feele no waight
Of humane dirt clogge. This is *Iulio's* bloode.
Rich musique, father; this is *Iulio's* bloode.
Why lives that mother?

ANDRUGIO. Pardon ignorance. Fly deare *Antonio*:
Once more assume disguise, and dog the Court

In fainèd habit, till *Piero's* blood
May even ore-flowe the brimme of full revenge.   [*Exit* ANTONIO.
Peace, and all blessèd fortunes to you both.
Fly thou from Court, be pearelesse in revenge:
Sleepe thou in rest, loe here I close thy couch.
        [*Exit* MARIA *in her bed,* ANDRUGIO *drawing the Curtaines.*
And now yee sootie coursers of the night,
Hurrie your chariot into hells black wombe.
Darkenesse, make flight; Graves, eat your dead again:
Let's repossesse our shrowdes. Why lags delay?
Mount sparkling brightnesse, give the world his day.

SIR WALTER RALEIGH ON NECROMANCY

It is true that there are many arts, if we may so call them, which
are covered with the name of magic, and esteemed abusively to be
as branches of that tree on whose root they never grew. The first
of these hath the name of necromancy or *gœtia*; and of this again
there are diverse kinds. The one is an invocation at the graves of
the dead, to whom the Devil himself gives answer instead of those
that seem to appear. For certain it is, that the immortal souls of
men do not inhabit the dust and dead bodies, but they give motion
and understanding to the living; death being nothing else but a separation of the body and the soul; and therefore the soul is not to
be found in the graves.

JOHN MILTON

From the masque of *Comus*, already alluded to:
Some say no evil thing that walks by night,
In fog or fire, by lake of moorish fen,
Blue meager hag, or stubborn unlaid ghost,
That breaks his magic chains at curfew time,
No goblin or swart fairy of the mine
Hath hurtful power o'er true virginity.

HENRY VAUGHAN

Henry Vaughan's religious poetry is remarkable, suffused with "celestial
light." His description of his "angel infancy" will raise the hair on the back
of your neck. In one of his minor works, *The Importunate Fortune*, he suggests that dead human beings are not likely to linger as ghosts but, freed
from the body, the soul will ascend into the heavens and join what Bishop
Berkeley called "all the choir of heaven," the angels and archangels, the
cherubim, seraphim, thrones, dominions, powers, principalities....

The Witch of Endor's necromancy brings back the dead for King Saul (left).

Get up, my disentangled soul, thy fire
Is now refined and nothing left to tire
Or clog thy wings. Now my auspicious flight
Hath brought me to the Empyrean light.
I am a sep'rate essence, and can see
The emanations of the deity,
And how they pass the seraphims, and run
Through every throne and domination.

TRUE RELATION OF THE APPARITION OF MRS. VEAL

In 1706, Daniel Defoe (1660-1731) published a version with this title of a ghost story that was the sensation of London at the time. It is a classic of the genre. Defoe's careful, almost dry narration gives it credibility. It demonstrates his famous ability to make fiction sound like fact and fact like fiction. In the story (based on real people who lived in Canterbury) Mrs. Veal's ghost visited a Mrs. Bargrave, to make up a damaged friendship. Mrs. Bargrave had no idea she was talking with a mere apparition. The two ladies had "an hour and three-quarters' conversation," though Mrs. Veal declined to accept a cup of tea. She did discuss a lot of books and poetry about heaven and the afterlife and told Mrs. Bargrave that Charles Drelincourt's *The Christian's Defense against the Fear of Death* (first published in 1675) was "the best....on that subject ever written." It transpired that she was in a position to know.

"I think you look as well as I ever knew you," said Mrs. Bargrave to the figure who turned out to be an apparition, and they parted friends again. Defoe ends with:

> This thing has very much affected me, and I am as well satisfied as I am of the best grounded matter of fact. And why we should dispute matter of fact because we cannot solve things of which we have no certain or demonstrative notions, seems strange to me. Mrs. Bargrave's authority and sincerity would have been undoubted in any other case.

JOSEPH ADDISON

In *The Spectator* for 1 July 1712, Addison wrote:

> There are many intellectual [he means intelligent] beings in the world besides ourselves, and several species of spirits, who are subject to different laws and economics from those of mankind.

WILLIAM BLAKE

Angels perched in the trees in his backyard in London, Blake claimed. One or more of them, he said, taught Blake how to draw. Blake wrote:

> Each man is in his Spectre's power
> Until the arrival of that hour,
> When his Humanity awake
> And cast his own Spectre into the lake.

This violent action is the sudden extension of the field of consciousness of which William James wrote. It is the insight that is depicted in cartoons as a light bulb lighting up. Before that we are plodding along as it were under the direction of some inner ghost; suddenly we are free of it. Colin Wilson in *The Occult* (1971 and reprinted) cites a number of examples. Here is part of a statement that struggles to put the almost ineffable into words. Wilson quotes it from Warner Allen's experience reported in *The Timeless Moment*:

> It flashed up lightning-wise during a performance of Beethoven's Seventh Symphony in the Queen's Hall, in that triumphant fast movement when "the morning stars sang together and all the sons of God shouted for joy." The swiftly flowing continuity of the music was not interrupted, so that what Mr. T. S. Eliot calls "the intersection of the timeless moment" [with time] must have slipped into the interval between the two demi-semi-quavers. When, long after, I analysed the happening in the cold light of retrospect, it seemed to fall into three parts: first the mysterious event itself, which occurred in an infinitesimal fraction of a split second; this I learned afterwards from St. Teresa to call the Union with God; then Illumination, a *wordless* stream of complex feelings in which the experience of Union combined with the rhythmic emotion of the music like a sunbeam striking with iridescence the spray above a waterfall—a stream that was continually swollen by tributaries of associated Experience; lastly, Enlightenment, the recollection in tranquillity of the whole complex of Experience, as it were, embalmed in thought forms and words.

The ghost of William Blake is said to have manifested itself to Allen Ginsberg when he was a student at Columbia University. It spoke in terms more direct than that. When Ginsberg was a colleague of mine at Brooklyn College CUNY, I always wanted to ask him if the ghost spoke, as Blake did, in Cockney tones, but I was always afraid that would be impertinent. Now it is too late to ask. The ghost of Blake, by the way, Ginsberg claimed to hear, not see. Ghosts need not be visible. Sometimes we hear them only, or we have auditory hallucinations.

Once I woke in the middle of the night, hearing my name called. My bed partner was sound asleep. There was no one else there. Next morning I discovered the voice was on my answering machine; I had not heard the telephone bell but my name had awakened me. Do you have similar explanations for mysterious voices calling your name, or have you never had the experience, asleep or awake?

AN OLD SEA DOG REACTS TO SEEING A GHOST

After a career as a naval officer, Frederick Marryat (1792-1848) became one of the best novelists of the sea in any language. He was the author of *Mr Midshipman Easy* (1834) and other renowned works. He saw the Brown Lady of Raynham and tried to shoot her.

Captain Marryat was visiting the great country house of the Townshends and bravely agreed to occupy a room many said was haunted by a lady in a brown Elizabethan gown such as appeared in an old painting on the wall. When the dead lady of the portrait appeared to him and a couple of companions, the captain took a shot at her point-blank. The bullet went right through her.

There were a number of other sightings, and in the 1920s Captain Provand and Indra Shira, two photographers, took what they said was a photograph of the Brown Lady. It went into the pages of *Country Life* magazine. Some people said they could vaguely see in the picture the ghost coming down the great staircase of the house.

The Brown Lady has been the subject of quite a number of literary reports. It is always interesting to see a Brown Lady, or a Gray Lady, or a Bloody Nun or some other ghost develop with the telling and retelling of a tale.

FROM "THE HAUNTED HOUSE" BY CHARLES DICKENS

This is from one of Dickens' many efforts to fill up space in a periodical he ran, so excuse the stretching out of material. Excuse also the snobbery of mocking the low-class accent (which Dickens doesn't even get right: such a person doesn't say "he 'ooted" but "'e 'ooted," of course). Still, it's amusing, as Dickens, prolix or not, invariably is. My colleagues in The Dickens Fellowship of New York (founded 1905) and Dickensians everywhere will be familiar with this passage:

> "This gentleman wants to know," said the landlord, "if anything's seen at The Poplars."
> "Ooded woman with a howl," said Ikey, in a state of great freshness.
> "Do you mean a cry?"
> "I mean a bird, Sir."

"A hooded woman with an owl. Dear me! Did you ever see her?"

"I seen the howl."

"Never the woman?"

"Not so plain as the howl, but they always keeps together."

"Has anybody ever seen the woman as plainly as the owl?"

"Lord bless you, sir! Lots."

"Who?"

"The general-dealer opposite, for instance, who is opening his shop."

"Perkins? Bless you, Perkins wouldn't go anigh the place. No!" observed the young man with considerable feeling, "he an't over-wise, an't Perkins, but he an't such a fool as *that*."

(Here the landlord murmured his confidence in Perkins knowing better.)

"Who is—or who was—the hooded woman with the owl? Do you know?"

"Well," said Ikey, holding up his cap with one hand while he scratched his head with the other, "they say, in general, that she was murdered, and the howl he 'ooted the while.'

Dickens' *A Christmas Carol* vividly limns the ghost of Scrooge's late partner, Marley, and Scrooge is treated to three Christmas ghosts as well. Four ghosts, for good holiday measure! Dickens is bested, however, by Sutton Vane's play *Outward Bound* (all but two of the cast are ghosts) and Hans Chlumberg's *Miracle at Verdun* (millions of soldiers killed in World War I rise from their graves).

DISAPPOINTED AS THE DICKENS

Edward George Lytton Bulwer-Lytton, the first Baron Lytton (1803-1873), added Lytton to his name when his first wife, the heiress Elizabeth Lytton (1773-1843), died. With her death he came into possession of the great country house of Knebworth, and to it over the years he invited a number of magicians, including the visiting French expert on transcendental magic who went under the pseudonym of "Éliphas Lévi." While visiting in England on one occasion this worthy once called up the ghost of Apollonius of Tyana. (I describe the scene in *The Complete Book of the Devil's Disciples*.)

Charles Dickens was one of those invited to one of Lytton's occult parties, and in a letter to a clergyman friend, dated 7 March 1854, Dickens wrote:

Said [Lytton] had a great party on Sunday, when it was rumoured "a count was going to raise the dead." I stayed till the ghostly hour, but the rumour was unfounded, for neither count nor plebian came

up to the spiritual scratch. It is really inexplicable to me that a man
of his calibre can be run away by such small deer.

By "small deer" (from *King Lear*) he means trivialities. Lord Lytton, however, was very serious about magic. He wrote about it extensively, and was
closely connected to a number of practicing French magicians and some
Englishmen dabbling in the black arts. Lytton tried to use magic in acri-
monious battles with his estranged wife. Apparently he felt more comfortable dealing with The Devil than with her.

CHRONONHOTOSTHROLOGOS

This is the astounding title of a burlesque of eighteenth-century tragedy,
written by Henry Carey, whom one writer of the time remembered thus:
"He led a life free from reproach and hanged himself October 4th, 1743."
That same year the play appeared in Carey's *Dramatick Works*.

The play mocks throughout the excessive posturing and weird names
of English heroic tragedy. For instance, the action begins in cliché style
with two characters meeting in the antechamber of the palace. One asks
the other where the king is. The first lines of the play are:

> Aldiborontiphoscophornio!
> Where left you Chrononhotosthrologus?

After that the plot and the language grow more complex. Death and ghosts
are part of the fun. At one point, the king—the title of the play is, of course,
his name—kills the cook and strikes a blow at his general, one Bombardinion. The general is enraged:

> *Bomb.* A blow! Shall Bombardinion take a blow?
> Blush! Blush, thou sun! Start back thou rapid ocean!
> Hills! Vales! Seas! Mountains! All commixing crumble,
> And into Chaos pulverize the world;
> For Bombardinion has received a blow,
> And Chrononhotonthologos shall die.   [*Draws.*
>   *King.* What means the traitor?
>   *Bomb.* Traitor in thy teeth!
> Thus I defy thee!   [*They fight—he kills the* King.
>   Ha! What have I done?
> Go, call a coach, and let a coach be called;
> And let the man that calls it be the caller;
> And in his calling, let him nothing call

But coach! coach! coach! Oh! For a coach, ye gods!
                                 [*Exit raving. Returns with a* Doctor.
    Bomb. How fares your majesty?
    Doct.   My lord, he's dead.
    Bomb. Ha! Dead! Impossible! It cannot be!
I'd not believe it though himself should swear it.
Go, join he body to his soul again,
Or, by this light, thy soul shall quit thy body.
    Doct. My lord, he's far beyond the power of physic;
His soul has left his body and this world.
    Bomb. Then go to t'other world and fetch it back.
                                                  [*Kills him.*

And if I find thou triflest with me there,
I'll chase thy shade through myriads of orbs,
And drive thee far beyond the verge of nature.
Ha!—Call'st thou, Chrononhotonthologos?
I come! Your faithful Bombardinion comes!
He comes in worlds unknown to make new wars,
And gain thee empires num'rous as the stars.
                                              [*Kills himself.*

            Enter Queen *and Others.*
    Aldi. O horrid! Horrible and horrid'st horror!
Our King! our General! our Cook! our Doctor!
All dead! stone dead! irrevocably dead!
O————h!   [*All groan—a tragedy groan.*

ALFRED, LORD TENNYSON

Here is a poem of Christian affirmation by another literary lord besides
Byron and Lytton. Tennyson wanted it to be placed at the end of all collections of his poetry. It makes one wonder: if indeed we meet God our
Pilot face to face when we die, why would anyone bother with their former earthly concerns and be a ghost, not an angel?

This poem comes from the bard of Victorian England, who sought
some comfort privately in the occult. Tennyson had problems with drugs,
difficult domestic life, loss, and depression, attributed to "black blood" in
the family, and also with homosexuality and insanity. Tennyson was said
to compose his poetry in trance states, while publicly adhering to established religion. Unconventional as he was in many ways, here he uses the
familiar imagery of life as a journey and reflects the basic love of the sea
of Britain's Island Race. *Crossing the Bar* is worth quoting in full:

        Sunset and evening star,
        And one clear call for me!

And may there be no moaning of the bar,
When I put out to sea,
But such a tide as moving seems asleep,
Too full for sound and foam,
When that which drew from out the boundless deep
Turns again home.
Twilight and evening bell,
And after that the dark!
And may there be no sadness of farewell,
When I embark:
For though from out our bourne of Time and Place
The Flood may bear me far,
I hope to see my Pilot face to face
When I have crossed the bar.

LAFCADIO HEARN

Regarded as an American author, this writer's Greek forename and Irish surname remind us of his foreign parents. He was born in Greece in 1850. He arrived in the United States in 1869. Attracted to a mulatto, he felt most comfortable among the creoles of New Orleans and eventually he moved to Japan and married a Japanese woman. "The stable conditions of a society to which [I] belong only by accident" never appealed to him. He said he had "nothing resembling genius" and was convinced that only some "curious study" could give him a notable place in literature. Among his curious studies were ghost stories.

His *Kwaidan*, fourteen tales of the supernatural in old Japan, is perhaps the best of all his strange works. It features ghostly samurai, women in the shape of foxes, and other marvels. His ghost stories include *Dead Secret*, *In a Cup of Tea*, and *The Story of O-Kamé*. The Japanese call him Koizumi Yakumo and oddly think he best reports them accurately to the West. See *Rediscovering Lafcadio Hearn* (ed. Sukehiro Hirakawa, 1997).

ARCHIE THE COCKROACH

Newspaperman Don Marquis (1878-1937) said that when he left food scraps around his desk he attracted a cockroach, named Archie, who began to communicate with him by jumping on the keys of his typewriter. Archie couldn't manage the shift key, so his philosophical remarks and tales of Mehitabel the cat, and other creatures, were all typed in lower case, no capitals.

Archie was profound. For instance, he admitted that the human race may be doing the best it can; that, he added, is an explanation, not an excuse. Here's what Archie said about ghosts:

> you want to know
> whether i believe in ghosts
> of course i do not believe in them
> if you had known
> as many of them as i have
> you would not
> believe in them either

BRITISH GHOST STORIES FOR CHILDREN

Phillipa Pearce's *Dread and Delight: A Century of Children's Ghost Stories* (1995) is a convenient survey with forty fine examples. It is a delight. We see that the British are not as afraid as Americans of frightening children (they welcomed more that we did the likes of Roald Dahl, for instance), so long as there is a reassuring conclusion to the tale. The British also prefer for these ghost stories everyday settings, as Alfred Hitchcock did for his films. Familiar settings make terror more unexpected and more startling.

Among UK writers of ghost fiction for children, Tom Deveson deserves more attention than he has enjoyed. *The Railway Phantoms* may be "too Yorkshire" for US readers and *The Weekly Ghost* to much connected with British school life, but *The Hidden Tomb* and *Stonestruck* should be fun for American young readers. It would be better for juvenile readers to be provided with ghost stories than frightened with vampires, werewolves, and other common kiddie horrors.

Children's literature may be (except for its wonderful illustrators) the writing field where the least talent goes the farthest. Therefore, if you are tempted to make a buck scaring the children, read George Edward Stanley's "Five Keys to Writing Scary Kids' Stories," *Writer's Digest* 75 (September 1996): 30-34, and get going. The competition is not too scary. However, handling witches in a nonscary way is even more lucrative. *TLS* and other serious commentators worry that tacky horror is keeping children and teenagers away from good literature. Perhaps horror and violence are simply preparing them for modern life, or offering them non-perilous escapes from real-life terrors.

GHOST RESEARCH

The Ghost Trackers Club, founded in Chicago by Martin V. Riccardo (who also started a Vampire Information Exchange), became the Ghost Research Society in 1981. It started as more of a fan club than an American equivalent of The Society for Psychical Research in London or the first of such organizations, the Ghost Club founded in London in 1862. A reincarnation of the original English Ghost Club achieved considerable publicity under the presidency of Peter Underwood (whose autobiography, *No Uncommon Task*, 1983, is full of interest, and to whom I have already referred as a leading light in the field).

The British societies seem to be in the responsible hands of researchers with only occasional kooks. Many US researchers seem more gullible, or at least more willing to accept the paranormal, and are crushed when the phantoms and faked photographs disappoint. Most of the hauntings that the Ghost Research Society investigates are in the homes of Roman Catholics, but that church is not called in for exorcisms, so their ghostbusting seems neither religious nor rigidly scientific.

As William James, who helped to found a Society of Psychical Research in the United States, wrote, ghosts are too persistent a belief to be ignored and too significant not to be studied with honesty and objective, reliable methods. Parapsychology is even more fascinating than psychology, but it will never become a science until it attracts hard-nosed scientists and conducts reproducible experiments.

Freaks and fans, zealots and 'zines are no real problem, but serious research is what is needed in parapsychology.

RECENT DIRECTIONS IN POPULAR CULTURE

Lynette Carpenter and Wendy K. Kolmer, eds., *Haunting the House of Fiction: Feminist Perspectives on Ghost Stories by American Women* (1991)

William A. Cohen, *Sex Scandal: The Private Parts of Victorian Fiction* (1996)

David Glover, *Bram Stoker and the Politics of Popular Fiction* (1996)

Larry N. Landrum, *American Popular Culture: A Guide to Information Sources* (1982)

David Lavery, ed., *Deny All Knowledge: Reading the "X-Files"* (1996)

Gwen Margaret Neary, *Disorderly Ghosts: Literary Spirits and the Social Agenda of American Women, 1870-1930* (University of California at Berkeley dissertation, 1994)

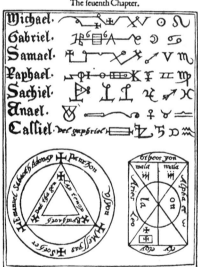

The charaćters of the angels of the feauen daies, with their names : of figures, feales and periapts.

The feuenth Chapter.

Thefe figures are called the feales of the earth, without the which no fpirit will appeere, except thou haue them with thee.

Reginald Scot's famous *Discouerie of Witchcraft* (1595) presents sigils and amulets and "seals" without which the angels assigned to the various days of the week, magicians said, could not be made to appear. Angels can be summoned, but they are not ghosts.

Spirit Voices.

Words and Music written expressly for the Shekinah.

Words by C. D. STUART.   Music by V. C. TAYLOR.

Very early spiritualism in the United States was connected with Protestant denominations and this music from the spiritualist journal *Shekinah* published in 1853 proves it had its own hymns. Later it added popular songs such as "Somewhere A Voice is Calling."

SCANDINAVIAN FOLKLORE ABOUT SPIRITS

Scandinavia did get some black books of magical recipes and rituals from German sources. On the whole, it has pretty much rejected general European superstitions about ghosts and demons. It has pictured The Devil in its folklore as more of a comic than a fearsome character. Christianity is only a thousand years old in Scandinavia, and has a weaker grip there, in my view, than it has in most parts of the world. There things are more Viking than Vatican, you might say.

Their own rich ideas and folklore serve the inhabitants of *Norden* well. Scandinavians are proud of old traditions. They cling to them. The Swedish milk company Arla educates the public in folklore with *gamla nyeter* (old news, which is to say folklore legends) on milk cartons.

With the assistance of Ola J. Holten, I translate the story on one:

A creature appeared at Green Stream and some of the children at Wood Farm encountered this dangerous fiddler when, without permission, they went down to the bank to bathe. Just as they were about to jump into the water, they heard the music of the fiddle. They became frightened, because they knew this meant a water nymph was after them. But everything turned out fine, thanks to the cleverness of the oldest girl. She was able to take a pin from her clothing, fasten it to a thorn, and pin the water nymph to the bottom of the stream.

Stories like this one have always encouraged the young not to fear ghosts and trolls and spirits in general; there is always something you can do to counter them.

Here is another, "Church Nearly Hit by a Giant's Throw":

On the eve of Sunday the ground in Hälanda shook when a giant threw three huge stones at the church. Jönnson saw this and rushed to the church tower to ring the big bell. His brave action chased the giant away. All three stones missed their target and you can see them today beside the church. The biggest one is more than 2 meters high. The giant was last spotted north of Korkberget. People of the region are advised to avoid that particular area where a marker to him is supposed to be.

Stories like this one are often used to explain odd geological formations and to keep people away from the haunts of The Devil, demons, giants, trolls, or other supernatural forces.

GOTHIC FICTION

When Horace Walpole, a wealthy eccentric, got tired of realism in the novel, he fled from English settings and "strict adherence to common life." He turned to mysterious Italian settings and the supernatural. He established the vogue for (and named) Gothic fiction in *The Castle of Otranto* (1764). Then the floodgates opened.

E. F. Bleiler covers over 7,000 stories in the genre in his standard *Guide to Supernatural Fiction* (1983). His examples range from 1750 to 1960. There are some works not in Bleiler to be found in Montague Summers' *Gothic Bibliography* (1941), but that book is to be used with caution. Marshall B. Tymn's *Horror Literature: A Core and Reference Guide* (1981) goes almost through the seventies. Frederick S. Frank's *The First Gothics* (1987) is strong on 500 selected romances dated 1764 to the 1820s in Britain, and in *Through the Pale Door* (1990) he treats 509 American examples 1786-1988.

Today Goths are in the discos, but also in the bookstores and the cineplexes. No year passes without several big ghost movies.

HUN HAUNTS

From the early days, the kingdom of France (what the Romans used to call Gaul) was invaded by barbarians from the East—frequently, in fact. In the reign of the eighth king of France, a nonentity called Caribert, the Huns swept into the territory with a new terror. They were said to have brought with them an army of the ghosts of their ancestors, who strangled the French enemies. A man with the delightfully apt name of Debonnaire in his *Histoire de France* says that the French were nonetheless able to beat back the Huns, living and dead. More recently, the Huns have defeated the French repeatedly and without the use of spectral armies.

GHOST LIGHTS

I mean not the marsh gasses of fact or the will-o'-the wisp of legend but real, electric lights. These ghost lights, as they are called by stage people, are single lights set up on standards in the center of the stages of closed-down theaters. Of course they keep people from falling off the stage into the orchestra pit, but theater people sometimes say they are necessary to keep content the ghosts who haunt theaters.

Could it be that the nightlights people keep burning in their bedrooms, hoping that light will banish bogeymen, are actually making the rooms more attractive to ghosts? A friend of mine (a hard-headed engineering genius) had this idea and installed a nightlight that is a representation of the Sacred Heart of Jesus. He believes "that will hold them."

FREEMASONRY

Banned by Roman Catholics, freemasonry is wrongfully thought by some people to be atheistic. Note, however, that the secret ceremony of admission to the Third Degree (Master Mason) ends with affirmation of this life as anteroom to the everlasting. After death, the ritual says, "we shall be summoned from this sublunary abode, [so that] we may ascend to the Grand Lodge above, where the world's Great Architect lives and reigns forever." There *can* be Masonic ghosts! There can, if there are ghosts possible at all, in fact be ghosts who were atheists or doubters in this life—and woke up to reality.

IMMORTALITY PROVED?

No Christian can question it, but the citizens of a hamlet near Machiasport, Maine, in the early nineteenth century were certainly delighted to have the affirmation of their own senses rather than the mere word of God for it. The Rev. Abraham Cummings in *Immortality Proved by Testimony of Senses* (1826) tells the story.

The wife of Capt. George Butler died. After that she appeared as a ghost on a number of occasions to groups as large as forty persons, both inside the Butler house and outside. She moved among the living as if alive but was free with both intimate knowledge known only to a few present and also with knowledge of the Next World. She may have been disconcerting at times but she was welcomed as, in fact, anything is that helps us believe in the comforting thought that we continue, somehow, in some form, after the death of the body. The death and corruption of the flesh we can accept, even eventually take as a release. But the extinction of the personality? Never!

Ruth Hussey and Ray Milland look apprehensive about *The Uninvited* in a Cornish mansion (1944). This may have been the best ghost movie Hollywood ever made.

A SCOTTISH GHOST

The *Colann gun Cheann* is said to be a headless ghost who, if bothered, throws his head at you.

SEEING GHOSTS OF PEOPLE NOT YET DEAD

An old British superstition says that if you sit at the church door at midnight on St. Mark's Day (4 April) you will see the spirits of all the people of the village who are going to die in the coming year. This may be connected with the Scandinavian superstition about seeing the dead of the coming year at midnight on New Year's Eve.

LATING

This is an old British custom now almost forgotten. It involves carrying a lit candle around the property at Halloween. This is supposed to drive off ghosts. As we say in Brooklyn, it couldn't hurt.

ANY MORE FARES?

If you put pennies on a dead man's eyes or a coin or two in the mouth of a corpse before burial the spirit will have the fare across the Styx and therefore will not return as a ghost or vampire. More on this and other superstitions connected to death and burial in the first book in this series, *The Complete Book of Superstition, Prophecy, and Luck*.

THE BANSHEE

This famous White Lady of Irish superstition had many equivalents in Europe, where warnings of imminent death are said to be brought by a number of supernatural means. In Kodom (Bavaria), for instance, the ghosts of dead herdsmen are said to bring death: if you see one or more you are doomed to die soon. Maybe from fright.

THE FIGURE AT THE SIDE OF THE ROAD

One of those persistent legends that Jan H. Brunvand so interestingly collects in books about urban folklore concerns a young girl, often in a prom gown or some other white dress, who gets a ride with a motorist and, somehow or other, is discovered to be a ghost of someone killed in an automobile accident. In *Psychology Today* for June 1980 and in subsequent books, Brunvand traced "The Vanishing Hitchhiker" story which, he said in the magazine article, "evolved from a 19th-century horse-and-buggy level into modern variants incorporating freeway travel."

In Yorkshire, a Mrs. Ann Kelly saw a child by the roadside, swerved to avoid him, and crashed into a parked car. But she did avoid the certain death that she would have suffered had she had a head-on collision with a car coming up the other side of the hill. Her first thought was, "Have I killed the child?" Not to worry. The child had been killed, it transpired, at that place some years before. His ghost she credited with saving her life.

An often-told story concerns a young lad who joins a hobo walking along the roads. The boy turns out to be a wandering spirit, apparently condemned to travel this way forever.

10 GHOSTS OF ANIMALS IN THE BRITISH ISLES

Bear: Ghostly bears haunt Worcester Cathedral and The Tower of London (England)

Bull: A black bull was reported to be haunting a Co. Clare castle in 1890 (Ireland)

Cat: The cat that haunted a Manchester house was headless (England)

Cow: A dun cow appearing as a ghost warns of the death of earls of Warwick (England)

Deer: A mysterious deer was reported haunting the Highlands (Scotland)

Dog: The *baquest*, a black dog of East Anglia, is an omen of death (England)

Donkey: A blue donkey is reported to have haunted Surrey (England)

Hare: The ghost of a girl who committed suicide appears as a hare (Cornwall)

Horse: Ghostly hoofbeats but no horse at Monagh (Ireland)

Wolf: Montague Summers reports a ghostly wolf in Wales in 1880 (Wales)

THE STORY OF GABRIELLE DE LAUNAY

Gabrielle was the beautiful daughter of the president of the tribunal of Toulouse in the mid-eighteenth century. Her story may or may not be that of a ghost.

As a young girl she fell in love with Maurice de Serres, but he was an officer who was going to the Indies and her father forbade the marriage, not wishing to lose his daughter thus. A couple of years later, Gabrielle was told that Serres had died overseas. Then she allowed her father to marry her off to an old man. A few years later still, Gabrielle died.

Serres was not dead. He returned to Paris, and when he learned of Gabrielle's death he went wild. He rushed to the cemetery of St. Roch and asked to view her remains. When the coffin was opened, he overcame the sexton and ran off with the corpse. The sexton did not report the incident because he did not want to confess he had taken a bribe to open the coffin. As far as people knew, Gabrielle still lay in the tomb.

Soon afterwards, Gabrielle's old husband happened to be in Paris and he thought he glimpsed Gabrielle in a passing coach. On the side of the coach he recognized the arms of Serres. He tracked down Serres and took him to court in 1760 with extraordinary charges: he allowed that Gabrielle was still alive and that she was posing as Julie, Maurice de Serres wife, who might, he suggested, have been murdered.

The verdict of the court was equally extraordinary. It declared that Gabrielle was buried in a catatonic state, had never been dead, had been rescued from the tomb by Serres, and must be returned to her legitimate old husband.

The woman called Gabrielle capped even that sensation. She returned as required to the house of her old husband but before going there she took poison, so that as soon as she appeared before him she gasped, "I restore to you what you have lost"—and fell dead at his feet. The old man was stunned. Serres, upon hearing of her death, killed himself. There's a movie "concept" in this!

IN MEMORIAM

For a long time after the death of his good friend Arthur Hallam, Tennyson's faith was shaken, but over the years he wrote a long poem to commemorate their friendship. It comes to the reassuring conclusion that in the long run everything will be all right, we shall after death be reunited with those we love, and that on earth we are only ignorant infants "crying for the light." The dead should inspire us to do more with our lives. It is better to have loved and lost than never to have loved. The spirits of the dead watch us benignly.

> Do we indeed desire the dead
>   Should still be near us at our side?
>   Is there no baseness we would hide?
> No inner vileness that we dread?
>
> Shall he for whose applause I strove,
>   I had such reverence for his blame,
>   See with clear eye some hidden shame
> And I be lessened in his love?
>
> I wrong the grave with fears untrue:
>   Shall love be blamed for want of faith?
>   There must be wisdom with great Death:
> The dead shall look me through and through.
>
> Be near us when we climb or fall:
>   Ye watch, like God, the rolling hours

> With larger other eyes than ours,
> To make allowance for us all.

THAT SINGULAR ANOMALY, THE LADY-NOVELIST

Victorian ghost tales in novels by women:

"Lucas Malet" (Mary Kingsley), *The Gateless Barrier* (1990)
Margaret Oliphant, *A Beleagured City* (1880)
Charlotte Cowan Riddle, *The Haunted River* (1877)
Clara Sicard, *The Ghost: A Legend* (1866)
Emma Whitehead, *The Haunted House* (1838)

BYZÉHIN MEADOW

Henry James was a great admirer of the story of this title by Ivan Turgenev (1818-1883). In this beautifully crafted tale of some young peasant boys herding horses and trading superstitious tales in a pleasant meadow on a lovely July day, there are references to the ghosts, nymphs, and other spirits in which the peasantry believe. One boy reports that a dead master haunts the Varnávitzy locality:

> "I should say so! In the worst way! The old master has seen the dead master there. He wears a dressing gown with a long skirt and they say he sighs continually, his eyes fixed on the ground, searching for something. Grandpa Trofimitch ran into him once."
> "What are you looking for, dear little father, Ivan Ivánitch," he said, "with your eyes on the ground?"
> "He asked him that?" Fédya, astounded, put in.
> "Yes, he asked him."
> "Trofimitch is a brave person to do that! Well, then what happened?"
> "I'm looking for saxifrage," he says, in a flat, hollow voice. "Saxifrage."
> "And what would you want with saxifrage, dear little father, Ivan Ivánitch?"
> "My grave is crushing me, crushing me, Trofimitch, and I want to get out, get out of it."
> "What a character!" said Fédya. "Probably he died too soon."
> "That's wonderful!" said Kóstya. "I thought dead people could be seen only on Relatives Saturday."
> "Dead people can be seen anytime," Iliúsha put in confidently. As far as I could tell, Iliúsha knew more than the rest about peasant superstitions. "But on Relatives Saturday you can also see any living person who is going to die that year. All you have to do is

sit on the church porch and keep watching the road and those who are going to die in the coming year pass right by. The peasant Uliyána, who lives in our village, sat on the church porch last year.... All of a sudden, she sees a little boy with nothing on but his shirt come walking along the road. She took a good look: it was little Ivan Feodósiev."

"You mean the kid who died last spring?" Fédya chimed in.

"'That's the one. He was sauntering along, not raising his little head... Uliyána recognized him right away. And then she took another look and it was a woman coming along. She stared and stared—Oh, my God!—it was Uliyána herself coming along the road!"

"You're sure it was herself?" Fédya asked.

"As God is my witness, it was her!"

"Yes, but what does that matter, because she isn't dead, right?"

"Well, the year isn't up yet. Take a look at her. She's about ready to kick off."

A LETTER TO THE EDITOR OF THE GENTLEMAN'S MAGAZINE 22 (1752), *173-174, SIGNED ONLY "A. B."* *(IN LIEU OF GIVEN AND SURNAMES)*

On the 23rd August, 1736, at noon, standing at the shop door with my mistress and maid-servant and Mr. Bloxham, then rider to Mr. Oakes and Co. (who now lives and follows the haberdashery trade in Cateaton Street [London]), we were choosing figured ribbons and other millinery goods, when I heard my father's voice call "Charles," very audibly. As accustomed, I answered, "Coming, sir" [but I did not go]. Being intent upon viewing the patterns, I stayed abut four minutes, when I heard a voice a second time call "Charles." The maid heard it then as well as myself, and answered, "He is coming, Mr. W-m-n." But the pattern book not being gone through with, I was impatient to see the end, and also being unwilling to detain the gentleman [Mr. Bloxham], I still tarried. Then I saw the door open, heard my father call a third time, in a strong, emphatic, angry tome, and [he] shutting the door I heard its sound. Both my mistress and the maid heard this last call, on which she [the mistress] pushed me out of the shop with, "Sirrah, get you gone, your father is quite angry with your stay." I ran over, lifted up the latch, but found the gate locked. Then going in at the backgate [I] saw my mother-in-law in the yard....I immediately went in, when I found no father.... Returning, I inquired of her [my mother-in-law] for my father; she said he was not come home, nor would dine at home that day.... I then went back to the company, whose consternation was as great as my own.... Whether all this was the force of imagination I cannot say, but I believe it may [have been]. I will not argue to the contrary, though two senses of two persons besides myself could not, probably, be so liable to deception. My mind and disposition from that hour received a new turn. I became another creature.... It is very remarkable that I had an only uncle (who was gunner of the "Biddeford," then stationed at Leith [Road]), that died there that same day and about the same hour.

A LETTER TO THE EDITOR IN
LONDON'S DAILY TELEGRAPH

Egyptian Hall, October 21st, 1881

Sir,—Having for many years been recognized by the public as an anti-Spiritualist and exposer of the frauds practiced by spirit media, it may surprise some of your readers to learn that I am a believer in apparitions. Several similar occurrences to those described by many of your correspondents have taken place in my own family, and in the families of near friends and relatives. The most remarkable one happened to my wife's mother some years ago. Late one evening, whilst sitting alone busily occupied with her needle, a strange sensation came over her, and upon looking up she distinctly saw her aged mother standing at the end of the room. She rubbed her weary eyes and looked again, but the spectre had vanished. She concluded it was imagination, and retired to rest, until the next day brought the news that her mother, at about the same time the apparition had appeared, had fallen down in a fit and expired.

John Nevil Maskelyne

THE END OF THE FLYING DUTCHMAN

Nineteenth-century spectacular melodrama, both nautical and nicely supernatural, can be illustrated with the rapid action leading to the absolutely sensational final curtain of a popular play which combines the appeal of both the British tar and the doomed outcast. It is *The Flying Dutchman*, by Edward Ball, called Fitzball (1792-1873).

Mowdrey had come to the rescue of the heroine Lestelle at The Devil's Cave, where she had been taken by The Flying Dutchman, Vanderdecken. "A terrific fight," but Mowdrey's stabbing cannot injure the supernatural Vanderdecken, who furiously throws him down.

VANDERDECKEN. Mortal, die! [*Thunder.*] Ah, what have I done! [*He displays bodily agony.*] I have spoken! [*Music.*] The spell which admits my stay on earth is destroyed with my silence. I must be gone to my phantom ship again, to the deep and howling waters; but ye, the victims of my love and fury, yours is a dreadful fate—a hundred years here, in torpid life, to lie entombed till my return. Behold! [*Points to the book—A Chord.*]

[*Enter Varnish...he runs across, and hides behind the magic book.*]

MOWDREY. Is there no hope?

VANDERDECKEN. None! seest thou this magic book; its mystic pages, consumed by the hand of a sailor's son, on ocean born, would set ye free; but never can that be accomplished, for in Vanderdecken's absence 'tis denied that human footstep e'er seek this cavern, or pierce those flinty walls. [*Varnish comes cautiously forward and snatches up the torch, which Vanderdecken has inserted in the ground—he sets fire to the mystic book, and advancing triumphantly to L., with the torch in his hand, exclaims, "'Tis done! 'tis done!"*] Vanderdecken [*after covering his face with his hands*]. Malediction! Malediction! you triumph. But I go to my revenge. Tremble, tremble! the rushing waves which rise to welcome the return of Vanderdecken shall bury ye deep, deep in their unfathomed darkness. Burst, stormy clouds, and overwhelm them; rise, ye many waters of ocean, cover them up for ever. [*Thunder.*] Rockalda! I come.

[*Music.—Vanderdrecken goes behind the rock table, whereon the magic book was placed, and sinks with the altar, amidst thunder and flames of red fire.—Exit Varnish...*]

VARNISH [*with a torch, on a projecting rock...*] Master, dear master, the rock, the rock—follow me; this way—I hear voices.

MOWDREY. 'Tis the voice of Varnish; he has found an outlet to liberty. Come, love, come. [*Exit Mowdrey and Lestelle, hastily...and they all appear on an eminence of the rock, R.U.E.* (right upper entrance, a stage location)]

MOWDREY. Alas, there is no hope!—Hark! hark! the torrent is rushing down on us. See! see! Assistance is at hand—help! help! help!

[*Waves handkerchief*]

[*Music.—Varnish continues waving his torch, and the agitated waters rush furiously into the cave, entirely covering the stage to the orchestra—the sound of the gong, and loud peals of thunder heard—a pilot, Peter von Bummell, with a torch, Captain Peppercoal, & Co., appear in a sloop from the very back—they come under the rock, R.U.E., and rescue Lestelle, Mowdrey, and Varnish aboard—sails are hoisted, with British flag, and as the cutter turns round to return, shout "Huzza!"—incessant noise, as on board a vessel, with brass, gong, and thunder, until the Curtain falls.*]

COMMENTS ON GHOSTS

John Aubrey, *Apparitions*:

> *Anno* 1670, not far from Cirencester, was an apparition [asked] whether a good spirit or bad? returned no answer, but disappeared with a curious perfume and most melodious twang. Mr. W[illiam] Lilly believes it was a fairy.

Percy Bysshe Shelley, "Hymn to Intellectual Beauty":

> While yet a boy I sought for ghosts, and sped
> Through many a listening chamber, cave, and ruin,
> And starlight wood, with fearful steps pursuing
> Hopes of high talk with the departed dead,
> I called on poisonous names with which our youth is fed.

Algernon Charles Swinburne, on mankind in *Atalanta in Calydon*:

> His speech is a burning fire;
>   With his lips he travaileth;
> In his heart is a blind desire,
>   In his eyes foreknowledge of death;
> He weaves, and is clothed with derision;
>   Sows, and he shall not reap;
> His life is a watch or a vision
>   Between a sleep and a sleep.

F. W. H. Myers on Henry James' *The Turn of the Screw*:

> "Do you mean to tell me that you seriously believe in the possibility of the Lesbian vice between the ghost of a governess and a little girl of six?"

Maurice, Count Maeterlinck, *The Bluebird*:
> "There are no dead."

J. P. Donleavy, *The Ginger Man*:
> "Well, ghosts won't bother me on a full stomach, and certainly never if I had a full sex life."

MORE BRITISH GHOSTS

R. H. Benson, "Phantasms Of The Dead," *Dublin Review* 150 (January 1912): 43-63

D. Hollis, "Sad Plight Of The British Ghost," *The Spectator* 138 (11 June 1927): 1015-1016.

W. R. Mitchell, *Haunted Yorkshire* (1969)

MOLLOY'S DARK VIEW

The right response to dubious life and definite death, pessimist prophet Samuel Beckett says, is ataraxy (you could look it up). In *Waiting for Godot*, characters say "Let's go," but they do not move.

In his novel *Molloy*, the character Molloy (also MacMann, son of man) says "I can't go on. I'll go on," and throwing away the crutches of faith and hope, he does. Molloy, the despairing observer of a world composed only of (to cite another Beckett title) *All that Fall*, and where everyone self-destructs or is destroyed, says that "to know nothing is nothing, but to want to know anything likewise, but to be beyond knowing anything, that is when peace enters into the soul of the incurious seeker."

Death brings either knowledge or a peaceful cessation of the struggle to know. Wait and see. Unlike Godot, it *is* coming.

Impatience with this fact is the reason that mankind worries about ghosts and the afterlife in general.

From the classic spoof of haunted-house movies, *The Cat and the Canary* (1927).

NEW AGE PHYSICS

The heroine of Ruth Brandon's novel, *The Uncertainty Principle* (1996), loses her daughter Laura to a hit-and-run driver. Nine years later she thinks there is a rent in the curtain between parallel universes that shows her Laura alive. As Ellen Beardsley puts it in her review of the book in the *The Times Literary Supplement* (20 December 1996):

> While working on a screenplay in Los Angeles, nine years after Laura's death, Helen is certain that she spots her child in a shoe shop. Bewildered, she returns to consult [her husband] Benny, who since Laura's death has relinquished his traditional Darwinist beliefs for the eccentric New Age physics advocating the existence of parallel universes and synchronicity. Alas, she finds Benny most certainly dead by his own hand, and this instigates her endless investigation into everything she has hitherto presumed to be true and certain.

Indeed, a rejection of the traditional explanations, Darwinist or other dogma, does raise for anyone immense questions, and the synchronicity studied by Jung and the parallel universes of science fiction today look attractive, if puzzling, to many persons. Could they explain ghosts?

GHOST STORIES BY WOMEN

See Lynette Carpenter and Wendy K. Komar's annotated bibliography, *Ghost Stories by Women*, and books that illustrate women's important contribution to the genre, including:

Richard Dalby, ed., *Modern Ghost Stories by Eminent Women Writers* (1994)
Vanessa T. Dickerson, *Victorian Ghosts in the Noontide: Women Writers and the Supernatural* (1996)
Edith Wharton, *Ghost Stories by Edith Wharton* (1985)

RECENT GHOST STORY COLLECTIONS

James Bowman, *Ghosts* (1986)
Brandi Anderson, ed., "East Texas Storytellers" issue of *Loblolly* 11 (Winter 1987)
Lloyd Auerback, *ESP, Haunting, and Poltergeists* (1987)
A. J. Wilson and D. Brogan, *Ghostly Tales and Sinister Stories of Old Edinburgh* (1992)
Ann Bradford, *Haunted!* (1992)
John Seymour, *True Irish Ghost Stories* (1992)
Marvin Kaye, *Ghosts: A Haunting Treasury of 40 Chilling Tales* (1993)
Brad Leithauser, *The Norton Book of Ghost Stories* (1994)

John Macklin, *The World's Most Bone-Chilling "True" Ghost Stories* (1994)
Steven Zorn, *Mostly Monsters* (1994)

"IT WAS A DARK AND STORMY NIGHT...."

This quote—it comes, by the way, from the nineteenth-century novelist Lord Lytton, whom you met earlier here—often begins spooky stories told around the campfire by or to children. I recall, as a King's Scout (the Canadian equivalent of an Eagle Scout) and as an assistant scoutmaster long ago, great success with "The Golden Arm." For some tales to tell yourself today, see the likes of:

Bob Hanson and Bill Roemmich, *Stories for the Campfire* (1983)
E. M. Freeman, *Campfire Stories* (1986)
"   ", *Campfire Chillers* (1994)
Rebecca Rizzo, *Campfire Thrillers* (1994)

And here is a version of "The Golden Arm":

> Once there was a man who decided that before he married he would find the most desirable woman in the world. He searched high and low, for years and years. He found pretty women who had no money and rich women who were very plain, highly-educated women and silly ones, women of all shapes and sizes and personalities. At long last he found a woman who was both beautiful and intelligent, young and desirable—and she had one arm of solid gold to replace an arm she had lost, when she was very young, in an accident.
>
> They lived together happily for years, and everyone envied him for her beauty and wit—and they said that anyone whose wife had an arm of solid gold was the luckiest man on earth.
>
> Then one day she died. After the funeral he went home and went to bed but he could not sleep. He thought it over and over and decided he knew what he must do. Stealthily, he crept off to the churchyard, opened the new grave, and stole her golden arm. Then he went home and, putting the golden arm underneath his pillow for safekeeping, he happily went off to sleep.
>
> In the middle of the night he woke to see that the curtains of his bed were being drawn back. There stood the ghost of his wife. Her face was set in an expression of great sorrow.
>
> "Where is your rosy complexion now?" he said.
>
> "All gone, all withered," the specter replied.
>
> "Where is your beautiful smile?"
>
> "All gone, lost in the grave."
>
> "Where is your golden arm?"

"YOU *have it!*"

With the last line, the teller of the tale suddenly seizes the nearest listener.

ANNE RICE

Most people are already familiar with the Queen of Scream, Anne Rice, the most successful of modern writers on the vampire theme. When her work is overlaid with a strong erotic (or homoerotic) theme, as in *Interview with the Vampire*, it has riveted public attention. She has a dedicated following, and she writes for persons alienated from society, who even feel like "monsters inside," so her potential audience is indubitably great. People who seldom buy and read any other books are avid to get and pore over hers. She fascinates them. She is showered with praise. She is one of the best known living American writers.

A review of the film version of *Interview with the Vampire* by Amy Taubin that appears in *Sight & Sound* (January 1995): 8, is more perceptive than most. Ms. Taubin notes that the film drowns the sex in blood, unlike better work by others, such as *The Addiction* and *Nadja*. Vampire stories have always been a way of talking about sexual violence and compulsive sexuality, even perversity (or, if you prefer, alternate lifestyle). Ms. Rice, who first wrote pornography (under a pseudonym) now can write it (as it were) under a metaphor. There is now a long shelf of her books and fan(atic) reference guides to them, too. She probably has done more for the vampire myth than any other twentieth-century writer.

A JEWISH VAMPIRE

This is not the joke Jewish Vampire who laughs when confronted with a crucifix; this is the Brooklyn Jew who is a struggling writer and practicing vampire in the "graphic novel" (sort of an adult comic book) by J. M. DeMatteis, *Greenberg the Vampire* (1986).

The protagonist, a caricature of a Jew, who perhaps surprisingly did not get the Human Rights Commission on the creator's tail for racist slurs, is one Oscar Greenberg. He finally breaks free of the vampire curse and improves his screenwriting career. For more vampires in fiction, see *The Complete Book of Vampires* in this series. The Jews have few vampire tales and not a lot of ghost stories. In the realm of the supernatural, they specialize in the *dybbuk* and the *golem*.

SIR WALTER SCOTT ON ELVES AND GHOSTS

The Little People, or Fairies, or Good Neighbors as they are called by those who are afraid to offend them, appear elsewhere in this series, but there is a tale told by Scott, the famous novelist, in his *Letters on Demonology and Witchcraft* (1830). It bears repeating if only because it is so strikingly unusual. He is recording folklore told to him as true incidents from "before the middle part of the last century" (that is, before 1750) in North Berwick, Scotland.

The tomb of John Donne in St. Paul's Cathedral, where he was dean, shows him in the kind of shroud in which corpses were customarily buried. Old ghosts might appear in such costume.

An industrious man, a weaver in the little town, was married to a beautiful woman, who, after bearing two or three children, was so unfortunate as to die during the birth of a fourth child. The infant was saved, but the mother had expired in convulsions; and as she was much disfigured after death, it became an opinion among her gossips that, from some neglect of those who ought to have watched the sick woman, she must have been carried off by the elves, and this ghastly corpse substituted in the place of the body. The widower paid little attention to these rumours, and, after bitterly lamenting his wife for a year of mourning, began to think on the prudence of forming a new marriage, which, to a poor artisan with so young a family, and without the assistance of a housewife, was almost a matter of necessity. He readily found a neighbour with whose good looks he was satisfied, whilst her character for temper seemed to warrant her good usage of his children. He proposed himself and was accepted, and carried the names of the parties to the clergyman (called, I believe, Mr. Matthew Reid) for the due proclamation of banns. As the man had really loved his late partner, it is likely that this proposed decisive alteration of his condition brought back many reflections concerning the period of their union, and with these recalled the extraordinary rumours which were afloat at the time of her decease, so that the whole forced upon him the following lively dream:—As he lay in his bed, awake as he thought, he beheld, at the ghostly hour of midnight, the figure of a female dressed in white, who entered his hut, stood by the side of his bed, and appeared to him the very likeness of his late wife. He conjured her to speak, and with astonishment heard her say, like the minister of Aberfoyle, that she was not dead, but the unwilling captive of the Good Neighbours. Like Mr. Kirke, too, she told him that if all the love which he once had for her was not entirely gone, an opportunity still remained of recovering her, or *winning her back*, as it was usually termed, from the comfortless realms of Elfland. She charged him on a certain day of the ensuing week that he should convene the most respectable housekeepers in the town, with the clergyman at their head, and should disinter the coffin in which she was supposed to have been buried. 'The clergyman is to recite certain prayers, upon which,' said the apparition, 'I will start from the coffin and fly with great speed round the church, and you must have the fleetest runner of the parish (naming a man famed for swiftness) to pursue me, and such a one, the smith, renowned for his strength, to hold me fast after I am overtaken; and in that case I shall, by the prayers of the church, and the efforts of my loving husband and neighbours, again recover my station in human society.' In the morning the poor widower was distressed with the recollection of his dream, but, ashamed and puzzled, took no measures in consequence. A second night, as is not very surprising, the visitation was again repeated. On the third night she appeared with a sorrowful and displeased countenance, upbraided him with want of love and affection, and conjured him, for the last time, to attend to her instructions, which, if he now neglected, she would never have power to visit earth or communicate with him again. In order to convince him there was no delusion, he 'saw in his dream' that she took up the nursling at whose birth she had died, and gave it suck; she spilled also a drop or two of her milk on the poor man's bed-clothes, as if to assure him of the reality of the vision.

The next morning the terrified widower carried a statement of his perplexity to Mr. Matthew Reid, the clergyman. This reverend person, besides being an excellent divine in other respects, was at the same time a man of sagacity, who understood the human passions. He did not attempt to combat the reality of the vision which had thrown his parishioner into this tribulation, but he contended it could be only an illusion of the devil. He explained to the widower that no created being could have the right or power to imprison or detain the soul of a Christian—conjured him not to believe that his wife was otherwise disposed of than according to God's pleasure—assured him that Protestant doctrine utterly denies the existence of any middle state in the world to come— and explained to him that he, as a clergyman of the Church of Scotland, neither could nor dared authorize opening graves or using the intervention of prayer to sanction rites of a suspicious character. The poor man, confounded and perplexed by various feelings, asked his pastor what he should do. 'I will give you my best advice,' said the clergyman. 'Get your new bride's consent to be married tomorrow, or today, if you can; I will take it on me to dispense with the rest of the banns, or proclaim them three times in one day. You will have a new wife, and, if you think of the former, it will be only as of one from whom death has separated you, and for whom you may have thoughts of affection and sorrow, but as a saint in Heaven, and not as a prisoner in Elfland.' The advice was taken, and the perplexed widower had no more visitations from his former spouse.

SOME TRULY ECCENTRIC BOOKS ON GHOSTS

Fred Gettings, *Ghosts in Photographs* (1978)
Frederick George Lee, *Glimpses in the Twilight* (1885)
Konstantine Raudive, *Breakthrough* (1971)
Ed Warren and Lorainne Warren, as told to Robert David Chase, *Grave-yard* [in Easton, CT]: *True Hauntings from a New England Cemetery* (1992)
Thomas Wright, *Narratives of Sorcery and Magic* (1851)
Rosemary Gabbert Musil, *The Ghost of Mr. Penny* (1939)
"Paul Pray" (Richard Hill Wilkinson), *The Ghost in the Belfry* (1941)
Arnold Ridley, *The Ghost Train* (1931)
Robert St. Clair, *The Ghost House* (1946)
Booth Tarkington, *The Ghost Story* (1926)

THE GRATEFUL DEAD

Folklore around the world tells us not only to fear the dead's wrath but also that we can benefit hugely if and when we can oblige one of them. The grateful dead are much discussed in Frazer, in Lévi-Strauss, and other anthropologists' works and appear even more in folktales. A corpse in the grave can be an ace in the hole if you can get the ghost on your side.

LADY HOWARD'S COACH

The folklore of England is replete with ghostly coaches rattling through the night. British friends of mine complain of a more modern nuisance, a ghostly motorcyclist in Wiltshire. However, an old story ought to be here. So, permit me to introduce Lady Howard and her entourage. They are among the leading specters of ghost-ridden Devon.

Tavistock is in Devon. Its abbey has long since been destroyed (though two huge thighbones of Ordulph, the founder of the abbey, are shown to visitors to the town even today) and the wool industry and tin mining which once made the town famous are only memories. But Lady Howard's ghost remains. Near Tavistock is Fitzford House, which this seventeenth-century woman is said to haunt. At midnight she leaves there in a ghastly coach made of human bones and decorated with human skulls at the corners, drawn (of course) by the standard headless horses of these ghost tales. She also has a dog—in some versions of the story a pack of them—which runs alongside. It is worse than the ordinary big black dog (sometimes called a *yeth hound*, that is a dog on the heath) of Devon ghost tales: this one has only one eye, right in the middle of its forehead. The dog has the task of going with Lady Howard's ghost to Oakhampton Castle. There it has to pluck just one blade of grass, which is then carried back to Fitzford House.

The legend is that this must go on until all the grass at Oakhampton Castle is gone, but of course that will never happen. The grass grows fast and the dog's efforts are limited. Curses involving unending tasks such as this are not unusual in folklore. Whether this particular curse is due to the fact that Lady Howard murdered three of her four husbands, as some say, I cannot judge.

FROM THE AMERICAN FOLK

American folklore features many ballads involving ghosts and hauntings (*Sweet William's Ghost* is a good one), from both native and foreign (mostly British) sources. From the sea comes *The Phantom Ship* and much more. There are vampire tales and poltergeist tales and ghost tales. The pioneers, backwoodsmen, riverboatmen, and miners seeking gold all met with the supernatural on occasion; and imported tales were refashioned by the Gullah speakers, Spanish speakers, and many others into real American ghost

stories. The ghost story is a rich and respectable department of our literature. The ghosts of the movies need a book of their own. The oddest ghost
in American cinema, for my money, is a dog. It's in a dog of a movie called
Face of Marble.

THE GRAVEYARD SCHOOL

In the eighteenth century such morbid ruminations as *Night-Thoughts on
Life, Death and Immortality* (by Edward Young, 1683-1765, published 1742-
1746) created what was somewhat derisively called The Graveyard School
of English poetry. The Rev. Robert Blair (1699-1746), a Scottish clergyman, contributed importantly to this fashion. Here is a snippet from *The
Grave* (1743):

> Oft in the lone church-yard at night I've seen
> By glimpse of moon-shine, chequering thro' the trees,
> The schoolboy with his satchel in his hand,
> Whistling aloud to bear his courage up,
> And lightly tripping o'er the long flat stones
> (With nettles skirted, and with moss o'ergrown),
> That tell in homely phrase who lie below;
> Sudden! he starts, and hears, or thinks he hears
> The sound of something purring at his heels:
> Full fast he flies, and dares not look behind him,
> Till out of breath he overtakes his fellows;
> Who gather round, and wonder at the tale
> Of horrid *Apparition*, tall and ghastly,
> That walks at dead of night, or takes his stand
> O'er some new-opened *Grave*; and, strange to tell!
> Evanishes at crowing of the cock.

NIGHTMARE ABBEY

This is the title of an extremely funny novel, which satirizes Samuel Taylor Coleridge and other romantics. It is by Thomas Love Peacock (1785-
1866), memoir writer about his friend Shelley, father-in-law of George
Meredith. Here is one of Peacock's typical dialogues:

> *The Rev. Mr Larynx.* We have such high authority for ghosts, that
> it is rank skepticism to disbelieve them. Job saw a ghost, which
> came for the express purpose of asking a question, and did not
> wait for an answer.
> *The Hon. Mr Listless.* Because Job was too frightened to give one.
> *The Rev. Mr Larynx.* Spectres appeared to the Egyptians during
> the darkness with which Moses covered Egypt. The witch of

THE CASTLE SPECTRE.

A DRAMATIC ROMANCE, IN FIVE ACTS.—BY G. LEWIS.

Ang.—"HEAVENS! THE VERY WORDS WHICH ALICE——"—*Act iv, scene 2.*

Persons Represented

OSMOND	MOTLEY	MULEY	HAROLD
REGINALD	KENRIC	ALARIC	ANGELA
PERCY	SAIB	ALLAN	ALICE
FATHER PHILIP	HASSAN	EDRIC	EVELINA

ACT I.—SCENE I.—*A Grove.*
Enter FATHER PHILIP *and* MOTLEY, *through a gate.*

F. Phil. Never tell me. I repeat it, you are a fellow of a very scandalous course of life. But what principally offends me, is, that you pervert the minds of the maids, and keep kissing and smuggling all the pretty girls you meet. Oh, fie, fie!

Mot. I kiss and smuggle them? St. Francis forbid! Lord love you, Father, 'tis they who kiss and smuggle me. I protest I do what I can to preserve my modesty; and I wish that Archbishop Dunstan had heard the lecture upon chastity which I read last night to the dairy-maid in the dark; he'd have been quite edified. But yet what does talking signify? The eloquence of my lips is counteracted by the lustre of my eyes; and really, the little devils are so tender, and so troublesome, that I'm half angry with nature for having made me so very bewitching.

F. Phil. Nonsense, nonsense!

Mot. Put yourself in my place. Suppose that a sweet, smiling rogue, just sixteen, with rosy cheeks, sparkling eyes, pouting lips, &c.—

F. Phil. Oh, fie, fie, fie! To hear such licentious discourse brings the tears into my eyes!

Mot. I believe you, Father; for I see the water is running over at your mouth; which puts me in mind, my good Father, that there are some little points which might be altered in you still better than in myself; such as intemperance, gluttony—

F. Phil. Gluttony! Oh, abominable falsehood!

Mot. Plain matter of fact. Why, will any man pretend to say that you came honestly by that enormous belly, that tremendous tomb of fish, flesh, and fowl? And for incontinence, you must allow yourself that you are unequalled.

F. Phil. I!—I!

Mot. You, you. May I ask what was your business in the beech-grove, the other evening when I caught

Endor raised the ghost of Samuel. Moses and Elias appeared on Mount Tabor. An evil spirit was sent into the army of Sennacherib, and exterminated it in a single night.

Mr Toobad. Saying, The devil is come among you, having great wrath.

Mr Flosky. Saint Macarius interrogated a skull, which was found in the desert, and bade it relate, in presence of several witnesses, what was going forward in hell. Saint Martin of Tours, being jealous of a pretended martyr, who was the rival saint of his neighbourhood, called up his ghost, and made him confess that he was damned. Saint Germain, being on his travels, turned out of an inn a large party of ghosts, who had every night taken possession of the *table d'hôte*, and consumed a copious supper.

Mr Hilary. Jolly ghosts, and no doubt all friars. A similar party took possession of the cellar of M. Swebach, the painter, in Paris, drank his wine, and threw the empty bottles at his head.

The Rev. Mr Larynx. An atrocious act.

Mr Flosky. Pausanius relates that the neighing of horses and the tumult of combatants are heard every night on the field of Marathon: that those who went purposely to hear these sounds suffered severely for their curiosity; but those who heard them by accident passed with impunity.

The Rev. Mr Larynx. I once saw a ghost myself, in my study, which is the last place where anyone but a ghost would look for me. I had not been into it for three months, and was going to consult [a book by] Tillotson, when, on opening the door, I saw a venerable figure in a flannel dressing-gown, sitting in my armchair, and reading my Jeremy Taylor. It vanished in a moment, and so did I; and what it was or what it wanted I have never been able to ascertain... .

Mr Flosky. I can safely say I have seen too many ghosts myself to believe in their external existence. I have seen all kinds of ghost: black spirits and white, red spirits and grey. Some in the shapes of venerable old men, who have met me in my rambles at noon; some of beautiful young women, who have peeped through my curtains at midnight.

The Hon. Mr Listless. And have proved, I doubt not, 'palpable to feeling as to sight' [a quotation from Shakespeare].

Mr Flosky. By no means, sir. You reflect upon my purity. Myself and my friends, particularly my friend Mr. Sackbut, are famous for our purity. I see a ghost at this moment... .

THE MOST UNUSUAL GHOST IN LITERATURE

I challenged myself to come up with the most unusual ghost in literature and I believe that after painful researches I have found him. He occurs in Gilbert & Sullivan's operetta *Ruddigore*. This is a work I liked even before I saw it, just from the title and story that I was told went with it. It seems that some woman made the mistake of congratulating Gilbert on "your *Bloodigore*." Gilbert objected that there was a difference between *ruddy* and *bloody*, and suggested it could be illustrated by the fact that while he admired her "ruddy complexion" he did not like her "bloody cheek." "Bloody cheek" is a British term for "damned impudence," you know.

The plot of *Ruddigore* is equally clever. This burlesque of old melodrama starts with a family curse: each baronet in the line is condemned to commit one crime a day or die. Every "bad baronet" in the past has tried to be evil but, sickening at last of crime, has stopped being evil, and perished. All that is left of them around the place are the giant ancestral portraits in the great hall.

The newest baronet is Sir Ruthven. His name, once actually banned in Britain, is suitable for an evil person, but Sir Ruthven doesn't want to be some sort of perverse Boy Scout doing an evil deed every day. He wants to be good, and to marry Rose Maybud. His ancestors' ghosts step down from their frames to threaten Sir Ruthven, for *Ruddigore* features a striking chorus of ghosts, all in period costumes from the paintings. Then Sir Ruthven finds a way out of his dilemma. To refuse to do his daily demonic duty will kill him. But if he does this deliberately that is tantamount to suicide. Suicide is a crime. That solves everything! Happy ending! Only someone with Gilbert's amusement at British law could have conceived of that. Remember, Gilbert & Sullivan's great success started with *Trial by Jury*.

Now to the most unusual of those ghostly ancestors, Sir Roderic. In life he was in love with Hannah—and comes back to her because he ought not to have perished at all. A ghost that returns to life! How's that for unusual?

THE PRIORY OF ST. CLAIR

A very minor writer in the popular Gothic mode was the Miss Wilkinson who wrote *The Priory of St. Clair* (1811). In this wordy but frightening tale young Julietta, in the tradition of the badly-treated innocent girl, is first of all shut up in a convent against her will, then drugged, and shipped off disguised as a corpse to the castle of the satanic Count Valvé. She regains consciousness just long enough to realize why: she is to be made a human sacrifice on the altar of his devilish rites. She gets her revenge by reappearing every night to haunt the hell out of the count. Ghosts walk in a great many novels and melodramas of the nineteenth century. Many are forgotten today, largely neglected even by literary critics and historians, but were immensely popular in their day.

THE WATCHER

In England of old you didn't want to be the first to be buried in a churchyard—The Devil might take you for his own. So sometimes a dog was interred when a new burial ground was needed so that the ghost of the first person interred would not have to be "The Watcher," for the first to be buried had to take on this duty.

STAYING PUT

There are, according to superstition, various ways of keeping a ghost from walking. You could nail the body to the coffin or stake it into the ground. You could put sharp spindles (nine was thought to be a good number) into the turf above the coffin. You could bury an animal *under* the corpse.

This last was not uncommon in olden times in Britain. Corpses thought to be somehow suspicious—suicides, gypsies, tramps, even strangers who happened to die passing through a village—were usually interred in the northern part of the graveyard and an animal buried with them. Or some other method might be used to make sure the ghost would not bother the living of the parish. Such corpses were thought to be especially dangerous when there was no one to pay for a headstone to keep the body down. You realize, of course, that headstones had a practical as well as a sentimental purpose. And don't forget to keep the lid on the urn if you retain the ashes of those cremated, not buried.

THOSE AREN'T MICE IN YOUR KITCHEN, THEY'RE GHOSTS!

In the *Journal of American Folklore* 71 (1958, 118-119), Edward Stankiewicz writes of the "perils of the soul" superstition among the Slavs. He quotes from one Nikiforovskij a belief of the Byelorussians:

> If you leave an unfinished loaf of bread in the house overnight, then spirits of the ancestors, assuming the shape of mice, will attack it; should, however, a cat catch one of the mice, disasters will fall upon the house because of the loss of an ancestor.

THE GHOSTLY HIGHWAYMAN

The best example of the common superstition that a road may be haunted by a modern driver or an old-fashioned highwayman involves Dick Turpin, a famous outlaw. I grew up with a Staffordshire figurine of him on a mantelshelf at home. (Why he was so honored I do not know, and on a similar shelf I now keep two Staffordshire dogs instead. They are supposed to be magical protectors, you know).

Dick Turpin (1706-1739) led a rather short life, as those dates indicate, but it was crowded with incident. He teamed up with the notorious Tom King and the two of them made travelers stand and deliver on the Cambridge road. In the long run Turpin was caught and convicted not as a highwayman but as a horsethief. He was publicly hanged at York. He made a brave show on the gallows. He was a kind of folk hero.

To that fame, pretty likely, we owe the folk belief that his ghost, mounted on Black Bess and sporting pistols, haunts Wroughton-on-the-Green or thereabouts (the B488) and also the area of Loughton and Epping Forest and even what Americans would call a throughway, the A11 between Norwich and London. Actually his old stomping ground also included Hounslow Heath, about where Heathrow, the international airport, now stands, so look out for him in that vicinity when you are flying in or out of London. He's a handsome fellow on a black horse; he's dressed in eighteenth-century garb as he was in that Staffordshire figurine. I'd recognize his ghost anywhere.

If you would like to read an exciting book about Dick Turpin, unearth a copy of *Rookwood* (1834). It is particularly amazing when you consider that the author, William Harrison Ainsworth (1805-1882), penned it "in less than twenty-four hours."

USEFUL BOOKS ABOUT GHOST STORIES

In addition to the introductions to ghost-story anthologies from the peerage (Lord Halifax, Lady Astor) to the priesthood (Rev. Montague Summers), there are whole books on the genre. Of those, I recommend:

Julia Briggs, *Night Visitors: The Rise and Fall of the English Ghost Story* (1977)
Elizabeth MacAndrew, *The Gothic Tradition in Fiction* (1979)
Eino Railo, *The Haunted Castle* (1927)
Jack Sullivan, *Elegant Nightmare: The English Ghost Story from LeFanu to Blackwood* (1978)

A VAMPIRIC GHOST

An earlier volume in this occult series (*The Complete Book of Vampires*), as you now know, dealt with the undead. A ghost is, by definition, not undead but dead, so these two ghastly figures can be separated for discussion. However, Prosper Merimée offers an interesting switch: a story in which a ghost acts like a vampire.

Prosper Merimée (1803-1870) is best known for *Carmen*, which first appeared in his *Nouvelles* (1843), but when he was just beginning in fiction he produced a set of tales that were fake translations of Illyrian folklore, so convincing that they even took in the great Pushkin.

In one story in *La Guzla* (*c.* 1825) there is a vampire. In another, *La belle Sophie*, there is this vicious ghost. Sophie dumps her fiancé in order to marry a much richer man. The fiancé, in true romantic style, then commits suicide. Later he comes back as a ghost—and bites her sadistically in the neck.

ME AND MY SHADOW

The part that becomes a ghost, the human spirit as separable form the human body, has been portrayed in various cultures in a variety of ways. One interesting example is found in the cultures of the far north of Europe, where the Norse *fylgior* (followers), which can be either *dyrefulgior* (animal followers) or *kvinnefylgior* (female followers), are companions to human beings throughout life, like their shadows. There are folklore beliefs in various European cultures about The Devil buying a person's shadow (that is, the soul) or vampires and such casting no shadows (having no souls).

GHOST MESSAGES

In the mid-fifties, American poet James Merrill and his lover, David Jackson, claimed they contacted through a Ouija board the ghost of a Greek Jew born in AD 8. He was a voluble fellow named Ephraim who somehow learned to express himself in arty American. In *The Book of Ephraim* this person, who says he was once a favorite of the Emperor Tiberius, has a lot to say (until he is pushed out of the way by angels, fallen and otherwise, who want to have their say), much of it very Politically Correct, about the dangers of nuclear holocaust and overpopulation on earth. Ephraim himself complains of "unrelenting fluency."

Some leading poets reveal that they wrote in trance. Merrill claimed to have taken dictation from a ghost.

SONG OF THE GHOST DANCERS OF THE SIOUX

The whole world is coming,
A nation is coming,
The Eagle has brought this message to the tribe.
The father says so,
The father says so.
Over the whole earth they are coming

The Buffalo, they are coming.
The Crow has brought this message to the tribe.
The father says so,
The father says so.

ONE MOTIVE FOR A GHOST'S RETURN

Richard Brinsley Sheridan, author of *The School for Scandal*, thought he as well as his comedy might be immortal. Just a little while before he died he said to Lady Bessborough (a former mistress) that he would come to haunt her after his demise. Why, she wanted to know, would he persecute her in death as he had persecuted her in life?

"Because I am resolved," Sheridan explained, "you should remember me."

You will recall the admonition of the ghost of Hamlet's father: "Remember me!"

THEATRICAL GHOSTS

There are no ghosts in Henrik Ibsen's *Ghosts*, but you will find some in Thomas Otway's *Venice Preserv'd*, David Belasco's *The Return of Peter Grimm*, W. Somerset Maugham's *Sheppey*, James Elroy Flecker's *Hassan*, Walter Ferris' *Death Takes a Holiday*, Paul Green's *Supper for the Dead*, Elmer Rice's *American Landscape*, Irwin Shaw's *Bury the Dead*, Thornton Wilder's *Our Town*....

There are many ghost dramas which were popular in their time. In the first half of this century, mystery, comedy, or melodrama plays, usually three acts but occasionally shorter (especially if designed for children's theater) were turned out rather amateurishly. They are usually pretty bad, not worth reviving, and maybe even Samuel French doesn't offer them anymore, but here are few titles. Some oldsters may recall one from a community theater or summer camp or church basement production of long ago.

Paul Dickey, *The Ghost Breaker* (c. 1914, novelized by Charles William Goddard, 1915)
"Nan Fleming" (Wilbur Braun), *The Ghost Plane* (c. 1948)
LeRoma Eschbach Greth, *The Ghost from Outer Space* (1958)
Alma Murphy Halif, *A Ghost on the Loose* (1948)
Frederick Jackson, *The Ghost Flies South* (1939)
Bill Johnson, *Ghost Road* (1950)
Lee Luilian, *The Ghost of Lone Cabin* (1940)
Homer Miles and John Ravold, *Double Trouble; or, The Ghost Fighter* (c. 1935)

There are still such plays and playlets being written, but I decline to embarass recent authors. I know of not one decent play for juveniles writ-

The Flying Dutchman.

ten in the last half of the twentieth century with a really frightening or even very entertaining ghost in it. Even the vampire and werewolf skits and dramas are better.

GHOSTS OF THE SEA

For the serious scholar, there are books such as:

Bassett, F. S. *Legends and Superstitions of the Sea and of Sailors in All Lands and at All Times* (1885)
Bassett, W. *Wanderships....* (1917)
Buss, Reinhard J. *The Klabautermann* [Man on Board] *of the Northern Seas* (1975)
Gerndt, Helge. *Fliegender Höllander* [Flying Dutchman] *und Klabauternamm* (1971)
Sébillot, P. *Croyances et superstitions de la mer* (Beliefs and Superstitions of the Sea, 1886)
Smidt, Heinrich. *Seemans-Sagen und Schiffer-Märchen* (Sailors' Stories and Ship Tales, 1835-1849)

For the ordinary reader, there are entertaining accounts such as the following from a British admiral's anonymously and privately published *The Life of a Sea Officer* (1830). Throughout this book I have sought to offer you not the easily-obtained material (so you may miss some of your favorites) but what you are unlikely to have found yourself. Out of an obscure but fascinating source I bring you this encounter in the Indian Ocean in 1787:

> We had now been at sea for some time, and were some hundreds of miles from the nearest land, still scudding before the gale, the ship's company's hammocks had been piped down, and I was hanging up mine abreast the main hatchway; on hearing a noise and bustle upon deck, I ran up without my hat, and found that a strange sail was seen broad upon our starboard bow, pretty close to us, carrying a heavy press of sail, and steering the same course as ourselves. The eagerness of all on board to see a living object was such, that all hands rushed upon deck and lined the starboard side and gangway as fast as possible, to get a good place to view her from; our ship's course was altered a little on purpose to speak the strange sail, and we were fast overhauling her, every one intent upon making her out, but when within two cables length of her, she broached to, and a sea struck her broad upon her beam; her sheets flew, her sails fluttered, and instantly split into ribbons; yells of distress and despair were heard by all the crew of the Vestal frigate; notwithstanding the force of the wind, and our distance of near a cable's

length from the distressed ship, her men were distinctly seen endeavoring to cut away the shrouds, that the masts might go by the board, but the nest sea made a clean breach over her, and we saw her hull no more, as we flew like lightning by the eddy she caused in the water when sinking, which, as we passed, her top mast heads shewed above water, but the white spray of the sea which hung in the hollow, between the waves, was so dense, that nothing but the tops of the waves were visible as we passed, there was therefore no possibility to render the least assistance, and we resumed our course. During these few moments, not a word was spoken, all was hushed, except the hissing noise from the boiling wake of our ship as she flew along; indeed, a feeling of horror seemed to have seized on all our ship's company from a consciousness of our inability to render the smallest assistance, but, after a few moments pause, a kind of half stifled sound from the forecastle confusedly murmured, "the Flying Dutchman!" "the Flying Dutchman!" dying away as it came to the people aft: on this I felt my hair erect from my head, and although I put my hand to press it down, so great was my sensation of surprise, that it scarcely yielded to the pressure.

It was some time before my usual spirits returned, nor was the ship's company less affected at this appalling sight, for instead of dancing as was their general custom every evening, until the watch was set, they kept huddling together in sixes and sevens, and walking backwards and forwards upon deck, wrapt in thoughtfulness, and then by degrees retiring, by twos and threes to their hammocks. The impression that was made upon the officers and ship's company after seeing the Flying Dutchman may more easily be conceived than described, therefore I shall merely state, what I used to hear after this upon the subject amongst the old seamen in their common chat to amuse each other, while upon deck in their night watch, and relating past events: viz., When the Dutch were advanced in trade with the East Indies, it was known that certain merchandise was very scarce in those parts, and a rich Dutch merchant freighted a ship at considerable expense with those commodities that were wanting in the East, and thought no other merchant would attempt the same thing, it not being generally known; but in this he was mistaken, for another merchant, equally alive, and actuated by the same spirit of trade, had in another port of Holland freighted a ship likewise for the East Indies with similar merchandise, having heard a report of this scarcity.

These two ships sailed form Holland, and arriving within a day or two of each other at the Cape of Good Hope, were equally surprised to find themselves bound for the same market with similar goods. The skippers, therefore, for the benefit of their owners, agreed to sail together, and in case of accident upon the passage, agreed mutually to assist each other, and upon their arrival in the East Indies not to undersell one another in the market. They left the Cape of Good Hope, but before they got to the eastward of the island of Madagascar, a strong gale of wind came on from the west, and after running their course together for some time, on a dark night, a little after the first watch had been set, one of the ships sprung a leak, which from the rolling of the ship increased so much, that all the exertions of the crew at the pumps could not keep her free. The distressed ship made signals of distress to her companion, by firing minute guns, and though their distance from each other was not more than one mile and a half, so that the flashes of the powder and report of the guns must have been heard, yet the other ship paid no attention to them, but holding counsel amongst themselves the skipper and crew agreed to leave their consort to her fate, calculating that should they get first to the market they would get a higher price for their merchandise. They did leave her to her fate, and made a good voyage, but the other ship was never heard of afterwards.

To commemorate this act of injustice, this act of inhumanity, which had its rise solely from the spirit of trade, it seems to have pleased Providence that the apparition of this ship in distress is still to hover and haunt those seas as a memorable beacon to remind others who navigate them of such cold-blooded cruelty. This phenomenon assumes various guises; I have been told sometimes as here related, at others as a ship always in company with you for days together, or as a large ship bearing right down upon you, so that you think that you will be run down, and then in an instant disappearing, leaving, I should suppose, similar lasting impressions upon the minds of all who have seen it, as it has upon mine. I have frequently met persons in company that had seen this apparition, who related to me the appearance this spectre ship put on to them, but fearing ridicule withheld themselves form touching upon it....

On our return to the Cape of Good Hope, we often related the circumstance to the people at whose house we were lodged. I was then at sick quarters, and we were invariably answered by them, "you have seen the Flying Dutchman," and that there were few ships navigating those seas, who had not seen this phantom ship, some under one guise, and some under another.

FOLKLORE

Browning School District 9 (Montana), *Sta-Ai-Tsi-Nix-Sin* [Blackfoot Ghost Stories] (1979)

Jan H. Brunvand, *The Vanishing Hitchhiker* (1981)

Tekla Domotor, *Hungarian Folk Beliefs* (1983)

Richard M. Dorson, *Folk Legends of Japan* (1962)

Dietrich Grau, *Das Mittagsgespenst* (The Ghost at Noon, 1966)

Moritz Adolph Jagendorf, *Ghostly Folktales* (1968)

W. Henry Jones and Lewis L. Kropf, *The Folk-Tales of the Magyars* (1889)

Eiko Kondö, *Japanischer Gespenster* (Japanese Ghosts, 1980)

Alan Lomax, *The Folksongs of North America in the English Language* (1960)

Herbert Mayo, *On the Truths Contained in Popular Superstitions* (1851)

G. Willoughby-Meade, *Chinese Ghouls and Goblins* (1918)

Patrick B. Mullen and Linna Funk Place, *Collecting Folklore and Folk Life in Ohio* (1978)

E. Hugo Meyer, *Mythologie der Germanen* (German Mythology, 1903)

Howard W. Odum, *Blue Moon, Black Ulysses Afar Off* (1931)

Annibale Piccoli, *Esistono i fantasmi?* (Do Phantoms Exist?, 1968)

Rennell Rodd, *The Customs and Lore of Modern Greece* (1892)

Harry A. Senn, *Werewolf and Vampire in Romania* (1982)

Stith Thompson, *The Folktale* (1946)

"   ", *Motif-Index of Folk Literature* (6 vols., 1932-1936)

Elwood B. Trigg, *Gypsy Demons and Divinities* (1973)

Elias Weslowski, *Die Vampirsage in rümanischen Volksglauben* (Romanian Vampires, 1911)

F. Wollman, *Vampyrické povésti v ceskoslovansy* (Czech Vampires, *c.* 1925)

GHOST FICTION COLLECTIONS

E. F. Bleiler industriously collected in various anthologies novels of the *golem*, the ghost stories of E. T. A. Hoffmann, Lord Dunsany, Montague Rhodes James, Algernon Blackwood, and Ambrose Bierce, *Three Gothic Novels* (Horace Walpole's chilling *The Castle of Otranto*, William Beckford's exotic *Vathek*, and John Polidori's *The Vampyre*, with fragments of Lord Byron's efforts on the same topic) and, most apt to mention here, *Five Victorian Ghost Novels*: Mrs. J. H. Riddell's *The Uninhabited House*, J. W. Meinhold's *The Amber Witch*, Aemilia B. Edwards' *Monsieur Maurice*, Vernon Lee's *A Phantom Lover*, and Charles Willing Beale's *The Ghost of Guir House*. Minor stuff indeed, but where else would you find it today?

Some authors have produced a series of anthologies, of which one already quoted in the present book, Jessie Adelaide Middelton's *Another Grey Ghost Book* (1914), is a good example. There are, naturally, local and national collections: an example of the latter is Daniel O'Keefe's *The Book of Famous Irish Ghost Stories* (1956), heavy on LeFanu. See *Books in Print*; use the internet.

Not sufficiently noticed and well worth looking for are the ghost stories in *Widdershins*. Their author was Oliver Onions, and I read all his work to write the entry about him in the *Dictionary of Literary Biography*. *Widdershins* was my favorite of all his books.

ON THE RECORD

In the seventies the Spoken Arts collections, especially from Caedmon, offered long-playing records which, to a generation that still could listen to the radio and use their imaginations, told ghost stories. Among recordings from Caedmon were *Tales of Witches, Ghosts, and Goblins* (1972), *Spirits and Spooks for Hallowe'en* (1973), and *A Graveyard of Ghost Tales* (1974).

SCANDINAVIAN GHOSTS

Ola J. Holten and myself have been working for some years in collaboration on a big book of Scandianvian folklore. It naturally will include a section of the soul system and detailed, scholarly examination of folkloric beliefs in spirit doubles, spirit followers, necromancy in the Norse tradition (for fortune-telling or other purposes), modern specters, and other superstitions. These *fulgya* (followers), *vardyvle* (a kind of *Dopplegänger*), sendings (dead persons summoned up by magic and set upon one's enemies), *draugs* (walking spirits of drowned fishermen), etc., have never been seriously discussed in English before.

Here is just one of many tales we translate from Icelandic traditions collected in 1862:

> At Eyrarbakki in Åmissysla there is a *draugur* which is called *Sels-Mori*. [The *mori* is a male ghost who traditionally wears a brownish-red sweater and a broad-brimmed black hat or what is called a "sheep-house cap" pushed back on his head. He carries a spiked staff.] The story goes that once upon a time there was a man named Einar who lived at Hraunshverfi in the eighteenth century. He chased away from his house a young man who came wandering along, with many others, at that time from Skaptafellssysla, after the eruption of the geyser Skaptareldurrin. That happened in winter, and the young man, hungry and scantily clothed, was forced to spend the night outdoors not far from Borg and was found dead in the dale called Skersflød. In spite of the fact that the young man's corpse was buried, it became ever clearer as time went on that his ghost followed Einar and his descendants.

In fact, whether called up from the dead by magicians to settle scores with enemies, or returning of their own accord to complete some task or exact vengeance, revenants are a lively part of Scandinavian folklore, both pagan and Christian. There is an obscure, scant, but interesting literature about them. It has never been completely collected nor translated into English. There is a very little bit about this in German, for it was from black books originating in Germany that Swedish and other necromancers learned their damned crafts in the middle ages. The Slavic ghosts also deserve more attention in English but in that part of the world vampires appear to get it all.

LITERARY CRITICISM AND THE GHOST

The Gothic romance, with the sensational appeal of the supernatural, was among the first really popular departments of British fiction. It had immense impact on the eighteenth-century novel, the Romantic movement, melodrama in the nineteenth century, the detective story, and more. Now it is still the rage (Anne Rice, Stephen King, Clive Barker) and the darling of popular culture, and feminist and other critics in vogue. Neil Barron (*Horror Literature*, 1990) offers the best overall guide; also see James B. Twitchell's *Dreadful Pleasures*, (1987). Stephen Jones and Jim Newman (*Horror*, 1990) offer a list of the 100 best books in the genre from Horace Walpole and "Monk" Lewis to today. The best writer in the genre is either Wilkie Collins (though he is more correctly seen as one of the creators of the detective story) or Joseph Sheridan LeFanu (author of *Green Tea* and the lesbian vampire tale *Carmilla*, which influenced the later and more famous *Dracula* by Bram Stoker).

Here are a half dozen examples of modern literary criticism involving phantoms and the like. The articles are chosen from recent foreign sources so as to indicate the worldwide interest in the subject that goes along with the hundreds of similar articles published annually in English:

Minaka Imuro, "*Gautier et ses danseurs fantomes*" (Gautier and His Phantom Dancers), in *Bulletin de la Société Théophile Gautier* 15:1 (1993): 153-169

José Enrique Laplana-Gil, "*Algunas notas sobre espectros y aperecidos en la literatura del Siglo de Oro*" (Some Notes on Specters and Apparitions in the Literature of the Golden Age), in *Le Peur de la mort en Espagne au siècle d'or* (The Fear of Death in Spain in the Golden Age), Paris, 1993

Martin Puvel, "The Perplexing Ghost of Banquo," *Neuphilogische-Mittelungen*...(Bulletin of the Modern Language Society, Helsinki) 94:3-4 (1993), 287-296

Shigeru Taniguchi, "The Vicissitudes of Spectres and the Development of Blake's Myth" in *Center and Circumference: Essays in English Romanticism* (Tokyo, 1995), 83-95

Margareta Terenius, *"Spoktro hos barn"* (Ghosts, Children, Folklore), *Tradisjon* (Tradition) 24 (1994): 115-122

Gero v. Wilpert, (The German Ghost Story...), Stuttgart, 1994.

THE GUINNESS BOOK OF GHOSTS

There isn't one. However, if records are ever kept I can suggest a few entries.

Silliest Relationship with a Ghost: the friendship between a teenager and a friend who has died of eating a bad hamburger, in TV's *Teen Angel.*

Silliest Dependence on a Ghost: Though over forty, [Marguerite] Radclyff Hall felt she had to obtain the go-ahead of her dead lesbian lover before cutting her hair short.

Silliest Appearance of an Important Ghost: Jesus Christ Himself appeared to the philosopher Søren Kierkegaard while he was at breakfast one morning and instructed him to chew more.

Most Dramatic Ghost: Anne Boleyn, "with her head tucked underneath her arm."

Most Famous Ghost: Hamlet's Father.

Georges Méliès' *Le Manoir du diable* (English title, The Haunted House), 1896.

Most European of Ghosts: those who delay a dinner party in Buñuel's *The Discreet Charm of the Bourgeoisie.*

Most Well-Costumed Ghosts: the ancestors in Gilbert and Sullivan's *Ruddigore.*

SOME GHOSTS OF THE SILENT FILM ERA

The Ghost Breaker
The Ghost Club
The Ghost Fakir
The Ghost Holiday
The Ghost Hounds
The Ghost House
The Ghost in the Garret
The Ghost of Mudtown
The Ghost of Old Morro
The Ghost of Rosie Taylor
The Ghost of Seaview Manor
The Ghost of Slumber Mountain
The Ghost of Sulphur Mountain
The Ghost of the Hacienda
The Ghost of the Mine

The Ghost of the Rancho
The Ghost of Tolston's Manor
The Ghost of the Twisted Oaks
The Ghost of the White Lady
A Ghostly Affair
The Ghost's Warning
Haunted
Haunted Bedroom
Haunted Conscience
Haunted by the Cops
Haunted Café
Haunted Castle

THE PHANTOM OF THE OPERA (1925)

Following up his success with the extravagant *The Hunchback of Notre Dame,* Lon Chaney scored as Erik, the phantom resident in medieval torture chambers and dungeons five cellars below the Paris Opera House. He appears as "the cloaked figure of a man who hides his face and will not speak." The owners of the opera are glad to sell and as they depart tell the new proprietors, "It is barely possible you may hear of a ghost, a Phantom of the Opera." And, of course, they do.

But Erik, escaped from "Devil's Island for the criminal insane," masked to hide his disfigurement (the cause of it not explained in this version but attempted in a later Claude Rains version), is not a ghost. The film can stand for many in which a criminal figure is thought to be a ghost but is revealed to be a real live human being.

10 TRULY UNUSUAL GHOST MOVIES

Uncle Josh in a Spooky Hotel (1900). A 1-minute silent from the Edison Studios.

The Ghost Breaker (1922). Paramount—Famous Players—Salky produced this 6-reel movie based on the stage success by Paul Dickey & Charles W.

Goddard (1909), but director Alfred Green was damned for making it inferior to a 1914 filming. Star Wallace Reid was accused of being semi-inert. Lila Lee and Snitz Edward tried to perk it up. Probably the most unusual Hollywood use of a ghostly stage property.

Terror (1928). A 55-minute feature with Tom Tyler and Janet Reid in which the horror film meets the western movie. Later we had ghosts with sci fi, with kung fu, etc.

The Silent House (a/k/a *The House of Silence*, 1929). A silent movie from Butchers. Haunted house with the predictable secret panel, clutching hands (which go back at least as afar as *La Main qui étreint* with Max Linder in 1915), the works.

The Mysterious Doctor (1943). No Sleepy Hollow fake headless ghost this time but a "real" (or "reel") headless ghost—with a knife. John Loder.

When Michael Calls (1969). James Farris' eerie novel becomes a screen thriller. Many novels of ghosts were made into films. But here there is a plot twist that is startling, at least for a while. Mothers whose kids never call will appreciate that in this icy outing Mom starts getting telephone messages from son Michael—who is dead. Elizabeth Ashley, Ben Gazzara.

The House that Wouldn't Die (1970). Barbara Stanwyck, Richard Egan, and a director with moxie (in fact, his name is Moxey) give us an unusual "old dark house" in that there is no fakery to drive people out, drive them crazy, get their money, play a trick on them, or cover a crime or dark secret. None of those movie clichés. The place is really haunted. Later more places are said to be inhabited by honest-to-goodness and even up-to-goodness ghosts (as the public becomes more superstitious and even angel-happy), but this movie is really scary. Newer houses may have poltergeists; older ones tend to have ghosts.

Frank R. Strayer directed this 1934 film which begins in the now-classic way: traveling in a rainstorm and finding the road blocked by a fallen tree, the principals seek shelter at a big old house nearby. It is Dr. Kent's mental hospital. An early surprise is that the ghostly hand that appears when the lights go out and, in fact, the actions of the household members, are all just the first act of a play. Prescott Ames has written it and contrived to get Broadway producer Herman Wood to see it in this unusual way. Spencer Charters plays the maniacal professor. The big old house has all the standard secret panels, useful in the second part of the drama, in which a woman is murdered but the Broadway producer is sure it's just more of the play!

No profenar el sueño de los muertos (1974). This is remarkable for something other than its various titles, which include *Fin de semana los muertos, Non se deve profenare il sonno dei morti*, *The Living Dead at Manchester Morgue, Breakfast at Manchester Morgue*, and *Don't Open the Window*. Winner of a prize at the Sitges Film Festival—*where?* You must be kidding, the Portuguese Provincetown?——this film, whatever you want to call it, a pastiche of paranoia and parody, did, in fact, have a certain distinction. Or two. It was the first horror movie in stereophonic sound. The first sound horror movie was *The Terror*, 1931. Of course the knife chord and the creepy background music have done much to help horror flix ever since then; it has contributed at least as much as makeup—and it has eliminated the title cards that could take up at the extreme half or more of the footage not to mention telling those who can't read how to react. It is very much reminiscent of George Romero's trilogy of "Living Dead." I like the way these corpses are brought back to life: blood is smeared on their eyelids and they awake. This one is Grausome (Jorge Grau was the director).

An American Werewolf in London (1981). Surprised to see a werewolf movie in a ghost list? I just want to remind you that, as in Shakespeare (*Julius Caesar, Macbeth, Richard III*), the ghosts of dead victims appear. This time they manifest themselves to the werewolf—in a sex cinema, no less, at the climax of a rather fine film. Griffin Dunne, one of the two Americans attacked by a werewolf at the beginning of the film, is killed and appears as a ghost to the other (played by David Naughton), who has been committing all the rest of the werewolf crimes. Dunne wants Naughton to kill himself and put an end to the werewolfery. The ghost who wants something (think *Hamlet*) is a standard apparition, of course.

The Imp (a/k/a *Xiong Bang*, 1981). Yu Yung-kiang, known in the US as Dennis Yu, started his American production company with this tale of an innocent wife about to have an evil-incarnate baby (think *Rosemary's Baby*) and the husband who tries to exorcize the spirit of a corpse in the basement (think *The Exorcist*) with the help of a priest (this time Taoist). With Charlie Qin (known in the US as Charlie Chin) and Dorothy Yu. Chinese film has always been big on ghosts, but Yu's study in the US gives this film a special twist. It is as American as chow mein.

SOME RULES FOR GHOST MOVIES

Haunted houses are never ranch style. Nor are mobile homes (read: trailers) haunted.

Ghosts never come back just for an inconsequential chat. On the other hand, they never give any useful information about The Beyond.

"When staying in a haunted house," some anonymous benefactor reminds me via the Internet, "a woman should immediately investigate any strange noises, clothed only in her most attractive underwear."

Ghosts can make themselves invisible even when wearing the clothes they died in but if they put on anything else, it shows and seems to float around when they are not seen.

Though conventionally buried naked, wrapped in a shroud, ancient ghosts must appear in the costume of the period in which they died.

Ghosts of whatever nationality all speak English, except in foreign movies.

HOLD THAT GHOST (1941)

This old film of little value (though I always like Joan Davis, who is in it) is Bud Abbott & Lou Costello in a supposedly haunted house. It can stand for all the novels and short stories and screenplays in which in the long run everything that is thought to be supernatural turns out to be a fake. Explaining away the thrills is a tradition that goes all the way back to the earliest Gothic novels, and some of us think it an unfortunate tendency in the genre.

SOME MORE ABOUT GHOST MOVIES

The subtle material used in *The Uninvited* (the ghost story which an archbishop of Canterbury told Henry James at a dinner party) and *The Haunting* (a film version of Shirley Jackson's unkillable *The Haunting of Hill House*) was atypical. Generally ghost movies, whether anthologies of quality like *Dead of Night* or B-movie second features, tried to outdo all previous efforts in terror. Barbara Steele, a British actress who was seen in a number of features, was no great shakes as an actress, but she could scream astoundingly. Other women could cower well.

Some of the ghost films are really possession movies: the spirit of a dead person takes over the body of a living one. As we learn in *The First Power* (1990), "a spirit can't really do anything without a body." Examples include Carole Lombard in *Supernatural* (1933), and *Back from the Dead* (1957), *Tales of Terror* (1962), *Nightmare Castle* (1965), *An Angel for Satan* (1966), *Dark Places* (1972), *The Possession of Joel Delany* (1972), *J. D.'s Revenge* (1976), *Ruby* (1977), *Nurse Sherri* (1977), *Beyond Evil* (1980), *Witchboard* (1986, which warns that using a Ouija board may get a ghost to take you over), *Retribution* (1988). Almost all possessing spirits are evil, but there are a few films in which ghosts can be helpful to the living, including *The Curse of the Cat People* (1944), *The Sender* (1982), *The Supernaturals* (1987), *The Lady in White* (1988), and Stephen King's *Pet Sematary* (1989).

Folklore long has had the Grateful Dead (from which a pop music group took its name); a helpful ghost appears, as I told you earlier, in the first dramatic satire in English (George Peele's *The Old Wives' Tale*) in

Shakespeare's day. In *Twice Dead* (1988), a ghost defends the new tenants of his haunted house from a gang of punks, colorfully knocked off one by one. Helpful ghosts are something like guardian angels, something like children's imaginary friends.... . "I came so that your childhood could be full of friendliness," says the ghost in *The Curse of the Cat People* (1944). "Now you must send me away."

Sometimes an object is possessed of an evil spirit, as in *The Skull* (1966), or a demon, as in *Ghostbusters* (1984). But diabolical possession is not ghostly business.

The business of most ghosts (like that of Hamlet's father) is revenge. Vengeful ghosts abound in the movies, many of them extremely nasty. Examples are found in the old silents and in such modern films as *Strangler of the Swamp* (1945, a ferryman unjustly executed for a crime wants revenge), *The Long Hair of Death* (1964, Barbara Steele in Elizabethan costume), *The She Beast* (1965, Barbara Steele again, this time as a hag in Transylvania), *Black Sabbath* (1964, a corpse's ring has been stolen), *Kill, Baby, Kill* (1966, also called *Curse of the Living Dead*), *2000 Maniacs* (1964, a whole town wiped out in The Civil War has waited 100 years to get back at the damn Yankees), *Hatchet for a Honeymoon* (1969, vengeful wife gets after serial killer of herself and others), *The Fog* (1980, pirates have waited 100 years for revenge), *The Changeling* (1980, ghost of a little child murdered and another, who is now a US Senator, put in his place), *The Nesting* (1981, staff of a whorehouse that was burned down are killed but not quieted), *Ghost Story* (1981, a girl accidentally killed blames fogeys of "The Chowder Society"), *Superstition* (1982, like Barbara Steele as a crone, this nasty has waited 200 years to come back), *Loves of the Living Dead* (1986, where we discover that ghost can be driven off by hair dryers which dispel their ectoplasmic fields), *Trick or Treat* (1986, a dead rocker who seems to be helping a nerd get revenge on his high-school friends turns out to have an agenda of his own), *The Wraith* (1986, the returning avenger is not nearly as interesting as his Dodge Turbo Interceptor), *Hello Mary Lou: Prom Night 2* (1987), *Prison* (1987, another executed criminal returns to wreck havoc), *Ghostriders* (1988, another 100th anniversary, this time for hanged Texas outlaws), *Grave Secrets* (1989, a ghost has lost her head—literally), *Horror Show* (1989, as in *First Power* an executed criminal returns).

Gimmicks that accompanied some of these films included a nurse in the lobby of the movie theater (in case you fainted), a guarantee to "bury you free if you die of fright," and a million-dollar insurance policy should you perish of fright at the film. William Castle turned a clinker into a hit with that last p.r. stunt.

Here are some other ghost movies, none as important as *The Innocents* or *The Uninvited*. These 10 oldies you ought also to try to see, for one reason or another, if you are an inveterate fan of ghost films.

> *Night Comes Too Soon* (1947)
> **Das Spukschloss im Spessart** (1960)
> *Carnival of Souls* (1962)
> *Tower of London* (1962)
> **Kwaidan** (1964)
> *The Ghost in the Invisible Bikini* (1966)
> *Dark Places* (1972)
> *The Haunting of Julia* (1977)
> *The Evil* (1978)
> *The Forgotten One* (1989)

You probably have seen most of the ghost movies of the nineties if you are a fan. Which do you think was the best?

ACADEMIC WOMEN AND GHOSTS

Kathy Anne Fedorko, *Edith Wharton's Haunted House: The Gothic in Her Fiction* (Rutgers University dissertation 1987). Abstract: *Dissertation Abstracts International* [*DAI*]48:7 (1988), 1769-A.

Maria Katrakis, *Gothic Patterns in American Short Fiction of the Nineteenth Century* (University of South Africa dissertation, 1988). Abstract: *DAI* 50:9 (1990), 2896-A

Barbara Constance Patrick, *The Invisible Tradition: Freeman, Gilman, Spofford, Wharton, and American Women's Ghost Stories as Social Criticism, 1862-1937.* (University of North Carolina dissertation, 1991). Abstract: *DAI* 52:2 (1992), 2555-2556-A.

Teresa Alice Goddu, *The Haunted Text: Form and History in the American Gothic.* (University of Pennsylvania dissertation, 1991). *DAI 52:11 (1992), 3928-A.*

POLTERGEISTS AND GHOSTS AND FOLKLORE

Diane Tye, "The Great Amherst Mystery: Linking Folk Belief and the Female Experience," *Collections of the Royal Nova Scotia Historical Society* 44 (1995), 105-119. Old tales—this one of a famous Canadian poltergeist "mystery"—can be used to fit into new agendas on women's studies and other special interests.

Christine H. Neby, "A Storyteller's Story," *Tennessee Folklore Society Bulletin* 49:4 (1983), 155-163. Ghost stories are important to ethnologists and anthropologists and often give hints about aboriginal peoples who belong to pre-history.

Larry Millet, "The Ghost of the Gateway: The Metropolitan Building, Minneapolis," *Minnesota History* 53:3 (1992), 112-115. Stories connected with buildings are part of local history. Urban folklore is an important if rather recent specialty.

GUIDE TO SCHOLARSHIP IN THE HUMANITIES

"Everybody's into weirdness right now."—A weirdo in the film *Repo Man* (1984).

HALF A DOZEN NEGLECTED FILMS INVOLVING GHOSTS

La Caverne maudite (The Accursed Cavern), Georges Méliès, 1898.
Photographing a Ghost, G.A.S. Company (UK), 1898.
The Haunted House, Lubin, 1899.
The Miser's Doom, Paul, 1899.
L'Evocation spirite (Raising a Spirit), Georges Méliès, 1899.

BRINGING BACK THE DEAD

The horror movies have suggested many ways of bringing the dead to life. One example is in *House of Seven Corpses* (1974), a horror movie that revolves around making a horror movie. Paul Harrison was the leading creative talent and the cast included John Ireland, John Carradine, Faith Domergue, Charles Macaulay, Carol Wells, and Jerry Strickler. In the plot, the Faith Domergue character brings the dead back to life by reading from *The Tibetan Book of the Dead*.

THE HAUNTED HOUSE

This short (25-minute) Buster Keaton film of 1921 has a criminal gang pretending there is a haunted house, to cover their nefarious activities. An accountant, played by Keaton, encounters the fake ghosts—and some real ones. There is a surreal quality in this film which has not been captured in many subsequent films about the occult.

A SHORT SHELF OF BASIC REFERENCE BOOKS
ON HORROR FILMS

Every good public and college library ought to have these, because the public loves this stuff.

Butler, Ivan. *Horror in the Cinema* (1970)
Clarens, Carlos. *An Illustrated History of the Horror Film* (1967)
Clifford, Dennis. *Movie Monsters* (1969)
Copyright Office, Washington, DC. *Catalog of Copyright Entries, Motion Pictures* (periodically since 1912)
Daniels, Les. *Living in Fear* (1975)
Derry, Charles. *Dark Dreams* (1977)
Dillard, R. H. W. *Horror Films* (1970)
Eisner, Lotte. *The Haunted Screen* (1969)

Everson, William K. *Classics of the Horror Film* (1974) and *More Classics* (1986)

Halliwell, Leslie. *The Dead that Walk* (1968)

Hardy, Phil & Tom Milne & Paul Willemen, eds. *Encyclopedia of Horror Movies* (1986)

Huss, Roy & T. J. Ross, eds., *Focus on the Horror Film* (1972)

Kaminsky, Stuart. *American Film Genres* (1974)

Prawer, S. S. *Caligari's Children: The Film as Tale of Terror* (1980)

Robinson, William R., ed. *Man and the Movies* (1967)

Scheuer, Stephen H. *TV Key Movie Guide* (1968)

Steinbrunner, Chris & Burt Goldblatt. *Cinema of the Fantastic* (1972)

Telotte, J. P. *Dreams of Darkness* (*re* Val Lewton's films, 1985)

Twitchell, James B. *Dreadful Pleasures: An Anatomy of Movie Horror* (1985)

Walter, Gregory A. *The Living and the Undead* (1986)

SOME INTEL(LIGENCE) INSIDE

Remembering that, along with the accurate and the interesting, what you get are often no more than the unfiltered opinions of the "booboisie" (as H. L. Mencken cynically called John Q. Public), turn to the internet and try searches using these terms:

Ghosts	Occult Sciences
Ghost Stories, American	Parapsychology
Ghost Stories, British	Unexplained Phenomena
English Short Story Collections	New Age
Short Stories (Anthologies)	Body, Mind, Spirit
Fiction	Spiritualism
Literature: Folklore And	Supernatural
Mythology	Poltergeists
Literature-Classics/Criticism	Haunted Houses
Occultism	Wonders And Curiosities

This book has been crated with the use of libraries, where materials can be obtained and checked, with professional bibliographies and authoritative sources. The authority expected of print demands that. However, there is also a whole world of casual browsing and chat available in cyberspace. You can express your opinions there, too, abut this book or anything it touches upon. Happy surfing. Just don't get caught in The Net.

STIGMATA

The term refers to the marks of The Crucifixion miraculously transmitted to a living ecstatic. Here it is used as the title of a novel by Phyllis Alesia Perry (1998) about "forever" black people who reincarnate or haunt: "We back and gone and back again." The sufferings of the past reverberate in the present.

In the novel, Lizzie DuBose inherits a quilt made by her grandmother and the diary of her great-grandmother's slaveship memories come to her in dreams. The relationships between the dead and the living are touched upon, though the principal concern is the connection between generations of women in an African-American matriarchal tradition. Ghost stories these days can be put to many uses.

HALF A DOZEN STRANGE EUROPEAN PLAYS WITH GHOSTS IN THEM

Lilliom (1909) is the best play by Ferenc Molnár, whose real name was Neumann. This Hungarian play was a flop at its premier in Budapest but a success later in New York (1921) and London (1926). It is more familiar in its musical version. You know it as *Carousel* (1945).

The Ghost Sonata (played by The Provincetown Players in the US as *The Spook Sonata*, 1924, and in London under that unfortunate title in 1926, with this better title translated by E. Sprigg in 1963) is in the Swedish original *Spöksonaten* (1907). It is one of the chamber plays of August Strindberg (1849-1912). He was a playwright much interested in the occult in both private life and public writings. It was written in 1909.

The Glittering Gate (1909) was one of the earliest plays of Edward, Lord Dunsany (1878-1957), the Irish playwright, who liked to use supernatural elements in fantasies. *Johnson over Jordan* (1938) starred Ralph Richardson as a recently-dead man full of vain regrets, but that was not enough to make it a success for J. B. Priestley, OM (Born 1894). He published it with an essay telling "All About It" in 1939. He also used the supernatural in *I Have been Here Before*, 1937.

La Signora é buttare (The Lady is to be Removed, 1967) is the best play by the Italian playwright Dario Fo (born 1926). In a US circus, the clowns die and go to a heaven and discover it is full of American consumer goods.

Kärlekens död (The Death of Love, 1952) is a work by the Finnish playwright Hagar Olsson (born 1893) in which a fake doctor (and real magician) helps the inhabitants of a old-folks' home. Maybe including this play under this rubric is stretching things, for the discarded humans are not exactly dead. But they might just as well be, because they are pretty much dead while still alive, ghosts of their former selves.

THE BEST EPITAPH

Some people collect epitaphs and have a great store of them. They certainly reveal a lot about what we think of the end of life and the fate of the dead. (W. C. Fields liked "On the Whole, I'd rather be in Philadelphia." One hypochondriac has, "I told you I was sick"). To choose the best of all is difficult if not impossible, but here are my two favorites. The first is an anonymous quatrain that is seen in various versions on a number of Puritan tombstones:

> Remember this as ye pass by;
> As ye are now, so once was I.
> As I am now, so soon you'll be.
> Prepare for death, to follow me.

The second is by a better poet. Just before his execution, Sir Walter Raleigh was calm and inspired enough to write in his bible, which he left in the gatehouse of Westminster, before going to have his head chopped off and entering what he called in his unfinished *History of the World* "the House of Death, whose doors lie open at all hours, and to all persons." What he wrote were some lines which he added, in this doleful circumstance, to a poem he had written some time before. The early lines, which begin "Nature that washed her hands in milk," are not much, but consider this:

> Even such is Time, which taks in trust
> Out youth, our joys, and all we have,
> And pays us but with age and dust;
> Who, in the dark and silent grave,
> When we have wandered all our ways
> Shuts up the story of our days;
> And from which earth, and grave, and dust
> The Lord shall raise me up, I trust.

GHOSTS

Henrik Ibsen's play, usually given this title in English, might well be called *Vampires*, because he says that persistent dead ideas drain the strength of the living. They persecute us. In the play, Mrs. Alving says:

> I almost think that all of us are ghosts, Pastor Manders... it is not just a question of what we have inherited from our father and mother that walks in us. It is all kinds of dead ideas, lifeless old

beliefs, and so forth. They have no vitality but they cling to life just the same and we cannot free ourselves from them. Every time I pick up a newspaper I seem to see the ghosts [of dead ideas] gliding between the lines. There must be ghosts all over the country, plentiful as grains of sand at the shore. And then we are, one and all, pitifully afraid of the light.

STONE SOUP

In concluding a book into which I have crammed so much, I want to mention something I did not include—except in brief reference, to give a sort of completeness to my coverage of the field—and that is the great mass of information available in cyberspace.

I could have made a book like stone soup, doing no more than collecting snippets from the Web. The expression *stone soup* refers to an old legend about how a couple of bold entrepreneurs made a product out of nothing. Setting a fire under a large cauldron full of water in the public square, they dropped some stones in. Then, as passersby asked what they were cooking, they replied that they were making stone soup, except that it lacked a few potatoes. So someone dropped some potatoes into the cauldron. Another, told it needed only a few carrots, supplied those. Another, onions. And so on, and soon there was a rich soup the clever pair was able to distribute to the crowd—presumably at a great profit.

Many books are made that way today. In collections of statistics or life stories or celebrity interviews or Web site reports or newspaper clippings they pretend to offer original books. True, in my books I have relied on historical information and quarried the materials out of a great many libraries. But I have contributed my own energy, expertise, and judgment, my own insights and opinions. I trust I have made something new and original—and tasty and nourishing as well.

Don't fail to take advantage, if you can, of the community of others out there who, like you, are interested in the kind of things you find in my books on the occult. I receive so many letters in the mail from readers who live in isolated communities and who want to chat about the occult. I see in cyberspace, for those who have access, a marvelous opportunity for the individual to connect to like-minded, supportive others.

I believe that *The Complete Book of Ghosts and Poltergeists* will give you readers much to think about and talk about.   What you read here, remember, is thoroughly researched, as reliable as I can make it. What you read on the computer screen (and cyberexpert Andrew Devries assures us that "Paranormal stuff is all over the Net") may be disinformation, deliberately or just incompetently incorrect. You may need organizations such as CSICOP, which attempts to debunk the more bizarre misinformation, the magazine *Skeptical Inquirer* or its website, websites such as *Urban Leg-*

ends (where David Nichols attempts to ride herd on pseudofacts), and more than a few grains of salt.

FINIS CORONAT OPUS

"The end crowns the work," and death is either the end or the beginning. Whether you believe in life after death or you do not, this life is full of joys and wonders. My advice is to enjoy it as much as you possibly can. As a character in Alice Walker's novel *The Color Purple* aptly puts it, "lay back and just admire stuff. Be happy."

As I conclude this book, last things are naturally in my mind. This book has been about death and the possibility of an afterlife. On these great matters I fear I can offer no certainties, especially to those who, whatever their religious beliefs are or are not, have no certainties of their own, only fear and hope. I offer, however, a thought from a religious text, albeit an apocryphal one. I speak of *The Gospel of Thomas*, an ancient document discovered again only in the twentieth century.

The Gospel of Thomas assures us that if we look into ourselves and find what is there we shall be saved, and if we do not do that, or if we look into ourselves and do not find what is there, we shall be lost. I say: Know thyself. That admonition goes back before the Gnostics, to the Greeks.

That process, if anything, will give you, if you have the determination to persevere and the courage to face what you find whatever answer we mere "items of mortality" (as Oliver Twist says) can grasp. That way you may indeed find the meaning of life and the answer to the mystery of death.

THE LADDER OF INTELLECT

Readers of earlier books in this series may be familiar with Raymond Lull, but even if you have never heard before any word of this writer on the occult, I want to show you before I end the present book Lull's ladder of intellect. The diagram is from his quite obscure *Liber de ascensu et descensu intellectus* (Book of the Ascent and Descent of the Intellect).

At the right is a flight of stairs (*scala*) with steps identified as Stone, Flame, Plant, Brute, Man, Heaven, Angel, God. Leaving aside any idea of the theory of evolution, we see that by the steps we rise to the house of wisdom (*scientia*), God (*Deus*, The Lord), and the divine mysteries hidden ("occult") in clouds.

At the left is a circular diagram related to the *scala intellectus* (ladder of the intellect). The inner sections are identified as the Intelligible, the Sensible, the Imaginable, the Doubtful, the Credible. We have been dealing in this kind of material throughout the present book, along with the incredible. The outer circle identifies the Individual, the Species, the Genus (states of categorization), Being, Act, Suffering (states of action), Action (the concept), Nature, Substance, Accident, Simple, Complex. Underneath, a scroll proclaims: Total Intellect. Latin verses (*disticon*) once underneath the picture may be translated thus:

> You must go up the steps three at a time.
> Whoever aspires to reach the higher levels must approach the heavens as a scholar.

What is the relevance here? This: That if you want like Lull the alchemist to transmute base matter into gold you must take the facts and opinions of this book and transmute them in the fire of what Samuel Taylor Coleridge used to call "the esemplastic power of the imagination." Use your creative powers to deal with the Doubtful and the Credible. Struggle with the Simple and the Complex. Make what you can of this book, and climb the steps, not toward Certainty (because we can never as mortals see what are the mysteries) but at least toward greater knowledge through the increasing use of our god-given intellects. There is no magic escalator. Climb the steps by determined and disciplined thought.

May you have a happy journey through life and enjoy what Cardinal Newman called "peace at the end."

-- IT IS LATER THEN YOU THINK --

● Time is passing ● ● ●
● ● ● Death is coming ▭

● God says, it is appointed unto man once to die, but after that the judgment, and every one of us shall give account of himself to God. Rom. 14:11-12. That includes you.

● Over 48,000 persons die every 24 hours.

● If it should be your turn to die to-night —

ARE YOU PREPARED
TO MEET YOUR GOD?

● Or will you wake up in Hell, begging to have your parched tongue cooled with a wet finger, like the rich man? See Luke 16:19-31.

● Every knee shall bow to me. saith the Lord and every tongue shall confess to God.

● Do not joke about hell, for if every living person knew what every departing Soul discovers, everybody would be saved today.

● Where is hell? Hell will be found at the end of a Christ-less Life. Beware -- Prepare!

Index